From Subordination to Revolution

From Subordination to Revolution

A Gramscian Theory of
Popular Mobilization

JOHN CHALCRAFT

UNIVERSITY OF CALIFORNIA PRESS

University of California Press
Oakland, California

Library of Congress Cataloging-in-Publication Data

Names: Chalcraft, John T., author.
Title: From subordination to revolution : a
  Gramscian theory of popular mobilization / John
  Chalcraft.
Description: Oakland, California : University of
  California Press, [2025] | Includes bibliographical
  references and index.
Identifiers: LCCN 2025010520 (print) | LCCN
  2025010521 (ebook) | ISBN 9780520416819
  (hardback) | ISBN 9780520416826 (paperback) |
  ISBN 9780520416840 (ebook)
Subjects: LCSH: Gramsci, Antonio, 1891–1937—
  Political and social views. | Mass mobilization.
Classification: LCC HM874 .C43 2025 (print) |
  LCC HM874 (ebook) | DDC 335.43092—dc23
  /eng/20250421
LC record available at https://lccn.loc
  .gov/2025010520
LC ebook record available at https://lccn.loc
  .gov/2025010521

GPSR Authorized Representative: Easy Access
System Europe, Mustamäe tee 50, 10621 Tallinn,
Estonia, gpsr.requests@easproject.com

34   33   32   31   30   29   28   27   26   25
10   9   8   7   6   5   4   3   2   1

To Julie, May, Pablo, and Marcelo

CONTENTS

ACKNOWLEDGEMENTS

This book owes much to the insight, support, and care of colleagues, friends, the press, and my partner. The book developed especially through four Gramsci conferences—at the Università di Bari in 2017, the Scuola Normale Superiore in 2019, the LSE in 2022, and Sapienza in 2023. Among the organizers and discussants, I would particularly like to thank Paola Caridi, Benoît Challand, Brecht de Smet, Michele Filippini, Gennaro Gervasio, Patrizia Manduchi, Alessandra Marchi, Alia Mossallam, Sara Salem, Andrea Teti, Rossana Tufaro, and the GramsciLab at the University of Cagliari. I am grateful to Daniel Wills, Dylan Stevens, and Mathilda Whitehead for their work on finding references. The manuscript has gone through many iterations and benefited greatly from readings and criticisms by Fadi Bardawil, Vincent Bevins, Benoît Challand, Laurence Cox, Michele Filippini, Julie Gervais, Mark Levine, Chun Lin, Zachary Lockman, Sumi Madhok, Alessandra Marchi, Jason Neidleman, Yaseen Noorani, and Sara Salem. Valued advice and support at key moments came from Ayça Çubukçu, Neve Gordon, Sa'ad Hossain, Refel Ismail, and Laleh Khalili. Michael Gilsenan has, as always, been a deep source of insight and subtle guidance. It was a joy and a solace after some hard times to work with the editor (Niels Hooper), the staff (Julie Van Pelt and Nora Becker), the copyeditor (Artemis Brod) and the readers at the University of California Press who have been outstanding—engaged, supportive, rigorous, and professional. I am grateful to Francesca Bosic for generously granting permission to use her original artwork, a mural of

Gramsci from Ghilarza, Gramsci's hometown, for the cover image, and to Alessandra Marchi for taking the photographs. My partner Julie Gervais has been there for me, through thick and thin, and I still feel that if I can get something past her exacting reading, then I stand a chance of it reaching the required standard.

Introduction

This book aims to put forward a theory of popular mobilization, defined as the many ways in which subordinated groups rearrange their relationships to challenge and overcome social domination. The book is based on the writings of the Italian intellectual and revolutionary socialist Antonio Gramsci (1891-1937) and on the voluminous research and activism undertaken in the living Gramscian tradition. The goal is to put forward a theory which can identify, situate, and connect the highly diverse elements of popular mobilization.

The book contends that existing theories, whether conservative, liberal, rationalist, or critical, are unable to achieve such a connecting theory. In some cases, this is because certain forms of spatio-temporality, identity, structure, or social force are unjustifiably privileged over others. This privileging fails to grasp the diversity that must underpin understandings of popular mobilization and tends, in practice, towards imposition, reduction, and divisiveness. In other cases, this is because the tendency is towards a conceptual situation where pluralism, diversity, difference, and deconstruction are eventually all there is, foreclosing the possibility of meaningful connections between the spatio-temporal, social, structural, and strategic elements of popular struggle, a recipe in practice for cacophony and ineffectiveness.

The book taps into the not always fully realized potential of the living Gramscian tradition to ground a connecting theory of popular mobilization. It contributes by gathering in a distinctive constellation the diverse and fertile concepts and elements involved; by engaging in an extensive theoretical articulation in relation to a wide variety of examples taken from all over the world; by offering some key points of theoretical renovation and making some key arguments, notably about organization and bloc formation. The objective is to offer a theory in which the many elements of popular mobilization can be linked together, both in theory and practice. The point, at a time of mass discontent, revolutionary weakness, and the ascendancy of the Right, is to contribute to thinking and constructing progressive forms and forces of renewal.

This introduction pitches the Gramscian tradition as a force for renewal, identifies the core puzzle and the theoretical challenge of the book, and briefly situates and summarizes the connecting theory on offer and its main arguments. The introduction ends by outlining the book's structure.

GRAMSCI: LODESTAR OF RENEWAL

> In Palermo . . . in the baggage room [in prison transit] . . . a formidable, superindividualistic and anarchistic type . . . [introduced me] to a Sicilian . . . arrested for various motives, a combination of political and common delinquency . . . [Whereupon the Sicilian] stared at me for a long time, then he asked: 'Gramsci, Antonio?' Yes, Antonio! I answered. 'That can't be,' he retorted, 'because Antonio Gramsci must be a giant and not such a tiny man.'[1]

Gramsci himself sought to be a 'fertilizer' not just a 'ploughman' of history. And Gramsci has been a powerful reference—a veritable giant, notwithstanding his small stature, hunchback, ill-health, peripheral origins, and incarceration—in a wide variety of theoretical and political renewals in many parts of the world. To read Gramsci in search of renewal in theory and practice is to join a long and vibrant tradition.

In Europe, for instance, Palmiro Togliatti aimed at renewal, under the sign of Gramsci, by forming a democratic, mass-based communist party in Italy in the 1940s, after the communists had been decimated by fascist repression, exile, and death, including that of Gramsci himself.[2] New revivals in Italy in the 1980s again arose when 'the "national roads to socialism" [associated now with Togliatti] . . . emerge[d] in all its narrowness'.[3] Mouffe's early writings expanded intellectually on the question of democratic socialism.[4] Those confronting Stalinist and Soviet Bloc bureaucratic dictatorship in Eastern Europe in the 1960s and 1970s turned to praxis, humanist Marxism, and Gramsci.[5]

In Britain, one of Gramsci's most significant literary interpreters, Raymond Williams, drew on Gramsci very much in order to think a new politics, a 'New Left' as it came to be termed, between Fabianism / social democracy on the one hand, and Stalinism on the other.[6] Stuart Hall, a Jamaican-born British intellectual and activist, seminal in developing 'cultural studies' and an interpreter of Gramsci, sought a 'hard road to renewal', a 'redefinition' of socialism to oppose Thatcherism.[7] Renewal meant reworking a Left caught between insular, economic-corporate, patriarchal, top-down, British Labour Party politics and economistic, sectarian forms of Marxism. In France, the Gramsci reference was part of the search for the de-Stalinization of the French Communist Party (PCF) in the 1950s and 1960s, 'to reform the PCF from the inside and thereby to create a "new left"' in the face of the fact that the PCF itself was 'confused and sceptical towards the de-Stalinisation process initiated by Khrushchev and Togliatti'.[8]

In Latin America, Gramsci featured against 'dogmatic Marxism' across the continent in the 1960s and 1970s. His work was heavily operative in thinking the renewal of Left strategy, moving from defeated guerrilla insurgencies (the war of manoeuvre) in Argentina, for instance, to the cultural and organizational struggles associated with Gramsci's 'war of position'. He was a reference in Left renewals against Peronism in Argentina and in Nelson Coutinho's democratic socialist response to dictatorship in Brazil and his challenge 'to renew the political culture' of the Brazilian Communist Party from within.[9] Ernesto Laclau's early work cited Gramsci's 'great originality' for overcoming 'economism and class reductionism',[10] for the concept of hegemony, for democracy, and for its critique of both Althusser and of reductive Marxist explanations for fascism.[11] More recently, subalternity has been related to decolonial thematics, including the search for a 'pluripopular' juridical education in Colombia.[12]

In Asia and Africa, appropriations of Gramsci have also been part and parcel of renewal. In the Arab world, for instance, Gramsci was taken up by intellectuals and activists in Lebanon in relation to democratic socialism and the renewal of communism against top-down and bureaucratic forms in the 1960s and 1970s.[13] The Gramsci reference appeared significantly in the 1980s and 1990s in the search for new forms of politics and civil society; it was a way to address the growing crisis of the formerly lustrous but now 'overstated' and dictatorial formerly Arab nationalist revolutionary states.[14] There also has been a Gramsci revival in understanding the revolutionary uprisings of 2011 and their aftermath.[15]

In South Asia, part of the impetus behind subaltern studies was a search for new forms of politics—not only in the face of colonial discourse and the 'dominance without hegemony' of post-independence middle-class nationalists but also against 'the official communist parties for their opportunistic and dogmatic use of Marxism' and in support of popular movements, such as the Naxalbari peasant movement.[16] In various ways, Guha writes regarding the intellectual formation of subaltern studies as a whole, 'Gramsci has been our guide', especially because of the 'openness' of his thinking, which 'encourages adaptation'.[17]

In China, Gramsci has been drawn on since the 1990s 'when the shocking consequences and social costs of China's economic boom started to be widely felt and . . . debates broke out against the neoliberal-developmentalist complex of market fetishism'.[18] As Wang has it: 'What will be the new forms of popular socialist politics for the remaking of the Chinese "people" in this brave new world, of course, remains to be seen. . . . We have to be patient and inventive in any forms of solitude, in order to be contemporary not only with Gramsci but also with Mao, Qu Qiubai, and Lu Xun.'[19]

In North America, Gramsci has been read to think new forms of democratic revolutionary organization. The diverse, anti-globalization protests in Seattle in 1999, for instance, stimulated Stephen Gill's concept of the 'postmodern Prince', a democratic re-reading of Gramsci's 'modern Prince', understood to be a new kind of global political agency opposing neoliberal globalization and aiming at a 'global and universal politics of radical (re)construction'.[20]

The themes of these renewals give strong indications as to where the Gramscian tradition is theoretically and politically operative: the emphasis is on global, and not solely Western, politics and histories; on civil society not the state; on wars of position not wars of manoeuvre; on humanism not scientism; on the grassroots not the party bureaucracy; on democracy not dictatorship; on the social bloc more than on the cloth-cap proletariat; on openness not rigidity; and on the importance of cultural activity not just the supposedly objective workings of capital. These appropriations also show the ways in which the Gramscian tradition is a living and updating one. And they demonstrate the very wide range and variety of struggles, strategies, and forms of organization for which Gramscian theory has been found useful.

A living tradition by definition undergoes renovation—and the Gramsci revival in the contemporary period has some suggestive features. First, there is a tendency to embrace Gramsci's diversity, his many 'pathways' and 'prisms', rather than to lament his ostensible antinomies.[21] There have been more open-ended and in-depth studies of the *Prison Notebooks*, for instance, than perhaps ever before.[22] Likewise there has arguably been a stronger emphasis on accepting the various incarnations of Gramsci in different political traditions and histories, on questions of translation, and on the 'travelling' Gramsci.[23] This emphasis has tended to replace complaints over the inabilities of scholars or activists to properly cite and comprehend the true Gramsci as he 'really was'. The contemporary revival is less focused on a specifically European Gramsci, and still less on the closeted figure of 'Western Marxism' diffusing throughout the rest of the world. It is much more about a search for a non-Eurocentric Gramsci that has already travelled, joined hands with alternative traditions, and indeed been made to live in a whole variety of renewals, including of the revolutionary kind on the global stage. Even theorists such as Spivak have rowed back on earlier, more categorical postcolonial epistemic exclusions in relation to Gramscian concepts.[24]

Second, Gramsci is no longer used so much for his ability to reveal the cultural dimensions of power and resistance. This job has already been done, as it were, by the New Lefts of the 1960s and 1970s. Instead, thinkers increasingly wish to draw on Gramsci to see how theory, the subject, and culture might be combined with practice, the object, space, nature, civil society, economy, and the state. Radical geographers, for example, have developed Gramsci's multi-scalar and *spatial* historicism.[25] And the Gramsci revival draws more saliently than before on the post-, inter-, and transnational themes in Gramsci's work, chipping away at the lockstep modernist connotative articulation of nation, state, and territory.[26] These moves have dovetailed with the fertility of studying articulation and translatability, as well as an increased interest in praxis—defined from a Gramscian perspective as the (incomplete) unification of theory and practice.[27] Finally, renewal in the

Introduction

contemporary period underlines Gramsci's uses for thinking 'politics as organizing'[28] and diverse and democratic forms of revolutionary organization.[29]

This book takes these contemporary tendencies to be salient. They are elements in a propitious terrain for drawing on Gramsci to put forward a theory of popular mobilization which can think and link together distinct aspects of mobilization.

AFTER THE SPRING

The puzzles, debates and arguments developed in this book have been strongly marked by the aftermath of the popular uprisings and occupations of 2011–13. During the Arab Spring, millions of ordinary people occupied squares and streets, overwhelming the brutal and formidable security forces, amid the collapse of the 'wall of fear'. They insisted collectively on the fall of the regime—in the name of bread, dignity, and freedom. Some lived the best days of their lives in 'freedom, dignity and revolution'. In the aftermath, however, even amid a profound and many-sided crisis, the popular demands for meaningful and even revolutionary transformation were unmet. As one of the leading Egyptian revolutionaries of 2011, Alaa Abd El-Fattah put it, in his own 'prison notebooks': 'Like Tunisia's, our revolution has not seized power, and . . . the counter-revolution and the old regime have taken the state hostage.'[30] Popular energy did not translate—at least in the short- and medium-term—into broader social or structural change.[31] Diverse groups and social classes went their separate ways. The revolutionary unity and effervescence of the squares was eventually divided and dispersed. Instead, the aftermath of the uprisings saw, for the most part, the ascendancy of the Right, counterrevolution, conservative nationalism, civil war, regime violence, imperialist intervention, and increasingly violent settler colonialism.[32]

The hopes raised by radically democratic styles of organizing (horizontalism); the promise of the internet and social media; the peaceful, liberal-democratic and human rights activism of the middle-class youth; feminism; and the socialist possibilities of the labour movement were largely disappointed.[33] Similar weaknesses and disappointments have dogged the mass mobilization that returned, against the odds, to the region in 2019 in Lebanon, Sudan, Algeria, and Iraq and then in Iran in 2022. For all their fleeting powers, it became highly plausible to conclude that these popular uprisings lacked the sustained organizational and strategic forces to bring change.

The Arab world did much to unleash a decade of mass mobilization around the globe—from Rio de Janeiro to Hong Kong and from Kiev to New York. But the course and consequences of much of this popular mobilization were similar in so many places. Even amid the long, ecological, and 'organic crisis' of neoliberal hegemony,[34] the popular energies and demands of these mobilizations have failed to bring significant structural change, whether in relation to the economy, civil society, culture, the state, or internationally. Instead, in country after country, right-wing forces have assembled their reactionary social blocs and put forward a vision of order and stability, of family values and national security, while progressive forces, who rightly identify these projects with racism, xenophobia, inequality, misogyny, imperialism, and violence, have usually (but not always) been unable to cohere as a leading social force. Divisions of group and class have been difficult to overcome sustainably. Sometimes issues of colonialism, class, race, gender, and sexuality—in theory and practice—do as much to divide the Left and progressives as they do to unite them.[35] Whatever strategic mistakes the British Labour Party under Jeremy Corbyn made after 2015,[36] for example, it is arguable that forging a bloc combining socially conservative, former working classes with educated, metropolitan social progressives was always going to be an extremely difficult thing to achieve.[37]

Occupations and horizontalist activism across the world in the 2010s meant a transformative experience for many. These mobilizations, building on the alter-globalization movement, politicized a new generation; they changed debates about inequality; they introduced the idea of the 1 percent.[38] But in various other ways, these important movements were diluted and appeared to lack effectiveness. They lacked the strategic and organizational capacity to bring about social and structural change. They were usually unable to defeat newly ascendant right-wing authoritarianism.[39] Hopes for social media, the internet, and peaceful 'civic resistance' have often been disappointed. Sajjad-Akhtar's Gramscian critique of progressive activism in Pakistan highlights the problems with social media: techno-optimism combines with frenzied, individuated, reputation-guarding online practices of opining and sharing.[40] Queer Palestinians have written of an 'empire of critique'.[41] Social media as 'civil society' can be a highly divisive and punishing environment, rivalling the Marxist polemics of old—even if expression, identity, and affect, not ideology and strategy, are the central modality.

It has also proven difficult to connect everyday struggles and forms of resistance, together with mass disaffection of various kinds, into an organized progressive force. Bubbles of autonomous activity have dissipated or been outflanked, repressed, or coopted. Progressive forces themselves are deeply divided, both in theory and practice. The coming to power of various Left movements in Latin America in the 1990s and 2000s, for instance, was a major achievement, underlining the possibilities for popular mobilization. But they have greatly divided opinions regarding such issues as compromising on principles of autonomy, Left populism, authoritarianism, and the limits of challenging capital.[42] Questions about Islamist formations, sole leadership, and anti-imperialism continue to divide the Left, including regarding pressing questions about solidarity with Palestinian liberation.[43] Further, potential progressives may not know how to imagine change or think of the practical steps along the road. Slothuus, writing in Britain, puts it in an interesting way: 'In the current moment, there is a twin development of increasing appetite for radical social transformation, particularly among younger generations, and an increasing despair about the impossibility of imagining both the path to and the endpoint of such transformation.'[44]

It is worth underlining that Gramsci's context also bore important resemblances to the present. Gramsci faced, amid the crisis of liberal capitalism, the inability of popular uprisings (the two-year Biennio Rosso, 1918–1920) to bring about a revolution in Italy. He faced division among progressive forces and the challenge of popular organization. Abroad, he faced the ascendancy of settler colonialism and, at home, the fascist dictatorship that imprisoned him. Amid appalling blows and pessimism of the intellect, he also mustered an optimism of the will. As Alaa Abd El-Fattah puts it from his cell in the present: 'You have not yet been defeated.'[45]

We can say, then, with Peter Thomas, a major philosophical interpreter of a Marxist Gramsci, that 'the uprisings and revolutions of the early twenty-first century have posed a fundamentally Gramscian question: how is it possible to coordinate the diversity of interests of our pluralised, pulverised, and dispersed peoples into a hegemonic force capable not simply of resisting the current order, but of initiating a constituent process, a construction of a socialist order in the forms of struggle already underway?"[46]

The puzzles and disappointments of the present point to the need for a theory that can understand and conceptualize all the processes whereby a scattered, dominated, and divided ensemble of the subordinate can change their relationships, overcome social domination, and form a new hegemonic force capable of bringing structural change, locally and globally.

THE ARTICULATION OF STRUGGLES

Any such theory faces a formidable set of challenges: it needs to be able to think, within a single framework, a very wide variety of struggles, sociologies, types of resistance, strategies, tactics, and forms of organization and social force and to do so in relation to broader processes of social and structural transformation. It needs to be able to connect very different axes and spaces of struggle over class, race, gender, sexuality, and anti-colonialism without setting one against any other, while allowing for the fact that—against any rigid or moralizing application of intersectionality—priorities, capacities, spaces, and histories differ. It needs to grasp ways in which popular energy can be translated into organized activity—as in the case of Podemos in Spain—or the question of how the proverbial streets can be connected to the convention hall, as in the case of Bernie Sanders in the United States.[47] It needs to think organization without vanguardism, revolution without maximalism, intellectuals without scholasticism; and it ought to be able to situate and valorize everyday resistance, autonomous politics, and direct action without either dismissing or romanticizing them. And it needs to be able to think together struggles and structural transformation on distinct fronts—economic, organizational, cultural, and political—and to be able to connect multiple scales, including that of the inter/transnational, notably against nationalist and statist silos and East-West binaries.

In short, a fertile theory of popular mobilization in the present can usefully aim to solve the problem of *the articulation of struggles*, defined as a linking together both in theory and practice of diverse elements of popular mobilization. The challenge is to do this without reductionism and authoritarianism on the one side, while avoiding eclecticism, dissipation, and forcelessness on the other. A parochial nationalism and statism on the one side and abstract cosmopolitanism on the other need to be avoided. It is necessary to steer between the Scylla of Marxism and the Charybdis of culturalism; to retain an eco-socialist content while jettisoning materialism and authoritarianism; and to avoid the pure, essentializing separation of West and East. The lesson of the last decade is surely that transformative activity is not a free for all—but nor can there be any return to the Left vanguardism, dictatorship, and Soviet-style imperialism of the 'short' twentieth century (1917–1989).

This book aims at achieving just such a connecting theory of popular mobilization. It does so by drawing heavily on a particular interpretation of Gramsci's oeuvre and on the living Gramscian tradition, participating in a mode of theory-building that is deeply historicist and organic. Gramsci's approach involves a 'live work' in which both theory and practice change over time; this distinctive feature underpins the rhythms of updating and renewal so often identified within Gramscian theorizing itself. Much of the analysis of connection that is to come depends on Gramsci's highly original historicization. Only thus—in stark contrast to abstracted, logico-deductive theory-building—can seeming opposites, such as 'weapons of the weak' and popular uprisings or autonomous and party activity, be linked together. Historicizing in the Gramscian tradition, as will be seen, means situating mobilization deeply within Gramsci's distinctive history of subaltern social groups, while keying such work into the analysis of the politics of hegemony and engaging at all times with the philosophy of praxis. The point is to offer insights into how the existing hegemony can be challenged and a new one brought out.

The fundamental approach is distinguished sharply from conservative, rationalist, and liberal approaches to popular protest, mobilization, human rights, and social movements. As I will argue, conservative approaches tend to fix subaltern social groups—in theory and practice—in their subordination by reinforcing hegemonic common sense and division. Rationalist approaches suffer from profound problems of false universalism, abstraction, ahistoricism, and Eurocentrism. In contrast, critical theory is a vital source for the book; but as readers will discover, the formulation is distinctive and cannot be easily assimilated to Marxism, cultural studies, intersectionality, or anarchism. There are also significant aspects of theoretical renovation in relation to the mainlines of specifically Gramscian critical theory—from Marxist Gramscians to subaltern studies to the politico-ideological theories of Laclau and Mouffe. Indeed, the aim is to dial up and enrich the living Gramscian tradition in ways that go beyond familiar readings of Gramsci in order to overcome problems of materialism, modernism, and Eurocentrism associated with Gramscian Marxism and problems of culturalism and 'backdoor Orientalism' associated with Gramscian theory that draws too heavily on postcolonial theory and cultural studies.

The book constructs a connecting theory of popular mobilization. The theory envisages a long spatio-historical journey from subordination to revolution and the many moments, faces, and above all *phases* of this drawn-out process of mobilization, organic unification, and becoming. In this theory, the plural ensemble of the subordinate, the subaltern social groups, overcome their conditions of domination and fragmentation, eventually forging a popular force capable of founding a new historical bloc and a new form of post-subaltern hegemony. The spatio-temporal process of renewal, counterposed to tendencies of decomposition and neoformation, is subtended at all points by organic intellectuals, the transformation of social being and social consciousness, and the remaking of the structures of civil society, culture, economy, and the state.

The long journey is parsed into four major phases: the torturous contradictions of domination, the wellsprings of autonomy, the expansive search for consent, and the roiling ferment of revolution. These phases are distinguished by social being / social consciousness (class, group, and bloc formation), spatio-temporality, structures (civil society, culture, economy, and state), and social and popular forces. The subaltern phase of domination is associated with marginalization, fragmentation, common sense, objectification, contradictory consciousness, and forcelessness. The phase of autonomy is associated with self-activity, subjectification, new forces, group and class consciousness, good sense, and the 'spirit of cleavage'. The expansive search for consent is associated with social bloc formation, ideological elaboration, organizational activity, and the war of position. While the revolutionary phase is associated with historical bloc formation, a rupture in the balance and relation of forces, philosophical deepening, a new common sense, and the remaking of the hegemonic apparatus. The phases and their various faces correspond to the main moments in the politics of hegemony, defined as combining leadership, domination, autonomy, and consent.[48] These four phases are simultaneously the central moments in Gramsci's historiography—that is, his history of subaltern social groups. They are equally present in the historical elaboration of the philosophy of praxis—which can only be fully realized in revolution.

Placing these four phases front and centre enables one to do justice to all the pressing questions of identification (the dialectics of social being / social consciousness), structure (civil society, economy, etc.), organic intellectuals, and social force within the ambit of the Gramscian tradition. It gets us beyond monist theories that depend on identity, or on one axis of identity, or on one structural element (such as economy or civil society), or on one kind of force (international, economic, political, or otherwise). It does so while avoiding shapeless eclecticism and enabling one to think the ways in which these diverse elements are connected.

Theorizing in this way also permits us to identify, parse, research, and work towards a coherent position in relation to a series of major debates about popular mobilization in relation to hegemony and subaltern social groups. As we shall see, studying a phase of domination gives space to debates about fragmentation, subalternity, passive and active adherence, weapons of the weak, common sense, contradictory consciousness, and the like. Taking up a phase of autonomy allows us to pose questions about the drive for autonomy, how it comes about (in relation to crisis), what forms it takes, the promises and limits of group and class consciousness, and whether self-activity and autonomous strategy can ever be sufficient—debates which have underpinned many of the controversies over horizontalism, people power, direct action, self-management, place and space, 'militant particularism', popular uprisings, and what Gramsci called 'good sense'. Third, taking up the problematics of the phase of consent opens a space for studying the key questions of organization, ideology, party activity, strategy, popular education, bloc formation, and state engagement, including questions of whether consent-winning can proceed without vanguardism on the one hand or reformism on the other. Finally, foregrounding a phase of leadership and revolution enables us to think the dynamics of popular revolution, posing questions about maximalism, leadership, and authoritarianism and about popular, organic formulations of leadership and revolution. Thinking in terms of these phases, and eventually their complex interconnections, including on the (trans)national terrain, enables us to address highly diverse debates while eventually yielding a coherent, connecting theory of popular mobilization.

The book puts forward some distinctive arguments. Avoiding either the romanticization or the dismissal of the torturous contradictions of domination, the book aims to show how domination can be destabilized amid contradiction and crisis. It presents a distinctive criticism of *autonomism*—defined as the fetishization of autonomy—while refusing the many dismissals of autonomy issuing from more Jacobin traditions; it valorizes what autonomy can achieve while marking its distinct limits. It argues that there is no by-passing the phase of consent, while arguing against vanguardist or single party approaches; it valorizes what consent can achieve and avoids reformism, especially through what I will call, following Gramsci, the 'organic party' and the formation of a 'social bloc'. Finally, it specifies the dynamics of a popular revolution, proposing the existence of a democratic and organic formulation, with the formation of a new historical bloc at its centre, that steers between maximalism on the one side and passive revolution on the other. The book underlines the significance of group and class formation but also, and more distinctively, the processes by which group and class are overcome, above all through the formation of a social and then historical bloc, including on the transnational terrain. The argument throughout is that popular mobilization (like the Gramscian tradition) can be seen as a process of renewal in relation to the twin threats of decomposition and neoformation.[49] Renewal is evident especially in the (fruitful) phase changes, which involve radicalizing and revolutionizing dynamics: the destabilization of domination, the drive for autonomy, the emergence of responsible leadership among autonomous actors, the development of new kinds of popular organization within and against the existing apparatus of consent especially during the popular revolution, the 'vigorous antithesis' to passive revolution, the dramatic periods when the hegemonic apparatus crumbles away and a revolutionary historical bloc is formed.

It is hoped that this theory of popular mobilization will enable a richer understanding of the articulation of struggles, paving the way for insights that, at a time of weakness and crisis, can enliven the organic formation of a popular force in the future.

STRUCTURE OF THE BOOK

This introduction has set out the aims of the book, introduced the living Gramscian tradition, identified the puzzle, and briefly situated and summarized the connecting theory to come. The next chapter (chapter 1) must take a step back to situate, develop, and justify in much more detail the theoretical framework and method and its relationship to existing research in order to underline the originality and fertility of the living Gramscian tradition. Chapter 2 builds on this to develop more concretely the relevant concepts at work, establishing a language, defining terms, and laying out the main phases and faces of popular mobilization. Chapters 3–6, then, treat the four main spatio-historical phases of popular mobilization in turn: the torturous contradictions of domination, the wellsprings of autonomy, the expansive search for consent, and the roiling ferment of revolution. The conclusion summarizes the theory of popular mobilization—the long journey from subordination to revolution—and lays out its main theoretical and practical implications.

CHAPTER ONE

The Originality of the Living Gramscian Tradition

This chapter situates, develops, and justifies the theoretical framework and method of this book, underlining the originality and fertility of the living Gramscian tradition. I will first develop the criticisms of conservative, liberal, and rationalist approaches briefly mentioned in the introduction. I will situate the Gramscian tradition in relation to critical approaches generally, pointing to the potential to overcome problems and weaknesses. The chapter then turns to readings of Gramsci, showing how there is room—between Marxist and culturalist interpretations—for a new reading and develops the case for the originality of Gramsci's intervention. Finally, I detail what a historicist and organic theory is and lay out a philological method.

CONSERVATISM

Conservative and Orientalist conceptions of popular mobilization continue to be produced in significant quantities in contemporary culture, civil society, and academic research all over the world. The hallmarks of such views are well known: popular challenges to the status quo are conceived in terms of disorder, chaos, subversion, barbarism, backwardness, recalcitrance, anger, irrationality, violence, and pathology. Arabs are angry; Muslims fanatical; Dalits polluting; Blacks violent or criminal; Jews sinister, money-grubbing, or self-hating; colonial subjects ungrateful; migrants and minorities threatening; women hysterical or impure. Feminists and LGBTQ people are snowflakes, deviant, demented, or woke. The urban poor are loiterers, welfare-sponges, harassers, and drug-addicts. Striking workers are militant and disruptive. Protestors in general are just disaffected opportunists. Or they are subversives, fifth columnists, and troublemakers. They are sometimes seen as being in hock to alien ideologies or inauthentic values or as the (un)witting agents of a foreign, Islamist, or Western agenda. In reactionary forms of populism, certain allegedly embattled social groups are singled out for their purity and authenticity—the white American, the pure woman, the real Hindus—and pitted against other groups, such as migrants or those considered impure or deviant. Progressive gains are siloed and used to divide: feminism is used as a stick to beat transgender people; antisemitism is weaponized against Arabs, Muslims, and Palestinians—even while the latter are massacred and starved by Israeli settler colonialism.[1]

Conservative theories have been widely criticized in liberal, radical, and Gramscian perspectives. Central to the latter is the point that these theories are premised on an uncritical approach to existing forms of hegemony; they tend to reproduce the forms of common sense diffused by the ruling groups, who are themselves engaged in suppressing and dividing popular mobilization. Referencing Antonio Bresciani (d. 1862), a Jesuit priest, novelist, and journalist known for his extended attacks on liberalism and democracy, Gramsci referred to reactionary, conservative, and populist theories as 'Father Bresciani's progeny'. Like the Catholic church, these theories cultivated superstitious beliefs to keep the 'simple' subordinate and used disciplinary measures to keep the clergy in line. Gramsci writes: 'To a social elite, the components of subaltern groups always have something barbaric or pathological about them.'[2] Subalterns who challenge the status quo are seen as a pathological (or exceptional) type—as a *genus*. They are conceived as abstract and particular. They are separated from history and politics or placed outside the community. There is no drive, in this conservative exceptionalism, to unify theory and practice, and the disunity is reproduced, in theory and practice, by some ahistorical mechanism of social domination: Nature, Order, Hierarchy, Stability, Purity, the Divine.

It is particularly important in the present not to cede the terrain of 'the people' and 'the popular' to right-wing, neoliberal, statist, and nationalist forces. Popular mobilization is not a species of *populism*. In the Gramscian perspective, populism refers eventually to the manipulation of the masses by adventurers and ruling groups. It refers to activity in which *logos* as rhetoric/politics outweighs *logos* as reason/philosophy. Populism can be criticized for nationalism and statism on the one side and for passive and romanticizing representations of subaltern social groups on the other. As Ciavolella writes, 'The first point to keep in mind about Gramsci is this: on one side, he strongly criticised any "populist" representation of popular classes; on the other, he interrogated their potentialities for emerging as a political subject.'[3] Stuart Hall read Gramsci to distinguish between, on the one hand, popular-democratic forces and, on the other, 'authoritarian-populism', which depicts a true national people supposedly menaced by a series of threatening Others.[4] Populism is read here as an alternative project of ruling groups, which operates by romanticizing and flaunting the supposed (especially national) authenticity of certain social groups, the better to divide and rule, including in statist ways. Hall's Gramscian approach fruitfully attempts 'to distinguish the genuine mobilization of popular demands and discontents from a "populist" mobilization which, at a certain point in its trajectory, flips over or is recuperated into a statist-led political leadership'.[5]

LIBERALISM AND RATIONALISM

Human rights, development, humanitarian, and conflict resolution work are widely seen as forms of activism and advocacy with change-making potential. Writing from Central America, in the wake of various failed socialist and Marxist guerrilla struggles and massive repression in the late 1980s, Fonseca wrote that '[i]t really seemed to many of us including those of us who were forced to go into exile, that the contractualist potential of civil society, struggles organized around human rights, and demands for the rule of law were certainly worth exploring . . . [seeking] progressive change through democratic politics and in the context of neoliberal globalisation'.[6]

Some have seen global civil society, and its forms of expertise, as a site in which new sustainable development norms can be worked out and then diffused.[7] Some have argued that transnational activist networks in the human rights field have created positive change, rolling back the arbitrary and abusive exercise of state power and institutionalizing human rights.[8] This approach has garnered new appeal in some quarters as a way to challenge a resurgent populism which cares little for due process and human rights.

Such research and activism, however, has been extensively criticized—as colonial, middle class, overly professionalized, dependent on foreign-donor agendas, and complicit with state domination and neoliberal capitalism. While it would be wrong to exclude categorically certain strategic uses of human rights, many of these criticisms are taken to be highly salient in Gramscian perspectives. Fonseca offers a nice summary: '[However,] the "transition to democracy" turned out to be, in fact, a transition to minimalist peripheral polyarchy, promoted and consolidated by Washington in combination with structural adjustment policies and free trade agreements as required conditions for joining the process of transnationally dominated neoliberal globalization.'[9]

Fonseca concludes that hopes in such a transition had been 'misplaced'. In order to pre-empt more fundamental social change, '[D]emocracy promotion is about the promotion of polyarchy and the discouragement, if not outright condemnation, of popular democracy in the Rousseauian-Marxist tradition.'[10] Knowledge is produced 'passively' so that policymakers (i.e., ruling groups) can decide what to do. One might add that in Gramscian perspectives, juridical equality is insufficient and procedural—including in relation to rights-based approaches to LGBTQ activism.[11] Civil society is turned into an innocent terrain, a public sphere, conceived as a form of abstract autonomy—rather than a concrete terrain where consent for the ruling classes is organized and contested, including at the international level. Liberal politics fails to 'reckon with the equal status of reason and passion'.[12] The oft-found liberal disavowal of all forms of coercion and force is too innocent (or naïve). Sharp's work, for example, on how nonviolent protest can overthrow dictators, for all its distinctiveness, is thin on the fundamental power relations at work in hegemony and too easily appropriated by Beltway actors looking to destabilize authoritarian enemies.[13] Gramsci criticized liberal formulae such as Kant's categorical imperative as a falsely universalist 'static, empty formula into which one can pour any actual historical content'.[14] Gramsci here gives the example of 'honour' killings: 'a jealous husband who kills his unfaithful wife thinks that all husbands should kill unfaithful wives.' Perhaps above all, in a Gramscian perspective, the most fundamental problem with these approaches is the multiple ways in which they remove subaltern social groups from the scene of their own emancipation. Like Mrs Pardiggle in *Bleak House*, distinguished for her 'rapacious benevolence',[15] these theories suffer from a distinctively colonial and middle-class form of false universalism.

The most widely used approach to contestation, especially in the Anglo-American academy, involves rationalist theories of social movements and contentious politics, including strategic interaction perspectives.[16] These approaches differ from conservativism in that they assume the basic rationality of protestors and movements. They also conceive of contention as involving more conflict and antagonism than approaches focused on 'passive, service-oriented NGOs'.[17] These theories obviously do not all agree with one another and have been revised significantly over time, even by their progenitors. Where they blend with conventional political science, they have often, but not always, been more strongly marked by positivism, natural science epistemology, and quantification. They have also been influenced by other approaches including social psychology.[18]

Social movement theories have been substantially critiqued, including by Marxists and Gramscians.[19] Such theories seem to have no way of probing or understanding power relations in general or hegemony in particular and are thin on how such relations can be transformed historically. Capitalism, state power, and social class have dropped almost entirely from view, while queer, anti-colonial, anti-racist, or feminist thinking are not seriously engaged. Social movements are, in familiar Eurocentric style, born in Europe and then diffused to the rest of the world. Older—but by no means discontinued—forms of social movements theory explain protest, as is well known, as flowing from various structures, such as political opportunities, or resonant interpretive frames, or social movement organizations. This causal logic, however, makes it impossible to see or imagine how such protest can bring about structural change. Framing processes[20] imply a campaigning view of social movements, offering a reductive, descriptive, movement-centric, instrumental, objectivist, and top-down scheme of 'frame' resonance and alignment. The concept of framing processes is in turn based on Goffman's 'frame analysis', the study of interpretive schema in the presentation of the self in everyday life. Goffman's approach examines frames—interpretive schema—by deliberately abstracting them from power relations, social class, practice, and social organization. Goffman's theory was an avowedly 'conservative' intervention, one which sidestepped many of the key structural questions—including around race, ideology, capitalism, and imperialism—raised by popular mobilization in the US of the late 1960s and early 1970s.[21] This was an uncritical, clinical, and detached starting point for a theory of meaning in mobilization. Frame theory does not identify social domination, let alone form part of a struggle against it.

Dynamic and interactionist approaches, on the other hand, for all their gains in relation to static and deterministic social movements theory, do even less to situate or parse forms of hegemony and, in so far as every form of structure is broken down into interacting elements, cannot picture the emergence of a new coherent social force. These theories are shapeless: they ignore or have nothing to say about fundamental social transformation; marked by rationalism and abstract universalism, they increasingly deploy positivist theories of causation. In relation to the interactionist approach, with its extensive reference to 'players' and 'arenas', we might well say with Gramsci that complex, antagonistic dialectical developments associated with emerging forms of subaltern politics are not a 'sporting game, with its umpire and its pre-established rules to be loyally respected'.[22] These theories focus very much on movements, campaigns, or contentious interactions, depicting actors or players pursuing interests and making claims. The tendency is to abstract from context, resulting in an ever-thinner capacity to grasp fundamental social and historical change, let alone to discuss emancipation. Gramscians see the gap between activists and academics in these increasingly professionalized fields as too wide, indicative of the negative figure of the 'traditional intellectual', scholasticism, and an untenable subject-object separation.

Gramscian perspectives provide a distinctive criticism of both elite, conservative, and populist approaches, on the one hand, and middle-class, liberal, Eurocentric, and rationalist approaches, on the other. The former are marked above all by genus-thinking and a hierarchical approach which keeps subaltern social groups in their place, even while sometimes championing alleged subaltern authenticity; the latter are marked by varieties of abstraction, false universalism, objectivism, individualism, and rationalism: subaltern social groups are either but a target for middle-class reform, or they disappear from view altogether, along with questions about social domination and how it can be overcome.

CRITICAL APPROACHES

There is a diverse critical constellation of perspectives on protest, resistance, and popular movements—including in Marxism, anti-colonialism, post-structuralism, feminism, anarchism, cultural studies, queer theory, critical race theory, post/decolonialism, and intersectionality. These critical approaches oppose conservative and liberal approaches in many ways: they attend to fundamental questions about power relations and their transformation and to oppression and emancipation. Gramsci's work has been a major reference in these approaches, and they in turn have much to teach a Gramscian theory with regards to thinking questions of how subordinated groups have challenged power, overcome domination, and built new and more emancipated ways of life, including transnationally. Nonetheless, these approaches have some gaps and weaknesses.

Marxism is a vast and highly diverse tradition, which in general terms foregrounds and prioritizes material relations, capitalism, and class. Challenging subordination within the cosmos of historical materialism means tackling the fundamentals of capitalist accumulation, exploitation, imperialism, unequal exchange, peripheralization, alienation, commodity fetishism and building up the powers of the international working class and working classes. Eventually, by abolishing capitalist property and socializing the means of production, it becomes possible to bring about some form of communism or socialism, locally and globally. 'Marxism-Leninism' underlines the importance of party organization and the seizure of state power as the correct way to complete this revolution.

The great strength of Marxist theory relates to the critique of political economy and the attention it gives to material relations and needs, capital accumulation, class and the working classes, the need for organization and strategy, and the importance of the state and of thinking internationally and globally.[23] Gramsci's oeuvre cannot be thought or understood as if it were separate from the Marxist tradition, and a Gramscian theory will always have much to learn from research in the Marxist tradition.

The weaknesses of Marxism, however, relate to forms of materialism, economism, class- and Eurocentrism, determinism, nationalism, state- and party-centrism, and authoritarianism. Gramsci devoted a substantial part of his *Prison Notebooks*, written between 1929 and 1935, to the critique of many of these problems. Gramsci rejected the priority of the material over the ideal and the priority of practice over theory. He rejected philosophical materialism and economic determinism. He argued against the authoritarian, positivist, and scientist degeneration of Soviet Marxism and Stalinism.

Gramsci's critique is arguably one of the most powerful criticisms of Marxism and 'Marxism-Leninism', in spite of and arguably because of Gramsci's commitments to Marx and to socialist transformation. Marxist theories, in particular, find it almost impossible to do justice to the articulation of struggles. Marx wrote that the interests of the working class can and must become the interests of all the other oppressed groups, but he did little to develop a theory of politics in which this articulation could happen. The 'Leninist' solution, however caricatured and contested in relation to the historical life and politics of Lenin, has travelled in vanguardist and authoritarian forms; its lesson has been for so many that professional revolutionaries, by virtue of their monopoly of scientific insight into the laws and motions of capitalism, supply correct consciousness and strategy through 'objective analysis' to workers and all other subordinate groups.[24] This beckons not the articulation of struggles but a monist imposition of a single struggle, and even a single line of interpretation. There is an elective affinity here with statist authoritarianism and imperialism and with division and left sectarianism. In Gramscian lights, conventionally Marxist theories of popular mobilization, notwithstanding the vital insights that the Marxist tradition continues to supply in relation to capital and class, are arguably insufficient: they almost always suffer from economism, monism, and authoritarianism; they need significant revision with far-reaching implications. Marxists, for all their importance, have no monopoly on either socialism or revolutionary politics.

Foucault and Foucauldian-discursive approaches have had a major impact on the study of power, knowledge, and resistance. Foucault introduced new concepts of capillary, discursive, and disciplinary power, along with more resistance-related concepts of counter-conduct, homosociality, and the ethics of care.[25] Foucault's original concept of discourse turned the subject and the object into effects of power. The illusion of subjectivity and objectivity were produced in an anterior, capillary, disciplinary terrain, an episteme, an archaeology of knowledge. Foucault did not prioritize theory/ the ideal over practice/the material or vice versa. He welded them together with great force—in schools, asylums, prisons, barracks, town planning, timetabling, regulations—and their microphysics of power. Discourse in Foucault's hands was neither theory nor practice, but a profound fusion of the two. Foucault's intervention lent great weight to the sense that social emancipation would require not only the abolition of capitalism but also the most fundamental overthrow of the deepest and most 'archaeological' epistemic formations. One of Foucault's great achievements—in his deconstructive mode—was to reveal the depth and extent, especially regarding sexuality, of epistemic processes of normalization.

Foucault teaches Gramscians to be acutely aware of the power of certain kinds of hegemony and their diffuse forms—including across borders. He reminds us of the importance of sexuality; of queerness; of the importance of the challenge to hegemonic heterosexual masculinity; and the salience of 'molecular' practices of care. Some of Foucault's interpreters, such as Eribon, by foregrounding the connection between Foucault the queer man and Foucault the thinker, have much to teach the Gramscian tradition about how to think through and overcome queer subalternity via a 'revolt against the powers of normalisation'.[26] There are ways to think Foucault's developing contribution in relation to popular mobilization, as will be suggested in chapter 4.

Nonetheless, Gramscians see significant problems in the Foucauldian tradition. Sanbonmatsu has put forward a wide-ranging critique of Foucault.[27] The philosophical disagreements are deep: humanism, social emancipation, and the dialectical unification of theory and practice, so important in Gramsci, are difficult to find concretely in Foucault, where there is no process of unification, because on the one hand, the unity of theory and practice has already been achieved in discourse and, on the other, subject and object are irretrievably mired together in 'discipline'.[28] With neither dialectic nor praxis, there is no way to conceive of transformation. If power is truly everywhere, then the whole concept of social force collapses. If there is no author anywhere, then there can be no collective will. Disciplinary power is not mediated through the organization of consent in civil society. Instead, it oozes amorphously across the social formation, in institutions which fuse together state, civil society, economy, and culture in an indivisible whole. In this framework, it becomes impossible to specify or understand how consent can be reworked and reorganized or 'governmentality' changed.[29] In Foucauldian perspectives, which can be read as eliminating social becoming, we can find ourselves back to pre-Hegelian fixed ontology of Being and Non-Being, Self and Other, a world that can be interpreted as reinstating some of the binaries and oppositions (such as

The Living Gramscian Tradition

West-East) that it sets out to denaturalize. Foucault, by sticking so close to the object to be overcome (i.e. normalizing discourse), eventually created the impression for many interpreters that normalizing discourse is all there is.

Foucault's work, especially in later years, opened theoretical space for some provisional and limited increments of autonomy, but these are little more than cracks and fissures in the dominant discourse. As Mumby puts it, Foucault and de Certeau both 'tend to situate resistance at the individual level and within the confines of the dominant disciplinary regime'.[30] In a Gramscian perspective, we are only in the start points of popular mobilization: the force of popular upsurges, the struggles for consent, broad social transformation, and the politics of revolution are not in view. For the most part, Foucauldian perspectives have meant among researchers an excessive scepticism towards resistance, voice, protest, ideology, uprisings, and revolutions of all kinds—even queer activism itself, which can be assimilated too completely into 'incitement to discourse' and imperialism.[31] In mainstream Foucauldian optics, popular mobilization or political ideology, for instance, are typically not living possibilities in the world but mere discursive effects.

Anti-colonialism, race, sexuality, gender, and transnationalism has long been written into theorizing about power, resistance, revolutionary politics, and social emancipation. A highly selective and truncated list of some of the major figures involved would include the great Black American race critic, W. E. B. Du Bois; feminists, such as Simone de Beauvoir; anti-colonial theorists and historians of Black liberation, such as Frantz Fanon and C. L. R. James; critics of Western imperialism as Orientalism, such as Edward Said; Black revolutionary feminists, such as Angela Davis; and gender and queer theorists, such as Judith Butler and Didier Eribon.[32] More recently, decolonial approaches challenge and aim to think beyond Eurocentric 'modernity/ coloniality'.[33] Against the lockstep link between nation-state and emancipation, further, Palestinian one-state intellectuals, indigenous organizers, and the postnationalist organic intellectuals of the Rojava Revolution, *inter alia*, propose a search for new transnational, plurinational and pluripopular forms.[34] One major achievement of all of this engagement has been to ensure that overcoming social domination cannot be theorized adequately without reference to colonialism, race, gender, sexuality, and inter/transnational questions.

Gramscian approaches in general and the approach taken in this book in particular accept, embrace, and learn from many of the achievements of this research. Gramsci himself addressed issues important to non-materialist critical theory.[35] He struck against Orientalism in his discussions of Islam.[36] He was not immune to all forms of Eurocentrism and colonial modernism, but he rejected naturalized or biological theories of race and racialized theories about the peripheral Italian South.[37] He opposed cultural imperialism and settler colonialism. Of anti-colonial uprisings after 1918, Gramsci wrote: 'For several years we Europeans have lived at the expense of the death of the colored peoples. . . . But today flames of revolt are being fanned throughout the colonial world. This is the class struggle of the colored peoples against their white exploiters and murderers. It is the vast irresistible drive towards autonomy and independence of a whole world, with all its spiritual riches'.[38] Gramsci clearly considered the national and the state to be a vital terrain of struggle, but he constantly posed the question of the international—whether in relation to the Comintern, the Catholic Church, or the question of North and South—beckoning towards transnational, plurinational, and pluripopular possibilities in contemporary readings.[39] Gramscians learn much from the decolonial and indigenous critique of nationalism and statism.

It is striking that a whole raft of Gramscian thematics—the national popular, cultural leadership and revolution, and 'organic intellectuals', for instance—were being engaged by contemporary anti-colonial and progressive thinkers and activists in the colonized world including C. L. R. James in the Caribbean, José Carlos Mariátegui in Latin America, and the Communist leader Qu Quibai (1899–1935), who died at the hands of the state in China. Such engagements occurred largely without any direct influence by or contact with Gramsci. The notable Chinese Marxist, Hu Feng (d. 1985), for instance, discussed cultural centres in mid-twentieth century Shanghai, in ways remarkably redolent of Gramsci's concept of civil society.[40] This Sardinian from Italy's racialized and marginalized South; this descendant on his mother's side of a Sardinian village family of middling status and on his grandmother's side of a moderately prestigious Italo-Spanish family; and this great-grandson on the grandfather's side of an Ottoman Greek-Albanian[41] was addressing conceptual problematics that were emerging in other parts of the world during the same period amid the struggles and transformations of colonial modernity. Since Gramsci's time, concepts such as that of the organic intellectual, in particular, has had a significant life in critical, Black, and anti-colonial traditions.[42]

Typical forms of patriarchy have been found in Gramsci.[43] But Gramsci challenged what he called 'masculinism' and understood why Nora left her family in Ibsen's *The Dolls House*.[44] Holub concludes that he believed in 'the non-negotiable and fundamental importance of women's complete emancipation for any liberatory agenda'.[45] Gramsci's 'emotional intelligence' from prison in relation to his wife and sister-in-law has been put in question—even by Gramsci himself;[46] but Gramsci did reject any rationalist priority of knowing over feeling. He admired his mother greatly for saving seven children against seemingly insurmountable difficulties.[47] He linked sexuality to hegemonic common sense and saw sexuality and the 'personal' politically in ways that challenged bourgeois public-private distinctions.[48] Overcoming social domination in the Gramscian tradition implies paying significant attention to the colonized and the 'Southern Question'; to race, gender, and sexuality; and very much involves the activities of a highly plural ensemble of subaltern social groups.

Gramsci's own oeuvre, furthermore, has been a substantial inspiration for major contributors to later cultural, postcolonial, feminist, and subaltern studies. Theorists in these fields have drawn substantially on Gramsci's concept of hegemony.[49] Edward Said, for example, saw Orientalism as a form of hegemony in the Gramscian sense. He writes: 'It is hegemony, or rather the result of cultural hegemony at work, that gives Orientalism . . . durability and . . . strength.'[50] Subaltern studies, old and new, has drawn major inspiration, in analyzing power and the diverse histories of castes, migrants, peasants, women, and workers in South Asia and far beyond.[51] The dialectics of subject and object, so important in Gramsci's philosophy of praxis, come out vividly in Fanon. They are central to his sense of oppression as a Black man in colonial France, and to his search for a new humanism.[52] These dialectics are conveyed (via Sartre) into Eribon's work on homosexuality.[53] Themes of praxis have been explored among feminists of many kinds.[54] They show up in striking ways among anti-colonial cultural theorists such as Sylvia Wynter—where praxis is the 'realisation of living'[55]—and in decolonial approaches.[56] Praxis plays an important role among radical educators.[57] And, in relation to ecology, there are intimations of a different relationship to nature—coexistence not conquest, interrelation not dualism—in the philosophy of praxis.[58] In short, the Gramscian reference should not be underestimated in the development of postcolonial, cultural, and subaltern studies itself.

Some of the most inspiring Gramscians have taken up questions of gender and sexuality. Decades ago, Stuart Hall declared the death of 'Socialist Man', with '"his" particular sense of masculinity, shoring "his" identity up in a particular set of familial relations'; this was the death of 'a particular kind of sexual identity'.[59] Hall likewise spoke of feminism as a 'new, socially revolutionary force' that should be part and parcel of left politics. He noted the vital importance of the 'uncompromising assault, spearheaded by feminism and revolution in gay and sexual politics, on patriarchalism and patriarchal forms of masculinity'. He relates these forces intimately to the search for 'a freer, more emancipatory kind of life', insisting that revolution involves a revolution in culture, against '[t]he tiny "family man" . . . still hiding away in the heads of many of our most illustrious "street-fighting" militants'.[60] Hall sought a 'project, a new social bloc which has learned to live positively with difference and diversity, rather than suppress it'.[61] Creative uses of Gramsci, indeed, have powerfully emphasized how struggles can and must learn from one another.[62] A Gramscian approach to social domination—as we shall see in detail—emphatically includes and embraces a plurality of struggles, and eventually can reach towards popular and plurinational forms.

Intersectionality insists on the existence, and intersection, of many different kinds of subordination and oppression—and underlines the importance of not prioritizing one axis of domination over another, including in thinking resistance.[63] These theories, together with contemporary revolutionary feminism, argue very strongly that there is no natural or *a priori* logico-deductive prioritization of either class, gender, race, or sexuality.[64] Monism—a theory of social emancipation based only on a single axis of class or identity—has been criticized in highly convincing ways for a long time.[65] Back in the 1940s, de Beauvoir convincingly explained to historical materialists, for example, why the paradox and situation and oppression of women should *not* be reduced, even ultimately, to 'private property', 'class conflict', reproductive 'tasks' or 'services', or 'the economic monism of Engels'.[66] There are problems, furthermore, with the forms of homogenization proposed in Eurocentric, nationalist, and statist conceptions.[67]

Gramscian approaches learn from, build on, and contribute to these themes. Gramsci himself criticized 'monism'.[68] In discussing social class, Gramsci drew attention to elements of culture (including gender, race, and sexuality), civil society and state; in discussing social groups, he drew attention to class and the capitalist economy. Gramsci, argues Morera, saw sexual liberation as a relatively autonomous and equal component of liberation, even thinking economy and sexuality together.[69] Gramscian approaches, therefore, are at ease and in dialogue with many of the insights of intersectionality.

There are nonetheless, in a Gramscian perspective, gaps and weaknesses in intersectionality and in cultural and postcolonial studies when it comes to building a theory of popular mobilization. Cultural and postcolonial theory reveals forms of social domination, which although an important and critical act, often remains in a negative register and does not point explicitly to the many concrete, political, and mobilizational processes by which social subordination can be overcome. And while these theories are strong on culture, they are undoubtedly weaker in relation to discussions of capitalist economy, civil society, and the state—and how these can be transformed. Attention to ideology, organization, strategy, and to what Gramsci calls the balance and relation of forces is often only marginal in much postcolonial theory. Revolutionary politics regularly goes missing. One problem is that if intersecting forms of oppression multiply sociological categories *ad infinitum* then any linking together of struggles appears to drown in a sea of differences. Another is that, where new axes of domination are discovered, the problem of how, if ever, particular prioritizations are possible is very difficult to solve. Cultural and postcolonial studies, moreover, often fail to grapple and connect with the lives, common and good sense, and material struggles of ordinary people and are sometimes discussed in registers that are inaccessible, reproducing the very divisions between mental and manual labour that Gramsci associated with traditional intellectuals. The importance of the transnational theme must not result in an abstract cosmopolitanism which fails to make an adequate reconnaissance of the national terrain or fails to do battle with the state. Finally, the risk with decolonial approaches, for all their importance in developing the criticism of nationalism and statism, is that they can be read as homogenizing and essentializing the West and, by the same token, the Other. By erasing syncretism and creative combination, they can feed Western narcissism, offering sustenance to armchair intellectualism's ability to tar the global majority with the brush of being epistemologically colonized. A renovated Gramscian theory, arguably, can point to ways to overcome these problems.

Finally, anarchist traditions of various kinds have gone to battle against statism and nationalism and explored a huge variety of previously unsung or autonomous forms of resistance—from the weapons of the weak, hidden transcripts, and the art of not being governed to direct action, horizontalism, prefiguration, and the spontaneous, revolutionary capacities of the intelligent multitude.[70]

Gramsci was never an anarchist, but he did champion the factory councils, he valued autonomous organization and self-activity, and he studied capillary and infra-political activity in ways that are underappreciated. Arguably, a Gramscian perspective is much more accommodating to themes of autonomy, radical democracy, and even prefiguration than a 'Leninist' interpretation such as that by Salvadori would have us believe.[71] There is a junction between autonomous thinking and Gramscian perspectives.[72] Stuart Hall keys a Gramscian perspective into a positive vision of the 'the mobilization of democratic power at the popular level'.[73] Boggs understood Gramscian perspectives to include an 'organic process of popular struggle that could prefigure the new communist society by gradually extending the domain of egalitarian, non-bureaucratic social and authority relations'.[74] As Hall puts it, 'Far from belonging exclusively to the left, we have mercilessly neglected [democracy's] force as a revolutionary idea over the years.'[75] He also believed that the 'advance towards socialism, is inextricably linked with the deepening of democratic life, and the widening of popular-democratic struggle'.[76]

Nonetheless, Gramscian approaches see gaps in relation to anarchism and horizontalism when it comes to theorizing popular mobilization. An important point has to do with the ways in which the romanticization of weapons of the weak can radically foreshorten political horizons, resulting in a 'discovery' of resistance and even, supposedly, revolution in the most interstitial and survivalist manoeuvres, which bring only the illusion of agency. A second key issue has to do with the slippage from the valorization of autonomous politics to the intellectual and ideological fetishization of autonomy (what I will discuss in chapter 4 as *autonomism*), which eventually limits the development and potency of popular mobilization and revolutionary politics. A related point is that autonomist approaches fail to grapple with the ways in which revolutionary politics involves the winning of consent, the defeating of enemies, and forms of revolutionary leadership, including an assault on the state. Horizontalism, in particular, is vulnerable to a Gramscian criticism as lacking strategic efficacy and an ability to build organic roots in subordinated groups, overemphasizing the liberatory powers of styles of organizing, and failing to attend to concrete problems of transformation in culture, group/class, the state, and the economy. How does the scattered multitude become an emancipated people? Gramscians can learn much from anti-statism and anti-nationalism, especially in the present, but Gramsci's optics also force us to recall that states and nations are crucial elements in the terrain to-be-transformed, and new forms of state and community—including the plurinational and popular—will need to be constructed.

Critical approaches, then, for all their overlap and synergy with the Gramscian tradition, also suffer from certain gaps and weaknesses in relation to theorizing popular mobilization. Marxism suffers from reductive materialism; Foucauldian approaches from the political constraints of discourse theory; postcolonialism and cultural studies from slippages into idealism; intersectionality from a lack of concreteness in relation to political struggle; and anarchism from political limitations and strategic inefficacy. In a sense, we have theories of politics (Marxist) which tend towards the authoritarian and theories of culture and power which are insufficiently political. These problems leave us with theories that do not allow us to think concretely about popular mobilization. They also make it difficult to think the articulation of struggles, because they seem to slight one or other of the important forms of group or class, one or other of the important fronts (cultural, economic, political, or civil) or strategies/tactics of struggle so it is hard to relate one to the other. The Gramscian theory of popular mobilization developed here aims to overcome these gaps and limitations.

READINGS OF GRAMSCI

Although there is much to build on, Gramsci's fertility as a theorist of popular mobilization is not always fully grasped, and sometimes it goes missing entirely, partly because Gramsci's texts are not always used as extensively as they might be—especially his writings on the history of subaltern social groups. But Gramsci's fertility is overlooked above all for profound theoretical reasons. This section takes up these arguments in relation to hegemony, Marxism, post-Marxism, subaltern studies and right-wing appropriations of Gramsci.

Many authors, perhaps even most, approaching Gramsci through his most famous concept, hegemony, take the latter to be a way of understanding the stability of the existing order (including with its 'overstated' states and hoary forms of nationalism), an overwhelming mechanism of control, and the reproduction of capitalism.[77] Or it is a way to grasp the *cultural* control of patriarchy, racism, Orientalism, and homophobia, *inter alia*. These understandings—especially when merged with the Foucauldian concept of discourse—often take us a long way from the study of progressive or revolutionary struggle, the study of how subaltern social groups make history. As Lipsitz puts it: 'Antonio Gramsci's ideas have gained popularity among scholars largely as a means of explaining the futility of efforts to change past and present capitalist societies. Above all else, Gramsci was a revolutionary strategist . . . [who] championed a political and ideological struggle for hegemony.'[78]

Lipsitz goes on: 'the Gramsci who appears in much contemporary scholarship is less a strategist of social struggle than a coroner conducting an inquest into the blasted hopes of the past.' Certainly, it is not enough, in Gramscian optics, simply to reveal to the *cognoscenti* how profoundly the existing order is entrenched in wide-ranging forms of complicity and consent: this would be an abstract knowledge, the property of traditional intellectuals, a matter of mere 'clairvoyance'[79] without a connection to a transformative, popular politics. This view, further, struggles to avoid presenting politics and history as a *marché de dupes*, a presentation that Gramsci warned against. These views on hegemony do very little to excavate a history of sub-altern social groups, and they usually sidestep—and offer little help for those seeking to theorize—the diverse problematics of popular mobilization, especially those which do not relate to cultural forms of consent and domination.

Gramsci's relationship to Marxism has long been contested, and at least four important positions exist. In one view, Gramscian perspectives are regarded negatively as something of a culturalist deviation from Marxism. Althusser, for example, criticized Gramsci's historicism in the name of a scientific reading of *Capital* and a deepening of dialectical materialism.[80] A second position sees Gramsci as more or less a Marxist-Leninist.[81] A third reads Gramsci in more positive mode as a Crocean of the Left, who justifiably gives culture, civil society and non-material factors a certain centrality, even priority.[82] Finally, one of the most widespread positions sees Gramsci positively as a creative Marxist, 'an original figure of Marxism', based on the emergence in the *Prison Notebooks* of 'a profound revision of Leninism and the Marxist vulgate'.[83] In this view, Gramsci opposed historical economism while holding to historical materialism, even while he often referred to the latter as the philosophy of praxis.[84]

These positions all have their problems. As for the first, Gramsci's contribution is not helpfully seen as some voluntarist deviation from Marxism but as an enrichment, and even as going beyond. The deviationist view takes us back to the narrow, class-centric view criticized earlier in this chapter. The second 'Leninist' reading is not simply wrong; it is dogged by problems of statism, vanguardism, and authoritarianism. I justify this criticism in chapters 5 and 6. The third, the neo-Crocean reading, takes Gramsci too far from material relations, capital, and class and tends towards idealism, turning popular mobilization too narrowly into a question of the superstructure (culture, civil society, and the state). The fourth reading—Gramsci as a creative, cultural Marxist—has born great fruit and is a major advance on economistic Marxism. The problem is first that sufficient evidence for its key postulate (that Gramsci prioritized material relations) arguably does not exist in Gramsci's texts. Second, it eventually, through however many subtleties, takes us back to a prioritization of capitalism and class and to the dangers of monism and a modernist Eurocentrism that does not, in the last instance, accord sufficient importance to the whole range and diversity of popular struggles, such as those relating to colonialism or to gender and sexuality.[85]

Chantal Mouffe and Ernesto Laclau's post-Marxist approach was built on a search for new forms of radical democracy and socialist strategy in a context of waning working-class activism and on an impressive, extended critique of Gramsci's supposed economism. These interpretations laid a heavy emphasis on the logics of democratic equivalence, forms of non-totalizing political-ideological articulation, and inclusive and democratic (left) conceptions of the people. They draw attention to the sorts of discursive articulation necessary among progressive actors to construct a people in contemporary struggles for a socialist, democratic hegemony.[86] This approach avowedly moves them beyond the Gramscian fold, even as they retain some of his terminology.

In Gramscian perspectives, Laclau and Mouffe, in the tradition of interpreting Gramsci in a neo-Crocean mould, do elevate superstructure over the structure, subject over the object, theory over practice, the ideal over the material, knowing over feeling, and social consciousness over social being. While the emphasis on democracy is salient, arguably the shift to idealism is not. Stuart Hall, for example, is convincing in the ways he 'definitively dissociated' himself from 'the discourse theoretical approach to the analysis of whole social formations'—a reference to Laclau and Mouffe—arguing convincingly that this was a species of neo-Kantianism.[87] In chapters 5 and 6, this book argues that Laclau and Mouffe, having determined (convincingly in this book's view) that the proletariat has no given or natural destiny to be the hegemon, end up jettisoning too readily the need for a continued connection in social emancipation to material relations, practice, and class—and the dialectics of social being and social consciousness. Left populism, because of the privileging of the ideal, the cultural front, and groups defined by representation, cannot connect such elements with other aspects and elements of popular mobilization—the material, the fronts of civil society, the state, and the economy—or with issues of class, body, and feeling. This is ultimately not satisfying in relation to the articulation of struggles, because it does not give sufficient space to mobilization aside from that involving politico-ideological rearticulation.

Third, subaltern studies has made extraordinary rich and important use of Gramsci's concept of subaltern social groups for several decades in rewriting the history especially of South Asia against colonialist and bourgeois-nationalist historiography, but also of many other world regions.[88] This book draws much from the way subaltern studies has brought history and politics 'from below' into focus, especially regarding the study of the colonized world, which is sometimes occluded in interpretations of Gramsci that emphasize the state (risking statism) and centre on the West.[89] These works have put a highly salient emphasis on the diversity of social groups and classes, generally avoiding monism and reductionism. They have treated a wide range of forms of resistance and contestation—in a richly historicized fashion. Subaltern studies has also made enduringly important methodological and theoretical contributions.

Subaltern studies has not pretended, on the other hand, to put forward a theory of popular mobilization and has often dwelt extensively on (important) topics or questions of theory not directly related to popular mobilization. Second, it often remains confined to the study of the dynamics of social subordination—whereas Gramsci's history of subaltern social groups extends all the way to revolutionary politics. 'Subaltern groups', writes Gramsci, 'are always subject to the initiatives of the dominant groups even when they rebel and rise up; only "permanent" victory breaks their subordination, but not immediately.'[90] The first clause of this quotation is often cited, holding great resonance, perhaps, in an age of defeat, but the second part is often unaccountably left out, as if even contemplating victory is impermissible.

Third, subaltern studies in general refers less to the detail of Gramsci's actual texts than one might think, making it less useful as a source for a theory of popular mobilization based on Gramsci's work.[91] Fourth, the view that the 'subaltern cannot speak', while insisting usefully on the interrogation of Eurocentric epistemology,[92] does not serve a theory about overcoming social domination very well and cuts against both Gramsci's point that some part of the subaltern is directive, active, and takes the initiative and against Gramsci's injunction that the 'integral historian' should find 'inestimable value' in '[e]very trace of autonomous initiative'.[93] Spivak, in fact, no longer claims that 'the subaltern cannot speak'; instead she puts the emphasis much more plausibly on the difficulties the subaltern has in being heard.[94]

Finally, where subaltern studies adopts a Foucauldian or a purely cultural register, it becomes very difficult to grasp popular mobilization at all, especially on fronts other than the discursive or cultural.

Finally, right-wing currents, reacting against the New Left while seeking to appropriate its tools, have cited Gramsci extensively (if superficially) since the 1970s—in Europe the 'New Right' and in the US neoconservative currents and, since the 2000s, the alt-right.[95] These thinker-activists cite Gramsci's insights on the importance of winning the cultural battle—'cultural hegemony'—as a prelude to winning political power. They are often heavily engaged in media activity and dissemination—'civil society'. Their criticisms of liberalism, reason, materialism, and individualism can sometimes ostensibly overlap with Gramscian critique. But their usages of Gramsci are almost always superficial and instrumental, based on numerous decontextualized citations and aphorisms.[96] These references are part 'political savvy' and part attempt to destabilize the Left by appropriating its language; they do not define a worldview—which instead draws on familiar conservative assumptions and thematics from de Maistre to Nietzsche to Heidegger—above all about the crisis of modernity and of 'Western civilization' and the loss of hierarchy, certainty, and purity. Hegemony is reduced to 'cultural hegemony', which is in turn reduced to a culture war. The history of subaltern social groups is nowhere to be found—only a stylized and polemical narrative, in which a putatively authentic (abstract) 'people' is corrupted by Left and liberal forms of hegemony. Right-wing Gramscians are best seen not as organic intellectuals or popular educators formed on the terrain of group, class, and bloc but as manipulators, populists, and culture warriors,[97] whose positionality ('truth-telling', 'rebellious') remains conceived as external to politics and history. This literature sheds light on the Right and its strategies and underlines Gramscian lessons about the importance of culture and civil society in politics, but it does not provide any genuinely Gramscian depth to a theory of popular mobilization.

GRAMSCI AS AN ORIGINAL THINKER

> The laceration which happened to Hegelianism [involving a lapse into spiritualism] has been repeated with the philosophy of praxis. That is to say, from dialectical unity there has been a regress to philosophical materialism.[98]

This book takes Gramsci to be a profoundly original thinker. His intervention is not just a tributary of Marxism but rather originates a new worldview, the headwater of a new and mighty tradition. Gramsci tends to be read, as we have seen, as either a Marxist/Leninist or a Crocean/Hegelian. However, Gramsci put forward, in the swansong of revolutionary Europe, a new synthesis of Bartoli, Croce, Hegel, Lenin, Machiavelli, Marx, and Sorel. In defending Marx against Croce, Gramsci developed a new reading of Marx, which he keyed into a wider synthesis. The many, deeply divided interpretations of Gramsci owe not only to ambiguity and difficulty in Gramsci's oeuvre but also to the ways in which Gramsci's highly original and deeply historicist intervention aimed to combine the material and the ideal, practice and theory, structure (economy) and superstructure (culture, state, and civil society), and working classes as well as other subaltern social groups. Marxists and non-Marxists alike have not been able to decide whether Gramsci was an idealist or a materialist because he was, or became, in the last years of his life, neither.

Gramsci was provoked into a vast and radical rethinking not only by the failures of bourgeois-liberal hegemony, revolutionary weakness and fascism in Italy, and the revolution in the European country *least* fitted for it according to Marxist theory ('backward' Russia) but also, and perhaps most painfully, by the authoritarian direction taken by the post-revolutionary Soviet Union, together with the unrealistic maximalist directives issued by the latter from the late 1920s onwards. No wonder Gramsci's language became so strong—going as far as to speak of the *laceration* of the philosophy of praxis. Gramsci is often read as providing a concept (hegemony) which could explain the survival of capitalism. Gramsci was just as concerned to understand what had gone wrong with communism—while holding onto its popular, socialist, and revolutionary content. This reading of Gramsci draws in various ways on exploratory, diverse, and open-ended uses of Gramsci[99] and finds a vast storehouse of evidence in the painstaking textual work on Gramsci of recent years.[100] Three points are fundamental.

The Philosophy of Praxis
First, Gramsci warns strongly against 'self-styled "orthodox" adherents of the philosophy of praxis' who 'fall into the trap and themselves conceive

their philosophy as subordinated to a general (vulgar) materialist philosophy just as others are to idealism'.[101] In this same note in *Prison Notebook* 11, Gramsci underlines his view, expressed in so many places in the *Prison Notebooks*, that materialism is of metaphysical origin. Gramsci even sees Marx as holding to a non-materialist philosophy: 'Marx always avoided calling his conception "materialist" and whenever he spoke of materialist philosophies he criticised them. . . . Marx never used the formula "materialist dialectic"—he called it "rational."'[102] A statement like this, whether accurate or not about Marx, reveals for my purposes here the extent to which Gramsci's Marx, Gramsci's founder of the philosophy of praxis, was not a materialist. Gramsci's most succinct and powerful definition of his own original understanding of the philosophy of praxis is as follows: 'It has been forgotten that in the case of a very common expression [historical materialism] one should put the accent on the first term—"historical"—and not on the second, which is of metaphysical origin. The philosophy of praxis is absolute "historicism", the absolute secularisation and earthliness of thought, and absolute humanism of history.'[103]

Not materialism nor idealism, then, nor the motions of capitalism—at the beating heart of Gramsci's deeply original philosophy of praxis are secularism, humanism and historicism. No less an authority than Giuseppe Vacca, argues that 'from the middle of 1932 onward, with the expression "philosophy of praxis", Gramsci intended to stress the originality of his own thought'.[104] Gramsci's philosophy of praxis supersedes materialism, while pushing against the Marxist 'abandoning' of philosophy.[105] For the purposes of this book, it gives philosophical meaning to the fact that overcoming social domination is a process of organic unification.

The Politics of Hegemony

Second, hegemony refers to Gramsci's theory of power relations, his theory of politics writ large,[106] developed above all from existing conceptions among Russian Marxists from 1926 onwards to 'combat economism'.[107] Power relations, Gramsci was saying, are not just a reflection of or solely determined by material relations; nor is the superstructure (civil society, culture, and the state) determined by the structure (the capitalist economy). Instead, the concept of hegemony adds the ethico-political to the economic-corporate; it combines structure and superstructure while broaching the fundamental issues of class, group, and bloc; space and time; and the balance and relation of forces. Hegemony is profoundly historicized; it is situated temporally, and built and won over time. Hegemony is taken in this book to be above all a rich and historicized analysis of power relations combining leadership, consent, autonomy, and domination. Gramsci's concept is fertile ground indeed for thinking the many forms, fronts, phases, and tasks of political struggle in general and popular mobilization in particular. It avoids idealism, materialism, and monism, and it allows for a variety of strategies and forms of organization. It is a powerful analytic for grasping the terrain inhabited and transformed.

The History of Subaltern Social Groups

Third, in relation to the history of subaltern social groups, Gramsci started to chart new territory from 1930 onwards. Although he had used the word subaltern mainly in bureaucratic or military contexts before then, the phrase 'subaltern classes' was used for the first time in June 1930, in *Prison Notebook* 3, §14, under the heading 'History of the dominant class and history of the subaltern classes'. The most complete expression of Gramsci's thinking comes in *Prison Notebook* 25, which is a Special Notebook (i.e. one devoted to a particular theme, not a miscellany). As we shall see, this was a historiography that broke decisively with the familiar Marxist emphasis on the history of the working class. Buey suggests that part of the immediate impetus for Gramsci's rethinking was his political disagreement with the (maximalist) leadership of the Communist Party under Stalin in the early 1930s: 'he began to write, from that moment on, on the "molecular work" that the subaltern classes have to carry out before they can conquer political hegemony.' [108] Gramsci was linking the successful creation of a new hegemony more closely with the necessarily bottom-up and 'popular' history of a diverse array of subaltern social groups—in short with all the granular processes of popular mobilization.

The original Gramsci thus takes conceptual shape in his philosophy of praxis, his politics of hegemony, and his history of subaltern social groups. These are the three fundamental pillars of a theory superseding historical materialism, capitalism, and the proletariat; it is a theory with still not fully realized potential for rethinking the rich diversity of popular mobilization, which includes theory and practice, subject and object, the ideal and the material, feeling and knowing, various classes and groups, structure and superstructure, time and space, the national and the transnational, and the balance and relation of forces. It is a theory which cannot be reduced to one or other of these terms. The original Gramsci is a promising start point for thinking diverse struggles, varied strategies, different phases, and battles on many fronts and for a theory of the articulation of struggles.

Gramsci praised Machiavelli's *Prince* for being a '"live" work' fusing ideology and science in the 'dramatic form of a "myth"'. He explains that 'the entire "logical" argument now appears as nothing other than auto-reflection on the part of the people—an inner reasoning worked out in the popular consciousness, whose conclusion is a cry of passionate urgency'.[109] Gramsci arguably saw his own thinking as just such an 'inner reasoning worked out in the popular consciousness', in other words, as elaborating organically on the challenges and dilemmas of subaltern social groups in search of emancipation. Gramsci's oeuvre continues to be a live work, fertile for the theoretical reconstruction of popular mobilization in the present, beckoning towards an approach which can connect struggles without reduction.

GRAMSCIAN THEORY AS HISTORICIST AND ORGANIC

What, then, is a Gramscian theory? History and theory are conventionally opposed, both in theory and in institutionalized academic disciplines. But history—and what Gramsci referred to as 'historical life'—is the lodestone of theory and theory-building in the Gramscian perspective. Marx is often seen, for example, as one of the greatest *theorists* of the nineteenth century. Gramsci roundly declared, on the contrary, that Marx was an *historian*. Gramsci meant it as a great compliment. In Gramsci's hands, theory is not positivist, objectivist, logico-deductive, or taxonomic but historicist, organic, interpretive, and engaged.

Theory is itself an activity, a task, a theoretical practice, an element of praxis; the task is to '"translate" the elements of historical life into theoretical language'.[110] 'Historical' does not refer to the distant past, or anything antiquarian, or mummified. It refers to a connection between past, present, and future.[111] It refers in some sense to the temporal depth reaching into the past of present activity, which is always, in turn, oriented to the future, because it involves the subject and a collective will which postulates in activity a certain direction in life and a certain kind of future or horizon. 'Historical' means that the social world is in formation over time and needs to be understood in the genetic movement and process of its formation. The term 'historical' needs also to be understood in the sense of 'making history', which is also layered in Gramsci with meanings of renewal and liberty, which eventually is a reference to overcoming domination, 'attain[ing] . . . historicity',[112] and bringing about liberation.[113]

'Life' (or 'life-activity') means praxis—the struggle to bring about the organic unification of theory and practice, subject and object, knowing and feeling. This struggle involves both coming into Being (e.g. growing up) and moving towards Non-Being (e.g. death). Life-activity refers to the actual historical (synthetic) path of becoming in which any thesis is threatened by an antithesis; but the dialectical passage of postulation, (determinate) negation, and reconstruction always leaves traces on the life-activity that passes through it. Our struggles, aiming to be socially conscious of our social being (the historical deposits of an infinity of traces) make us who we become. The dialectical struggle for unification *is* the real—that is, it is fundamentally operative in processes of actualization, or better still *realization*, the process of *making real*, which also contains within it an element of subjectivity (given the double meaning of the word 'realize'). Realization is a useful term as compared, for instance, to production, which suffers from economism and productivism (in a Marxist register), and to discursivism in a Foucauldian register, in which effects of the real are 'produced' and the subject only ever arrives too late to intervene. Realization is neither complete nor certain; it is experimental, involves trial and error, and is subject to reversal, as well as to change and development.

Theory is a *translation*: historical life is translated into language, while remaining as faithful as possible to historical life. The notion of translation presupposes neither identity (isomorphism) nor radical difference/incommensurability but immanent connections, oppositions, and distinctions between the theory and historical life. Language is words that make meaning, that interpret and make sense of the world, forming conceptions of it. Language is a matter of both precise and defined meaning but also of metaphor; a matter of both semantics and culture, of expression and force; and it is always historicized, being 'at the same time a living thing and a museum of fossils of life and civilisations.'[114] To think of theory is to think of the science of language (i.e. Gramsci's reference to philology). *Theoretical* language forms ever more encompassing, connecting, and fertile conceptions of the world.

Theory is interpretive; at some level, then, it makes meaning, not laws. It discovers connections, distinctions, and opposites, not constant conjunctions. Theory can discover relatively automatic and predictable processes and reactions, but these are a result of the balance and relation of forces situated in forms of hegemony and are ultimately historicized in ways that make them subject to change and transformation. Objectivist natural science models, positivist necessity, and regularity are very much excluded,[115] an exclusion that is at the heart of the meaning of praxis as an ongoing experiment. As Gramsci writes: 'It is not a question of "discovering" a metaphysical law of "determinism", or even of establishing a "general" law of causality. It is a question of bringing out how in historical evolution relatively permanent forces are constituted which operate with a certain regularity and automatism.'[116] As Gramsci writes, such forces can be economic, military, or international: they can also be political, meaning that they depend in part on the construction of the collective will, which in turn depends on the development of shared understandings and meanings, which in turn depend in part on theoretical language.

How does Gramsci expect such a theory to be truthful, reliable, or valid? Theory proves its this-sidedness in practice. It is 'proven' not by a series of abstract, positivist, or experimental tests—falsifiability, statistical verification, and so on—but more by the quality and rigour of the philological methodology, which demonstrates connectedness to historical life, and by 'practical-critique'—that is, how the theory fares in its translation into practice. The latter connects the theory to historical life not just to prove that it is 'correct' but in order to update it. Practical-critique determines whether the theory can realize itself in practice, the way it might be put to use in provoking meaningful social transformation. This epistemology is a deep strike against scholasticism, while at the same time underlining the political significance of both intellectuals and theory.

Theory provides a language which becomes richer, deeper, and more fertile the more such language—and the concepts and meanings specified and expressed in it—connects, contextualizes, and historicizes. Theory makes explicit the concepts implicit in practice and returns to inform practice.[117] Every interpretation, writes Gramsci, is a transformation. Theory is developed above all not by serene, scientistic figures who separate themselves from the historical process, peer down on the social formation as if from on high, and act as 'traditional' intellectuals, consecrating theory apart from practice, but by organic intellectuals, who are intimately and passionately connected with the life-activity and history of groups or classes in formation. Theoretical practice transforms the scientist himself. Full theoretical realization can only be achieved in relation to a process of liberation. The purpose of theory is not to generate theory, or to satisfy the demands of a formal logical scheme, or to be a prized artefact in a 'scientist's cabinet'[118] but to establish a new translation back into historical life. Theory is a live work—it does not stem from timeless concepts or principles and must update and renew itself over time to avoid ossification. It is no static, hypostasized scheme, but necessarily a living tradition. Theoretical language is not 'innocent' but implicated in power relations, in lines of social force, in the construction of this or that collective will. It is a not a grey wisdom, coming retrospectively and too late to change things, but an implicated and 'thrown' knowledge, stimulating rejuvenation and renewal. Prediction becomes a matter of constructing a collective will, not a matter of the discovery of an objective law or abstract cause in a social world radically distinct from the theorist. Organic theorizing (or 'living philology') can amount, in Gramscian optics, to leadership. It is a necessary aspect of hegemony.

LIVING PHILOLOGY

Gramsci wrote that theories must respond to 'actual concrete, living history, adapted to the time and the place'. They must be something that springs 'from all the pores of the particular society which [has] to be transformed'.[119] A theory cannot be born of another theory, but instead must be developed based on historical life.[120] Philology translates the elements of historical life into a theoretical language—while the reference to 'living' philology underlines the need for a reciprocal translation into historical life and emphasizes

The Living Gramscian Tradition

that these translations are both theoretical and political. The process is one of renovation (not creation ex nihilo). Initial particulars might be abstract— in the sense of being necessarily abstracted from a larger whole because of the initial uncertainty of the 'integral historian' in selecting them. But the methodological movement (of renovation) is to link them to a larger whole, to travel from the abstract particular towards the concrete universal, via ceaseless iterations from evidence of activity (the object of study) to theoretical development (the subject of study) and vice versa. Understanding the relationship to a wider whole will simultaneously be a process of discovering what is both 'stable and permanent' and 'distinct' in the 'material'.[121] 'Scrupulous accuracy and scientific honesty' are fundamental.[122] Gramsci himself was highly meticulous.[123] The historical context and political repercussions of both the subject and object of study, points which are bound up with the social positioning and purpose of the researcher, are emphatically in play. As critical historians have averred, the source materials, their production, the reading process, linguistic medium, and the researcher must be thought together.[124] The purpose of the researcher is necessarily present because researchers are assumed to be engaged, passionate, and implicated in social change. This engagement in turn is anticipated to result in knowledge that can matter and be useful for non-researchers who are also seeking change.

These methods set a high bar, but this book has attempted to use them— or draw on work that has—in its efforts to read Gramsci's life, his texts, and to interpret secondary research on both Gramsci's texts and on historical cases. The most important Gramsci texts are the *Prison Notebooks*, the 29 notebooks (*quaderni*) he wrote in prison under very difficult conditions between 1929 and 1935. The only comprehensive edition of the *Quaderni del Carcere* in any language is the 1975 Einaudi (Italian) edition completed under the direction of Valentino Gerratana.[125] The main English language *selections* from these notebooks were published in 1971 and 1995,[126] while the only comprehensive translation of notebooks 1–8 was published in three volumes in 1992, 1996, and 2007.[127] This book makes particular use of the recent, critical edition of Gramsci's late notebook, *Prison Notebook* 25, which gathers and translates for the first time all Gramsci's prison writings on subaltern social groups.[128] Another important source for Gramsci's cultural writings includes both selections from the prison notebooks and from his journalism and criticism between 1913 and 1922.[129] This book also makes use of Gramsci's pre-prison political writings,[130] some of his youthful work,[131] and his letters written both before and from prison.[132] This book thus owes a major debt to the translation and annotation of the Italian texts. I have also used vital resources such as the *Dizionario Gramsciano*, in which the prison notebooks become fully searchable.[133] The concordance tables (available online) of the International Gramsci Society are extremely helpful for cross-referencing.

Reading, in my case, has involved a productive suspension of disbelief. Some of Gramsci's texts are very difficult to understand and even apparently contradictory. Not for nothing did Perry Anderson write about Gramsci's antinomies.[134] Anderson gives many examples of concepts, such as civil society or the state, which change their meaning, merge together, or are highly distinct. I have found it productive—and perhaps this hazardous method of reading can only work when one is dealing with a great and original thinker—to continue to push on through the sense of difficulty and contradiction, to suspend the feeling of dissonance, and try to figure out how a concept or sentence could possibly take on the meanings that Gramsci appears to be giving it. It is shocking how Gramsci's concepts can seem to alter their meaning. An example of this, which comes in chapter 6, is the temporality of the war of position. There, Gramsci writes that the war of position is not only a long arduous *preparation* for the war of manoeuvre but can also come *after* the 'frontal assault' on the state, amidst a revolution. This felt almost like a step beyond what was plausible. But I have found that sticking with the apparent intended meaning eventually works. Part of the secret is to appreciate that Gramsci is not building a static photograph or a synchronic logico-deductive system but a profoundly historicized theory, in which cases and forms of mobilization, together with social structures, have to be understood in all their connections and temporal variations.

I have also drawn on the significant 'philological' and open-ended readings of the *Prison Notebooks* of recent times,[135] as well as the vital work now available in a range of Italian, Portuguese, and Spanish studies translated over the last decade into English.[136] I have made use of a series of classic studies—such as Boggs, Femia, and Salamini[137]—and taken much from interpreters such as Stuart Hall and Raymond Williams, as well as drawing for Gramsci's life on key biographies such as that of Fiori.[138] This material reaches enough detail, arguably, to permit judgements about Gramsci's work amid his own 'historical life'. These judgments have been further assisted in this book by 'further reading' into the relevant theoretical and cultural terrain—Bukharin, Croce, Engels, Feuerbach, Hegel, Labriola, Lenin, Luxemburg, Marx, Sorel, Togliatti, inter alia—a terrain which helps considerably in understanding Gramsci's intertextual universe, his sometimes subtle or obscure references and lexicon, and thereby the import and meaning of his interventions.

I have also made use of several hundred research studies carried out on cases of popular mobilization or related themes in all parts of the globe. Most of these are Gramscian studies, but I have also looked outside of the Gramscian tradition, especially at major and even organic intellectuals, to develop the range and depth of the analysis. Some of the best of these studies clearly use philological methods, enhancing their value. I have used this material for theoretical articulation—that is, for purposes of explanation and enrichment—and to work some forms of renovation on the theory itself. My own training as an historian interested in theory has in some ways helped me grasp the importance of Gramsci's own historicism for theory-building. Thirty years of research into history and politics 'from below' in South-West Asia and North Africa—and seeking a framework overcoming problems in Marxism, poststructuralism, and Orientalism—is the fundamental backdrop for and driver of the reading of Gramsci undertaken here.[139]

An academic such as myself, working in and subject to career logics in a neoliberal university, engaged in various ways as I have been, should not be mistaken for an organic intellectual.[140] Gramsci left university while still an undergraduate, operated far outside the walls of the academy, and, after eleven years of fascist incarceration, died for the cause. Much of Gramsci's learning came from political struggle. I have learned much from my own political engagements—about, for example, Zionism, Orientalism, racism, British ruling complicity, and above all about civil society and the war of position in relation to a transnational mobilization. But these engagements, although passionate, have been minor. There are limits to the extent to which a researcher, especially one that is white, male, middle class, straight, and formed in British colonial culture, can unlearn the positionality of the traditional intellectual and the problem of knowing but not feeling. I have been deeply alienated by the neoliberal university. But I have also found positions and sites of flourishing within middle class and intermediary structures. And one should never assume any unproblematic link between alienated intellectuals and oppressed groups. Almost all the time, the links are tenuous at best, and difficult to construct, as Gramsci was acutely aware. Note also that this book is not philological: the theory presented here *is* largely based on another theory (one stunningly superior to anything I could possibly come up with), albeit a theory developed by an organic intellectual. My aim has been to give a certain meaning to an already highly elaborated language and not to add new terms, something even Gramsci mostly avoided.[141] I have aimed, in Gramscian spirit, and with figures like Laurence Cox and Alf Nilsen neither to polemicize, in masculinist or sectarian fashion; nor to impose an orthodoxy, nor to express or to vent—but to contribute to a broader, collective tradition and cause.

Overall, my position in this book in relation to the Gramscian tradition is something like a gathering together and a setting out—a passing on of what I have grasped, having been privileged to have the time and space to engage with what are, after all, fiendishly complex puzzles. My position is neither one of postmodern irony nor is it draped in any sort of authenticity. It is alienated, uneasy, contradictory, Janus-faced. It is convinced by the need for unlearning, certain of the need to build, searching for renewal amid crisis. Perhaps a book, emerging from the university, by an author striving to be what Gramsci called an 'integral historian'—which I take to be an engaged historian who connects history to philosophy and politics—could potentially set out 'detailed observations useful for awakening an interest in effective reality and for stimulating more rigorous and more vigorous political insights'.[142] This was Gramsci's definition of political science, one which clearly breaches the institutionalized behavioralist and positivist opposition between 'normative political theory' and 'empirical political science'.[143] I aim to have applied such a science, as an historian, to the question of popular mobilization.

CONCLUSION

This chapter has situated, developed, and justified the theoretical framework and method, underlining the originality and fertility of the living

Gramscian tradition. The chapter has argued that conservative approaches suffer from genus-thinking and from a hierarchical perspective which maintains subaltern social groups in their place, while liberal and rationalist approaches are marked by varieties of abstraction, false universalism, and objectivism in which popular mobilization eventually dissolves into either static structures or shapeless, interacting mechanisms. I have argued that the Gramscian tradition has offered much to critical approaches and learns much from them in turn. But ultimately the chapter contends that this tradition is uniquely positioned to overcome the materialism of Marxism and postcolonial culturalism. The chapter maintains this argument also in relation to readings of Gramsci, arguing that the key to grasping the originality of the Gramscian tradition, and its capacity to ground a connecting theory of popular mobilization, lies in assimilating Gramsci neither to Marxism nor to cultural and postcolonial studies. The chapter has fleshed out this case by outlining the keys to a Gramscian approach: the philosophy of praxis, the politics of hegemony, the history of subaltern social groups, historicist and organic theory building, and a method of living philology.

CHAPTER TWO

The Faces and Phases of Popular Mobilization

The living Gramscian tradition permits us to understand and link together the highly diverse faces and phases of popular mobilization. This chapter explains what this means, laying out the main definitions, language, interpretive criteria, and conceptual architecture of a Gramscian theory of popular mobilization, drawing very much on the writings of Gramsci himself. The chapter takes up the question of the people and the popular, of subaltern diversity and bloc formation, of the place of intellectuals, of revolutionizing praxis; and of structure, space and time, popular forces, and renewal—the 'faces' of mobilization—before turning to the key phases of this complex morphology of transformation. It establishes the conceptual architecture on which the remainder of the book expands.

THE PEOPLE AND THE POPULAR

In Gramsci's hands, 'the people' and the 'popular' do not refer to a homogenous, pre-existing authentic group, or to a juridical subject, or to the industrial proletariat writ large but to the living, internally differentiated, historicized *ensemble* of the dispossessed classes and groups. These terms refer to the sum of all subaltern social groups, all those at the 'margins of history' who, qua group, are subordinated, objectified, and oppressed. The people, writes Gramsci, refers to 'the ensemble of the subaltern and instrumental classes of every form of society that has existed thus far'.[1] As the Gramsci Dictionary has it: 'The adjective "popular" in the Q[uaderni] indicates what belongs or is widespread among the people, understood as the ensemble of the subordinate.'[2] The popular then, in Gramscian perspective, can be defined as the plural ensemble of the subordinate.

Gramsci, however, is no academic hypostatizer of social categories. Nor was his horizon in any way limited by studying the dynamics of social subordination. His concern with the popular and the subordinate is a revolutionary one; it relates to the overcoming of subordination and the emancipation of subaltern social groups. Green argues that the 'underlying impetus' of the investigation into the history of subaltern social groups was that 'the analysis of subaltern classes incorporates an examination of the elements necessary for them to transform their conditions and liberate themselves'.[3] As *Prison Notebook* 25 makes abundantly clear, Gramsci seeks out a tendency of organic 'unification', a line of development from the most subordinated positions to a point of culmination in 'permanent victory'. The term popular thus contains a tense combination of opposites—domination on the one hand and liberation on the other, beckoning towards a dialectical overcoming. Gramsci, Boggs writes, was thinking in terms of 'a world-historical struggle for a classless society, the realisation of which would for the first time unify subject and object'.[4]

In thinking popular modalities of overcoming social domination, Gramsci, inspired by Machiavelli, had in mind a wide-ranging process: the transformation of a loose multitude with only particular interests, people in a 'diffused' and 'molecular' (here meaning individuated) state, into a socially emancipated people (*popolo*). As Fontana writes:

> [F]or a stable state, Machiavelli required that the 'Prince' and the people should negotiate and share common goals. The precondition for this is that individuals should be converted from a 'multitude' (*multitudine sciolta*, in Machiavelli's phrase), in which each member looks to his or her private interests or *bene particolare*, into a collective subject or a 'people' (*popolo*) with a public interest or *bene comune*: that is, the people are created as a potentially hegemonic force in a 'public space' where the moment of force is transcended through dialogue and agreement is reached between prince and people, leaders and led.[5]

A scattered multitude of the subordinated, characterized by social domination, separation, individuation, disaggregation, dispersal, private interests, and an absence of mediating institutions and 'organisms', was to be overcome in the making of an emancipated people. These people would be connected to each other and organized organically as a social force in the pursuit of the common good, overcoming, amid collective will formation, the many varieties of social domination, along with the division between ruler and ruled, in a new form of collective self-rule. The people and the popular, then, suggests a work in progress, a point of arrival rather than one of departure.[6] Much depends, as will be seen in chapter 6, on whether the *popolo* in question eventually makes up a *national* community. In the contemporary world, when nationalism either fails to oppose or actively collaborates in forms of social domination, we can put Gramsci to work in ways which think beyond nationalism and homogenizing representations of the popular, renovating through an engagement with translocal and transnational forms.

The processes of group, class, and popular transformation in view are understood as a process of social becoming. Those on the margins of history are to have a history. Gramsci overcomes all forms of (historicist) determinism, not to mention class and group reductionism and essentialism, by thinking in terms of the historical self and the formation of a historical personality. The question 'Who am I?' and 'Who are we?' is always related in historicist and humanist fashion to the question 'Who can I/we become'?[7] The Russian violinist who married Gramsci, Giulia Schucht (1896–1980), put the tension clearly in a letter to Gramsci. She wrote: 'I ask myself which of the two people that there are inside me is the authentic one: the one that I want to be, or the one that I am?'[8] For her husband, *social being* (who I am / we are) is the self as the 'précis of all the past',[9] the self produced by 'the historical process to date', the 'infinity of traces' deposited on the self by that past. *Social consciousness* (who I/we wish to become) is developed through the critical compilation of an 'inventory' of these traces.[10] The dialectics of social being and social consciousness mark the passage at work in the process of historical social becoming. The passage is difficult, to say the least, because it cannot be fully realized until social domination is overcome.

MOBILIZATION

Gramsci does not use the word 'mobilization' very often, but this nonetheless is arguably an apt single term for referring to the many forms and processes involved in the popular overcoming of social domination, in the diverse ways in which popular and subordinate groups aim to or can challenge subordination. In the Gramscian register, it refers most fundamentally

The Phases of Popular Mobilization

to the rearrangement, recombination, and rearticulation of molecular (granular, individual, sub-individual, and micrological) elements and relationships in ways that can create new forms and unleash new energies, derived from the creative combination of previously disconnected, distinct, or opposed elements. Mobilization is a useful term for grasping the diverse, molecular, and *generative* processes involved in challenges to domination. It is a much more open-ended and relational concept than that of 'social movement', which is more particular, specific, continuous, and organized—and notoriously difficult to define, precisely because so many different sorts of activity are involved and because there is so much change over time in the life of a given movement. Mobilization can apply to the activism of diverse groups and classes and can refer to change over time and to a very wide range of activity, including everyday forms of resistance, non-movements, intellectual labour, alternative economic activity, popular uprisings, social-movement campaigning in civil society, party activity, unions, popular education, courts or assemblies, and armed struggle, inter alia.

Molecular rearrangement (mobilization) of the popular kind has a capacity to generate new social forms. Such capacity is easily overlooked and scorned because of the lowly status of many of the component elements. However, just as the molecular changes and energy releases in physics or organic chemistry bring into being new compounds, reactions, and forces, so too can the social rearrangement of 'molecular' relationships, even among the weak and the oppressed, bring into being new forms and social forces. *Pace* Hegel, even the addition of the same (i.e. of *quantity*), to a given combination, could eventually bring about a transformation in *quality*. An increase in the number of participants, for instance, can turn a demonstration into a popular uprising. Further, a collection of elements or individuals, when combined in a certain way, could become more than the sum of its parts. 'It will be said', writes Gramsci, in a discussion of necessity and freedom, 'that what each individual can change is very little, considering his strength. This is true up to a point. But when the individual can associate himself with all the other individuals who want the same changes . . . the individual can be multiplied an impressive number of times and can obtain a change which is far more radical than at first sight ever seemed possible.'[11] Mobilization, then, refers to new associations and combinations, which can be studied for their potential to generate new forms and social forces, capable of challenging social domination.

C. L. R. James's classic work, *The Black Jacobins*, charted the ways in which Black slaves were transformed from 'trembling in hundreds before a single white man' into an emancipated social force which could 'organize themselves and defeat the most powerful European nations of their day'.[12] Popular mobilization refers to all the molecular processes through which subordinated groups rearrange their relationships to create new social forms and forces in challenging and overcoming social domination. As we shall see, it eventually pushes beyond the national and any singular representation of the popular.

SUBALTERN DIVERSITY AND BLOC FORMATION

Subaltern social groups are highly diverse. Gramsci 'does not conceive of them [subaltern social groups] as a single or homogenous entity, which is why he consistently refers to them in the plural'.[13] 'He refers to slaves, plebeians, common people, the protoproletariat of the medieval communes, peasants, and the modern industrial proletariat as subaltern classes.'[14]

In *Prison Notebook* 25, the shift in terminology is from subaltern classes to subaltern social groups. Green argues with considerable persuasiveness that this is not an attempt to conceal references to class, not a code to fool the prison censor, because references to class continue to be present in the *Prison Notebooks*. Green writes that it was more likely 'a greater emphasis on the heterogeneous nature of subalterns, stressing the problematic issue of the relationship and difference between "the categories of 'people', 'classes', and 'social groups'"'.[15] Green suggests that in Gramsci 'classes are constituted in specific historical contexts and in relation to other contributing forms of disaggregation and marginalization, such as relations of race, religion, and gender, among others'; class analysis is intertwined with structural, cultural, and ideological specificities.[16] One should add that in Gramsci, *group* analysis is also intertwined with the economic.

The old thesis that the usage of the phrase 'subaltern social group' was only a code for 'proletariat' used by Gramsci to avoid censorship has been substantially discredited. It is not that Gramsci was the predominant twentieth-century thinker of gender, the colonized, race, and sexuality—

but it is convincingly demonstrated that subaltern social groups included women, Blacks, Jews, Southerners (internally or externally colonized groups), slaves, peasants, and serfs. Gramsci compares American Blacks in the early twentieth century with Jews in eighteenth century Europe. He considers the possibility of a future shift from a negative consciousness of a 'despised race', which he argued was 'the result of a struggle carried on by whites to isolate and depress them', to a positive consciousness of a national character. He took note of movements which saw the African continent as a mythic fatherland—Liberia as the Zion of 'American Negroes', an African Piedmont.[17] Judy has argued that Gramsci, in ways comparable to W. E. B Du Bois, the great Black American intellectual and activist, completely avoids 'biological or ethnographic race' and insists on the historicity of Blacks and their formation.[18] Gramsci's scattered notes on sexuality make very clear that he rejects the claim that sexuality is defined by nature, as well as the colonial connotative articulation of savagery and unbridled or deviant sexuality.[19] Gramsci also clearly adopts a sceptical attitude to calls for a resurgence of 'masculinism' in the face of feminism and rejects the ways in which the 'aesthetic' ideal of woman oscillates between the conceptions of 'brood mare' and of 'dolly'.[20] Gramsci also compares race, class, and gender in relation to subaltern social groups: 'Often, subaltern groups are originally of a different race (different religion and different culture) than the dominant groups, and they are often a mixture of different races, as in the case of slaves [in Rome]. The question of the importance of women in Roman history is similar to the question of the subaltern groups, but up to a certain point; "masculinism" can be compared to class domination only in a certain sense and, therefore, has greater importance for the history of customs than for political and social history.'[21] The history of 'customs' can be read as highly limiting: but given the vital importance of culture in Gramscian perspectives, perhaps we do not have to read it this way. Many would agree that class domination and masculinism are comparable, but non-identical.

Overcoming social domination involves a genuinely plural ensemble of the subordinate. The implication for a Gramscian theory of popular mobilization is twofold: on the one hand, there is the imperative to do justice to a wide variety of social groups and classes, including those whose existence does not map without domination or erasure onto a cartography of nations and states. On the other there is the need to study questions of bloc formation—that is, how different subaltern social groups and classes can forge alliances, including transnationally, especially in relation to the diversity and unevenness in relation to self, structures, time, space and popular forces. As we shall see in chapters 5 and 6, much turns on whether bloc formation is conceived in democratic or authoritarian ways.

THE PLACE OF INTELLECTUALS

While some theorists of popular politics and many histories 'from below', Marxist and non-Marxist, either ignore or assign a negative role to intellectuals in general, Gramsci distinguishes between traditional and organic intellectuals, making the latter one of the central moments in popular mobilization.

Traditional intellectuals are likened by Gramsci to a closed caste. They are supposedly objective and detached. They peer down serenely from on high at culture and society. They restrict, in a scholastic mode, their activities to theory, which they see as having a continuity and complete existence of its own.[22] Traditional intellectuals do not build the new but represent the old; they continue to live 'in the worm-eaten integument of old history'.[23] They tend to view the social world as an object to be contemplated, controlled, or reformed. They contribute to the oppressive split between mental and manual labour, blocking the unification of theory and practice, the development in practice of critical consciousness from subordinate positions—and are associated with social domination.[24]

Organic intellectuals, on the other hand, are intimately connected with the historical life of a particular group or class.[25] They contribute to the 'awareness' and 'homogeneity' of the group. They are not just thinkers, artists, or rhetoricians; they are also involved in 'active participation in practical life, as constructor, organizer, "permanent persuader" . . . [not just] "specialised" . . . [but also] "directive" '.[26] They are thus economically active, culturally active, and even active in the state. Gramsci says that they particularly operate in civil society, wherein the connections between groups/classes, culture, the state, and the economy are mediated and where consent is organized and contested. Organic intellectuals are associated with the living unification of theory and practice, subject and object, with overcoming social domination. As Gramsci writes: 'A human mass does not "distinguish" itself and does not become independent per se without organizing itself (broadly speaking); and there is no organization without intellectuals, that is, without organizers and leaders.'[27]

In relation to popular mobilization, the extremely difficult, threatened, and precarious task of an organic intellectual is to remain intimately connected with the subaltern effort to overcome social domination. It is a process that is 'long, difficult, full of contradictions, advances and retreats, breakups and regroupings, in which the "loyalty" of the mass is, at times, severely tested'.[28] Such an intimate connection cannot be sustained by windy cosmopolitanism, but equally, in the contemporary world, it cannot simply imply the nationalization of intellectual life.

REVOLUTIONIZING PRAXIS

Revolutionizing praxis is, pace Marx's *Theses on Feuerbach*, 'practical-critical activity', the coincidence—and tense combination—of self-changing and the changing of circumstances. Gramsci referred to 'il rovesciamento della praxis'.[29] Not only is group, class, social becoming, and people formation at stake—self-changing—but so too is the making of new forms of structure (economy) and superstructure (civil society, culture, and the state)—the changing of circumstances.

The self as the ensemble of social relations, as 'the process of his [*sic*] actions',[30] cannot be transformed nor can an emancipated *popolo* be formed without modifying the 'ensemble of these relations'[31]—that is, forging new forms of production, civil society, culture, and state. Gramsci makes clear that the history of subaltern social groups is profoundly intertwined with the histories of civil societies and the state.[32]

Revolutionizing praxis is thus not only a profound insight into the roiling heart of popular mobilization but also an indication that a theory of popular mobilization should study not just processes of social becoming (all the questions of group, class, and bloc pertaining) but in addition the intimately connected question of structural change: the transformations wrought (or not) by popular mobilization on civil society, culture, economy, and state.

CIVIL SOCIETY, CULTURE, ECONOMY, AND THE STATE

I cannot do justice here to the extensive debates about these structures, but a Gramscian theory of popular mobilization needs to define these terms. I take each in turn, in alphabetical order, to indicate no priority. Gramsci writes, 'Between the economic structure and the State, with its legislation and its coercion, stands civil society.'[33] Civil society is the site where consent is won and organized. It is the 'hegemonic apparatus' of the ruling groups and a terrain of struggle for popular and others social forces seeking to win consent. It is the site where the ethical content of the state—of the common good—is worked out. It links together state, culture, and economy and is the engine room of the diffusion of ideology and common sense. It is a product of specific modern historical developments and involves typically voluntary organisms: churches, schools, media, syndicates, unions, political parties, cultural associations, and the like—all marked by the 'private' initiative of social groups and classes.[34] Civil society spreads far and wide across national and regional boundaries and must not be conceived as merely domestic; it is also transnational. For the purposes of this book, civil society is a key terrain, both national and transnational, on which popular mobilization must do battle—and one, as Gramsci writes, which 'must be radically transformed'.[35]

Culture is another crucial front of political struggle and of popular mobilization.[36] It is intimately intertwined with both social being and social consciousness. It is at work in civil society, economy, and the state. It is a deeply historicized '*intersubjective* universe of beliefs and values',[37] much of it being inscribed in language, and is crucial for the formation of a collective will.[38] Gramsci called ideological struggle 'a necessary moment of revolutionizing praxis'.[39] Cultural formations are syncretic, do not exist in national containers, and diffuse across national borders, especially through multiple processes of translation. In this book I have in mind two key points. First, for Gramsci, culture involves all the *drama* (and catharsis) of the organic passage between feeling and knowing and reaches for understanding.[40] Second, it gives a structure, or an inner formation, to the self and to social becoming as a fortification and a necessity rather than as a luxury, an instrument, or an item of consumption. It includes art, literature, music, theatre, film, poetry, novels, periodicals, fashion, and so on, as well as common sense, good sense, ideology, and philosophy. Culture is thus a work in progress, a matter of translation, including between national languages, and popular mobilization, as a process of moral and intellectual reform, must enrich and deepen its forms and capacities.

Gramsci's conception of the economy and capitalism is another major area for debate. In Vacca's Gramsci, the critique of political economy and capitalism is woven in throughout.[41] Cospito mines the *Prison Notebooks* for Gramsci's economic theories.[42] It is important to point out that Gramsci did not reduce 'economics to the technical relations of production'.[43] It is possible that Gramsci, influenced somewhat by a non-idealist reading of Croce, saw the economy as an aspect of human sensuous activity oriented towards 'the useful'—towards the production of 'real things rather than profit'.[44] He embedded economic activity in all the other elements of social life, against the Marxist tendency to prioritize all matters economic. It is also clear that Gramsci aimed to think economy at multiple scales—from the local to the hemispheric—and had a profoundly historicist understanding of capitalist formations and development, did not believe in ineluctable economic laws, and sought constantly forms of politics that could transform capitalism along with its forms of objectification, exploitation, and oppression into socialism. Economic tasks are fundamental to the struggles of popular mobilization.

The state is another major area for debate in Gramsci scholarship, and a crucial element in the 'superstructure'.[45] As Gramsci reminds us 'every political struggle always has a military substratum'.[46] This book follows much of Gramsci scholarship in working with two different meanings. The state in the narrow sense is defined as the 'apparatus of state coercive power which "legally" enforces discipline on those groups who do not "consent" either actively or passively'.[47] This state—political society—is contrasted with civil society. It is associated not with the state as a whole but 'refers only to the coercive relations embodied in the state apparatuses'.[48] It is often seen as similar to the *stato carabinieri*—the military and nightwatchman state— defending property rights and monopolizing powers of coercion, regulation, law, and taxation. State coercion, it is important to note, reaches across borders, especially in forms of imperialism.

The second meaning refers to the state in the larger sense, the 'integral state', sometimes compared to the *stato etico*. It is a 'sociopolitical and socioeconomic order'[49] defined as the 'entire complex of practical and theoretical activities with which the ruling class not only justifies and maintains its dominance, but manages to win the consent of those over whom it rules'.[50] Here authors have also invoked the 'extended state' and the 'educator state', which includes activities such as education and subsumes forms of civil society; or, perhaps, as in the regulated society, the state is 'integral' because it is made minimal and subjected to popular democracy and an ascendant civil society. Morera usefully suggests that the state becomes an educator in certain historical or political situations in order to maintain control and to continue to encompass civil society.[51] Popular mobilization can be read against statism and nationalism, but it must equally do battle on the terrain of the state and the integral state, which are both intertwined with imperial, international, and transnational elements and flows.

This book follows Cospito's reading, which argues that Gramsci 'no longer believed in the validity' of the view that structure (the economy) determines the superstructure (civil society, culture, and the state), even in the last instance.[52] Rather, Gramsci is concerned, first, to discover the complex relations between civil society, culture, economy, and state; second, to probe and understand the balance and relation of forces that determine these relationships; and third, and above all, to study a structural terrain to grasp the ways in which it can and should be transformed—that is, how there can be an intervention into the balance and relation of forces. Popular mobilization, then, operates within this structural terrain, both on the domestic and the international levels, and is precisely such an intervention. It can and must be understood solely neither in relation to whether this or that movement achieves its goals nor in relation to 'self-changing' but also in relation to the ways in which popular mobilization transforms the structures and circumstances in which it is so intricately enmeshed or fails to do so.

The long revolution at stake here carries a major philosophical charge, a rationale and motivation as profound as those associated with religion, precisely because it is only through the revolution in the secular and 'earthly' basis of the social formation that alienated forms of religion, the latter understood as in Marx's *Theses on Feuerbach* as a powerful and deeply felt search for the other world to save us from oppression and soullessness in this world, will be overcome. For this reason, the long revolution, as a replacement in relation to religious life, must mirror and discharge many of religion's profound moral and motivational elements and functions. The search for a new people is a matter of liberation; it promises an end to oppression and alienation. It is not just a matter of economy and state, for example, but a question of a long moral and intellectual reform: the formation of a new philosophy and a new culture on a global scale, a transformation comparable to transformations such as—albeit taken from European history—the Protestant Reformation or the Renaissance. The Protestant Reformation disestablished the Catholic Church; in the contemporary world it is perhaps more a matter of disestablishing the nation.

SPACE AND TIME

Social becoming and structure are also constructed amid space and time. Kipfner underlines that 'spatial differentiation and temporal nuance were both at the heart of Gramsci's historicism'.[53] Space is not given but constructed on many scales—including the transnational—amid hegemony. It is clear in *Prison Notebook* 25 that what was—or appears—marginal is in fact central in relation to the history of subaltern social groups and eventually becomes central in both Gramsci's thinking and in historical renewal. What is spatially fragmented, disaggregated, divided, and dispersed starts to become connected and organized. New forms of place and new horizons and forms of space are constructed on ever wider scales. In popular mobilization, the disaggregation, division, and carceral practices imposed by ruling groups, including forms of statism and nationalism, are also overcome, especially by translocal and transnational flows and linkages (supra- and sub-state connections across national and state boundaries).

Temporality is a connection between the past, the present, and the future, and in Gramsci this connection is not just out there, an objective fact of nature, but has to be forged.[54] In popular mobilization, what is episodic— that is, what occurs not continuously but only sporadically, in fits and starts—now becomes the focus of a continuous stream of temporal unfolding, capable of connecting past, present, and future; of having a history (and thus a future); of being 'worth' a history; of having a past 'worth remembering'; and of being narratable diachronically in a connected fashion (with a beginning, a middle, and an end). The apparently seamless temporal continuities of official history and ruling class narratives are themselves to be interrupted and challenged by the new politics, new imaginaries of the past. It turns out that subaltern social groups do have a history, including an ancestral one, that does not march lockstep with nationalist historiography, and can stretch back many centuries. Realizing such connections, and their particular temporalities, which at the outset are not conspicuous, is a work in progress, sometimes yielding dramatic results. Gramscian geographers have developed the vital insight that space and time are *connected* (not fundamentally separated) in Gramscian theory—building spaces is related to how temporalities will be made, and vice versa.[55]

POPULAR FORCES

Popular mobilization is not only a process of social becoming, structural transformation, and spatio-temporal change. It must also construct—at the same time—popular forces. Popular mobilization intervenes in and changes the balance and relation of forces—economic, political, military, and international.[56] The question is whether new combinations and rearrangements (forms of mobilization) can 'win new energy from the connections newly entered into' as Marx puts it in the *Eighteenth Brumaire*.[57]

Gramsci makes clear that forces cannot be assessed solely with reference to quantities—sheer numbers of persons, resources, arms, or local or global allies—because a force, just as in physics, is not an intrinsic property (like mass) but, like weight, directional and depends on interactions. Quantity is always being transformed into quality.[58] One cannot determine the outcome of a struggle by the quantitative capacity of the adversaries at the start point. To become a force, quantities have to be arranged, acquire certain new characteristics, and be set in motion—formed up and organized or directed in a certain way. Cultural factors, such as ideology, are particularly relevant in the construction of *political* forces, especially amid party activity. Popular forces can partly be determined by 'an evaluation of the degree of homogeneity, self-awareness, and organization attained by the various social classes'.[59] We might say that force combines social consciousness with social being in a certain way—including in relation to space and time. Factors such as morale are important: one cannot assume, for instance, that even amid a widespread economic crisis, ruling groups, not to mention the foreign governments who might back them, will automatically lose confidence, morale, or simply give up.[60] Gramsci's analysis of forces is undertaken not for purely academic purposes, but to determine how best to intervene strategically—to find points of least resistance, for example, or to determine tactics, including how to launch a campaign, which language will best be understood by popular groups, and so on.[61] The question of force, then, is always accompanied by a strategic analysis.

The analysis must not confine itself to the national. Forces include 'great power' politics, 'the combinations of States in hegemonic systems', 'small and medium powers', and the differential meanings of 'independence and sovereignty' in these contexts.[62] International relations also intertwine with the 'internal relations of nation-states', 'creating new, unique and historically concrete combinations': 'A particular ideology, for instance, born in a highly developed country, is disseminated in less developed countries, impinging on the local interplay of combinations.'[63] The diffusion of ideology and culture—including statist and nationalist ideologies, on the one hand, but also ideologies which can confront them, on the other—across national borders is a key element in a Gramscian theory of popular mobilization, based as it is on the 'interplay of combinations'. Popular political force can acquire leverage by connecting transnationally against interstate power politics, although this is by no means guaranteed.

There are also other intersections of the national and transnational. 'This relation between international forces and national forces is further complicated by the existence within every State of several structurally diverse territorial sectors, with diverse relations of force at all levels (thus the Vendée [during the French revolution] was allied with the forces of international reaction, and represented them in the heart of French territorial unity).'[64] The balance and relation of forces in a local setting amidst a revolutionary process, in other words, is combined with and impacted by transnational flows and international forces.

Popular forces owe much to the construction of an organized collective will—a will that otherwise is by no means given in any law-like structure or objective cause but is a collective volition and desire that is constructed, worked on, produced, and organized. Collective will is necessary because the revolution will not just *come* (for instance, through the autonomous construction of alternative forms of economy or ways of life) but needs to be *made* amid various forms of conflict and antagonism. Gramsci situates his most famous discussion of collective will in notes on language. The logic here is that organic intellectuals translate historical life into theoretical language, which in turn furnishes the shared understandings necessary for building a collective will, which in turn is crucial in the construction of popular force.

In modern times, the will is not individual (the traditional Prince) but a collective protagonism (the modern Prince). That it cannot be supplied by an individual, a hero, a Prince, or a charismatic deliverer is fundamental to Gramsci's approach. As we shall see in chapters 5 and 6, much depends on whether one reads Gramsci's modern Prince as a single, vanguardist party oriented above all toward the nation and the state and based on a 'correct' interpretation of the motions and laws of the economic structure or whether, as this book will argue, leadership involves a more plural, democratic, transnational, and non-monopolistic form of transformative organization. This organization combines many opposites and distincts associated with the postmodern Prince[65] or what Gramsci himself foreshadows in his discussion of the 'organic party'.

In relation to Machiavelli's *Prince*, Gramsci wrote of the 'myth-Prince', whose function was to forge a *popolo*. Gramsci gives, at one level, a very particular, positive meaning to myth via his interpretation of the French syndicalist philosopher Georges Sorel. Myth here is a profound motivation and a belief in eventual victory. It gives a specific content and horizon to an 'optimism of the will'. It contributes a vital revolutionary morale[66] to the formation of a 'collective will' amid suffering, despair, and fragmentation. While for Machiavelli and Gramsci the myth of the national popular was front and centre, it may be that in the contemporary world it is the positive myth of the plurinational—or what I will refer to as the transnational popular—that is arguably more compelling.

RENEWAL, DECOMPOSITION, AND NEOFORMATION

Popular mobilization presents a stream of renewal. It is the steps that overcome social domination that make history, in the sense of producing a stream of meaningful events marking 'new times', or renewal. History is closely associated, in this regard, with liberty.[67] The word 'history', in this register, is Gramsci's non-speculative version of Hegel's 'Spirit'. Overcoming social domination is also associated with 'making live' (renewing) because it involves the organic unification of theory and practice. These presuppositions offer another set of interpretive criteria for thinking and understanding the most positive face, as it were, of processes of popular mobilization. They return us also to the strong sense in which popular mobilization involves constructing new temporalities and histories.

Thinking in terms of renewal and its opposites is also key in identifying how popular mobilization is deformed, defanged, and broken down. Gramsci writes, in a little remarked sentence, about how subaltern efforts to overcome social domination play a role in 'determining processes of decomposition and renewal, or neoformation'.[68] Decomposition refers to forms of death, ossification, rigidification, mummification,[69] morbid phenomena, and to becoming an anachronism—as well as to the sense of disaggregation into constituent parts, the severing of connections and bonds newly made—and hence to dissipation and decay. Popular mobilization can decompose—'dissipate like steam not enclosed in a piston box'[70]—or become mired in spatial or social division, or fail to build an 'adequate quality superstructure', or fail to keep up with changing times. Decomposition can include the loss of temporal continuity, the sapping of positive myth and morale, the crumbling of the ideological bloc, and the loss of cohesion of language and collective will. Quality can be turned back into quantity as coordination fails and private interests prevail. Popular mobilization can also be deformed through *neoformation*: the creation of new forms of social domination. This can happen within the ranks of the mobilizers, when leaders become maximalists or dictators, when organic intellectuals become traditional intellectuals, or when representatives or delegates become detached from their popular base and join the ruling class or ruling bloc, or when ruling classes themselves engineer ways for popular mobilization to be absorbed—including within an authorized site of autonomy—within the existing hegemony. Gramsci's theory of popular mobilization is anything but a romanticization. It is not a jargon of authenticity. Popular mobilization is constantly threatened and 'interrupted'. Emancipation is very far from being guaranteed. The direction of change is redefined over time. Gramsci's approach is a foil for thinking through the weaknesses, failures, and dead ends of popular mobilization—understood here through the terminology of decomposition and neoformation—as much as it is a way to think the hard road to renewal.

DOMINATION, AUTONOMY, CONSENT, LEADERSHIP

> The upheavals in the Moroccan countryside [in the late nineteenth and early twentieth century] are . . . not to be put in one and the same category. The real revolts, which did not have an essentially tribal base, were those of Mahdist inspiration—one of which, indeed, eventually overthrew the system. In the other, more numerous cases, [revolt] was a means—for those under regulation—of expressing a grievance, participating in power (for the leaders), [and/or] consolidating a more or less recognized autonomy.[71]

Popular mobilization is not a quick fix. Revolutionary politics, notwithstanding the continued significance of the seizure of power, and the rupture in the balance of forces, is not a lightning bolt that brings about the millennium. Even a critic of Gramsci such as Perry Anderson eventually concedes the importance of Gramsci's thinking about the before and the after of revolution: 'while Gramsci took the overthrow of the capitalist state to be indispensable . . . there was also a sense in which he thought that the construction of a revolutionary bloc before the conquest of power, and the consolidation of the new communist order after it, were deeper and harder tasks.'[72]

A theory of popular mobilization, particularly one so invested in generative transformation over time, needs to find a way to think this temporal depth, while allowing for the fact that sometimes there really are rapid qualitative shifts, 'weeks when decades happen'. As Laurence Cox reminds us, if revolutionaries think a quick fix is nigh, they are apt to be disappointed. One needs to find a way to think popular mobilization as a process that scales up over time and simultaneously operates on multiple scales; we must avoid becoming localist, narrowly nationalist, or statist on the one hand, and excessively globalist or abstractly cosmopolitan on the other.

On many occasions, Gramsci invokes the word 'phases'.[73] The term 'phase' was drawn from discoveries in molecular physics, in which, at bottom, matter was no longer seen as something solid and static but instead as composed of ever smaller and smaller particles which were in some determinate sets of relationships with each other and in certain sorts of motion. Gramsci is suggesting that different *situations*, which he analyzes as being formed amid a balance and relation of forces, when located in relation to a line of renewal, could be understood as phases, in a way analogous to the different 'molecular phases'[74] of physical matter (chiefly, solid, liquid, gas, plasma). A phase, then, is a configuration of relationships.

'History is thorough,' wrote Karl Marx, 'and goes through many phases when carrying an old form to the grave.'[75] Gramsci singles out in *Prison Notebook* 25 six phases ranging from the 'objective formation' of subaltern social groups all the way through to revolution ('formations that assert complete autonomy').[76] In other notes, Gramsci makes a distinction between an economic-corporate phase and an ethico-political phase. The former is associated with trade unionism, group or class consciousness, and forms of autonomy 'within the old framework' and is associated with economic activities, demands, and interests. The latter is a more advanced phase in which economic demands and interests are included within a more developed political project—one involving ideology, party organization, 'integral autonomy', the transformation of the 'old framework', and the formation of a broader social bloc. Gramsci writes of how a 'subaltern group' is involved in 'growing beyond the economic-corporative stage and rising to the level of ethico-political hegemony in civil society and domination of the state'.[77]

At stake in assessing the various phases is the degree to which social classes and groups attain force through cohesion, awareness, and organization.[78] The 'first and most elementary . . . is the economic-corporate level: a tradesman feels *obliged* to stand by another tradesman'. The last and most developed phase is that in which hegemony is attained.[79] The developments in question correspond 'to the different levels of political consciousness as they have manifested themselves in history up to now'.[80] Phases are understood in relation to social becoming, spatio-temporality, the transformation of structures, as well as the building up of popular forces.

Gramsci establishes some vital criteria for differentiating between key phases when discussing the various passages of ascent the 'innovative forces' of the Italian Risorgimento underwent on their way to leadership in the state:

Many criteria of historical research can be constructed by studying the innovative forces that led the national Risorgimento. . . . To become a state, they had to subordinate or eliminate [the forces they were struggling against] and obtain the active or passive consent of [certain auxiliaries or allies]. The study of the development of these innovative forces—from subaltern groups to leading and dominant groups—must, therefore, look for and identify the phases through which they gained autonomy from the enemies they had to defeat, as well as the phases through which they gained the support of the groups that actively or passively assisted them, for this whole process was historically necessary for them to join together and become a state.[81]

Gramsci suggests, then, that we need to 'look for and identify' the various phases in the passage from subalternity to leadership and goes on to explain that 'the level of historical-political consciousness progressively attained by these innovative forces in the various phases' is measured by both the achievement of autonomy ('separation from the previously dominant forces') and the building of active and passive consent, whereby a social class or group or bloc unites 'the people around itself'.[82] Usually, Gramsci adds, the former is 'the only criterion employed and the result is a one-sided history, or, at times, a failure to understand anything. . . . The Italian bourgeoisie proved incapable of uniting the people around itself and this was the cause of its defeats and the interruptions in its development.'[83]

This note puts forward four major criteria for locating the various phases which mark the temporal passage of the innovative forces from subordination. The first has to do with the not-to-be neglected phase of subordination, subalternity, and *domination*—from which the innovative forces emerge but in which the collective will is dispersed and (subaltern) groups and classes are fragmented and lack force. In a second phase, the innovative forces achieve some form of separation and *autonomy* in relation to previously dominant forces. A third phase, which can be closely associated with the second, involves the drive to secure *consent* from allies and followers. The final phase involves *leadership* in a new state. What this note suggests are criteria for distinguishing four major phases in the passage from subordination to revolution, in the transformation of hegemony at local, national, and transnational scales. These phases are above all evaluated by the way classes and groups and their associated social forces are related to domination (*dominazione*), autonomy (*autonomia*), consent (*consenso*), and leadership (*direzione*).

The phases are constructed in relation to enemies who must be defeated, potential allies, followers, and elements which must be subordinated (both on the national and the international stage). Gramsci writes, for instance, that a party of the ruling groups may emerge very much as a reactive attempt to control the new initiatives of subaltern social groups. The line of renewal in phases occurs, then, in relationship to the existing hegemony—with its own elements of *leadership*, modalities of *consent*, spheres of authorized *autonomy*, and forms of *domination* and its own alterations, including forms of decomposition, neoformation, and passive revolution.[84] The line of renewal must counter this hegemony and eventually provide an alternative to it, with its forces holding onto 'the spirit of cleavage' even amid accusations of divisiveness and actual concessions from governing classes.[85] The phases are thus situated in relational antagonism and confrontation; they are highly contested and subject to the balance and relation of forces. In such a system of power relations, collective will weighs in the balance, and the line of renewal and ascent is by no means guaranteed but is subject to decomposition and neoformation.

The phases of renewal are at one level diachronic. A line of renewal can be traced from domination to leadership. Each phase builds on the previous one. '[E]very real historical phase', writes Gramsci, 'leaves traces of itself in the succeeding phases, which in turn become its best document, in a certain sense'.[86] First movers can light the passage, establishing new forms of good and common sense, in ways which then make once radical phase shifts now seem normal and natural—in situated ways. Once, union formation, female education, or nationalism was radical, 'extremist', illegal. Later, it was considered normal, legitimate, 'common sense'. The significance—not to mention affect (*feeling*, in Gramscian language)—of autonomy is hardly grasped without an understanding of the prior history of domination from which autonomy emerges. If Tahrir or Kasaba Square, for example, had not been such theatres of regime power, occupying them would not have meant nearly so much as it did.[87]

Note that the temporal order of the phases can be reversed. If, at one point, nationalism promised leadership, for example, later it might only mean a form of autonomy. The dramas of 'each phase . . . will soon be transcended, and will no longer be of interest'.[88] Earlier phases then fade from view; what matters to protagonists, fundamentally, changes in relation to the line of renewal.

Each phase also contains elements of all the other phases. For instance, organization (consent-winning) involves elements of leadership, as do apparently 'spontaneous', fleeting confrontations with the police, for example, under conditions of domination. Some part of the subaltern, Gramsci writes, is autonomous and directive. Elements that are present but not predominant in one phase can subsequently come to the fore. For instance, forms of leadership that are implicit in consent-winning will then come to the fore if these forms of leadership take power. This is why prefiguration, properly understood, has its place even in Gramsci's work.[89]

The phases are also juxtaposed, intertwined, and internally differentiated. Subaltern social groups are highly diverse: some groups may be fragmented, wrestling with contradictory consciousness and social domination—others may be already group or class conscious, organized, and searching for allies. The terrain is uneven and relational. The phases need to be embedded in various spatial scales, including that of the international and transnational. The party activity of subaltern social groups (in seeking consent) has 'repercussions . . . across the entire terrain of subaltern groups'.[90] One party or popular organism might exclude one or other subaltern social group, while another co-opts, and another includes, and yet another goes on the attack. Some subaltern groups might 'exercise a certain hegemony [over a variety of subaltern social groups] through a party'. Other parties—including those of the dominant groups—may seek to include not only elements of the 'leading' subaltern social group but elements from other subaltern social groups. In other words, there is a complex field of competition in relation to the organization of subaltern social groups at various scales, which may also divide and fragment them, or bring them together, or co-opt them, depending on the case.[91] The phases are therefore not radically separate: the phase of consent-winning is intertwined with the phases of domination, autonomy, and leadership.

Moreover, Gramsci underlines that historical analysis must include 'the repercussions [of subaltern party activity] on the attitudes of the dominant group'. Consent-winning can therefore impact the forms of *direzione* pursued by ruling groups, including reactions by trans/international forces. Further, the analysis 'must also include the repercussions of the much more effective actions—because they are propped up by the state—of the dominant groups on the subaltern groups and their parties'.[92] Gramsci also makes the fertile point that local ruling groups in peripheral states collaborating with economic imperialism may dress themselves up as nationalists to discredit domestic forms of popular mobilization.[93]

Domination, autonomy, consent, and leadership are criteria for grasping configurations of relationships (phases), not a rigid taxonomy. This means that phases can be broken down into subphases embedded in wider scales, or given complexity, or even combined, while the historical criteria remain the same. As Gramsci cautions: 'These phases can be listed in even greater detail, with intermediate phases or combinations of several phases.'[94] Sometimes phases are brief or multiple. When thinking of the path to revolution in Italy in February 1924, Gramsci writes to Rome from Vienna: 'That the situation is actively revolutionary I do not doubt and therefore that within a limited span of time our party will have the majority with it; but if this period will perhaps not be long chronologically it will undoubtedly be dense with successive phases, which we will have to predict . . . in order to be able to maneuver and not to fall into errors.'[95] Here the idea of phases is invoked in relation to party activism in fighting wars of position and building up the necessary consent and collective will. On other occasions the temporality is slower: there are long phases when the molecular motions are slow, when there is indifference, when new energies and connections are lacking, or when the balance and relation of forces is so hostile that renewal fails or is crushed.

Popular mobilization, then, involves a lengthy, non-linear, and unguaranteed process of dialectical unification, involving various phases and subphases, wherein the old hegemony can be transformed and the new hegemony built on multiple spatial scales, including the national and the trans/international. The phases are distinguished in relation to domination, autonomy, consent, and leadership: these criteria define phases that are temporally diverse, juxtaposed, intertwined, and internally differentiated.

CONCLUSION

This chapter has specified the main definitions, language, interpretive criteria, and concepts of the faces and phases of popular mobilization. The aim has been to outline for popular mobilization a distinctive theoretical language—which is not just a form but 'an ensemble of certain notions and concepts'.[96] The chapter has put forward and justified several key definitions—above all, of popular mobilization—but also of phases. It has aimed to establish a consistent language—for instance regarding 'renewal', 'structural transformation', 'decomposition' and the like. It has put forward the key faces of popular mobilization—diverse subaltern social groups searching to overcome social subordination, bloc formation, organic intellectuals, the transformation of civil society, culture, the economy, the state, spatiality, temporality, and popular forces (including collective will and myth). It has depicted the positive side of popular mobilization as a process of renewal, while referring to degenerative processes in relation to decomposition and neoformation. It has underlined some of the guiding notions behind these moments, for example, the concept of revolutionizing praxis or the concept of social becoming (built of the historicized dialectics of social being and social consciousness). It has argued throughout that popular mobilization operates on the national, international, and transnational terrains. It has, finally, put forward various interpretive criteria for conceiving the phases of popular mobilization, arguing that the initial phase of popular mobilization can be understood in relation to domination, the second in relation to autonomy, the third consent, and the final phase in relation to leadership. It has argued that these phases are internally differentiated, heavily contested, and intertwined in various ways. The rest of the book unpacks each of these phases in turn.

CHAPTER THREE

The Torturous Contradictions of Domination

I am an invisible man. No, I am not a spook like those who haunted Edgar Allan Poe; nor am I one of your Hollywood-movie ectoplasms. I am a man of substance, of flesh and bone, fiber and liquids—and I might even be said to possess a mind. I am invisible, understand, simply because people refuse to see me. Like the bodiless heads you see sometimes in circus sideshows, it is as though I have been surrounded by mirrors of hard, distorting glass. When they approach me they see only my surroundings, themselves, or figments of their imagination—indeed, everything and anything except me.

Ralph Ellison, *Invisible Man*

This chapter takes up the start points in the long temporality of popular mobilization. In view is activity at the margins: a subaltern phase of diffuse, capillary, marginal, 'spontaneous', episodic, and tactical intervention and protagonism, including 'latent instability and rebelliousness among . . . large popular masses'.[1] In view are the daily, 'molecular' struggles of subaltern social groups.[2] Gramsci refers suggestively at one point to 'popular intervention . . . in the "diffused" and capillary form of indirect pressure'.[3] 'One may say', writes Gramsci, 'that the element of spontaneity is . . . characteristic of the "history of subaltern classes" and, especially, of the most marginal and peripheral elements of these classes, who have not attained a consciousness of the class per se.'[4] In this phase, subaltern social groups— persons 'of substance, of flesh and bone', possessed, even, of a mind— wrestle with, accommodate, negotiate, reproduce, challenge, try to ignore, suffer from, and agonize over social domination. It is a phase of daily, 'small-scale reactions that remain on the infrapolitical level . . . tactical forms of resistance of dispersed subjectivities'.[5] In this subaltern phase, fleeting and episodic confrontations with domination are a common occurrence. But subaltern social groups have not yet gained a consciousness of their strength; they remain objectified, they do not know how to build alternatives, and they do not know—in matters of collectivity, strategy, ideology, alliance, and so on—how to escape.

Invisibility is—as in the Ellison quotation above—one deeply disturbing feeling among the subordinated—an intuition of domination. 'We were like ghosts, unseen', wrote a Syrian migrant worker-intellectual, regarding his situation doing construction work in Lebanon in the early 1970s.[6] Invisibility, note, is not exclusively 'not being seen'. Something is, in fact, seen: 'everything and anything except me'; what is seen is a faceless object, not a person ('mirrors of hard distorting glass'). What is seen, for instance, amid the awkward hypervisibility of a carer in a *hijab* (headscarf) collecting a child from a public school in contemporary Paris, say, is not a person but a certain piece of cloth, with all of its overdetermined structures of feeling. Invisibility involves not only a putting out of sight, then, but also involves tense dramas around objectification and domination, dramas that are central in the subaltern phase of popular mobilization.

The paradox, drama, and point of departure at the centre of this phase, in the Gramscian tradition, is the question of how those at the margins of history attempt to make their own history. Gramsci was highly original in posing the question in this way, in historicist terms, and in taking this granular, micrological, and 'molecular' question extremely seriously. He was interested here in the start points of the long labour that gives birth to a new collective will, start points where the masses exist only in a '"diffused", "molecular" state'.[7] Gramsci's oeuvre offers an interrogation of the elusive, diverse, ambiguous, and contradictory phase of not fully hegemonized subaltern activity 'at the margins'. This activity—with its layers of common sense, contradictory consciousness, popular culture, utopia and myth, subversivism, indifference, passive/active adherence to dominant formations, subaltern formation, and forms of 'spontaneous philosophy'—precedes the appearance and crystallization of a collective will, a certain leadership, a current of opinion, or a given movement while confronting new forms of control from above. Gramsci understood that such activities also carry on alongside (simultaneously with and in distinct spaces) movements, leadership, and associational and party activity. He understood that many spatial scales were at stake. He also proposed—foreshadowing the later monographic output on this topic—that the monograph was the best format for presenting work on this theme, which required the collection of a vast amount of fragmented material.

Gramsci insisted on various vital 'methodological criteria': that some part of the subaltern is directive and responsible and that it is the task of the integral historian to seize on every trace of autonomous initiative. He argues that subaltern social groups, however objectified by domination, are never merely objects or things. He makes clear that different degrees of active or passive consent by subaltern social groups to dominant formations matter in larger temporalities and transformation. Gramsci's insistence on the inexistence of congenital or dumb passivity has certainly been resoundingly confirmed by subsequent research. However, Gramsci never conflated activity with agency—a fraught concept indeed, as feminist scholarship especially has explored.[8] For Gramsci the ambiguities, contradictions, and incompleteness of this phase of activity are what is essential. The development out of this phase is neither guaranteed, nor is it a moralizing precept or *mission civilisatrice*. Contradictory consciousness, intimately bound up with activity at the margins, is historical in the sense that it relates back to and expresses 'profound historical contrasts' and in the sense that it has a major relevance for the subsequent phases of popular mobilization. Hegemonic common sense must be transcended but also engaged with, reworked. The growth, expression, education, developing coherence, and intellectual elaboration of the phase of subaltern activity—its unification (albeit provisional), its participation in renewal (albeit episodic, and subject to decomposition or neoformation)—are what is in view here. The paradoxes, dramas, and contradictions of activity at the margins are deeply connected to the subsequent growth of popular mobilization, but in ways that are still not commonly fully appreciated. This deep connection is what explains Gramsci's interest in a phase which many Marxists have ignored or dismissed, and, even more interestingly, which Gramsci also himself criticized—with a constructive and reconstructive aim in mind. What is striking about the Gramscian approach is that it takes the subaltern phase seriously, without any possible sense of romanticization. Gramsci's position here expresses, as ever, Gramsci's favourite maxim: pessimism of the intellect, optimism of the will. This chapter argues that a Gramscian theory offers a rich, important, and underappreciated way of seeing everyday resistance and daily struggles against domination.

DEBATING DOMINATION

The primitive, the backward, the violent and the angry are leitmotifs of Orientalist, racist, and elitist conceptions and research. 'Men rebel', according to Ted Gurr, because of 'frustration-aggression'.[9] For liberals, there is usually a sense that subaltern individuals need to be civilized or paternally tutored—including regarding reason, liberal education, and property rights.[10] In new religious politics, there is the claim that the subaltern—whether Muslim, woman, or otherwise—is benighted, heathen, fallen, or deviant, and in need of saving or of 'summoning' (*daʿwa*) to the faith. In these formulations, discipline from on high, whether in the form of temperance, morals, true piety, or the application of the standards of middle-class respectability, looms large. Rationalists tend to attribute some founding kernel of reason or self-interest to the activities of those who challenge 'the polity', a well-meaning corrective to the irrationalist collective behaviour school. Still this corrective is inadequately abstract when compared with the Gramscian sense in which feeling (passion, care, non-rational motivations) and knowing (reason, strategy, rational motivations) are intertwined.

There are those Marxists who are apt to scorn the 'lumpen', disorganized, 'brawling' aspects of subaltern daily life or those who draw uncritically on Marx's critique of peasant politics in the age of the Napoleonic code or on his assertion that peasants are unable to represent themselves, like 'potatoes in a sack'. Such a critique may only be implicit, revealed by omission, for instance, in the hundreds of working-class histories that pay no attention at all to activities at the margins. The insistence that such struggles are 'pre-political' is understandable, as politics here are implicit or immanent, not explicit or developed. Nonetheless, the appellation 'pre-political' has pitfalls indeed: it is apt to obscure the connections to the more explicit politics of subsequent and distinct phases of popular mobilization. Certainly, a contemporary theory cannot follow research, including among Marxists, which does not fully break with nineteenth-century schemata of civilization, teleology, modernism, and Eurocentrism. Hobsbawm's book *Primitive Rebels*, with its focus on 'archaic' social movements, only complemented his deeply problematic claim in *Age of Extremes* that the makers of history in the Third World were 'elite minorities'.[11] Hobsbawm's modernizing vision tends to ignore subaltern daily resistance—eliminating the principal drama of the Gramscian approach regarding this phase. Although Hobsbawm was reading Gramsci as early as the 1950s, it is arguably unfair to attribute his Eurocentrism to Gramsci, who took a more complex and differentiated view of the subaltern phase.[12]

In Guha's important early work there is perhaps too much emphasis on the 'elementary', the inchoate, the backward, and the traditional regarding the daily struggles of peasants in nineteenth-century India.[13] This emphasis belies or occludes the sophistication, the perforce in-depth knowledge, and the great care, in a context of significant hazard, that many a subaltern deploys in knowing and negotiating the fraught field of domination.[14] For many, E. P. Thompson's strictures against the 'enormous condescension' of posterity are a sufficient corrective—but it needs to be mentioned here that E. P. Thompson did not himself mount any sustained or serious assault on modernism, masculinism, or Eurocentrism and does not explicitly develop a distinctive perspective on the subaltern phase. It is not that resistance used to be elementary and now is more sophisticated, that resistance used to be backward but now is modern—these assumptions reflect the globalized temporality associated with teleology and Eurocentrism. It behooves us instead to identify, past and present, the embryonic and fraught forms of capillary, diffused, and episodic collective challenge that are present under conditions of domination.

There is critical work in anarchist, autonomist, and postmodern traditions that arguably finds too much autonomy in the contradictions and ambiguities of the subaltern phase. A Deleuzian approach informs the valorization of the fugitive, hybrid lines of flight, the 'power of exodus' achieved by nomadic subaltern figures, such as migrants.[15] The practices of everyday life do ultimately wind up in the recuperation of a certain form of autonomy—a suggestive proposition, but hard to square with the larger condition of subordination in play.[16] Other anarchist inflected work seems to deny the existence of resistance in everyday tactics—arguing that they above all serve to reproduce the state.[17]

Scott's widely-cited work on 'weapons of the weak' among peasants in a Malaysian village in the 1970s, which was informed by a certain rationalism, individualism, pragmatism, and autonomism, made the boldest claims for the transformative—even revolutionary—potential of such 'small arms fire in the class war' as pilfering, foot-dragging, arson, false compliance, slander, parody, and the like.[18] Writing about poor rural-urban migrants in the aftermath of a revolution (in 1979) that 'devoured its children', Asef Bayat argued—in a more collective and less atomistic or rationalist vein than Scott—that the 'quiet encroachment of the ordinary' among rural-urban migrants, which includes fleeting confrontations with authorities, brought change 'no less significant than the one the Islamic Revolution [of 1979] was to bring about'.[19] Others make more modest, but nonetheless positive claims. Singerman's study of informal avenues of participation in Cairo does not speak of revolution but certainly argues that the informal economy and informal networks, often constructed by women, play a role in economic redistribution and in politics, generously defined, at the national level.[20]

Some Gramsci-inflected research takes up autonomous possibilities in subaltern lives and daily struggles. There is plenty to think about here and no basis for any abstract dismissal of the possibilities for the incremental acquisition of forms of relative autonomy amid peripheral activity. But it should be noted that the emphasis on autonomy in early subaltern studies[21] has also been criticized for projecting the 'self-originating self-determining individual', the classic figure of 'Western liberal humanism', onto subaltern persons and conditions.[22] The most striking problem, arguably, with the emphasis on autonomy regarding the subaltern phase is precisely that the subaltern phase is marked above all by domination, subordination, and *heteronomy*. The emphasis on autonomy, then, which can only refer to some form of self-determination, to encompass the subaltern phase—when and where the collective will is above all extraneous and imposed—does come across as problematic. Gramsci's position, as Ciavolella avers, is very far from 'a populist insistence on a people's capacity to express its cultural autonomy and creativity as a way of resisting dominant culture' whereby the populist goes to the people and thereby creating a new myth, an authentic subject able to contest power. It is instead 'a historicist invitation to politically go beyond . . . embryonic popular forms of cultural rebelliousness'.[23]

Much of the Gramscian research on everyday struggles strikes a critical note—in keeping, in some respects, with Gramsci's own scathing criticism of peasant resistance. The peasant, writes Gramsci,

> erupts in violent revolt against the 'gentry' every now and then, but he is incapable of seeing himself as a member of a collectivity (the nation for the landholders, the class for the proletarians), nor can he wage a systematic and permanent campaign destined to alter the economic and political relations of society. . . . [T]heir defence against exploitation . . . was merely individualist . . . inspired largely by guile and feigned servility. Class struggle was confused with brigandage, with blackmail, with burning down woods, with the hamstringing of cattle, with the abduction of women and children, with assaults on the town hall—it was a form of elementary terrorism, without long-term or effective consequences.[24]

Consistent, for instance, with this general line, and taking aim at Scott's rationalism and individualism, and invoking the way in which cultural hegemony defines in civil society what is rational and possible, Mitchell offers a strong challenge to Scott's rural 'weapons of the weak'. He makes a strong argument that Scott was studying a village at a moment of significant demobilization and that many weapons of the weak, such as cheating on weights at harvest time, only give an illusion of autonomy, which delivers only microscopic gains to the subordinated, and acts as a tolerated 'safety-valve' ultimately reinforcing existing forms of hegemony.[25]

Also working with the optics of cultural hegemony, Willis's classic study showed how masculinist resistance to a vaguely conceived class hierarchy in secondary schools in Britain in the 1970s actually contributed to the ways in which working class lads withdrew from educational attainment and thus ended up in working class jobs, reproducing the class structure that they set out informally to resist.[26] Burawoy's well-known work on 'manufacturing consent' shows how competitive work—arrangements orchestrated by employers in factories—engage the willing participation of individualistic workers seeking to maximize their income.[27] Jackson Lears has shown vividly how 'rugged', masculinist, property-owning individualism informs

The Contradictions of Domination

quotidian struggles—including in rural areas—in the United States.[28] My own historical ethnography of Syrian migrant workers in Lebanon, which draws on Gramsci, shows that stigmatized, hard-working migrants cultivated self-discipline and an inconspicuous 'heads down' public comportment in order to keep their jobs, avoid assault, and send back remittances in the hope of a better future. The argument is that these are all small-scale activities which reinforce unequal structures of accumulation at wider scales.[29] Wedeen's research on domination and symbolic control in pre-2011 Syria shows the ways in which subordinates acted as if the hegemonic narratives of the state were actually true in order to demonstrate an outward loyalty that they did not feel, a wooden conformity at once pulverizing of subordinates' subjectivity and subtly reinforcing of the regime's narratives and cult of personality.[30]

The point of departure, here though, against the romanticization of weapons of the weak on the one hand but also against the argument that daily struggles are ultimately seamlessly complicit in hegemony, is to stress the way in which the living Gramscian tradition situates daily struggles in a larger history of subaltern social groups and always considers the potential for overcoming social domination:

> Some of the theories mobilizing Gramsci content themselves with the idea that the politics of the subaltern . . . is effective and productive only if it emerges from, but also remains inside, the margins. . . . This view tends to reduce subaltern politics to an issue of resistance, piracy, smuggling, circumvention, informality and daily tactics of survival outside the direct engagement with power and state. Gramsci's idea of a potential politics of the subaltern then becomes no more than that of an actual politics of the excluded or the marginalised. For Gramsci the latter are important not so much for their daily efficacy, but for their potential to move up from the "infrapolitical" dimension to that of transformative and emancipatory politics.[31]

Indeed, Gramsci's insistence on the fractures, complexity, and sociological, living substance of the always plural 'subaltern social groups' refuses to make a binary, abstracted choice between 'the subaltern [who] cannot speak' on the one hand and all of those who speak for and represent the subaltern on the other.[32] Gramscians have rightly argued for reading documents

The Contradictions of Domination

against the grain[33] or for a 'search for "traces" offered by the subaltern'[34] which is clearly less categorical.

We should not have to choose, by the same token, between the missionary activities of a 'Gay International' that speaks for and imposes on gay men a single identity-politics model of gayness the world over and a rigidified, authentic, unchanging Arab same-sex activity shorn of identity—a choice which Massad's optics, inflected by the early Foucault, arguably impose.[35] Language is neither completely hegemonic and pellucid nor completely incomprehensible; it is almost always a work in progress, situated between coercion and consent. And as many have argued, the complexities of gay life-activity in the Middle East cut against such a binary.[36]

The rest of this chapter aims to identify what it means to avoid this kind of binary and to specify what it means to speak about the potential and importance of the phases of diffuse, capillary, episodic, and contradictory activity and consciousness.

SUBALTERN SOCIAL GROUPS

The exposition begins with the life-activity of the subaltern social groups that Gramsci places front and centre in *Prison Notebook* 25—a start point that is thoroughly intertwined with the humanism of the philosophy of praxis. Domination instrumentalizes and objectifies. The accent is on 'objective formation', but domination does not expunge the mind, the subject, social consciousness, historicity. Gramsci writes of a phase in the history of subaltern social groups involving 'the objective formation of the subaltern social groups through the developments and the changes occurring in the sphere of economic production; the extent of their diffusion; and their descent from pre-existing social groups whose mentality, ideology, and goals they preserve for a period of time'.[37]

Manual labour does not eliminate mental labour. *Homo faber* never quite excludes *homo sapiens*. Dehumanization does not eliminate the human, and subaltern social groups preserve an inherited culture for a time. Social being is reduced by domination to nature, epidermis, menstruation, genitalia, manual or muscular capacity, 'human resources', manpower, genetics, primordialism, the animal, the beast, the 'genus'. 'Woman has ovaries, a uterus' writes de Beauvoir, 'these peculiarities imprison her in her subjectivity, circumscribe her within the limits of her own nature. It is often said that she thinks with her glands.'[38] As Eribon has it, 'the inscription of the sexual order as a matrix of inferiorisation happens in those bodies and minds that contravene the norms.'[39] Gay men or lesbians are 'reduce[d] to the state of an object within the categories of the dominant discourse'.[40] Yet, a thinking subject remains. As Ellison's character tells us, 'I may even be said to possess a mind.' As Gramsci insists, everyone is an intellectual, or a philosopher, carrying on a conception of the world. Social being—an infinity of traces deposited historically in the body—is always in a relationship with social consciousness, which can seek to compile an inventory of those traces.

It is striking that Simone de Beauvoir's *Second Sex*, published ten years after Gramsci's death poses the question of 'woman' as encompassing a not entirely dissimilar paradox and drama as to that invoked in Gramsci's sense of subaltern social being. She writes: 'The drama of woman lies in this conflict between the fundamental aspirations of every subject (ego)—who always regards the self as the essential—and the compulsions of a situation in which she is the inessential. How can a human being in a woman's situation attain fulfilment?'[41] The terms of the 'drama' and 'conflict' are not identical, but like Gramsci, de Beauvoir posits a subject and a self even amid extensive objectification, anatomization (e.g. menstruation), and otherization.

Zene evokes the tormenting drama of subalternity for Dalits in South Asia as follows: 'The adoption of the term Dalit as self-designation springs out of the awareness and perception of the oppression/humiliation . . . they have to endure: the real subaltern in Gramscian terms. When the word Dalit is spoken by a non-Dalit, it might have the character of a derogatory remark. Yet for Dalits themselves, the term has become a place of resistance and a reason for struggle.'[42]

The question of subaltern social being is posed by Gramsci, as one would expect, within the framework of the philosophy of praxis and the ontology of becoming. It is not above all a question of being or non-being, to be or not to be; it is a question of becoming. To fix social being ahistorically and for all time (or for a perpetual present)—to classify, to categorize, to assign to this or that genus or this or that essence, whether Arab, Muslim, Jewish, Black, Oriental, Masculine, Feminine, Gay, Untouchable, and so on—is an oppressive act of objectification and domination. It is a matter of eternalizing and naturalizing what is in fact historical. Subaltern social being cannot be wholly understood in terms of who one is but also in terms of who one wishes to become. This point has been underlined in Zene's research on Dalits and other untouchable and low-status castes in India:

> After much time spent among these Rishi groups, it became easier to ask them how they saw themselves. Initially, in fact, their comments were a reflection of what others—caste Hindus, Muslims, missionaries, police, teachers—said about them. Only later did they feel at ease to let me know what they thought about themselves. At times I judged their statements false, until I realised that they were projecting a vision of themselves in the future, not just as they were seen by others but most of all as they 'wanted to be' seen. . . . I . . . remembered a passage in Notebook 14, where Gramsci discusses 'Pirandello's Theatre', introducing a variation on the question 'what is the human being?' 'It seems to me that "one's real nature" is determined by the struggle to become what one wants to become.'[43]

Subaltern social formation is not solely a question of taxonomy from on high but is the subject and object of a fundamental drama; a set of paradoxes and tensions; a struggle over becoming; a clash of what presents itself as dominant, objective, and factual and what is present in consciousness in terms of shame, honour, desire, aspiration, and the like.[44] The point is also made in Black feminism. Michelle Wallace writes, 'When I began this book, I thought it would be about what the black woman is, but. . . . [s]he has yet to become what she is.'[45] What one wants to become is not set in stone, defined in advance, or free from hegemonic influence. What matters is the existence of tension and the drive to overcome it—an element in a provisional process of unification.

Gramscians, drawing on anti-colonial thought, have situated the Black radical tradition in terms of a struggle intertwined with the oppression and exploitation involved in the European encounter with Africa: 'The violent generative process of that encounter created different historical processes of conquest, racialisation, alienation and human exploitation, but also what Aimé Césaire called the process of "thingification." '[46] Judy goes on:

> [T]he phrase 'black radicalism' suggests a tradition of resistance to capitalist modernity that develops a dialectic of liberation out of the material historical

conditions of racialised oppression. It is a tradition of resistance, rehumanisation, and revolution as well as one that reframes radical questions in ways that challenge the more predominant forms of Marxism because the subject of revolutionary change is neither bourgeoisie or proletariat but rather the dehumanised subject—the figure created by the historical force of "thingification"—that, rejecting the anthropology of modernity, presents an alternative understanding and practice of sociality and individuation.[47]

The question of thingification, of 'objective formation', as Gramsci puts it, is intimately involved with Gramsci's humanist account of subaltern social being under conditions of domination. There is a not wholly produced subject—a subject in part inherited, historical—but one under huge pressures of objectification.

We need to grasp how objective formation can work its molecular effects on social being. Subaltern social being may become such through a negative molecular process, whereby conditions of life are 'written on the body', bit by bit, quantitatively, until a negative phase change occurs; one quality of person becomes another. Gramsci writes: 'People also speak of "second nature"; a certain habit becomes second nature.'[48] A prisoner, for example, becomes 'institutionalized'—incapable of living outside of prison. In prison, Gramsci wrote that 'he was sinking deeper and deeper into a realm of the ocean depths where there was an "absolute immobility" and where "even the most formidable storms no longer make themselves felt"'.[49] Cleaners literally cannot sit down in the employer's living room as it is no longer their place; a back becomes permanently hunched after repeated bowing and scraping; after years of doing a stupid and repetitive task, a worker loses faculties. 'Don't stay here,' I was urged, by a veteran of twenty-two years in a manual job in a bread factory, 'or your brain will go to mush.' Antonio Labriola, who was an important influence on Gramsci, made a similar point: 'The greater portion of mankind, by the quality of their occupations, are composed of individuals who are disintegrated, broken into fragments and rendered incapable of . . . development. . . . From the relative liberty of the few is born the servitude of the greater number, and law has been the protector of injustice.'[50]

In this way, for Labriola, industrial and scientific progress, on the one hand, and law, on the other, were tied to oppression and servitude in relation to the formation of social being and culture. Objective and subjective elements in the formation of social being work together. As Eribon has it, 'to be insulted is to be branded on the shoulder by a red hot iron'; 'the act of naming produces an awareness of oneself as other, transformed by others into an object'.[51] Social being becomes object-like in theory and in culture as well as in practice.

This process, pace sensuous humanism, is painful. Gramsci himself writes of the 'atrocious destiny' tormenting those who must pay 'the ineluctable compensation that nature demands from its exceptions'.[52] Kapadia underlines the 'hideous degradation' attendant on the way in which Dalits in India are understood to be irredeemably polluted.[53] Roy writes of the pervasive shame and stigma in India among lesbians, whose desire is seen as unthinkable, marginalized, and invisible.[54]

Subaltern social consciousness does not, in the subaltern phase, identify the subaltern social group as a meaningful and operative collectivity. Recall Gramsci on the peasant in revolt as 'incapable of identifying himself as a member of a collectivity'. Consciousness is fragmented—or preserves an older consciousness which does not yet recognize or understand the new conditions. Thomas speaks of a 'lack of conscious or self-direction'.[55] Objective formation is at work in terms not just of the reduction to an object but of the ways consciousness of social being is elusive in the current phase / phase of domination. Subaltern social groups, writes Thomas, are 'seen as subaltern insofar as they are unable to progress to forms of self-representation through the formation of their own strata of intellectuals, but instead remain represented as objects of contemplation by and for the discourses of the dominant classes'.[56] Subaltern social groups are represented (i.e. depicted) by the powerful, but their capacity to represent themselves in relation to their actual social being, or in civil society, or in relation to political representation is sharply limited—a situation that is reinforced by state violence deployed against those who 'speak truth to power'.

In keeping with this, the phase of diffuse and capillary intervention is characterized, as Gramsci writes, by a period in which the 'great labouring masses are disorganized, dispersed, and atomised into a confused multitude'.[57] Gramsci writes that certain subaltern social groups are excluded from 'any organized collective life of . . . [their] own'.[58] Under conditions of domination, in which revolution is still premature or doomed to failure, the 'great popular masses . . . [are] still amorphous, still fragmented'.[59] To be subaltern is to be 'subjected to the political initiative of the dominant classes'.[60] The terrain of social being in the subaltern phase is one—paradoxically perhaps—in which no fused community or self-determining group actually exists except as an instrument of dominant groups and classes or as a genus-like element in hegemonic common sense, such as '"the eternal feminine" . . . "the black soul" and . . . "the Jewish character"'.[61] The implication is that any too rapid homogenization—whether in terms of fearful and prejudiced elite caricatures or romantic revolutionary wishes and projections—is false and problematic.

Subaltern social groups are thus a multitude. Multitudes appear 'as a social subject of less determinacy', writes Liguori, 'than a "class" or "social group", and with a negative connotation'.[62] The paradox of the subaltern is to be on the one side a genus—that is, apparently united—but on the other side profoundly disaggregated and atomized: disunited, looking only to their private interests, a *multitudine sciolta*. Social being and social consciousness is fragmented, cacophonous, like an orchestra tuning up.

There is an association, an elective affinity perhaps, between the scattered multitude and the deployment of coercive domination. Gramsci mentions the forms of social dislocation operative in enabling colonial military occupation. A 'nondemocratic leadership based purely on force' can, 'according to Machiavelli's *Discourses* . . . "build fortresses" and "keep a good army always ready to take the field" or to "scatter, disorganize and destroy" the people as a collectivity and reduce them to individuals'.[63] Indeed, the very way to maintain domination by force, writes Machiavelli, is to divide up the people and reduce them to competing individuals, each looking only after private or particular interests.

De Beauvoir makes homologous points about dispersal and fragmentation in the case of women. She writes:

> [W]omen lack concrete means for organizing themselves into a unit which can stand face to face with the correlative unit. They have no past, no history, no religion of their own; and they have no such solidarity of work and interest as that of the proletariat. They are not even promiscuously herded together in a way that creates community feeling among the American

Negroes, the ghetto Jews, the workers of Saint-Denis, or the factory hands of Renault. They live dispersed among the males, attached through residence, housework, economic condition, and social standing to certain men—fathers or husbands—more firmly than they are to other women. If they belong to the bourgeoisie, they feel solidarity with men of that class, not with proletarian women; if they are white, their allegiance is to white men, not to Negro women.[64]

However we read the comparisons and contrasts made here, the subordination of women is linked to spatial dispersal; a lack of commonality in relation to religion, race, history, and interest; a lack of organizational means; and a series of personalistic, vertical attachments. What is underlined is a Gramscian sense of the amorphous, fragmented, divided, and *dispersed* nature of the subaltern social group and a sense of a search for a group or class consciousness that could escape this position of interiorized fragmentation, Otherization, and forcelessness.

By the same token, in the phases of domination, subaltern consciousness may not identify the other major operative social groups and classes or the forms of unification at work in the (dominant) historical bloc and various social blocs. Instead, the main targets of subaltern oppositional consciousness may be particular individuals or leaders; forms of corruption; moralizing tales; conspiracies; supernatural, divine, or mystical agencies; other subaltern social groups; now-outdated social institutions and agencies; or even themselves and their own failings and weaknesses. Social consciousness may in fact involve subversivism (*sovversivismo*), a rather crude and diffuse hatred of state officials, officialdom in general, or even of relatively minor local officials, who are poor and of relatively low status, as they were in much of the Italian South. Or the workers of Turin may have internalized or inherited stereotypes about the 'lazy' and racially inferior peasants of the Italian South. Or masculinist workers may direct homophobic abuse and insults against gays.[65]

Under conditions of domination, when social being is amorphous and dispersed (lacks internal coordination) and when class/group consciousness is not present, space is fragmented and time discontinuous: 'One may say that the element of spontaneity is therefore characteristic of the "history of subaltern classes" and, especially, of the most marginal and peripheral elements of these classes, who have not attained a consciousness of the class per se and who, consequently, do not even suspect that their history might possibly have any importance or that it might be of any value to leave documentary evidence of it.'[66] Here, the term 'spontaneous' refers precisely to the fact that activity appears to be—and in some sense actually is—temporally disconnected from past and future. In Apostilidis's in-depth study of precarious Mexican migrant workers and temporality in the US, 'precaritised workers are "out of time" inasmuch as their jobs block them from consciously and collectively intervening in capitalism's . . . historical temporalities. . . . [W]orkers are caught in the prevailing social condition of time's condensation into a present with neither forward- nor backward-looking trajectories.'[67] This is a Gramscian meaning of spontaneity, where activity, under huge pressures, is reduced to the activity of the present. To speak of spontaneity is to say that something happens, rather out of the blue, and then is immediately lost. In such a case, burdened with *fortunà*, historical consciousness is not necessary or relevant. Thus, there is apparently no imperative to leave documentary evidence of such fleeting, fly-by-night, and discontinuous activity, as the purpose of documentary evidence is to leave a record for the purposes of memory or history—both of which assume the possibility of constructing a diachronic, even narrative, connection, neither of which are present in the perpetual present of spontaneity. This very condition contributes to historical marginalization. Nonetheless, just as Apostilidis has it, precarious subalterns are not passive but engaged in a 'fight for time'.

COMMON SENSE

In the subaltern phase, social consciousness—and life-activity at the margins—is intimately connected to, shaped, and informed by common sense (*senso comune*). Common sense is a vital and oft-mentioned theme in Gramsci's prison notebooks and is included in the list of sixteen main topics that Gramsci laid out in February 1929 in his first notebook.[68] 'Every social stratum', writes Gramsci, 'has its own "common sense", which is ultimately the most widespread conception of life and morals.'[69] It is a 'sedimentation' left by philosophical currents 'which have entered into common usage', the 'folklore of 'philosophy'' with a tendency to ossification over time, being as it is 'a more or less rigidified phase of a certain time and place'.[70] Salamini notes suggestively that '[c]ommon sense is the typical Weltanschauung [worldview] of the masses in their subaltern phase of development'.[71] Common sense is not just an excrescence of ruling ideas (the conventional view), but also operative, in its own right, within the overall actualization of domination and subaltern social being within hegemony.

Common sense is absorbed by subaltern social groups from their immediate social formation, social group, and its intellectuals; from civil society, ruling classes, religions, and heresies; and from past scientific and philosophical currents. It includes the 'sedimentations of past historical epochs'.[72] Gramsci suggests that social life begins with 'a conception of the world mechanically imposed by the external environment, i.e. by one of the many social groups in which everyone is automatically involved from the moment of his [or her] entry into the conscious world (and this can be one's village or province; it can have its origins in the parish and the "intellectual activity" of the local priest or aging patriarch whose wisdom is law, or in the little old woman who has inherited the lore of the witches, or the minor intellectual soured by his own stupidity or inability to act)'.[73]

Gramsci here—drawing on his own experiences in Sardinia in Italy's South—invokes for the sources of common sense the local and immediate social group and the local aspects of civil society and its traditional intellectuals—the priest, the patriarch, the wise woman, or the minor intellectual. Here there is obviously an accent on youthful social formation and thus on relatively narrow horizons. There is an accent on inheritance and historical depth. Common sense also comes from a far broader cosmos of influences like religions, heresies, popular movements, and scientific concepts from the past.[74] In other words, the sources of common sense are both local and global, both present and past. Common sense and social group formation—that is, combinations of social being and social consciousness—are closely intertwined.

As the reference to mechanical imposition suggests, common sense is a tissue of conceptions absorbed in an acritical fashion. It is, Gramsci writes, 'the conception of the world acritically absorbed from the various social environments in which the moral individuality of the average person is developed'.[75] Common sense, argues Crehan, is 'the term Gramsci uses for all

The Contradictions of Domination

those heterogeneous beliefs people arrive at not through critical reflection, but encounter as already existing, self-evident truths'.[76] Here, Liguori writes, 'the greater part of subjects are not *mobilized*, but *defined* (in their subjectivity, in their individual and collective way of being).'[77]

Gramsci's position is not exactly the conventional view of common sense, in which the latter is seen as an expression of what is generally accepted to be true, sensible, or practical. The difference is Gramsci's insistence on 'the historical, ideological and political characteristics of common sense'.[78] Conversely, and in spite of the reference to 'stupidity', we should not embrace the view that common sense is fully understood through the overly rationalist or 'Jacobin' lens of false consciousness or the materialist Marxist lens of ideological mystification. It is not systematic or programmatic like an ideology; it is not deliberately created to mislead; it is not simply irrational, as it is also historical; and it is not simply false, as it is operative. Nor is it entirely imposed by a dominant group or hegemony. It also, as we will see, contains crucial elements of value which deserve to be developed.

Common sense is in formation—in relation to social groups, civil society, religion, popular periodicals and multiple social relations; it involves a process of acquisition over time. It is not a single preformed chunk. Gramsci speaks in this context of 'acquiring one's conception of the world'.[79] Nor does common sense, rigidified and solid as it is, remain static, but it transforms slowly, through shapeless, molecular motions that do not involve major change regarding the overall function. In a discussion of types of periodicals, Gramsci refers to attempts in popular periodicals 'to modify the average opinion of a particular society, criticising, suggesting, admonishing, modernising, introducing new "clichés". If they are well written . . . they can have a large circulation and exercise a most important function.'[80]

Common sense has some important characteristics. Unlike philosophy, common sense is certain about the objective existence of reality—a certainty that Gramsci argues comes from religion.[81] In some respects, common sense sees the world as an 'objective formation'. It is thus immanently connected to the 'objective formation' which is the predominant route into subaltern social being. Gramsci adds that '[i]n common sense it is the "realistic", materialistic elements [of Catholicism/religion] which are predominant. . . . [T]hese elements are "superstitious" and acritical.'[82] Gramsci draws on Marx to refer to the seeming solidity and imperative nature of common sense.[83] Common sense naturalizes—makes 'second nature'[84]—social domination and forms of hegemony.

However solid it may appear, common sense cannot be the basis for verifying philosophical truth, though it may contain some truths, given that all sorts of things can indeed be found in common sense. '[C]ommon sense is led to believe that what today exists has always existed.'[85] In other words, common sense erases its own historicity, it creates a kind of perpetual present, naturalizing the present for all time, believing 'that what exists has always existed'. This erasure of historicity, the forgetting of historical origins, is not only a seemingly solid, certain, and imperative form, but it is also oppressive: 'the ossification of an eternal present'.[86] Common sense is acritical and ahistorical and far from evoking an 'historical personality'. In relation to social being, it eliminates the dialectic with consciousness by genus-thinking. For instance, in relation to gender and sexuality, Gramsci mentions that '[t]he popular proverbs, "man is a hunter, woman a temptress", "the man who has no choice goes to bed with his wife", etc., show how widespread the conception of sex as sport is even in the countryside and in sexual relations between members of the same class'.[87] One of the most important characteristics of common sense is that it is diverse, multiform, ambiguous, and contradictory. It comes 'in countless different forms', 'even in the brain of one individual'.[88] 'Common sense is a chaotic aggregate of disparate conceptions.'[89] It is incoherent; it is 'disjointed and inconsistent'. It contains an 'infinity of traces' deposited in individuals from the past.

This ambiguity (in social consciousness as common sense) is intimately related to the amorphous and multitudinous nature of subaltern social being:

> By virtue of one's worldview, one always belongs to a particular group, namely, the group of all those social elements that share the same mode of thinking and acting. All conform to some conformism or other; there is always mass-man or collective man [or woman]. The question is: What historical type of conformism or mass-man does one belong to? When one's conception of the world is not critical and coherent but disjointed and inconsistent, one belongs simultaneously to a multiplicity of mass groups and one's personality is a strange composite: it contains aspects of the caveman

and the most advanced scientific principles, narrow-minded prejudices from every historical era, and intuitions of a future philosophy that will be embraced by a unified humanity all across the world.[90]

Underlining the main point, Gramsci writes that '[t]he fundamental characteristic of common sense consists in its being a disjointed, incoherent and inconsequential conception of the world that matches the character of the multitudes whose philosophy it is'.[91] Fragmented, amorphous and multitudinous social being is accompanied by common sense.

The use of the term 'inconsequential' in the above passage is indicative. Gramsci links common sense to passivity, to ineffective activity, to subordination, to domination, and to a lack of collective social force. Liguori explains that 'on the basis of common sense, the subaltern classes cannot mount a real challenge for hegemony'.[92] Common sense means 'the passive adaptation of *the led* when faced with the *leaders'* elaboration of the necessary conception of the world'.[93] As Gramsci explains, 'common sense . . . cannot be reduced to unity and coherence. . . . Or rather . . . [it] cannot be so reduced "freely"—for this may be done by "authoritarian" means.'[94] The implication is that a common-sense conception may require, or be required by, activities associated with domination and subordination. Gramsci is clear that the form of subjectivity associated with common sense is, in a negative sense, passive and subordinate. He writes: 'Is it preferable to "think" without being critically aware of doing so, in a disjointed and inconsistent manner? . . . [T]o "participate" in a conception of the world mechanically "imposed" by the external environment. . . . Or is it preferable to elaborate consciously and critically one's own conception of the world and, through the labors of one's intellect, choose one's sphere of activity, participate effectively in the creation of world history, and be one's own guide, rather than passively and supinely let external factors shape his personality?'[95]

Gramsci writes that when a group has, 'for reasons of submission and intellectual subordination, adopted a conception which is not its own but is borrowed from another group and it affirms this conception verbally and believes itself to be following it, [this is] because this is the conception which it follows in "normal times"—that is, when its conduct is not independent

The Contradictions of Domination

and autonomous, but submissive and subordinate'.[96] The reference to 'normal times' is helpful here in suggesting that we are dealing with ordinary, daily struggles and activities that are not fixed for all time. There is a glimpse here of the fact that this subordinate absorption and reproduction of common sense is only a certain phase.

For the time being, however, common sense is a powerful element in keeping the subaltern in their place; solidifying the established order; and reinforcing its 'objective formation', static immobility, and the attendant disunity of theory and practice.[97] Authoritarianism, order, and common sense create an illusion of harmonious coordination—an illusion of the unity of theory and practice.

Hall's classic work establishes powerfully the role of common sense in Thatcherite authoritarian populism in Britain in the 1980s. 'To a significant extent', Hall writes, 'Thatcherism is about the remaking of common sense: its aim is to become the "common sense of the age". . . . The hope of every ideology is to naturalise itself out of History into Nature, and thus to become invisible, to operate unconsciously.'[98] Thatcherite ideology, as a species of authoritarian-populism, selected aspects of popular common sense and mobilized them for their congruence with neoliberalism, thereby creating a new common sense, which enshrined individualism and stigmatized social protection.[99]

Nonetheless, the ambiguities and incoherence of common sense cut deep, beckoning reconstruction. Gramsci's great attention to common sense is not intended above all to explain the seamless reproduction of hegemony. Instead, Gramsci insists on 'the negative "face" of this lower segment of the ideological continuum. . . . [in order to elaborate] a line of political activity that could shift the relations of force and again open up the struggle for hegemony, thus transforming common sense'.[100] As Gramsci writes, 'The philosophy of praxis does not tend to leave the "simple" in their primitive [sic] philosophy of common sense, but rather to lead them to a higher conception of life.'[101] As the next chapter will discuss, common sense contains glimmers of good sense, fragments and traces of quotidian sense-making which can be recombined, renovated, and reconstructed along lines which challenge social domination.

ORGANIC INTELLECTUALS

In the subaltern phase, the split between traditional intellectuals as a separate, closed caste, supremely distinct, reflective, and 'peering down from on high' and subaltern social groups is at its most acute. Gramsci was thinking of the relationship between Benedetto Croce, the great cultural intellectual and philosopher of nineteenth- and twentieth-century Italy, and the popular masses of the South, where Croce was from. Gramsci, also from the South, was an intellectual with a very different relationship to the region. Gramsci believed that Croce's posture, and the split it embodied, was intimately related to domination. 'According to Gramsci,' writes Levy, 'it had been the inability and unwillingness of Italian intellectuals to abandon their elitist cosmopolitanism that left the masses without proper leadership.'[102] Gramsci believed that organic intellectuals had to engage—at least in the first instance—with domination, common sense, and group formation in local, immediate, and concrete forms.

Scattered, fragmented, 'humble', and subaltern forms of 'conscious leadership' and activity encompass intellectual and cultural activity at the margins: the activity, in the subaltern phase, of organic intellectuals. These intellectuals are involved in practical activity as well as in representation. In some cases, their practical-critical activity involves the struggle to develop an effectively expressive language in the face of domination; in other cases, it involves the struggle to speak, to have a platform, to write and to publish, which, from the margins (as opposed to where traditional intellectuals sit) is very often a difficult task. Gramsci refers to the 'first representatives of the new historical phase'; they engage in ideological critique of the old conceptions of the world.'[103] Expression itself is a practical activity—a daily struggle—in and of itself. Words may not be available, or their meaning may be snatched away. Publications are refused or inaccessible or unreadable; censorship is active; seminars are banned; intellectuals are imprisoned; study is unaffordable; new economic, social, or political initiatives are shut down; venues defunded or closed. Gramsci himself managed to write, in the face of fascism and ill-health, from a prison cell—his writings only saved by his sister-in-law, Tatiana Schucht.

As an 'Oriental', an Arab and a Palestinian, Edward Said wrote from the margins—despite his tweed jacket, his educational privileges, and his prestigious institutional position. As a gay man, likewise Foucault. The French novelist George Sand published by passing as a man. Michelle Wallace and bell hooks wrote in the face of the exclusions of white feminism and masculinist Black anti-colonialism. Betty Friedan was a white woman with educational privilege, but she wrote against the 'slow death of mind and spirit' occurring in the 'comfortable concentration camp' inhabited by the American housewife.[104] Frantz Fanon was an accomplished psychiatrist of social standing in Martinique, but in France, a child calling out to their mother, crystallizing a whole world of epidermal domination, had the power to freeze him: 'Look a . . . Negro! I'm frightened.'[105] The subsequent fame and prestige of many an organic intellectual often contrasts shockingly to the pilloried, degraded, excluded, or poverty-stricken conditions under which such figures lived and worked. Gramscian approaches strike against the confusion of high intellectual endeavour with cultural elitism. Gramsci insisted that all people are intellectuals, and that everyone carries on some philosophy or other. We must be attentive to the ways in which vast and vital areas of cultural production are indeed organic—rooted in the experiences and daily struggles of subaltern social groups.

Organic intellectuals, in the subaltern phase, one might argue, have a specific set of functions. In the face of the genus-thinking that virtually encompasses social being in the phase of domination, they counterpose the living, historical person. In the face of objectification, they resurrect the subject: '[Jean] Genet', writes Sartre, 'invents the homosexual *subject* [emphasis in original].'[106] In the face of a frozen, perpetual present, they compile a connected temporality, a narrative. In the face of marginalization, they make new space in explicating the real relationship between the margin and the centre, the colonial South and the colonizing North. They discern the forms of objectification, the objective formation, of the subaltern social group: the theories, practices, and histories—capitalism, racism, statism, sexism, colonialism, and so on—that have generated social domination as such. Prior to any publication on these themes, prior to any coming out, or raising of the head, there is a long subaltern phase of gestation, of cogitation behind closed doors, of troubled reflection, of turbulent and even contradictory activity and consciousness, of second-guessing, of trial and error in practice, of fear, and even of avoiding 'the strain involved in undertaking an authentic existence'.[107] Many are the confessions and manuscripts that were not published; common, here, is posthumous recognition.

Gramsci, as we have seen, suggests a start point in the 'inventory of traces'. This is the project of knowing thyself and understanding what is still a fragmented, disjointed collectivity and where it has come from. This means confronting the tissues of common sense and beginning the project of reconstruction. A stunning example of an explicit project of this kind comes from Edward Said, who writes that his own dissection of Orientalism, a Western style of representation and domination of the Orient, relied on a Gramscian inventory of traces: 'In many ways my study of Orientalism has been an attempt to inventory the traces upon me, the Oriental subject, of the culture whose domination has been so powerful a factor in the life of all Orientals.'[108]

Said became a leading twentieth-century public intellectual and cultural and postcolonial critic. *Orientalism* was perhaps his seminal work. And Said's inventory of traces led him to see Orientalism as a form of hegemony in the Gramscian sense. Said was a major Palestinian intellectual and activist, an 'organic intellectual' of the Palestinian cause. His life and work was in many ways a democratic and humanist struggle to grasp the Palestinian subaltern situation (as the Other) and to transform it. In the process, he unearthed the 'humanly objective' formation of the Palestinian 'politics of dispossession', showing, against the dominant common sense in the West, the intimate relationship between Zionism and Orientalism. 'Palestine was seen', writes Said, 'by Lamartine and the early Zionists—as an empty desert waiting to burst into bloom; such inhabitants as it had were supposed to be inconsequential nomads possessing no real claim on the land and therefore no cultural or national reality.'[109] 'Orientalism', he goes on, 'governs Israeli policy towards the Arabs throughout.'[110] In Zionist, Orientalist discourse, 'Arabs are . . . as one in their bent for bloody vengeance . . . psychologically incapable of peace and . . . are not to be trusted and must be fought interminably as one fights any other fatal disease.'[111] Said's writings not only were a product of a struggle against domination—an inventory of traces at the start points of critical consciousness—but also provide, for vast masses of Palestinians who are themselves struggling against domination, a framework, a consciousness, a way to conceive of their social being, a way to start to unravel, challenge, and change the oppressive, Orientalist, and racist common sense associated especially with the diffuse subaltern phase of ambiguity and contradictory consciousness.

POPULAR CULTURE

The inventory of traces—knowing thyself and developing a historicized sense of social being under conditions of acute domination—is also at stake in popular culture: songs, music, poetry, theatre, art, stories, tales, proverbs, graffiti, oral histories, popular novels, films, 'village museums'—in all activities and forms of popular memory.[112] In the 1920s, Gramsci engaged as a critic with early forms of industrialized, commodified, and degraded popular culture—'the production and manipulation of needs and desires' in ways which reinforce 'acceptance of a static status quo'[113]. He did not see popular culture as a repository of the true, the pure, the uncorrupted, the original, and the authentic. Gramsci, like subsequent figures such as Stuart Hall, rejected any 'flat, populist', uncritical celebration of popular culture.[114] But Gramsci did not adopt the entirely pessimistic view, often associated with the Frankfurt School, in which all forms of popular culture become merely ciphers of commodified capitalism or all invocations of popular culture doomed to Adorno's 'jargon of authenticity'. A Gramscian perspective, arguably, maintains a powerful critique of the ways in which popular culture is constantly absorbed and commodified—not to mention of blind passion, sectarianism, sexism, and racism—but the critique is deployed for a fundamentally constructive and reconstructive purpose. Here, Gramsci avoided 'romanticised visions while still considering subaltern cultures as possible grounds for a politics of emancipation'.[115]

Popular culture, popular memory—along with culture in general—has both rich and degraded forms in Gramsci. Cultural richness is understood not in conventional terms of high versus low but in terms of its capacity to develop the organic passage from feeling to knowing, and vice versa, a capacity often found in forms of catharsis. In this context, in the subaltern phase, popular cultural forms continue to enable the discovery and articulation of meaning even under acute pressures of domination. They enable the oppressed to hold body and soul together. They have this necessary quality. They must not be forms of exit or opium but intimately connected with mental and physical survival itself—with the internal formation of the self. Gramsci's reading of Dante's Canto X enabled Mussolini's prisoner to extract some meaning from his own excruciating, 'damned' situation in which he 'had no knowledge of the present' in relation, above all, to his son.[116] Culture is not only a sign of the group: keeping 'our' traditions alive, demonstrating our unity and group consciousness for a more or less implicit or explicit political purpose, 'acceptable' to this or that leadership; it is living and changing. It speaks to subaltern persons by making both sense and nonsense of their situation, by working passages from feeling to knowing and vice versa. Culture does not resonate or edify; it enables and is part and parcel of a living, meaningful, necessary working through. Cultural life does not and cannot come in a political straitjacket.

Gramscians have continued to make distinctions of value in their studies of popular culture. Why, for instance, was Billie Holliday 'far better than other popular singers'? Because 'her voice can be argued to find a form of expression for a complex range of feelings and experiences toward which others can only gesture'.[117]

De Martino, an anthropologist who investigated popular politics, was politicized by the Resistance against the fascists, and worked with Gramscian concepts went to Romagna, in Italy, in the post-1945 period 'with a research project on the traces of political antagonism and the spirit of emancipation in popular imaginaries, songs, discourses, and stories'. He considered these to be 'folklorist manifestations in a direct relationship with the popular experiences of social subjectivation (*soggezione sociale*), of protest, of rebellion, of struggle or even of victorious emancipation'.[118] Here was a wide-ranging appreciation of a variety of tissues of popular culture. Part of the conceptual interest here has to do with De Martino's sense of the ways in which popular culture, even when not apparently or directly about 'resistance', involved a certain form of 'social subjectivation', which can be read as a reference to a certain kind of cultural activity or a cultural life as against and in opposition to the 'objective formation' and objectification of the subaltern social group.

This sort of sensibility has informed and been developed in various explorations of the popular culture in the Black radical tradition. Blues, jazz, cosmology, and other aspects of Black popular culture have been studied for

The Contradictions of Domination

the ways in which they have maintained temporal continuity with the fear-some ruptures of an enslaved past; for the ways they unearth an inventory of traces; for the intuitions, rhythms, sensibilities, intuitions, inheritances, and the like which are able to give some cultural content and meaning to peoples and groups who have undergone racial slavery.[119]

UTOPIA AND MYTH IN THE FAR DISTANCE

Even in phases marked by domination, the question of Utopia and myth is important for Gramsci and has a subtle place—neither wholly negative nor wholly positive. In some senses, Utopia and myth have a negative relation-ship to popular mobilization. Gramsci identifies Utopia with abstract ration-alism. Utopian prophesies can proliferate amid fears of change. Fear-inducing changes are in the air, and prophesies appear as a way of resolving such fears in an evasive way. Utopia involves a kind of a metaphysics, an eva-sion of history, which attempts to 'reconcile, in a mythological form, the real contradictions of historical life'. '[T]he fall of the present oppressive order is thinkable not in the historical future "of this world", but in a place outside history where everything is orderly and organized. With utopias, "humanity tries to evade the narrow limits of the existent organization which is crush-ing it", through "imagination and dream". This is particularly visible in pop-ular literature, especially the kind that insists on dreams and utopias.'[120]

Utopia in this sense, arguably, involves a kind of an abstracted and ahistorical—a purely imaginative—construction of a harmonious world in which there is a falsely completed unity of theory and practice. The attempt is to reconcile real contradictions, including forms of alienation and oppres-sion, through an abstract construction in some great (spatial and temporal) beyond. But this does nothing to induce or develop the practical and creative capacities of those that such myths engage. At one level, this applies to reli-gion. As Gramsci writes: 'religion is the most gigantic utopia, that is the most gigantic "metaphysics", that history has ever known, since it is the most grandiose attempt to reconcile, in mythological form, the real contradic-tions of historical life.'[121]

At another level, myth has an extremely negative dimension as a rather acritical and degenerate populist and 'military' mass 'loyalty'. Gramsci puts it as follows:

The Contradictions of Domination

[T]here is a type of party constituted this time not by an élite but by masses—who as such have no other political function than a generic loyalty, of a military kind, to a visible or invisible political centre. (Often the visible centre is the mechanism of command of forces which are unwilling to show themselves in the open, but only operate indirectly, through proxies and a 'proxy ideology'). The mass following is simply for 'manoeuvre' [posturing in front of the crowds] and is kept happy by means of moralising sermons, emotional stimuli, and messianic myths of an awaited golden age, in which all present contradictions and miseries will be automatically resolved and made well.[122]

Gramsci almost certainly has fascism in mind here.

Even Marxism is critiqued for its mythological dimensions. Gramsci goes as far as to say that the materialist Marxist proposition that the proletariat will inevitably triumph because of the workings of capitalism is another myth, a 'substitute' for the religious notions of 'predestination' and 'providence' and a deeply problematic example of mechanical determinism.[123]

So far, so critical. However, in terms of the problematic of collective will formation, Gramsci writes of the '[i]mportance of utopias and of confused and rationalistic ideologies in the initial phase of the historical processes whereby collective wills are formed. Utopias, or abstract rationalism, have the same importance as old conceptions of the world which developed historically by the accumulation of successive experience.'[124] This is quite an extraordinary statement. Conceptions built up by accumulated experience, Gramsci is saying, are no more important in the *initial phase* (the phase of domination, of collective will formation) than those stemming from Utopia. What can this mean?

First, it is important to note the contrast here: Gramsci is pointing on the one hand to abstract rationalist Utopianism—the most 'unrealistic' flight of the imagination, the flightiest aspect of 'theory'. But on the other hand, Gramsci is putting in counterpoint to this the earthiest of knowledge: 'old conceptions' which have been built up through practice and experience. True to the search for the unification of theory and practice, Gramsci does not deny the significance of either 'extreme'. The dynamic, presumably, comes in part in the tension between them. The sharp contrast between these two orders of activity is part and parcel of a disunity of theory and practice itself.

But what can be constructive here? It is less the ways in which Utopia and the philosophical novel have functioned as 'political criticism' by highlighting the deficiencies of the present order. Such deficiencies, indeed, are relatively easy to spot in an abstract way, especially by alienated middle-class intellectuals. Instead, Gramsci states that 'one of the most interesting aspects to consider is . . . [these Utopias'] unwitting reflection of the most basic and most profound aspirations of subaltern social groups, including the lowest strata, albeit through the minds of intellectuals governed by different concerns'.[125] Gramsci goes on: 'some of this literature expresses the interests of the dominant or deposed groups and has a backward-looking and reactionary character.'[126] But he also writes that '[u]topias are produced by individual intellectuals . . . who essentially reflect, albeit in a very distorted way, the latent instability and rebelliousness among the large popular masses of the time'.[127] He goes on: 'Through utopias, individual intellectuals sought a solution to a set of problems vitally important to the humble; that is to say, they sought a connection between the intellectuals and the people.' He makes the point elsewhere that 'the sexual question plays a very large, often dominant role in "utopias"'.[128]

Finally, in relation to the Marxist myth of inevitable proletarian triumph, Gramsci writes, 'For those who do not have the initiative in the struggle and for whom, therefore, the struggle ends up being synonymous with a series of defeats, mechanical determinism becomes a formidable force of moral resistance, of cohesion, of patient perseverance. "I am defeated, but in the long run history is on my side." . . . In reality, though, even in this case, the will is active; it intervenes directly in the 'force of circumstances', albeit in a . . . covert and veiled manner.'[129]

In other words, mythological thinking and Utopia can reflect a latent rebelliousness; express profound popular aspirations; key into popular problems and feelings; make connections between intellectuals and subaltern social groups; and engender, amid defeats, a force of moral resistance and patient perseverance. Thus, they do not always operate as an expression of fatalism but sometimes as a certain kind of 'covert' assertion of the will. In other words, there are some positive dimensions of myth in the phase of defeat and suffering. Certainly it has been argued that, for Dalit women in India, Pentacostalism, with its redemptive message of Jesus dying for their sins and millenarian beliefs in the second coming, meant emotional solace; some forms of female sociability and solidarity; and a challenge, at least at some level, to racism and casteism.[130] What must be underlined is the macrological scale and temporality of myth, which is operative even in the carceral, perpetual present imposed by social domination. Myth has wings. It is a nomad in the positive sense. It is almost impossible for rulers to eliminate it completely. Here is the import of the common-sense expression, 'You can't kill an idea.'

For Gramsci, myth meant the possibility of a covert assertion of the will, even in appalling conditions of domination and dispossession.

SUBVERSIVISM

> If I negate powdered pigtails [i.e. the German status quo c. 1840], I am still left with unpowdered pigtails.
>
> Karl Marx, 1844

Gramsci's concept of subversivism (*sovversivismo*) and the form of sporadic, 'nomadic', contradictory, populist rebelliousness to which it refers is another important component of a phase of marginal activity under conditions of domination, especially in relation to the state and its forms of coercion, extraction, and domination. The concept can help us capture the limits and potential of a culture and politics of rejectionism—an apparent rebelliousness, a particularist negation—which is attractive to some for its sweeping denunciations and passions but highly limited as a meaningful 'revolutionary force' for challenging domination.[131]

'The purely Italian concept of the "subversive"', Gramsci writes, 'can be explained as follows: a negative rather than a positive class position—the people is aware that it has enemies, but only identifies them empirically as the so-called *signori* [gentlemen].'[132] We can speak of 'hatred of the official'. Certain kinds of individuals or cliques are denounced, but not civil or political society as such. Subversivism was to be found in the countryside, where it was directed against the minor, provincial state officials, who Gramsci referred to as the *morti di fame*. This phrase, meaning 'starved to death', indicates the intense poverty of many of these officials—and thus the insignificance in class terms of hatred directed against them.

Subversivism includes a relatively unelaborated mood of revolt, one that could easily swing back to a mood of fatalism.[133] It included the sudden, hasty, and usually all-too-temporary mobilization of volunteers for this or that political cause, which Gramsci traced in the history of Italy from the Risorgimento to the disastrous fascist March on Rome (1922).[134] Subversivists also existed among charismatic leaders on the Left, who 'used a radical stance as a form of blackmail against the political ruling class, because at the decisive moment these chiefs invariably threw their lot in with the forces of order'.[135]

Gramsci related *sovversivismo* to Italian social conditions: the narrowness of the ruling class, the underdeveloped nature of civil society, the lack of the rule of law, the thinly developed form of consent, and the existence of large numbers of white-collar workers and minor rural officials. Levy also argues convincingly that the origins of Gramsci's concept can be found 'in his polemics with anarchists and syndicalists during the period 1916–1920 [through which he sought] . . . to differentiate his libertarian Marxist/Gentilean/Sorelian communism of workers councils from the "subversive" variety of libertarian socialism' and anarchism.[136]

If Benedetto Croce was the figure of a traditional intellectual to whom Gramsci had once been attracted, Benito Mussolini was associated with the figure of the subversivist to whom Gramsci (at least before 1914) had also been attracted.[137] We might also add that Gramsci's own father was a minor provincial official who suffered imprisonment as a result of accusations of corruption, leaving the Gramsci family to struggle with shame and radically reduced resources. Perhaps Gramsci saw in these accusations a whiff of subversivism, an overdeveloped and less than productive hatred of minor local officials.

Subversivism, then, was both a problematic and misdirected way in which subaltern social groups wrestled ineffectively with state domination and also—and complementary with—a form of political populism enacted by charismatic, adventurist, manipulative political chiefs. Here we see the linkages and connections between two rather different phases of popular mobilization. It is quite possible to imagine developments of the concept regarding the deeper understanding of conspiracy theory and various kinds of sectarian and masculinist rebel populism.[138]

Conspiracy theory (as distinct from knowledge of actual conspiracies) can perhaps be conceived as a kind of subversivism, a negative elaboration of good sense away from good sense. Unlike the pragmatic basics of common sense, which help explain the world according to the terms of the existing hegemonic ideas, conspiracy theory builds initially on the basic premises of *good* sense: 'us and them', 'rich and poor', 'exploiters and exploited', the 'powerful and the weak'. It starts from conditions of powerlessness and situations where occasionally there are actual conspiracies from on high (such as, in the case of the Middle East, the Tripartite Aggression of 1956, when Israel, France, and the UK concerted behind closed doors to invade Egypt); in other words, it contains elements of good sense. But then, progressively and by increments, it hews away from good sense, putting *sovversivismo* in place of good sense or its development towards class and group consciousness, giving what was good sense an increasingly detailed and elaborate content, which departs further and further from any sort of real insight into the actual dynamics of social being and social consciousness, domination, popular mobilization, and hegemony. In Proudfoot's research, Syrian workers in Lebanon are endlessly spectating the uprising: they are passionately sharing images; they are concerned and moved; they are constantly on their mobile phones; they are following every detail—but, for the most part, this is a passive, social-media facilitated spectatorship. Conspiracizing, arguably, has an elective affinity with such passivity; given that the whole system is thought to be rigged and the large popular masses are the primary victims, there really is no line of collective action that one might, under such conceptions, conceivably follow.

Conspiracy theory is thus a kind of subaltern savoir faire: we are not fooled; we know *exactly* what is going on—even at global scales in space and long timelines (e.g. of the Free Masons). Conspiracy theory is a nomad in the negative sense. It does not remain in the subaltern phase but has its own manipulative development in civil society and culture. Still it is very close to subversivism in terms of content and ineffectiveness. It has a radical appearance in that it entirely rejects existing hegemonic explanations. And like subversivism, it is perfectly complementary with, and rather promoted by, forms of right-wing populism, the adventurism and blackmail of this or that manipulator of the masses. It makes its connection to and appearance at the highest levels of the state.

Subversivism is an almost wholly negative figure in Gramsci—though we should not fail to note that even here Gramsci spotted 'glimmers' of class and group consciousness, implying that such unpromising terrain could also contain elements which could be developed in new directions.

One hypothesis in regard to such a line of development could relate to the ways in which encounters with state officials (including police and security forces), originally based on a more or less subversivist cultural politics, could—through fleeting confrontations, the activation of new solidarities, the need to coordinate further, neighbourhood solidarities, and the like—result in developments away from the merely subversive. Building up group consciousness, elaborating a narrative history and a popular memory, and involving the new coordination of bodies and the acquisition of particular skills, and so on could lead to the incremental acquisition of forms of partial autonomy within a predominantly subaltern phase of domination.

Boeddeling's Gramscian fieldwork on young and un- and underemployed men in Tunisia's 'South'—the economically and politically excluded provincial periphery—argues strongly for this kind of trajectory. His research shows how subaltern political activity can start to break through the 'ceiling' associated with 'everyday politics, hidden resistance, and defensive mobilization'.[139] Police violence, humiliation, and insults all drove both fear and hatred, while the police represented the state.[140] As one interlocutor stated: 'In our mentality, the police were the state. When you saw a policeman, for you it is he who prevented your livelihood. He is responsible for your empty pocket, your frustration, your poverty, the injustice you feel etc.'[141]

Part of the reason the police represented the state was the fact that such subaltern youth did not encounter state officials in any other capacity.[142] Boeddeling traces the emergence 'of an insurgent vector of mobilization which, although evolving in a complex relationship with the union, was largely independent from formal politics' and from the various associations of civil society.[143] One start point involved straightforward 'taking revenge' on the police and the ruling party, coordinating covertly in small groups, attacking by night and rapidly withdrawing, and recovering some of the masculine pride lost in daytime humiliations. Said one protagonist: 'We would meet at a PlayStation gaming room. Everyone in the neighborhood went there. And there [the planning] started. . . . We jumped on the RCD premises at night, surrounded it with tires and set it on fire. You set fire and you fled. . . . We burned, and we left, we did not stay. Burn and get lost!'[144]

More open, daytime confrontations with the police, involving stones and tear gas, took place at football matches. 'Experience with clashes in stadiums provided subaltern youth with vital knowledge and skills in confronting the police.'[145] Prior to 2010, a larger political language was not at work. However, Boeddeling posits a complementary relationship between these kinds of clashes and the ways in which larger categories of group consciousness—around region and tribe—were being elaborated through the oral telling, activation, and elaboration of memories of revolt from the periphery, going back to the nineteenth century.[146] In the development of these categories, the good sense of 'us' and 'them' is to some extent elaborated into a more specific sense—in reference to history, local realities, and popular memory. The outlines of new forms of collectivity start to come into view.

Amid the action, indeed, conspiracist or subversivist tissues of culture may start to be revised. The talents that were put into a certain kind of subaltern savoir faire—linguistic skill, research on the internet, powers of persuasion, arrangements of the facts, pursuit of this or that argument—start to serve different arguments, different hypotheses: those that are much more about the elaboration of good sense. Spaces (e.g. the PlayStation gaming room) were 'repurposed', inhabited for different reasons, made to contain something different, and friendship ties became the informal networks for collective action. Here were some incremental gains: limited, but nonetheless vital elements of unification.

A WHOLE SUBTERRANEAN WORLD

Gramsci saw another kind of life in the margins, especially in the prisons and prison transports that he was subjected to during the last eleven years of his life. In his letters from San Vittore prison, he wrote of 'that subterranean world [including exiles, prisoners and non-Christians] which lives and reproduces itself on the margins of the other world . . . Bedouins from Cyrenaica, Sicilian *Mafiosi*, Neapolitan *Camorristi*, pale imitations of Farinata [an aristocrat, military figure, faction leader, and heretic, who was posthumously executed by the inquisition and mentioned in Dante's inferno] and seemingly harmless thieves'.[147]

Gramsci, far from dismissing, patronizing, scoffing, or romanticizing, spoke of 'a whole subterranean world . . . extremely complicated, with its own life of emotions, of points of view, of points of honour, and formidable, iron hierarchies'.[148] The reference here is to a subaltern formation built on the basis of its own codes, hierarchies, and emotions. This formation involved a kind of autonomy against the law. It comprised interstitial activities seeking neither transformation nor self-universalization but guarding spaces of particularity and invisibility, including across borders; using the above-ground world in the service of alternate norms and ends; and developing a concrete particularity. Research in the living Gramscian tradition on the 'subterranean world' is underdeveloped. It is a theme that is wide open for new studies.

PASSIVE AND ACTIVE ADHERENCE

Gramsci writes of an early phase in the history of subaltern social groups involving 'their active or passive adherence to the dominant political formations; their efforts to influence the programs of these formations in order to impose their own demands; and the consequences of these efforts in determining processes of decomposition and renewal, or neoformation'.[149]

This is a very important area in Gramscian optics on popular mobilization, more or less impossible to capture in terms of a 'romantic' model of resistance. The latter is an extensively critiqued view in which subaltern activity is conceived somehow inherently in terms of opposition, resistance, and revolution.[150] This romantic model differs sharply from a Gramscian perspective in which questions centring on passive and active adherence, the complex of demands and claims by differentially positioned subordinates, and their repercussions in relation to temporality and hegemony have seen significant research. The living Gramscian tradition, equally, is at odds with a model that romanticizes power or that sees power in terms of a top-down and purely imposed monologue, as only *diagnosed* by resistance. The above quotation signals the tension: passive and active adherents are led and incorporated in some sense, but they also make efforts, have demands, and these all have consequences.

Passive and active adherence signal the ways in which subaltern social groups are neither entirely excluded, outside, or in some immaculate external space; nor are they fundamentally included. Their situation can be ambiguous, both to themselves and to onlookers, both in practice and in theory. It is not a matter—here—of constructing a binary agency/non-agency, being/non-being, or even West/non-West, which is used, drawing on Foucault, to overdetermine these kinds of debates.[151] It is not a passive or submissive characteristic of the 'East', of the colonized, or of Muslims to offer passive or active adherence from below to a dominant formation. Gramscian and social movement perspectives alike join hands in finding such forms in global politics in general. Researchers have often drawn on the concept of hegemony to understand passive and active adherence from below in post-1945 Europe in terms of both class compromise and in terms of elections and votes.[152]

Adherence is a concept that encompasses loyalty; can involve elements of consent; and does not just mean inactivity, indifference, absenteeism, or being 'of no account'. It encompasses various activities, lines of social force, and includes subaltern attempts to influence and make demands. At stake can be a certain sort of 'protest politics', involving the expression and redress of grievance under domination via appeals to authority. 'We are exploited, the ruler will put it right.' Here there are forms of unequal reciprocity; tense, negotiated arrangements across power differentials; Gramsci's 'unstable equilibria'. There are engagements from subordinate positions and sociologies, with existing forms of leadership and consent, and the various repercussions of these engagements.

In living forms of hegemony, adherence is tended from above. Authorities do not here take passive or active adherence completely for granted. E. P. Thompson's studies of the moral economy in eighteenth-century England referenced Gramsci to explore these forms of structural reciprocity and their 'customs in common', with the gentry often responding with concessions to plebeian protests around bread prices, hoarding, and profiteering, thus shoring up the late eighteenth-century British paternalistic cultural hegemony.[153] Petitions from peasants, weighers, and measurers in nineteenth-century Egypt, which articulated official languages of loyalty and justice, were able to achieve investigation and redress, as well as to colour dominant languages on welfare and rights with subaltern views and interests.[154] The combined and uneven advent of political economy did not eliminate the importance of moral economies. Bread riots took place across the world in the face of neoliberal restructuring from the 1970s to the 1990s, achieving some concessions.[155] Authorities grappling with popular protest can find it difficult to dismantle redistributive bargains of earlier epochs.[156] 'Reform' can be dangerous. It signals that things did not have to be as they once were: calling into question either the authorities as they were or the previous adherence of the subaltern social groups.

Pressure from below by active and zealous followers (those who are 'more Catholic than the Pope') can cause authorities to proclaim their views more loudly and thoroughly, to enact policy in a more determined way and bolster elite determination and morale. For instance, following the demonstrations that broke out against Nasser's resignation in 1967, Nasser rescinded his resignation and returned to power. Some demonstrations are actively solicited. The Al-Sisi regime in Egypt, for example, called for (and obtained) demonstrations, seeking a popular mandate ('delegation') to 'deal with' (violently repress) Muslim Brotherhood sit-ins opposing the coup of early July 2013. Other leaderships can feel compelled to act in certain ways following interpellation from below. In Orwell's 'Shooting an Elephant', for instance, the young colonial officer feels forced to enact a colonizing script demanded by the crowds.

Concessions amid unstable equilibria are not simply unilateral and imposed. They need, at some level, to be compelling or, at a minimum, to make sense to subordinates. There is some form of bargain and dialogue at stake here—albeit a highly unequal one. Hoarders, profiteers, and state officials threaten or fail to uphold the moral economy, but the moral economy, a nexus of theory and practice, continues, in the eyes of those making the demands, to be savable. Under conditions of classical patriarchy, a breadwinner fails in his masculinist duties to provide for the household and is confronted by his wife, who needs to prepare the supper for several hungry children. It is a question of shoring up the integration of the subaltern social group within the larger hegemony. Kandiyoti has argued that everyday bargains with patriarchy, in a context of resource pressures on the patriarchal household, result in appeals to patriarchal protection.[157] Integration remains a matter of active adherence from below. In the first case there are plebeians seeking to shore up the terms of the paternalist moral economy anchored in the social domination of the gentry. In the second case the woman-as-homemaker—including in the face of the erosion of resources—seeks to shore up the terms of the patriarchal 'bargain' anchored in the social domination of men. In these cases, some minor actual, perceived, or threatened disunity of theory and practice, some challenge to a would-be organic activity structure, some tear in the existing hegemonic fabric, gives rise to a round of activity aimed at repair. Some of these forms of mobilization are 'everyday' in so far as they reflect the generally unreliable and tense integration and the instability of the equilibria at work in the relationship between subaltern social groups and leading and ruling classes.

Active adherence does not mean that dominant norms have been internalized in a wooden and puppeteering way: it may be that interpretations differ slightly or even very greatly. The self-described loyal subject, for instance, may believe that recent reforms at the top actually mean radical changes at the bottom. For instance, the *tanzimat* reforms in the Ottoman Empire, aimed at state centralization, juridical forms of equality between religious communities, and the construction of new forms of Ottoman citizenship, were interpreted by a non-literate poor muleteer and blacksmith, who would become the leader of a popular uprising on Mt Lebanon in 1858, to mean the end of feudal privilege and the equality of commoners with notables.[158] Even social bandits seeking liberty against the law have been known to proclaim a mandate from this or that ruler.[159] Intense forms of loyalty can coincide with intensive and extensive forms of popular mobilization—and even drive it forward. Further, subaltern social groups can continue to believe in policies and principles that the authorities have abandoned, and thus, in a search for 'hegemony from below', can mobilize to recreate those principles locally. Paulo Drinot has studied such a search for 'hegemony from below' in Lima (Peru) in the 1920s and 1930s among print workers, who continued to search for state protection for labour long after the 'Patria Nueva' had abandoned them. These workers mobilized for closed shops and even joined communists, not to bring about communism, but to improve their bargaining power and bolster the union movement in a search for a thicker form of state-labour relations.[160] Those engaged in mobilization may not be dupes of ruling or revolutionary ideologies; they may have their own purposes.

Writing in relation to slavery in nineteenth-century East Africa, Glassman gives a clear sense of the ideological meaning of a diffuse adherence to a dominant ideological formation among the enslaved: 'In most cases slaves defined [their] . . . humanity in terms of some variant of the hegemonic ideologies [Swahili paternalism]. . . . Slaves therefore struggled to be accepted as personal clients who shared with their patrons a devotion to Islam, commerce, and the other values of urban life.'[161] Here, those who have been radically excluded from the community as a dehumanized Other struggle to negotiate a subordinate yet partially included, humanized position as personal clients, aiming to avoid a social death as commodity and property. In this case, even the formerly radically excluded are not simply 'revolutionary'; they may seek to negotiate terms of subordination that align with dominant forms of culture.

Subaltern social groups may perceive unevenness within dominant formations and single out some 'intermediaries' as corrupt, profiteering, or unjust in some way, while proclaiming and demonstrating adherence to the ruler, top leadership, or the ideologies and worldviews (including of the transnational kind) with which the leadership are identified. This has been a common feature of labour protest in Egypt. A stream of loyal protest characterized workers' work-in strikes in Egypt in the 1960s. Here workers took over factories in a form of disruptive challenge to employers—a strike in the sense that they withdrew their labour from management control—but they then applied their labour, on their own terms, to actually raise production during the 'work-in'. They demonstrated a loyalty and active adherence to the terms of the existing Nasserist hegemony, while joining intensive battles with local management and union structure.[162]

Glassman points more broadly to the ways in which plebeian and agrarian rebels have been motivated 'not by coherent awareness of their discrete class interests but by an ambiguous consciousness fashioned out of fragments of the hegemonic ideologies which they had found at hand. Most useful to them were ideals of community, which they often transformed and manipulated to form the basis of popular new rebellious traditions.'[163] Appeals to authorities to uphold a valued community now presumed shattered, a *status quo ante* or a mythologized past, should not be dismissed as solely conservative or backward-looking. They are, rather, 'an effort by the relatively powerless to negotiate actively the terms of change while using the ideological tools available to them'.[164] Borrowed or 'old' languages in new contexts can potentially mean new things.

Passive and active adherence is not just a matter of subjectivity, belief, and ideas but also of practice, the material, and the object. In the moral economy, households need their bread; in the patriarchal household, children are actually hungry—and even pursuing their own demands, from a subordinate position, in relation to mothers. In Peru and Egypt, workers were seeking to improve their pay and conditions. In Mossallam's research on Nasserist hegemony among High Dam workers and Nubian communities in Upper Egypt, alongside the affective and intimate languages of poetry and song, there was also the promise and reality of education, skills acquisition, social mobility, and national and anti-colonial economic development.[165] Both the structure and the superstructure do double duty in these streams of passive and active adherence. The effectivity of the culture is intertwined in subtle ways with state and economy. Algeria's starring position in Third World national liberation struggles in the 1970s was undermined just as much by the economy as by a changing forms of politics and culture.[166] By the same token, the Algerian bread riots of 1988 were not just about bread, or even the moral economy, they were also about moral *polity*: subaltern social groups, drawing on long-standing traditions and customs actually brought from the countryside, sought to be included in decision-making and rejected the deep-seated 'contempt' (*hojra*) directed at them by 'the regime' (*le pouvoir*).[167]

Unstable equilibria are, as the name indicates, unstable: lines of development and regression are possible. Subaltern social groups continue to be vulnerable within them in a relatively structural sense. There is no guarantee that active or passive adherence will succeed in bringing about or maintaining desired forms of unequal reciprocity—repairing the tears and rips in the hegemonic fabric. There are limitations to this subphase of popular mobilization, dynamics that create pressures for change. In E. P. Thompson's research, the shift from moral economy to political economy, which accompanied the diffusion of French revolutionary politics and shifts in capital accumulation, started to disable and undermine the possibilities held out by the older moral economy tradition. A whole paternalistic hegemonic complex was surpassed and new modalities of mobilization, including new forms of active and passive adherence, were then sought out.

Glassman explains, 'At the end of the nineteenth century [slave-clients] suffered major setbacks in this quest for acceptance, as the rapid spread of commodity production made them more valuable to their masters as subordinate producers of market goods than as personal clients.'[168] In this case, the changing terms of accumulation, alongside the appearance of a more distant (Omani) planter class, worked against these popular struggles. In late nineteenth-century Egypt, petitions appealing to the justice of the ruler started to become less effective as the bureaucracy developed and centralized.[169] Instability thus has a Janus-face. On the one hand it means that a stream of meaningful concessions can be forthcoming. On the other, it means that such a stream can dry up: hegemony and existing forms of unequal reciprocity can wane or, in the language of Alan Knight on the ruling party in Mexico in the 1950s, become 'thin'.[170] At a certain point active and passive adherence, and its various kinds of demands and influence start to lose traction; these modalities then start to lose the capacity to command the overall acceptance of the subaltern social groups. Sites of hegemonic articulation, components of the 'hegemonic apparatus'[171]—whether petitions, elections, strikes, union mechanisms and so on—start to break up. There are problems in the relations between represented and representative. Those who are used to having some say through passive or active adherence or who implicitly held some faith in the status quo now find their voice and their faith challenged. Either new forms are found and put into place or there are the beginnings of a 'crisis of authority' or a variety of regressions come into play.

INDIFFERENCE

One condition against which Gramsci polemicized was indifference. It is arguably an important ingredient in the subaltern phase—a component of subordination. The 'passivity of the masses, their indifference and fatalist submission to an external, mechanical law of necessity explains why given groups and institutions become dominant'.[172] Gramsci writes: 'What comes

The Contradictions of Domination

to pass . . . is due not so much to the initiative of the active few, as to the indifference, the absenteeism of the many.'[173] Writing in 1917, regarding the 'future city', Gramsci writes passionately against indifference: 'I hate the indifferent. . . . It is the swamp that surrounds the old town (*città*) and defends better than the thickest walls, better than the chests of its warriors, engulfing the attackers in its quick-sand, decimating and daunting them, and sometimes making them abandon their heroic enterprise.'[174]

These metaphors strongly convey the sense of an active leadership, placing power under siege, searching for the engagement of subordinate groups, and failing to obtain it. Defeat results more from the quagmire of indifference on 'their own side' than from the strengths of the opposition. It is an 'undialectical' indifference that empties their ranks, lowers their morale, and even drives them to give up in despair. The subaltern social groups thus remain in their subordinated condition.

Indifference is a deadweight preventing not only the fulfilment of practical activities, but also theoretical activity. Indifference is the 'raw material', writes Gramsci, that 'ruins intelligence'. As Salamini puts it, 'the passivity of the masses generates and sustains extra-historical or suprahistorical values and beliefs, such as religion, human nature, science.'[175] Elites get away with it and subordinates continue to lose out, reinforcing a sense of divine predestination or appointment, statistical and mechanical (faux-scientific) social laws, or natural passivity—genus-like views of groups or of human nature in general. 'The fatality that seems to dominate history is precisely the illusory appearance of this indifference.'[176] Indifference and absenteeism are thus paradoxically reconstituted in Gramsci as a certain kind of inverted social force, a kind of dark matter, allowing narrowly based forces, groupings, or combinations of elements to come together and to operate without hindrance or disruption. History then appears as 'nothing but an immense natural phenomenon', at which point 'it is the indifferent ones who get angry, who wish to dissociate themselves from the consequences. . . . And while some whine piteously, and others howl obscenely, few people, if any, ask themselves this question: had I done my duty . . . had I sought to make my voice heard, to impose my will, would what came to pass have ever happened?'[177] The point is that for history to be made, for subaltern social groups to make their own history, forms of indifference and absenteeism will need to be overcome, and new forms of collective will constructed.

SUBALTERN FORMATIONS AND FLEETING CONFRONTATIONS

> Here in Ustica there are thirty of us political prisoners: we've already initiated a series of elementary and general culture courses for various groups of prisoners.[178]

In *Prison Notebook* 25, Gramsci wrote of a phase in the history of subaltern social groups involving 'the formations created by the subaltern groups themselves to press claims of a limited and partial kind'.[179] Hoare and Nowell Smith suggest that this references trade unions.[180] This is a possible interpretation, though it has not been elaborated. Gramsci does offer alternative clues as to the meaning of this phase at other points. Gramsci explains that the most elementary form of political force in the context of 'objective formation' has to do with the economic-corporate ways in which 'a tradesman feels *obliged* to stand by another tradesman, a manufacturer by another manufacturer, etc., but the tradesman does not yet feel solidarity with the manufacturer'.[181] Gramsci's reference here is to a phase in the emergence of the bourgeoisie under feudalism when no form of bourgeois class solidarity existed. Gramsci describes this also in more general terms—terms that could apply to the subaltern phase of working-class existence. He writes of a situation in which 'the members of the professional group [e.g. shoemakers, textile workers] are conscious of its unity and homogeneity, and of the need to organize it, but in the case of the wider social group [e.g. the proletariat] this is not yet so'.[182]

Even in a context of instrumentalization, then, Gramsci suggests that forms of unification are possible—the first developments anticipated being in reference to local forms of solidarity—where, for instance, there are rudimentary feelings of obligation and solidarity based on professional or face-to-face (social) ties between those doing the same job. Arguably it is these kinds of limited and partial formations, which involve some part of a subaltern social group or class but not all of it, that are at stake in relation to the 'formations created by subaltern social groups themselves'. In this subphase, vital, incremental gains can be made, while ultimately, there are key limits (the claims involved are only 'limited and partial' and may even only refer to increments of space and time) which will need to be overcome.

The thematic here is that captured by Stuart Hall, when he writes that 'people become empowered by doing something: first of all about their immediate troubles'.[183] It is a theme that plays an important role in Cox's analysis of the everyday start points of critical social movements.[184] It refers to the fact that some part of the subaltern is always directive and responsible. Such formations are at stake among a wide variety of subaltern social groups. They involve new spaces and places, however delimited, and new forms of continuous temporality, even if only on an episodic basis. They give rise to new sorts of social relationship (regarding social being) and new kinds of largely informal or unrecognized social organization; fleeting confrontations with authority; and new kinds of social consciousness and culture, even if only in glimmers of good sense and in iterations of popular culture and movements in spontaneous philosophy. They also represent an initial nodal point regarding the incipient presence of a new social force, organic to the subaltern social group. They are almost always informal, often fleeting, and can be barely registered at the time—sometimes even by the participants themselves. New gay-friendly spaces, writes Eribon, 'make encounters possible'.[185] Often their full significance only starts to become clear later.

Rather than large bureaucratic trade unions, then, in focus here in relation to the economy and organization are informal groups of workers meeting in various social spaces, initiating cooperation or mutual help, and overcoming total fragmentation with incipient forms of solidarity. Informal associational activity—in cafés, plant canteens and corridors, families, and neighbourhoods—was the organizational basis for much worker strike action in Egypt in the 2000s. In this case, these subaltern formations appeared when the existing sites of consent—the forms of active and passive adherence to the dominant formation (the statist union)—started to lose traction.[186] Community association based on locality, neighbourhood, and kin was a crucial layer of solidarity involved in the road blockages and protests by precarious youth against Petrofac in Tunisia over unemployment and underdevelopment in the 2010s.[187] In this phase, there is a felt need to form up, to coordinate, to organize, to structure a stream of activity. But such a formation is at this point only incipient, partial (in relation to the wider group or class), tentative, or informal.

Gramsci also considered latent possibilities regarding the emergence of various forms of group identification. He writes that '[i]n Rome, slaves could not be recognised as such. When a senator once proposed that the slaves be given a distinctive dress, the Senate defeated the measure fearing that the slaves might become dangerous if they came to realise their great number.'[188] Here is a clear indication of the latent possibility of group consciousness emerging amid an otherwise fragmented, isolated, and oppressed subaltern social group—in this case, a possibility glimpsed by the ruling classes in Rome. The example also gives us a sense that ruling classes in themselves may not be certain about the best way to impose domination on a given set of persons, a sense that presupposes the incomplete and processual nature of the exercise of hegemony. Gramsci goes on to suggest that the lines of power around which groups can or cannot appear in public as such—in festivals, parades, and so on—are fraught. He continues directly: 'In this episode one finds the political-psychological reasons that determine a series of public displays: religious processions, corteges, popular assemblies, different kinds of parades and, to some extent, also elections (the participation by some groups in elections), and plebiscites.'[189]

Gramsci is here underlining the fact that 'political-psychological' layers of activity are at work (not just economic processes of enslavement). We also note that even elections are included in terms of demarcating a certain category of those who can appear in public—in this case, the citizens—to the exclusion of non-citizens. These points underline the fact that the formation of social being and its relation to social consciousness is an ongoing process, that it is related to the structure (the slave economy) and the superstructure (the activities of the Senate). Without underestimating the social force of domination, the point is that subordination, regarding social being and social consciousness, is not fixed.

In eighteenth- and early nineteenth-century England, enslaved Africans were overwhelmingly represented in metropolitan theatre as racialized stock characters and stereotypes—including during the period of abolition. Black voices offstage, however, and marginal, quotidian performances of a different kind were never completely erased. Mary Prince was born an enslaved woman in Bermuda and freed herself in 1828 after being brought to England. Amid the acute pressures of social domination—in relation to her owners and middle-class white abolitionists—she was able episodically to evoke something of her past and present, of the tortures inflicted upon her body and person. Using wit, linguistic dexterity, encoding, and parody, she referred to the experiences of the enslaved as a collectivity, gathering audiences in specific scenes of fleeting confrontation, in the household of her 'owners', on the street, and among abolitionists.[190]

Eribon charts the ways gay people 'have tried to create spaces—practical spaces as well as literary and theatrical ones—in which to resist subjection and in which to reformulate oneself'.[191] Roy has written about the origins of Sappho, a lesbian collective in India in 1999: 'Two to four, four to six, six lesbians in the heart of the city of Calcutta exchanging laughter and tears—who had thought that such a day would come in our lives? When we would be able to speak our minds freely without fear or shame, share jokes with people of a similar mindset?'[192]

The novel and particular character of the space; the new, embodied, and felt social relationships that are generated by such a formation ('laughter', 'tears'); the great gain in relation to the surrounding experiences of domination and stigma; the idea of a break in a long life lived otherwise; a new form of temporality; the immediate relationship to life-activity; the new forms of language and communication ('to speak our minds'); and the sense of freedom—where lesbians can 'speak freely'—that such a formation allowed are all expressed here. The sense of incremental gain via molecular addition 'two to four, four to six', with the whole then creating something larger than the sum of its parts, is also evident in this account. A key element of this in Roy is the 'need to imagine and institute new spaces and forms of care, relationality, and sociality, *as queers* [emphasis in original]'.[193] New practices of care, in other words, start to matter in such subaltern formations.

An informal group or collective formed for its own purposes (e.g., in the case of sexuality or gender, to escape or cope with social stigma, violence, or insult or to find housing or make a living) may end up pressing claims to fulfil its goals or become embroiled in fleeting confrontations with authorities. In Bayat's research on Iran, rural-urban migrants seeking housing and

The Contradictions of Domination

livelihood along with increments of dignity and autonomy (but not ideology or programme) set up informal housing in unregulated areas and informal street vending activities on public pavements, generating in the process 'passive networks'—a minimum formation involving a kind of social recognition of those in similar situations. The authorities move in to bulldoze 'illegal', 'dirty' homes and to 'cleanse' and make orderly the pavements, resulting in fleeting collective organization and confrontations with the police.[194] Cronin makes the point that subaltern histories and struggles in the Middle East and North Africa were rarely revolutionary and generally 'defensive', involving limited formations in passing confrontations with authorities in defence of small gains.[195]

Police repression, nonetheless, is not always the end of the story. For instance, certain elements from among the subaltern social group may decide to mount revenge attacks, in response to the abuse they have experienced at the hands of the police. This pattern is present in the 'fleeting' attacks on police stations studied in Salwa Ismail's ethnography of young men from the popular quarters of Bulaq Al-Dakrur in Egypt.[196] It is also vividly at work as seen above in Boeddeling's study of young, marginal, and unemployed men on the eve of the uprising in Tunisia in 2010. While masculinist honour tropes and subversivism may rule the roost, there may also be unintended consequences of this activity: young men, for instance, may gain skills in physical confrontation with the police which may later serve a useful purpose, becoming something else when a wider crisis of authority comes.

When popular sectors are used to 'making do' and solving their own problems, which have their origins in the 'deficiencies of the public authorities', sitting down in front of the government and making demands may also be part and parcel of these practical activities and the form of consciousness (i.e. government failing) that it implies. In Nouakchott, for instance, urban subalterns 'develop various informal practices (locally called *tieb-tieb*) and other coping strategies which allow them to survive and evolve within the interstices of the city and the powers which, more or less, control its development. Strategies for illegally appropriating land (*gazra*), poaching, or piracy (especially of water and electricity) are among the subaltern's many responses in the face of the deficiencies of the public authorities.

Occasionally, the inhabitants of peripheral neighborhoods mobilize collectively. For instance, it is common to see women demanding water or plots of land directly in front of the presidential palace.'[197]

Here coordination for 'making do' morphs almost seamlessly into coordination for making demands. The two modes of formation are strongly overlapping and, at one level, may appear to be part and parcel of the same thing. Khalil's research on a village in Egypt's Delta in the 2010s found that organization and confrontation for local socioeconomic demands was strongly *dissociated* in the minds of villagers from demonstrations and protests—the latter being stigmatized and associated with educated youth, the city, disorder, ideology, and even terrorism.[198] Here subaltern formations engage politically while eschewing a political consciousness. This may not, of course, lead to any qualitative shift. Laveille's research on popular mobilization in Upper Egypt in the 2010s shows subaltern formations which come into being—for instance in an informal group that makes demands against corrupt officials for a local football field—but then melt away.[199] Other collectives worry that they only exist in a bubble. The lesbians in South Asia studied by Roy realized that there was a need to go beyond the privacy and intimacy of a 'support group', which would not change the larger structure and even 'replicate the dynamics of a ghetto'.[200]

Indeed, there is no guarantee that subaltern formation will develop further in relation to the wider group or class. Nor should this be considered a natural or normal development—it must be constructed actively. Teleology here is a high road to passivity. There is considerable doubt, for instance, over whether the labour movement in China in the 2000s was undergoing such a development. As Gray writes, 'Workers' protests have taken the form of direct collective actions, such as strikes, sit-down demonstrations, protests outside government offices, traffic blockades, riots, etc.'[201] However, Gray argues that '[t]heir demands were mostly concerned with the security of their jobs, the standard of the payment of economic compensation, and the punishment of corrupt managers', and there is arguably no 'politically-conscious organized working-class movement'.[202] As elsewhere, developments must be contextualized. In China, the movement operates in a post-socialist context and amid the legacies of a 'workers' state', implying dilemmas faced by both the state (regarding legitimation) and workers in

The Contradictions of Domination

relation to whether and to what extent once dominant languages can be deployed.[203]

On the other hand, incipient subaltern formations may scale up, developing more extensive and formal forms of organization and ideology, giving rise to forms of identity and solidarity, feelings of empowerment, and actual gains in terms of social force. In researching incipient coordination among workers in Detroit in the 1930s, for instance, Rick Fantasia analyzes a form of 'transformative associational bonding' in which new forms of worker solidarity and identity are activated amid informal association with a view to strike action: solidarity (which may well not be revolutionary) is 'created *and* expressed by the process of mutual association'.[204] In Featherstone's account, internationalist and interracial solidarity is a 'transformative political relation' discovered and forged in political activity itself, capable of forging 'subaltern geographies of connection' beyond nation and state.[205]

Even where such subaltern formations do not scale up, they can have interesting, partially unintended repercussions, such as hollowing out existing forms of hegemony. In Singerman's research on inner city neighbourhoods in Cairo in the 1980s, informal networks built in the informal economy at the community level often by women to secure resources and protections for the urban poor formed according to locally determined rules and norms undermined 'what Gramsci called the ideological hegemony of the state'.[206]

Practices of care in local contexts, under great pressure, great misery, and considerable degrees of subordination have a powerful significance as part and parcel of a subaltern formation. Bringing blankets, books, and food to a prisoner; finding a way to get a driving permit from the local authority; cooking; helping a loved one through relationship difficulties—these are all directive and responsible; they are not pregiven in any structure; they require initiative and care; they may end up generating forms of solidarity and foster aspects of good sense that can eventually become autonomous. Gramsci admired his mother, who coped while her husband was imprisoned, who managed to care for the young Gramscis against heavy odds. We can see a similar point in Tatiana Schucht's reminders to Gramsci that her care for him as his sister-in-law was neither self-evident, 'what women do' (as in the masculinist genus-thinking), nor was it valueless (as in much Marxism), nor was it simply functional for capital (as in social reproduction

The Contradictions of Domination

theory). Instead, she valued it in and of itself. Schucht, who had a doctorate in natural science from the university of Rome, did not believe that 'the satisfaction of creaturely needs was a function unworthy of serious and constant attention'.[207] It was a practice of care that was difficult for Gramsci to understand fully, but it is a theme that has been taken or can be taken up in Gramscian feminist perspectives. It is a thematic that overlaps strongly with the place of feeling in a Gramscian theory of popular mobilization.

CONTRADICTORY CONSCIOUSNESS

Contradictory consciousness is a crucial component of the subaltern phase. It has great value as a genuine expression, however fleeting and dimly registered, of contradictions in existing forms of hegemony. It is consciousness torn by the gap between how things and persons are supposed to be in practice and in theory according to the dominant hegemony and how things and persons are experienced in practice and in theory by subaltern social groups. Contradictory consciousness is the contradictory coincidence of two kinds of consciousness in one consciousness. On the one side is a consciousness 'logically affirmed as an intellectual choice' or 'uncritically absorbed'[208]: it is a form of consciousness either voluntaristic or doxic; associated with and intertwined with hegemony, dominant worldviews, civil society, capitalism, and the state; and present and structuring as common sense in the life-activity of subaltern social groups. On the other side is a consciousness that is present, implicit, and intertwined with the life-activity, practices (economic, embodied, social, cultural, or political), and experiences of subaltern social groups; it is a consciousness 'which emerges from the real activity of each man [or woman], which is implicit in his [or her] mode of action'.[209] When contradictory consciousness occurs in the lives of great masses, writes Gramsci, it is not a matter of 'self-deception', bad faith, or hypocrisy, but 'the expression of profounder contrasts of a social historical order'.[210]

Contradictory consciousness is a double consciousness existing in and rending apart a single consciousness. It is half articulate in that it does not in and of itself have a language or a conception of the world, and certainly does not have a developed politics. It can often be expressed in mixtures of parody, satire, nostalgia, irony, rejection, dissent, and desire of widely varying political significance.[211] It is not false (as in vanguardist conceptions), angry (as in Orientalism), or irrational and mired in custom and tradition (as in rationalist Jacobinism) but is linked to the painful, contradictory structure of life activity and of common sense in a given hegemony: it is only incoherent and unsystematic insofar as it expresses the contradictions of social and historical order. It is the gap between social situations and dominant interpretations thereof.[212] It expresses a situation, in the words of an anthropologist not using an explicit Gramscian referent, in which 'the gap between act and narrative, social reality and agent's consciousness . . . [is] no longer a matter of individual failure to establish congruence between seeming and being, it . . . [is] a collective experience'.[213] In other words, its very incoherence is revealing and vital rather than simply wrong or obfuscatory. Contradictory consciousness is not what Gilles Deleuze rightly dismisses as a 'little, private affair', an individual psychological trauma or deviation requiring expert, individualized therapy, but a vital, lived, tormenting drama and dissonance to be elucidated, attended, and understood, with a possible pathway towards catharsis.[214] It is not the putative weakness of a woman who needs the strong counsel of a man. Gramsci states, in considering how conceptions are formed and common sense transcended, that contradictory consciousness—'the coexistence of two conceptions of the world, one affirmed in words and the other expressed in concrete action—is not always attributable to dishonesty . . . [instead] a social group may have its own, albeit embryonic conception'.[215] Thus contradictory consciousness is a collective form of unrest that calls for, and indeed searches out, the insurgent act of 'only connect', of articulation in relation to the development of the embryonic conception implicit in the practices of the wider group or class.

Femia cites significant survey evidence in favour of contradictory consciousness: ordinary people do express, in the abstract, 'a great deal of agreement with the dominant ideology'. Whereas on the situational plane, they reveal 'not outright dissensus but a diminished level of commitment to the "bourgeois" ethos, because it is often inapposite to the exigencies of . . . class position'.[216] Most people are neither revolutionaries nor entirely mystified by a belief in the 'absolute efficacy of the established universe of discourse and action'. Femia concludes that Gramsci's approach is therefore more valid than consensus or conflict models: the former fails to look at power relations, while the latter looks often and only at 'rational calculations of personal advantage'.[217] A suggestive example comes from research based on fieldwork among Dalit and Other Backward Class (OBC) informal workers in Ahmedabad, India, in the context of Hindutva and development ideology. Desai found here 'ambivalent subjectivities' involving 'sentiments of support and admiration . . . expressed within the same interview with anger, cynicism and despair': neither passive acquiescence nor active resistance, identification nor otherness, but ambivalence.[218]

Contradictory consciousness is bound up with hegemonic contradictions and 'profound' historical contrasts. As Gramsci writes: 'Since the ensemble of social relations is contradictory, human historical consciousness is contradictory. . . . Among subaltern groups, given the lack of historical initiative, the fragmentation is greater; they face a harder struggle to liberate themselves from imposed (rather than freely propounded) principles in order to arrive at an autonomous historical consciousness.'[219]

Gramsci notes, against the insistence of the ruling class, the lack of complete coherence even in ruling conceptions.[220] Different ideologies, intellectuals, and political forces propose different solutions and meanings. Sites of articulation can break down. The state can also run into a far-reaching crisis of authority' (i.e. of hegemony) brought about in part by the failings of ruling groups in major undertakings, for which they had previously won or forcibly extracted mass consent. Here previous patterns of subaltern passive and active adherence are thrown into disarray. Common sense, furthermore, as we have seen, is not a seamless, singular expression of the dominant worldview—but highly fragmented and contradictory. The inventory of traces may suggest new meanings, histories, or identities for individuals or the group. At its most fundamental, contradictory consciousness expresses in some incipient way the forms of objectification and subjectification—the forms of oppression, the disunity of theory and practice—at work in the existing hegemony.

Contradictory consciousness is Janus-faced: 'elements of intellectual and moral approbation coexist in unsteady equilibrium with elements of apathy, resignation and even hostility.'[221] Contradictory consciousness is in one sense an important feature of subordination, a source of weakness and forcelessness. The anti-colonial Egyptian activist Abdallah Al-Nadim (1843-96) lamented how 'Orientals' are 'riven with contradictions and capitulations, constantly turning to foreigners for aid'. He wrote that 'the folly of the

Orientals has made them like the logs devoured in a fire so that others may forge metal'. He was searching for a single voice, mutual support, and the arousal of 'slumbering energies' in economic, political, and social action.[222] Neo-Gramscian research on the movimento negro of Rio de Janeiro and São Paulo, Brazil, 1945–1988, puts forward substantial evidence to document the great difficulties experienced by Afro-Brazilian activists in identifying racially specific patterns of violation and discrimination.[223] Hanchard here argues that the danger is in being subsumed by the contradictions that the dominant forms of hegemony (proclaiming a racial democracy) produce. Rancour and withdrawal can be also associated with contradictory consciousness. Satire can be a mere safety valve, and everyday resistance but necessity and survivalism. Femia writes that even though 'workers . . . may sense the contradiction between the positive official definition of reality and the starkness of their own subordination, they are unable even to locate the source of their discontent, still less remedy it'.[224] On the other hand, contradictory consciousness is a moment of incompleteness in the existing hegemony. It signals a site of disarticulation; is pressurizing; and provokes a practical-critical activity, involving a search for a new voice, a new language, a new conception of the world. Glassman puts it well: 'Within the minds of the subordinate population, fragments of ideologies from many different sources vie for dominance; the slave, peasant or plebeian absorbs many hegemonic ideas but finds that his day-to-day experience as slave, peasant or plebeian may contradict them. The resulting contradictory consciousness often produces frustration and an apparent acquiescence to domination, but sometimes various ideological elements are recast into internally inconsistent ideologies of popular rebellion.'[225]

Rebellion, then, is not excluded. Desai suggests that the very ambiguities and ambivalences at work in contradictory consciousness could well be 'what makes discursive formations—or articulations—so open to change, especially at certain moments when there is a crisis in the prevailing system of signification'.[226] Indeed, in thinking how new streams of activity can suddenly appear rather creatively, and seemingly spontaneously, ex nihilo, we should bear in mind Gramsci's view that it might be possible find 'a widespread state of affairs and corresponding state of mind which only mechanical, external, and hence transitory causes prevent from being expressed'.[227]

CATASTROPHES OF CHARACTER

On the other hand, appalling conditions, state violence, and other forms of oppression common among subaltern social groups do not necessarily provoke new forms of solidarity or any constructive line of development. Gramsci identified in prison and suffered through what he called 'catastrophes of character'. Here there was a kind of molecular transformation in reverse, amid appalling physical and bodily suffering, in which numerous illnesses went poorly diagnosed and treated within the prison system and its forms of domination. Gramsci reflects in 1933 on 'catastrophes of character'. He asks himself what needs to happen for 'normal people who have become the victims of a shipwreck to end up accepting the idea of cannibalism and putting it into practice.' He answers that a

> process of 'molecular transformation' occurs during the shipwreck between the moment in which cannibalism presents itself as a pure hypothesis and the moment in which it becomes an immediate necessity for some: these people both are and are not the same people that perhaps we once knew. He concludes that cannibalism apart, something similar is happening to him: what he feels is a 'splitting of the personality', such that a part of himself observes the process, and the other part suffers it, with the peculiarity, in his case, that the observing part, which regulates self-control, is aware of the precariousness of its *own* state and anticipates that it will not be long before its own function disappears, with the consequence that his personality will then undergo a metamorphosis as he becomes a new individual [in terms of] . . . impulses, initiatives and modes of thinking.[228]

Here the body, social being, is under immense pressure, undergoing suffering and sickness; the mind, social consciousness, is observing the deterioration, but weakening itself. After the suffering of the body and the concomitant collapse of the increasingly fragile mind, what was initially 'pure hypothesis' (i.e. some abstract alternate conception of the world or norm of conduct of an entirely alien kind) is eventually adopted within a new kind of subject, informed by new kinds of conceptions; initially only implicit in the changing, oppressive circumstances, it eventually becomes the explicit, ruling norm of conduct. The will observes the shipwreck—the suffering motions of the body—and gradually loses its capacity to control, to regulate, to take initiatives. Eventually it succumbs, fragments, is led back-

wards rather than forwards by bodily necessity. It is a retreat and disintegration rather than an advance or unification. This is a 'catastrophic phase'.[229]
Gramsci writes, as someone who had certainly endured and overcome a fair
amount of physical suffering in his time, 'I did not believe that one's physical
being could so overwhelm one's moral strength.'[230] Buey argues that this
point—the idea of the disintegration of the personality and the catastrophe
of character—was hugely important for Gramsci as it is one of the few things
which appears both in the letters and in the *Prison Notebooks*.

Buey writes that Gramsci calls attention to 'the *gradual* transformation of
people who do not stop being what they once were all of a sudden, as in the
case of the political defector or the intellectual chameleon'. Instead, Buey
explains, they transform 'little by little, through a molecular modification of
their whole being, during which process they observe and fear the change
which is happening within them, as if from the outside'.[231] In relation to
shop stewards' feelings of betrayal in the car plant at Cowley in Oxford, Harvey and Williams write: 'Betrayal is a process, not an individual and it is not
always conscious.'[232] A section of the movement changes tack and develops
an alternative trajectory.

Here is a harsh form of 'decomposition' indeed—involving collapse,
implosion, catastrophe and the like. The concept involves the disunification
of theory and practice, the way the body (as object) outruns the subject (as
mind), and eventually brings about a catastrophe. The body is starring in a
drama in which the mind did not agree to participate.[233] Not so much the
moralizing form of corruption but a fundamental process of disintegration.
Note that neither cannibalism nor Gramsci's state is being read as a mere setback on a longer journey of becoming or as a crisis out of which diverse pathways might emerge, but as a catastrophe—certainly the lexicon is distinctive—without much room for a positive development. It is a reverse
movement, a very decisive regress, a shift from leadership to domination.

CONCLUSION

This chapter has taken up the study of resistance at the margins—everyday
struggles with domination, the earliest and most marginal phases in the
history of subaltern social groups—as a way to study the most everyday,
inconspicuous forms of popular mobilization in the face of domination and

weakness. The predicaments, paradoxes, and tormented dramas of subaltern social groups, of those with a history at the margins of history, are at the centre of this phase. In philosophical terms, the phase is marked by fundamental forms of dehumanization; a lack of immanent connections; frozen dialectics; an absence of becoming; social being as genus—an object, a type, an essence, an ahistorical abstract particular, an 'internal, dumb generality which naturally unites the many individuals';[234] and a far-reaching disunity of theory and practice, with its attendant forms of contradictory consciousness. The most important concepts here are subaltern social groups, common sense, organic intellectuals, myth, subversivism, adherence to dominant formations, indifference, subaltern formations, contradictory consciousness, and catastrophes of character. In these notions it is possible to trace forms of development, as well as regressions, in relation to the diffuse and capillary activities at the margins, of those who are situated in ambivalent sites of inclusion/exclusion in relation to hegemony, but who can seek to overcome forms of domination.

We have seen that this phase and its various subphases contain the possibility of incremental gains and quantitative additions and connections in relation to the following: partial changes in social being / social consciousness; new constructions of time and space; the glimmers of good sense that exist in common sense; the positive aspects of myth; the pressures exerted by passive or active adherence to dominant formations which can win concessions; and new subaltern formations, which imply new forms of coordination from below, can deliver goods and services, and in time raise new demands on authorities. Even in subversivism, there is a faint possibility that 'hatred of the official' can effect a passage towards a less personalistic understanding of the structures of regime or state power. In contradictory consciousness, there is a search for resolutions, and specific forms of instability in relation to cultural hegemony. Popular culture can imply ways to keep body and soul together. In the inventory of traces and the incipient activities of organic intellectuals, new ways of seeing and acting are possible. It does not seem unreasonable, then, to agree with Salamini when he writes that '[t]he masses, whether they have been absorbed in the general ideology of society (ruling class) or consented to it, are always a potentially disruptive force within a given historical bloc'.[235] It is these potential disruptions, glimmers, incremental gains, and possibilities which form the hard kernel of a tendency to unification in the subaltern phase of wrestling over domination.

On the one hand, there is no guarantee as to the positive direction of change or the positive content of the various forms of activity in the subaltern phase. Gramscian perspectives provide plenty of scope for critique. Subaltern social groups are placed under significant pressures of objectification. Common sense is usually amorphous and ineffective. Popular culture can be debased, commodified, or sectarian. Myth can remain highly abstracted and otherworldly. Subversivism and conspiracy theory can become widespread, while passive and active adherence to dominant formations can continue for long periods and take new forms. Contradictory consciousness is Janus-faced, indifference can swamp even bold initiatives, while catastrophes of character can bring about more fundamental forms of disintegration.

We do not know, in fact, in advance, if the diffuse, spontaneous, capillary initiatives of subaltern social groups will add up to a wider transformation. In this sense, it is pointless to either damn or romanticize them. Ciavolella is surely right to argue that 'one should question the impact of small-scale reactions that remain on the infrapolitical level' and the emancipatory role that political theories, which refuse collective strategies, give to tactical forms of resistance of dispersed subjectivities.[236] In a Gramscian perspective, to suggest that 'weapons of the weak' amount to revolutionary transformation looks romantic and misguided—an extraordinary foreshortening of the history and politics of popular mobilization. It looks to be the brainchild, surely, of an epoch of demobilization and shattered hopes. In Gramscian optics, the literature on everyday resistance fails to pay sufficient attention to questions of consciousness and culture, let alone questions of politics and the state, or those relating to more macrological forms of economic accumulation. It fails to grapple seriously with the range of political questions at stake in the making of a new hegemony.

On the other hand, the view that diffuse and capillary activity at the margins is generally and fundamentally complicit with hegemony, nothing more than an illusion, and at best but a site of authorized autonomy in a larger all-encompassing system is too reductive and seamless. It does not do justice to the torturous nature of domination or to the complexity of the picture presented either by Gramsci or by subsequent Gramscian research. The major point, indeed, of the history of subaltern social groups is to focus on, without illusions and with the pessimism of the intellect, the ways in which subaltern social groups could begin to make history in the senses developed above and thus to start to construct forms of social force. The forms of ambivalence at work in the subaltern phase are also part and parcel not just of subordination, but of routes towards overcoming domination—for instance, regarding the possible instabilities of contradictory consciousness. Not only can diffuse and capillary activities at the level of the subaltern social group prepare the ground for more transformative collective actions, they are, as a Gramscian perspective avers, an 'indispensable premise' for the latter.

The Contradictions of Domination

The Wellsprings of Autonomy

Gramsci wrote of a phase in the history of subaltern social groups involving 'new formations that assert the autonomy of the subaltern groups, but within the old framework'.[1] Hoare and Nowell Smith suggest that this refers to 'reformist parties'.[2] This is a potential interpretation, although not developed. Perhaps, in fact, the reference to popular autonomy cuts against the top-down, bourgeois activities typical of reformist political parties. Indeed, noting that Gramsci's list of key phases is short and very encompassing, it is possible to argue that Gramsci is referring to a much broader range of activity associated with a distinctive phase of 'popular self-activity',[3] in which the autonomy of subaltern social groups is asserted, albeit within certain limits.

Autonomy is asserted in relation to the various faces of popular mobilization. There is a new development of social consciousness (e.g. of class, race, gender, or sexuality, or the anti-colonial). There is the establishment—by self-activity and direct action—of new forms of economy, popular authority, association, and counterculture. New forms of place are made, alongside new kinds of temporality and memory. New popular forces are operative, engaging in forceful confrontations, even those capable of shaking the established order and remaking strategic calculations. Popular mobilization in this phase is qualitatively distinct from the subaltern phase, growing out of the incremental gains made in that phase and interacting with wider circumstances, above all, crises of authority. The passage is from instrumentalization and heteronomy to self-determined ends and autonomy. While the drama of *dominazione* is at the centre of the subaltern phase, the drama of *autonomia* is at the centre of the wellsprings of popular self-activity. The chapter argues that there is much to be gained from reading popular self-activity—against autonom*ism* on the one side and dismissal on the other—as a phase: situating it historically, affirming its vital importance, but engaging with its transcendence.

HISTORIES AND THEMES

Gramsci drew for his understandings of popular self-activity in part on the two dramatic 'red years' of the Biennio Rosso, 1918-1920, a vital phase in Gramsci's own formation. These years saw the origins of the revolt against the Italian Socialist Party, linked above all to Gramsci and his young comrades linked with *L'Ordine Nuovo* group; the push back against the bureaucratic trade unions; the 'revolution' against the 'old ideology' of official, materialist, and scientific Marxism; wild-cat strikes; factory occupations; self-management; and forceful confrontations. The Biennio Rosso represented a crisis of authority, an organic crisis of liberal capitalism on the one hand, and on the other, a vast outpouring of popular-self activity in parts of Italy and more widely in Europe, in the context of the Russian revolution. Gramsci also studied the 'hot' years of the Risorgimento, notably the period between 1848 and 1849 and the successes achieved for a time by the Mazzinian, radical, democratic, and popular current.

Popular self-activity is not limited to the Biennio Rosso and the revolutionary situation in Europe after the First World War. The post-war crisis of authority was not just an affair of the colonial centres. As Gramsci registered, there were uprisings and insurrections in Egypt, India, Ireland, and Palestine. There were also risings in the Maghrib (North Africa) and the Mashriq (the Levant) and in other parts of Asia, Africa, the Caribbean, and South America.[4] Further examples, before and after Gramsci's lifetime, include the Paris Commune of 1870-1; the Russian 'revolution' of 1905; May 1968 in France; the popular uprising in January 1977 in Egypt; people power of 1986 in the Philippines—and South-East Asia's many forgotten uprisings since the 1980s;[5] the Palestinian intifada (shaking off, uprising) of 1987-1991; the 'people power' uprisings in Eastern Europe in 1989; the popular uprisings of the Arab Spring in Egypt, Libya, Syria, Tunisia, Bahrain and Yemen in 2011—and in Iraq, Lebanon, Sudan and Algeria since 2019.[6] One can also think of the occupations in St Paul's, London, in 2011; Zuccoti Park in 2011; Gezi Park in 2013; the Maidan in Kiev in 2013. Self-activity would also include experimental subjectivities; expressivism; and horizontal, rhizo-matic, and participatory organizing of the alter-globalization movement in the 2000s and since.[7] The Rojava Revolution in south-eastern Kurdistan since 2011 has exhibited many powerful features of democratic autonomy. There are also many smaller scale insurrections, crowd actions, bread riots and jacqueries—past and present—in the colonial metropole and the Third World, including in more recent times, the too-often forgotten riots in Brit-ain in the summer of 2011.

One of the most significant waves of popular power, or *poder popular*, in recent history unfolded in struggles against neoliberal hegemony in Latin America from the 1990s until the 2000s and to some extent since. Popular power has been 'one of the collective grammars running through Latin America's great social mobilizations'. It 'has embodied a dynamic visible during periods of revolutionary crisis (as in Cuba or Chile) but also in multi-ple local experiments limited to a particular neighborhood, factory, or terri-tory'.[8] It has involved 'a series of social and political experiences arising "from below", with the creation of new (and often limited) forms of collec-tive appropriations that are opposed in whole or in part to the dominant social formation and the established powers'. Such experiments mean 'putting into question the ways in which work is organized, social hierar-chies are established, and the mechanisms of symbolic, racial, gender, and material domination come into being'. Latin America was 'shaken' in many parts of its territory by these 'sparks of self-management' and this 'praxis of self-organization'. Crucially, such a praxis 'is also very often mistreated, suffocated or repressed, or simply the victim of its own limitations'.[9]

The problematics of popular self-activity clearly go beyond the Biennio Rosso: 'The general *content* of the issues raised by the factory council struggles—popular self-management, social revolt, prefigurative politics—cannot be reduced to their specific historical *form*.'[10]

One of the richest, albeit rather critical, summaries of this content is given in Sanbonmatsu's Gramscian account, referencing May 1968 in France and the 1960s in the United States. Key themes include counterculture; the 'visceral impulse to tear down'; the refusal of the verities of ideology (espe-cially Marxist) and of the party, especially in its vanguardist variant; a rejec-tion of the state; a rejection of formal political involvement and traditional organization (especially in existing civil society); the valorization of social movements; denunciations by established parties, including the Communist Party, as 'adventurist'; favourable attitudes to anarchism, spontaneity, self-expression, direct action, grassroots, or participatory democracy; decentralization; local organs of popular authority, including councils of manual and intellectual workers; autogestion; a sense of 'utopian vitality'; a millenarian flavour; an attachment of value to feeling-laden and 'aesthetic expression'; an opposition to detached analysis; an embrace of 'participation and experiential recollection' and of improvisation; a value attached to authenticity as well as to the knowledge gained from personal experience. Here acts of creation are valued compared to results obtained, and calls for a shift from protest to politics, for channelling radical opposition into establishment political parties, are regarded as politically naïve. In some currents, the awakening of communal feeling and 'Black power' in the face of 'state-sanctioned terrorism' was counterposed to white, bourgeois illusions about 'racial equality'. By 1965, questions of strategy and organization 'stank of "elitism", hierarchy, structure' according to many members of the Students for a Democratic Society. There are also themes of anti-intellectualism and of identification with the most marginalized and oppressed sectors of society and an implicit faith in the 'propaganda of the deed'.[11] This summary certainly captures much—albeit in relation to particular histories and politics in France and the US in the 1960s. One of the only things missing is prefigurative politics: the idea that the means used must be connected with the ends desired and that the new society must be practiced in some sense in advance in the ways in which revolutionary activity is organized.

SIGNPOSTING GRAMSCI'S APPROACH

Gramsci, in opposing anarchism throughout his life, struck against the maximalist embrace of popular self-activity. While seeking autonomy, he eschewed autonom*ism*. He never explicitly renounced his years with *L'Ordine Nuovo* and consistently opposed bureaucratic centralism. In his work, the search for *autonomia* remains a key problematic—arguably a 'phase'—in both his own life and in that of his history of subaltern social groups. Boggs assesses Gramsci's writings during the *L'Ordine Nuovo* period as 'infused with a spirit of impatience, optimism and confrontation. While never an

The Wellsprings of Autonomy

abstentionist, he believed that a truly revolutionary movement would have to sustain its autonomy and identity outside of the main political institutions in capitalist society—e.g., parliament, the party system, state bureaucracy, trade unions and local government. While these forms could be utilised for limited tactical purposes, only the local organs of proletarian democracy could serve as the . . . basis of socialist transformation.'[12] These themes capture very much the positive dimensions of Gramsci's sense of popular self-activity.

Nonetheless, as we shall see, Gramsci saw limitations in popular self-activity. Gramsci had no time for the pathologizing thesis as to the madness of crowds, the 'panicky fear of . . . every active intervention of the great popular masses as a factor of historical progress'.[13] This point set him apart from conservative views but also from those of liberals who shrank from breakages, violence against property, non-rational/feeling-laden phenomena, or things that did not conform to the precepts of middle-class respectability. Nor was Gramsci the kind of respectable social democrat of the British Left, rattled 'by the spectacle of the popular classes on the move under their own steam, outside the range of "responsible" guidance and leadership'.[14]

Gramsci was neither what Marx called a 'brawler' nor was he an anarchist. Arguably his understanding of the problems of popular self-activity had to do with this grasp of popular mobilization itself: that popular 'tumults' of the kind expected by Machiavelli were to be expected and understood as part and parcel of the escape from a phase of domination. It was not so useful to moralize, as Trotsky once wrote, about 'the forcible entrance of the masses into the realm of rulership over their own destiny'.[15] As Gramsci wrote, defending the approach of L'Ordine Nuovo: '[W]e simply made the mistake of believing that only the masses can achieve the communist revolution, and that neither a party secretary nor a president of the republic can achieve it by issuing decrees. Apparently this was also the opinion of Karl Marx and Rosa Luxemburg, and is Lenin's opinion.'[16] The birth of the factory councils throughout Europe, writes Gramsci, is 'a major historical event—the beginning of a new era in the history of the human race. For now the revolutionary process has burst into the light of day, and entered the phase where it can be controlled and documented.'[17] Even amid the excitement and the grandiose expressions of the Biennio Rosso, millenarianism is attenuated and the language of phases—and even of control (leadership)—is present. In the first part of the clause, the apocalypse; in the second, the language of phases, of control, and documentation. One thing is certain: there has been a 'sunburst', a qualitative shift, an end to one phase of subordination, and the beginnings of a new phase.

It is Gramsci's dialectical, historicizing mode of thought that, as elsewhere, forms the basis for his highly distinctive take on popular self-activity. Gramsci's overall view and approach, arguably, is not contradictory but still fresh and suggestive, even after decades of extensive debate—but also because of decades of research and activity in Gramscian mode. As Boggs has it, the 'vital challenge for Gramsci was how socialists could help advance pre-political struggles beyond spontaneity, how they could integrate expressions of alienation, despair, and anger into a viable revolutionary movement'.[18] Gramsci, writes Leontidou, is as painfully relevant today as in the 1920s, as he 'affirms spontaneity, but also proposes to raise it to a higher plane politically, with the help of leadership, in order to prevent its absorption by right-wing forces'.[19] The main point, arguably, far from either romanticization or dismissal, is to situate popular self-activity as a crucial phase with enormous potential and crucial limits within the larger journey from subordination to revolution.

DEBATING AUTONOMY

There should be no underestimating, however, the depth and importance of the debate on this issue, especially in left and progressive circles, at least since the anarchist split from the Communist International in 1872. As Sorel put it in 1907, autonomism (which here meant revolutionary syndicalism) was not a 'first, confused . . . youthful error' but involved arresting 'a threatened deviation towards middle-class ideas'.[20] The partisans of spontaneity and Rosa Luxemburg, one might say, have long vied with the partisans of party and Vladimir Lenin. Hal Draper inspired a whole generation with his insightful essay on the 'two souls' of socialism: one bottom-up, democratic, and autonomous and the other top-down, Jacobin, vanguardist, and organized.[21] In the 1960s, the direct, unmediated working-class struggle proposed in Mario Tronti's *operaismo*, which sought to bypass 'the ancient little world of civil society' amid the take-off of modern capitalism in Italy, inspired the autonomist extra-parliamentary Left in Italy against the by this time heavily institutionalized—and, for many, too thoroughly reformist— Italian Communist Party of Palmiro Togliatti.[22] In France, May 1968 signalled a great division between the autonomism and extra-institutional radicalism and experimentation of situationists and student radicals as against the bureaucratic and hierarchical French Communist Party and 'scientific' theorists of capitalism such as Louis Althusser.[23] Martin Breaugh's full length treatment of what he calls 'the plebeian experience' in Western history— 'the passage from a subpolitical status to one of a full-fledged political subject', with a 'refusal to submit to political domination' at its core—explores and valorizes many of the fundamental themes of autonomy.[24] Debates about autonomy have resurfaced in many parts of the world during more than a decade of mass protest since 2011,[25] and theorists of autonomy have acknowledged problems and aimed to get beyond them, proposing, in one important intervention, the possibility of *tactical* forms of leadership.[26]

In the Latin America of recent times theoretical and political divisions in significant measure 'pivot on the political weight in different left traditions allotted to party and government hegemony versus subaltern autonomy'.[27] The popular protests, for example, that followed a bus-fare hike in Salvador, Brazil, in 2003 pitted activists loyal to the Communist Party (PCdoB) against neo-anarchists.[28] Sara Motta enjoins us to take seriously forms of subaltern self-activity and autonomy in the face of the inability to see it adequately in the optics of orthodox Marxism and social democracy. She argues, for instance, that a 'movement's attempts to develop autonomous, self-governing communities . . . are not a retreat from the political in its rejection of the political party form, the state form and the politics of representation. Instead, they are attempts to reinvent the meaning of political struggle and social change based on popular rationality, struggle and experience.'[29]

Francisco Panizza, on the other hand, defends the social democratic parties in relation to macroeconomic stability, competitive economies, social justice (realistic redistribution), and representative democracy.[30] These debates are not easy to resolve: it is worth mentioning, for instance, that it was the least revolutionary and 'the most institutional, gradualist, and moderate versions of the political left that broke through [electorally] in most countries'.[31] This point could imply that radical autonomists are unrealistic and constantly risk self-marginalization; or it could imply that radicals should not go to the ballots as it involves unacceptable compromises.

In debates centred on the United States and Europe, there are divisions between horizontalists and the partisans of the revolutionary party.[32] While Graeber identifies many of the problems with would-be leaders defining agendas and imposing their preformed programmes on passive audiences assembled in rallies, Dean points to the way horizontalism can be another word for a disabling individualism, wrecking collective, coordinated action. Some studies of the alter-globalization movement come out firmly in favour of horizontal, expressive, deliberative, diverse, and experiential modes.[33] Others are more equivocal on the tensions and collaborations between such subjective modes and methods based on reason, knowledge, expertise, and representation.[34] These questions are also intertwined with debates—attentive to place and space—about the possibilities and problems of scaling up in relation to 'militant particularism'.[35]

In depth empirical treatments of autonomous action have taken very different positions. For instance, Asef Bayat's ethnography *Revolutionary Life* puts a very strong and positive accent on the autonomous social forms that came out of the Arab uprisings, freighting them with the significance of a quiet, social revolution. Bayat writes, 'These new subjectivities, if sustained, would serve as a precursor for changes to power relations, social roles, values, and expectations that altogether coalesce to a social transformation. A quiet revolution transpires in those layers of society that often remain invisible and undetected.'[36] On the other hand, Barbara Epstein's history of the post-1960s history of non-violent, creative, non-hierarchical, autonomous protest in the United States underlines the ways in which such formations, failing to solve problems of sustainability and effectivity, tended eventually to retreat into themselves, melt away, or fail to bring about lasting change: 'large and intoxicating protests have been followed by organizational collapse.'[37] Bevins's investigative journalism cautions that the fetishization of horizontalism can inadvertently pave the way for organized right-wing ascendancy.[38] Sanbonmatsu's critical Gramscian approach to autonomy captures much in terms of the weaknesses of expressivism—the problem with the privileging of 'emotive and aesthetic expression of an inner, "radical" nature over considerations of strategy, theoretical coherence, or the patient construction of a counter-hegemonic movement'[39]—as well as the problem that autonomism often fails to 'yield more than slight reforms in the system'.[40] Others point to the failures and oppression unleashed by more centrally organized and vanguardist modalities, and their all-seeing strategies, as well as the importance of feeling in mass mobilization.

Finally, a challenge to the fundamental concepts and categories used in debates about autonomous politics comes from a certain reading of the poststructuralist and postmodern tradition, associated with names like Foucault, Deleuze, and Baudrillard, which can be read as denying the very existence of autonomy. Ironically enough, such approaches have been joined with Gramscian theories of hegemony and subaltern studies in ways which tend to see autonomy as either inexistent, Eurocentric, or as a hegemonic effect, an authorized site tending to preserve and extend the system, rather than challenging its overall reproduction. In Graeber's critical summary, poststructuralism, dominant in academic cultural studies, 'tends to see the system (whether it is now labelled capitalism, power, discourse, etc.) as so all-encompassing that it is constitutive of the desiring subject him- or herself, rendering any critique of alienation, or possibility of revolution against the system itself, effectively impossible'.[41]

A Gramscian theory very much grasps the importance of authorized sites of autonomy in hegemony: it contests, however, the binary, categorical, and ultimately contradictory stricture that new forms of autonomy do not exist or cannot be formed.

CONSCIOUSNESS OF GROUP AND CLASS

A start point in the living Gramscian tradition is to think popular self-activity through the historicized and tormented questions of social being and social consciousness. Transformations take place among people and how they see themselves—above all among those who suffer in the subaltern phase from objective formation and domination. The incremental gains of the subaltern phase give way, at a certain threshold, to a qualitatively new phase—in which class and group formation is no longer at best incipient or marginal, but a real possibility in social activity. Subaltern social groups— workers, women, queer people, and so on—move 'from an amorphous collection of individuals into a homogeneous structure'.[42] What is at stake is the increasing development of the 'homogeneity, self-awareness, and organization' attained by the various social classes and groups, and the way this impacts on the balance of political forces.[43] It is a phase of corporate— meaning 'social collectivity'—formation. It is a matter, as Gramsci put it on many occasions, of the 'progressive acquisition of historical personality', a process in which social being and social consciousness are intertwined.

Imperialism, race, gender, and sexuality, not just class, are at stake. As Morera puts it regarding women:

> Gramsci considers the issue of the 'formation of a new feminine personality' to be 'the most important ethico-civil question tied to the sexual question'. This question, however, cannot be solved by the party or by any group of legislators. It can only be solved, he writes, 'when women have attained independence vis-à-vis men' and have developed 'a new conception of themselves and of their role in sexual relations.' Any attempt to legislate on sexual questions before this new feminine self-image is achieved, he warns, must proceed with great caution, for 'the sexual question will be rich with morbid characteristics'.[44]

We note that in the above formulation, the question of 'independence' (autonomy) comes to the fore. We also note the temporal priority given to group formation over legislation. Any attempt to legislate before a new kind of femininity emerges will stifle renewal. Social being and social consciousness— 'historical personality'—are at stake here for women, as well as for workers, 'despised races', queer people, and the colonized.[45]

Gramsci identifies a deeply inspiring start point—the much cited 'inventory' of traces: 'The starting point of critical elaboration is the consciousness of what one really is; in other words, "knowing thyself" as the product of the historical process that has unfolded thus far and has deposited in you an infinity of traces, accumulated without the benefit of an inventory. One must start by compiling such an inventory.'[46] This is clearly a site of intellectual endeavour. But the process of renovation involves an engagement in and learning from the practical activity and life experiences of the subaltern social group.

Gramscian research has been sensitive to the moments when female workers, for instance, start to think of themselves in terms of their womanhood in new ways, in ways that place questions about women, femininity, and feminism in the forefront in ways that previously were marginal. The process operates via incremental rearrangements or by appropriating models that are already circulating. In Britain, for instance, the Women's Liberation Movement was founded in 1970 as 'as an autonomous movement'—that is, in contrast with male- dominated labour and left unionism: 'Women from the Scunthorpe WEA [Workers' Educational Association] women's group also actively organized within the Labour Party, won the post of Labour Party secretary, and were elected as Labour borough councillors. . . . The group identified with the women's liberation movement of the 1970s with women-only consciousness-raising sessions and debates on socialist feminism.'[47]

Noteworthy here is the reference to women-only sessions. This is a striking reminder of the centrality of the *group* to the progressive acquisition of historical personality. In this phase, it is not a matter of 'listening to all points of view', of bringing in men for their supposed wisdom. Here the liberal language of inclusivity is inadequate. As usual it raises the question of who gets to decide what should be included, and who is congratulated for all this inclusion, and who or what gets to define and control the centre in terms of which of all those peripheries-to-be-included are understood and arranged. Against all this liberalism, in a Gramscian theory of popular mobilization, the margins battle their way into the centre, which ends up defeated, dispersed, and discomposed. What is central instead—in the phase of popular self-activity—are the feelings and experiences of the group in question: hence the need for spaces in which such feelings can be exchanged and expressed, where an inventory of traces can be compiled—the need for organizations to coordinate the group.

Steve Biko—in relation to the struggle for Black consciousness in the anti-apartheid movement in South Africa—captures the point: justifying an all-Black union, he writes, 'It seems sometimes that it is a crime for the non-white students to think for themselves. The idea of everything being done for the blacks is an old one and all liberals take pride in it; but once the black students want to do things for themselves suddenly they are regarded as becoming "militant." '[48] The centrality of the group, and the *development* of the group are central here. In this autonomous formulation, the group learns from itself, developing its own memory and history, its own experience, and so on. Having been struggling for so long against objective formation, the group is finally in the process of recovering its own subjectivity, its own memories, defining what it means by oppression and domination. As Biko put it, expressing a spirit of cleavage, 'The blacks are tired of standing at the touchlines to witness a game that they should be playing. They want to do things for themselves and all by themselves.'[49] Autonomy can of course be expressed in a vernacular, rather than in the formal national language, and focus on community self-understanding.[50]

The headline approach to group formation is historicizing—rather than moralizing about its lack of diversity; or its sectarian, separate, communitarian, supposedly anti-republican nature; or the 'wokeness' of its freedom-stifling safe spaces. But a historicizing perspective also eschews fetishization. As elsewhere, the point is that such group activity is a vital phase, but only a phase, in the larger processes of popular mobilization. The vernacular will not be the only language at work: 'national-popular rhetoric, informed by state's spirit, refers to the phase when such a community goes beyond its social boundaries and embraces a hegemonic project.'[51] We should also note that this phase of group formation is not fully autonomous but keyed into wider movements and experiences, including ideologies. In the case mentioned above, socialist feminism, language, liberation, and the women's liberation movement in general were involved.

In relation to the initial emergence of class consciousness in the economic field Gramsci writes the following: 'Already at this juncture the problem of the State is posed—but only in terms of winning politico-juridical equality with the ruling groups: the right is claimed to participate in legislation and administration, even to reform these—but within the existing fundamental structures.'[52] Gramsci is here marking a clear limit of a certain threshold in the development of popular mobilization—undergirded by a consciousness delineated by the solidarity of interests of a previously more scattered and less socially or class-conscious group. He is registering a gain, but also tracing the confines of this mode of political appearance. This is a mode of political representation in civil and political society of this kind of class or group consciousness which accepts the existing fundamental structures of (state) power (asserting autonomy within the existing framework).

Zene, in his research on Dalits in India, points out another (external) limit on group consciousness—the ways in which, if it leaves capitalist structures intact, it can end up being marketized: '[T]hese groups [of newly self-aware Dalits], like other subalterns, are exposed to manipulation by unscrupulous "entrepreneurs"—the "jackals of development"—who see them as exploitable assets on the international market.'[53] The question of the limits of group/corporate autonomy is again posed.

Conversely, forms of class consciousness, if not articulated with other forms of group consciousness, can be disabled. A vital example comes from Mumby's analysis of a neglected aspect of Willis's oft-cited study on why working class 'lads' got working class jobs in Britain in the 1970s. Part of the explanation, writes Mumby, has to do with the fact that the lads do not transcend their 'hegemony of commonsense' in which mental labour is associated with inferior, passive, fragile, conformist 'teacher's pet' femininity and manual labour with valued (tough, goal-oriented, active, defiant) masculinity.[54] In short, while the lads have a lively good sense regarding class subordination, it is disabled by a layer of masculinist common sense. There is a powerful cultural dimension, in terms of common sense, to habitual and feeling-laden masculinism, which numbers among the reasons for the continued class subordination of the lads, as these cultural tissues channel them into manual labour. Here class exploitation and masculinism work together. Meaningful challenges to class exploitation here would require a simultaneous challenge to class and to masculinism—only this would avoid the hegemonic reabsorption of the lads. Popular mobilization, then, envisages eventually a movement beyond class or group, and towards a broader bloc formation.

Frantz Fanon, the great thinker and activist of Third World and Black liberation, who has often been compared to Gramsci and seen as an organic intellectual, situated 'the Manichean racial dualism' in liberation movements as but a 'first phase' of anti-colonial confrontation. He also analyzed the 'degenerative' tendencies of nationalist and Black identity politics. True decolonization, he argued, requires a political practice that is at once 'national, revolutionary, and social', which can counteract the descent into 'primitive tribalism'.[55] Likewise, Gramsci underlines 'the problem of whether it may be possible to create a "conformism", a collective man, without unleashing a certain amount of fanaticism, without creating "taboos", in short, whether it is possible to do so critically, as the consciousness of necessity that is accepted freely because it is recognized as such "in practice" by figuring out the alignment of means and ends, etc.'[56] A critical conformism, a kind of strategic essentialism, is enjoined: a sense of group and class in relation to necessities and exigencies. There is always the possibility that new forms of identity—including national identity—can become stifling and conformist after their capacity for renewal has worn off.

The Spirit of Cleavage

An important element in the social consciousness of the autonomous phase is a concept that Gramsci borrowed from Sorel: the 'spirit of scission' or 'spirit of cleavage'. 'Gramsci', writes Del Roio, 'really lived the "spirit of cleavage" that pervaded the working class at the time [of the Biennio Rosso].'[57] Gramsci writes: 'What resources can an innovative class set against the formidable complex of trenches and fortification of the dominant class? The spirit of scission, in other words the progressive acquisition of the consciousness of its own historical personality, a spirit of scission that must aim to spread itself from the protagonist class to the classes that are its potential allies—all this requires a complex ideological labour, the first condition of which is an exact knowledge of the field that must be cleared of its element of human "mass."'[58]

This spirit of cleavage—a dramatic image picturing us against them—is thrown into the battle. It is a social force, a powerful motivator in its own right. It must be taken en bloc. As Gramsci puts it: 'Every antithesis must necessarily pose itself as the radical antagonist to the thesis, to the point where it resolves to destroy and replace it completely.'[59] The 'human mass' is 'cleared'; it is no longer mere quantity, no longer passive and subject to the statistical laws and regularities that were supposed to govern its behaviour, and to some extent do, in the previous phase. Instead, quantity is now transformed into quality. Instead of a quantity of matter, as in 'mass', we now have a force, as in 'weight', with qualitative characteristics and powers of attraction and disruption. Wholly comprehensible, in this context, are slogans such as 'Black is beautiful' or 'Gay is good.'[60] Gramsci himself as a teenager 'became an ardent Sardinian patriot with a mission to struggle for the autonomy—even for the complete independence, if necessary—of his native island'.[61] When the spirit of cleavage is operative, the group or class starts to become the central issue, the central subject and object of activity, the central locus of feeling and knowing, whereas in the subaltern phase this issue was shadowy, undefined, and in the margins. It was a spectre glimpsed in fits and starts, not a fully formed reality.

The spirit of cleavage is powerful, but double-edged. The risk is of degeneration into monism—either identity politics or an exclusive class politics. Here the 'truths' of one group or class trump all the others.[62] On the ground, and in theory, the 'spirit of cleavage' is a powerful start-point, but it is not enough. An ideological development is heralded. Gramsci was to leave Sardinian nationalism behind, for example, without ever dismissing Sardinian autonomy.

GOOD SENSE

The glimmers of good sense within common sense are a crucial element in the drive for autonomy. Gramsci affirms that there is within common sense a 'healthy . . . component . . . which can, in fact, be called good sense and which deserves to be developed and made more uniform and coherent', an element which can give 'one's activity a conscious direction'.[63] Good sense is not created ex nihilo from on high by abstract or logical theory but is already going on in common sense, in daily lives, in so far as 'everyone is a philosopher' with 'a spontaneous philosophy' (which includes religion, common sense, good sense, and language). This means that 'the point is not to introduce a totally new form of knowledge into "everyone's" individual life, but to revitalize an already existing activity and make it "critical"'.[64] Popular, quotidian sense-making—struggling with contradictions about identity, structure, and force—is the material through which the passage out of common sense and its forms of domination proceeds. It is a vital point that Gramsci hints is obscured by the polemical, confrontational stances associated with revolutionary theory.[65] Shifting common sense to the left, notes Rehmann in his discussion of Bernie Sanders in the US, 'is much more revolutionary than the many hyperradical discourses that have no consequences outside narrow academic circles and only [as Gramsci writes] create individual "movements" and polemics'.[66]

In Gramsci's writing, good sense exists in popular fragments, simple dictums, and traces, which are and can be expanded, rearticulated, connected in new, more coherent ways in relation to new forms of becoming, structure, and force. For example, he sees the common-sense expression 'a certain habit becomes second nature' as first a powerful insight into how common sense as *second* nature itself is formed and how it operates by naturalizing what is in fact historically constructed. Second, he sees it as having the capacity to question the very idea of *first* nature. Gramsci writes: '[B]ut was the "first nature" really "first"? Is there in the common-sense mode of expression some [good-sense] indication of the historicity of human nature?'[67] If so, this would be a revolutionizing proposition, fundamentally contrary to genus-thinking about social being, and firmly aligned with the philosophy of praxis.

Another example involves the common-sense dictum that in times of trouble, one has to be philosophical. Gramsci suggests that in this common-sense enjoining of perseverance there is a kernel of good sense; he treats the injunction as an invitation from the grassroots themselves to reflexivity, to stepping back, to not reacting with merely a violent impulse or passion, to adding an element of conscious direction. Such good-sense reflexivity, common sense as practical, or subaltern savoir-faire[68] is at a premium under conditions of social domination, where mistaking red lines, acting impetuously, or putting a foot wrong can cost livelihoods and lives.

There is a productive ambiguity here. On the one side, such savoir-faire expresses a dominant rationality about how to 'get on in life'—which internalizes and reproduces an existing hegemony. One must keep one's head down or deflect with a joke, even when the boss touches your body; one must work in the sweatshop 'like a son'; one must get married, as a respectable woman; one must control one's walk to the bus stop so as not to be appear effeminate; one must not, in order to get a job, be 'too Black', and so on. On the other hand, getting the judgement right on daily matters may contain a glimmer of understanding regarding the operative, real, and true power relations at work: the real, rigidified *disunities* (or fusions) of theory and practice. 'Knowing one's place' is thus Janus-faced. It contains glimmers of good sense, capable of being joined to others and becoming part of a broader understanding.

Good sense starts to denaturalize the order of social domination. As Gramsci puts it: 'One of the commonest totems is the belief about everything that exists, that it is 'natural' that it should exist. . . . [B]ut only gradually through experience . . . [a real movement] learns from the facts that nothing which exists is natural . . . but rather exists because of certain conditions.'[69] The development of good sense also accompanies the growing consciousness and social cohesion—in opposition to common sense—of a formerly divided and fragmented subaltern social group.[70]

Researchers in the Gramscian tradition have paid attention to these formations of good sense under conditions of inequality, exploitation, and social domination. Stuart Hall writes that 'living at the exploited end of a system creates a powerful tendency to see the world in terms of "us" and "them": the governing and the governed, the powerful and the powerless, the possessing and the possessed. "Us" and "them" is the spontaneous consciousness of all exploited classes and oppressed people everywhere: what Gramsci called their "good sense." '[71] In this case, good sense contains a broad—if vague—understanding as to the landscape of social domination. Good sense here may not indicate any developed collective will or strategy, but it involves a certain 'conscious direction' in the subaltern lives navigating this field and glimmers of significance about relations of class, group, and power.

Rehmann usefully juxtaposes common and good sense regarding the economic crisis in the United States: '[T]he predominant neoliberal version [of 'common sense'] is that the fiscal debt is not sustainable; that the government is driving the country to ruin by spending too much, in particular for the wrong people, namely the urban poor, blacks and other minorities, as well as "privileged" unionised employees in the public sector; that Hispanic immigrants are taking our jobs etc.'[72] He continues: 'A second layer of common sense, more akin to Gramsci's "good sense," manifests itself as awareness of the income polarity between rich and poor, which it sees as unsustainable and morally scandalous—a view which usually sees the main culprit as the speculative part of capitalism, its financial sector.'[73]

Here, common sense targets state spending and subaltern social groups. Good sense, rooted in experiences of foreclosure, redundancy, and environmental destruction, raises questions about social class and capitalism and ruling classes. Rehmann adds that the further development of this good sense, which is limited by moralizing and populist tendencies, remains mostly latent, because it is blocked by the lack of a democratic socialist alternative and by 'fear of being ostracised as radical lunacy'.[74]

Good sense is not some immaculate site of resistance, unalloyed, ideologically pure, or correct. It can combine, for example, a consciousness of autonomy and group with elements of ideologies left over or appropriated from existing or past leaderships and existing forms of consent and civil society. Gramsci believed that a lack of socialist consciousness, not just problems of organization, held back Italian workers during the Biennio Rosso.[75] According to Glassman's study of slave rebellion in late nineteenth-century East Africa, 'The maroons . . . built [new free] communities along the lines of their masters' culture. . . . Their motivating consciousness was a 'bizarre combination' of paternalist ideologies, which integrated ideals of patriarchy, commerce and tributary submission to an Omani overlord.'[76]

In short, even when good sense is strongly present, a further ideological and ethico-political development is anticipated to secure a further unification and renewal.[77]

MYTH CLOSE AT HAND

The previous chapter analyzed the operations of utopia and myth amid the torturous contradictions of domination. The phase of popular self-activity is qualitatively different. While in the subaltern phase, utopia and myth are what Kelley calls, in relation to the Black radical imagination, 'freedom dreams'.[78] At a huge distance from daily struggle, they only make up metaphysical (ahistorical) unifications, elements in perseverance, and glimpses of fundamental popular aspirations. In the phase of popular self-activity, they are radically and suddenly operative, near at hand, and intimately intertwined with autonomous activities. There is a great, translocal time-space compression.

Sorel had written in his revolutionary syndicalist work *Reflections on Violence*, 'Men who are participating in a great social movement always picture their coming action as a battle in which their cause is certain to triumph. These constructions . . . I propose to call myths; the syndicalist 'general strike' and Marx's catastrophic revolution are such myths.'[79] Apocalyptic

The Wellsprings of Autonomy

Christianity, the Reformation, and the followers of Mazzini also constructed such myths, which are 'groups of images' that encapsulate instinctively the entirety of a great struggle, including its fundamental aspirations, and 'must be taken as a whole (*en blocco*), as historical forces'. For Sorel, it was not about whether such myths were in fact accomplished into the future, but about how they motivated future-oriented action in the present. Myths are vital as 'expressions of a determination to act'.[80] Against intellectualist and scientistic analyses, to understand myth is to understand intensive motivations and self-sacrifice, even unto death, to grasp the 'forces which really move men [and women]'.[81] A myth, for Sorel, made the difference between revolt and revolution: 'As long as there are no myths accepted by the masses, one may go on talking of revolts indefinitely, without ever provoking any revolutionary movement.'[82] Sorel associated Utopia with intellectual construction, pedantic argument about functionality, and reform; he associated myth with direct action and transformation.

Gramsci wrote of Sorel's myth as 'a political ideology expressed neither in the form of a cold utopia nor as learned theorising, but rather by a creation of concrete phantasy which acts on a dispersed and shattered people to arouse and organize its collective will'.[83] The sense is that Gramsci found this aspect of Sorel's argument compelling. Arguably he recognized aspects of popular self-activity in this kind of theorizing. He recognized elements of his own subjectivity during the period of the Biennio Rosso—a subjectivity which was more grandiose, mythical, voluntarist—and certainly youthful—than it was to become. Gramsci recognized the power of non-rational elements of feeling and passion in motivating activity. He took neither a scholastic, rationalist view, showing myths to be false, nor a postmodern, ironic view. Gramsci accepted, one can argue, the fact that myth is a historical force, which needs to be taken 'en blocco'. Sorel's myth here offered a pathway for grasping the qualitative shift from a dominated, subaltern phase of a 'dispersed and shattered people' to a new phase of autonomous popular self-activity. Myth also gave free reign to the effervescent and apocalyptic temporality of the insurrection. A Gramscian theory accepts that the 'spirit of cleavage', the sense of antithesis of one class or group against another bound up with Sorel's myth, is a fundamental element in the development of popular mobilization—part of a way of defining a unity, albeit in a relatively abstract way, and part of the social force of newly mobilized subaltern social groups. The mythical content of the emancipated community can be defined by a wide variety of elements, including forms of cultural appropriation across national, regional, and even imperial borders, and across great reaches of time.

Gramsci, however, pursued a discriminating critique of Sorel's myth. First, Sorel did not advance 'from his conception of ideology-as-myth to an understanding of the political party, but stopped short at the idea of the [syndicalist] trade union'. Second, Gramsci did not accept that the general strike was the highest achievement of practical action; instead it was a 'passive activity', so to speak, of a negative and preliminary kind. Third, Gramsci sought, beyond the General Strike, an activity which 'envisage[s] an "active and constructive" phase of its own'. Fourth, Gramsci rejected the sweeping rejection of planning of any kind, the idea that 'every pre-established plan is utopian and reactionary', as this left outcomes to chance, to the irrational, and to spontaneity.[84] Above all, Gramsci argued that myth could not 'conceivably be effective' because it left 'the collective will in the . . . elementary phase of its mere formation, by differentiation ("cleavage")'. Gramsci believed that such a collective will, 'with so rudimentary a formation' would 'at once cease to exist, scattering into an infinity of individual wills which in the positive phase [i.e. the phase of actually constructing new social relations] then follow separate and conflicting paths'.[85] Gramsci goes on to argue that, appearances strongly to the contrary, Sorel's conception conceals a hidden and unacknowledged determinism. In other words, Sorel fails to appreciate that a collective will can be refined and made more precise and effective over time and thus fails to appreciate what can actually be achieved eventually by a more developed form of politics. Sorel's view stops short at the generalized bluster of the apocalypse, which for Gramsci is too chaotic to add up to something more developed than a mechanical conception. As Gramsci points out, to great effect, 'The abstract character of the Sorelian conception of the myth is manifest in its aversion (which takes the emotional form of an ethical repugnance) for the [emphatic political leadership of the] Jacobins.'[86] Overall, Gramsci was in the business, in this passage, of preferring the Machiavellian concept of myth, the 'myth-prince', over Sorel's, because of the more developed politics it contained—including the way it grasps politics as a construction in phases.

Gramsci's double, historicizing, dialectical view of myth contains a good deal of vital importance regarding understanding popular mobilization in general and the wellsprings of autonomy in particular. On the one side, Gramsci recognizes the social force of myth, its translocal and transtemporal powers, and its applicability for understanding popular self-activity, especially the insurrection; on the other side, he expects, requires, and assumes that Sorel's conception of myth will involve development in a subsequent or simultaneous phase that contains a much more developed politics. His claim is that myth is vital in a certain phase—in the passage from domination to autonomy, in the formation of group and class consciousness, in the shift from common sense to good sense—but ultimately, myth in Sorel's sense is too empty to pass muster, to achieve anything more than what Gramsci calls 'autonomy but within the old framework.' Gramsci, then, is no indiscriminate follower of the translocal and the transtemporal. Interestingly, though, there is no decisive rejection of myth, as one finds in so much Marxism. The concept is put to work via Machiavelli, as we shall see. Gramsci indicates that myth cannot be as Sorel suggests it to be. He asks, 'Can a myth . . . be "non-constructive"?'[87] Gramsci thinks not.

SOCIALIST SELF-MANAGEMENT

An important moment in the reworking of social being and social consciousness, in the phase of popular self-activity, is the reworking of relations of production themselves: a first really distinctive and autonomous, if for the time being incomplete, transformation in capitalist relations. In the subaltern phase, capitalist relations of commodification, marginalization, and wage-labour are vital in the objective formation of social being and the struggles of consciousness. In the phase of popular self-activity, there is a stream of socialist self-management, which refers to a qualitatively different kind of activity—to capitalist management, to the trade union structure, and to the established parties. This was the core of what was so inspiring to Gramsci about the factory councils. At a time when they were associated (through the experience of the Soviets) with communist revolution, they were the nucleus of socialist relations of production, and they were established within the belly of the beast. Capable of expanding to become a new structure, they implied concomitant superstructural transformations and the building of a new socialist hegemony and way of life. As Boggs has it, in Gramsci's opinion, 'Tasca failed to see the qualitatively new character of the councils, which were subject to their own logic and momentum—not that of the unions or party.'[88] Unlike in Lukács, the whole commodity system does not have to be destroyed before a new liberated form can appear.[89] It seems that socialist relations of production can develop under capitalism, just as capitalist relations could develop under feudalism. In late 1920, Gramsci is still maintaining that 'proletarian and communist forces of production . . . were developing within the very heart of the society dominated by the capitalist class'.[90]

While most pre-war socialism was premised on ideas of trade union and party activity, the eventual seizure of state power, and then the imposition of socialist economics from above, Gramsci saw in the factory councils a different route into communism, which did not require such a potentially authoritarian or reformist pathway through the state. The possibilities for communism were at hand, thought Gramsci, at his most enthusiastic. The factory councils, he writes,

> strove to render 'subjective' that which is given 'objectively'. What does objective mean in this case? For the individual worker, the conjunction of the requirements for technical development with the interests of the ruling class is 'objective'. But this conjunction, this unity between technical development and the interests of the ruling class is only a phase in the history of industrial development and must be considered transitory. The nexus can be undone: technical requirements can be thought of concretely as not only separate from ruling class interests but even tied to the interests of the class that is still subaltern. For a conclusive proof that such a 'break up' and new synthesis are historically ripe, one need only look at the fact that this process is understood by the subaltern class—which, for this very reason, is longer subaltern; that is, it manifests the drive to emerge from its subordinate position. . . . This acquired consciousness manifests itself externally and politically precisely in those organisms that look at the factory as the producer of real things rather than profit.[91]

This passage captures the ways in which, in Gramsci's view, new organisms of economic self-management could challenge objective formation and directly remake relations of production in a socialist rather than a capitalist way. The question is very closely tied into the shift from subaltern class to no longer being subaltern—that is, from the acquisition of social consciousness and from subordination and domination as wage-labour to the production of real things in, by, and for life-activity. From this passage we can discern how the question of self-management was keyed into the larger problematics of hegemony and the overcoming of domination, subalternity, and capitalism.

We also detect in this passage, and in others linking factory self-management to the sense among the masses of being creators of history, the link to a larger historicism and the philosophy of praxis. Implicit in self-management are matters far from purely technical. As André Gorz had it in 1960s, the repression of creative praxis and the replacement of it by the mere reproduction of capital meant that 'only "*auto-gestion*" (self-management) can bring back "praxis" into the factory'.[92] Gorz's formulation captures the sense in which self-management at the level of the factory, against 'objective formation' (commodification), brought back into dialectical relationship subject and object in the factory, unifying through praxis a social activity in which theory and practice, mental and manual labour, are put asunder and disunified. *L'Ordine Nuovo*, Gramsci says, 'was developed around a concept—the concept of liberty . . . and concretely developed, on the level of the actual making of history, around the hypothesis of autonomous revolutionary action by the working class'. The working class, from being an instrument of production dominated by financial capitalism, realizes its autonomy, reversing the old hierarchical scale.[93] Popular self-activity in production sets in train this mentality and practice of being creators of history—amid everyday practices—avoiding 'a manipulative, elitist approach to revolutionary politics'.[94] What matters is local: everyday, working lives. Autonomy here involves not demands of authorities or management but self-activity in the making of new forms of livelihood and economic relations.[95]

In relation above all to Pakistan, Sajjad-Akhtar has written that 'contemporary hegemony in the postcolonial world is founded precisely on the notion, however illusory, that the toiling majority, including the self-employed, can in fact secure upward mobility through strategic insertion into circuits of capital'.[96] It very much the task of socialist popular self-activity to break down this hegemonic element and the activities attendant on it, building new forms of socialist production and exchange that interrupt the circuit of capital.

Gramsci—and later Gramscians—have seen a variety of limitations to the economic self-management of the factory councils. In relation to the structure, there is the too-close association with production as opposed to finance, trade, and services, while there is a too-close association with a minority class—industrial workers. In some respects, the petty bourgeoisie, the peasantry, the rural and urban subproletariat, the informal sector, migrants, women engaged in domestic unpaid labour and care-work, and other subaltern social groups—the majority of the population, especially in the colonized world—were left too much out of account. The centrality of the industrial proletariat to this vision of popular self-management would have to be reworked. Further the question of ecology and the environment, only implicit in Gramsci's work but of growing importance since, has given rise both to alternative, autonomous lifestyles and new theory about experiments and forms of ecological and eco-socialist self-activity. Indigenous initiatives in autonomous economy, for example, have put forward the concept of a 'pluripopular economy' to account for the importance of ancestral community knowledge.[97]

Gramscian perspectives on autonomous socialist activity have come to encompass a very broad range of economic activity. In one study, villagers in Indonesia sought direct access to forests from which they were excluded by forestry companies; they engaged in forms of 'counterterritorialisation'.[98] They faced the dilemma of needing permits from the state, which eventually, these authors argue, reinforced state hegemony, while opening up certain new spheres of authorized autonomy.

Finally, for Gramsci himself, self-management risked putting too much emphasis on the structure as opposed to the superstructure. The latter would have to be changed too. Even the most developed forms of economic production (Fordism) could not build a hegemony without civil society, for instance. The same went for socialist production. Both cultural and political transformation were also required. Subaltern social groups would need to develop shared languages, understandings, and forms of collective will. Without such transformations, internal divisions and external repression were ever-present dangers. In the 1920s and 1930s, Gramsci himself started to develop his view, especially through the concept of the hegemony, that the route to socialism would require a much more substantial ingredient of party and state action after all. None of this vitiates the importance and centrality of building new forms of autonomous socialist economic activity, a vital principle in the development of democratic socialism.

THE ECONOMIC–CORPORATE PHASE AND ITS LIMITS

In the light of the theory of hegemony, to stick only with the structure, with the economy, was to remain trapped in an economic-corporate phase in the history of subaltern social groups. Gramsci believed that the militant occupations of factories by workers in September 1920 and the factory councils failed to bring socialist revolution, perhaps above all, because of a 'skillful co-optation process' that played out on economic-corporate lines involving the government, premier Giovanni Giolitti (d. 1928), the progressive industrialists, and the trade unions, with willing accomplices in the socialist party. It was 'the final, gallant moment in the pre-war scheme of *trasformismo*'; an attempt to save Italian capitalism through an 'elite-engineered "reformist solution"'. Capitalism 'needed the crutch of *trasformismo*'.[99] Here the energies and revolutionary potential of popular self-activity and insurrection, the productive-transformative potential of self-management, were defanged; they were absorbed by redistributive economic concessions into an, albeit tottering, liberal-capitalist structure, and the existing frameworks of culture, civil, and political society. The necessary forms of broader reformation in the superstructure—in culture, civil society, and the state—remained lacking in the socialist self-management at work during the Biennio Rosso. Above all, economic-corporate changes implied changes to markets, consumption, and distribution, but they did not challenge the extended reproduction of capital. As Boggs has it, there was 'a dialectic of radical upsurge and reconsolidation combined in the same phase of activity'.[100] Arguably this deformed dialectic (this 'neoformation') is a common aspect, a familiar danger, in relation to the formation of pockets of autonomous activity in economic, social, political, or cultural life. Indeed, economic self-management has been co-opted by and absorbed into the bureaucratic institutions of the state in other cases, such as Algeria in the 1960s and in post-revolutionary Iran (1979–1982).[101]

Without a transition to the ethico-political phase, self-organization in the structure is at great risk of economic-corporate co-optation, of remaining only in the interstices and side-pockets of a broader capitalist hegemony which reigns unchecked. In other words, the shift to the ethico-political in Gramsci is not just a matter of an unnecessary idealism or voluntarism: on the contrary, it is highly relevant to strategy and social force. Indeed, at a certain point in the development of popular mobilization, to define the struggle as solely about bread-and-butter issues, wages, and conditions is to run the risk of cooptation and of failing to develop. It is even convenient for ruling classes. As Gramsci writes about the apolitical, passive posture of French trade unionists before 1914, 'The purely "economic" struggle did not displease the ruling class, not in the least.'[102]

The gains at stake in the economic-corporate phase, the limitations attendant on a failure to preserve and transcend these gains, and the possibilities at work when new developments at the level of the ethico-political are pushed forward are usefully exemplified in Meek's research on Brazil's Landless Workers Movement, the *Movimento dos Trabalhadores Rurais Sem Terra* (MST), in recent times. The MST, in its own words, 'is a mass social movement, formed by rural workers and by all those who want to fight for land reform and against injustice and social inequality in rural areas'.[103] It was formed by direct autonomous action, the occupation of *latifundios* (large landed estates), and became a national movement in 1984. Since its inception, hundreds of thousands of families have participated in thousands of occupations of several million hectares of land. The MST pushes for and builds cooperatives, schools, agricultural credit, and health provision. It has a publishing house, featuring work by Gramsci.[104] In one settlement,

> 19 percent of inhabitants described their participation in the MST as 'high' at the time of the settlement's creation, [but] at present only eight percent see themselves as being actively involved in the MST. As one MST activist opined, 'Everyone's got their television, their house, their motorcycle. They have enough food, and can go and hang out with their cell-phone in the central square. What need do they have for the movement?' Other activists within the community continue to see the MST as a fundamental organizing force of the community, arguing, 'The struggle is continual. When one struggle ends, another begins.'[105]

On the one side, the satisfaction of immediate economic-corporate interests and the acquisition of much needed leisure time are important gains, even if to various constituencies this implies that there is no need to engage in further popular mobilization. There can be a 'relapse' into common sense and dispersal and an end to popular mobilization. On the other side, there are elements that are profoundly unhappy with this, given that, notwithstanding the undoubted socioeconomic gains, larger structures of exploitative, commodifying, marginalizing, and environmentally destructive capitalism are left intact. The living Gramscian tradition is capable of analyzing and bringing out this dilemma, which, arguably, is particularly prominent regarding the phase of popular self-activity. The dilemma also points to the unfinished dialectics of popular mobilization. A new contradiction emerges out of the very gains of the previous struggle: 'when one struggle ends, another begins.' When problems of fundamental poverty have been solved, new questions as to the system of exploitation more broadly start to arise, questions which are bound to reach deep into the analysis and transformation of the superstructure. It is tempting to read into this example both the ways in which popular mobilization can disperse amid economic-corporate gains, while on the other hand there are elements that push forward to a qualitatively new threshold, a phase change, in which questions of structure and superstructure are posed together.

POPULAR AUTHORITY

For Gramsci, the factory councils were new organs of popular authority. Political, superstructural questions were implicitly (and to some degree explicitly) at work in these forms of activity. The councils were not just self-organizers of production. They broached issues of legislation and control,[106] they were due to become the state; they were the post-subaltern state, albeit in some embryonic and under-developed form. Not for nothing did Gramsci raise the slogan 'All State power to the Workers' and Peasants' Councils.'[107]

These self-governing communities, it is important to remember, involved *all* the workers in the factory (not just those who were unionized), giving them an embryonically state-like quality—as they were not just voluntary, civil society associations. They raised new questions: for example, '[W]hat are the forms, practices and attitudes appropriate to the creation of democratic socialist authority relations? What are the constituent elements of a [post-subaltern] . . . non-bureaucratic state? How can revolutionary sensibilities be translated into everyday life?'[108] As Boggs puts it, 'Gramsci was to become one of the few Marxists to conceptualize the transition to socialism in non-economistic terms, as a process that would transform social and authority relations as well as the mode of production.'[109] Far from a vanguardist view, in which state power (static, pre-existing) is captured, political autonomy involves re-founding state relations from the bottom up.[110] It is not that these new organs really are the state and can act like one— or indeed *should* act like any of the existing states. Nor is it sufficient simply to seek inclusion or representation in the institutions of the existing state. The strategic imperative in this phase, which is not just a matter of expression or performance but practical instantiation, is precisely 'not to *conquer* the existing state apparatus but to create new popular organs of authority *before* the overthrow of the bourgeois state'.[111] At stake is the reconfiguration of state relations themselves, the re-posing via self-activity of fundamental questions of authority, coercion, and legislation; a search for participatory collective will formation and self-rule, for popular democracy.

This principle responds to Gramsci's point that *everyone* is in some sense a legislator. 'The concept of "legislator"', writes Gramsci, 'must inevitably be identified with the concept of "politician". Since all men and women are "political beings", all are also "legislators". But distinctions will have to be made. "Legislator" has a precise juridical and official meaning—i.e. it means those persons who are empowered by the law to enact laws.' Gramsci goes on, 'But it can have other meanings too.' Gramsci offers the following:

> Every man [*sic*], in as much as he is active, i.e. living, contributes to modifying the social environment in which he develops (to modifying certain of its characteristics or to preserving others); in other words, he tends to establish "norms", rules of living and of behaviour. One's circle of activity may be greater or smaller, one's awareness of one's own action and aims may be greater or smaller; furthermore, the representative power may be greater or smaller, and will be put into practice to a greater or lesser extent in its normative, systematic expression by the 'represented'.[112]

An ordinary person, Gramsci writes, 'continues to be a legislator even if he accepts directives from others—if, as he carries them out, he makes certain that others are carrying them out too; if, having understood their spirit, he propagates them as though making them into rules specifically applicable to

The Wellsprings of Autonomy

limited and definite zones of living'.[113] In other words, self-activity is engaged in the remaking of these rules and norms, as it configures represented and representative, leaders and led, in new patterns.

Sara Motta's prefigurative Gramscian approach captures the significance of this process in popular power in Latin America. In defending self-activity against the charge that it involves a flight from politics and the political, especially regarding Venezuela, she writes: 'The politicisation of place, social relations and subjectivities that these attempts involve is not the localisation, and, therefore, continued impotence of their political struggle. Instead it constitutes a creative negation of the forms of social life that have been the communities' experience of capitalism and an attempt to build something beyond and against such an organization of social relations.'[114]

Gramsci uses the now-jarring pronoun 'he' and refers to 'man'. However, he intertwines these ordinary modes of legislation with gender relations, striking against, at least in a limited way, the naturalization of masculine subjectivity. He writes, 'A father is a legislator for his children, but the paternal authority will be more or less conscious, more or less obeyed and so forth.'[115] Authority and legislation has a gendered component, and the reproduction of patriarchy is not smooth or inevitable, even in ordinary times, as consciousness and obedience is variable.

The association of elective principles with bourgeoise domination has generated a 'structure of feeling' on the Left which can sometimes slide into authoritarianism (where voting and elective principles are rejected altogether) or into autonomism (where voting of any kind is eschewed in favour of deliberative consensus seeking). As ever, Gramsci approaches, in a discriminating and historicizing way, the principles of election and the question of whether and how to use voting mechanisms to confer positions of political representation (one might say 'translation') and decision-making authority—and he relates them to hegemony. Gramsci's discussion of elections include a strongly developed critique of the way they are turned into a project of class domination, especially at the national scale; but it should be emphasized that Gramsci's factory councils were a form of shopfloor democracy that enshrined popular democratic principles of election, delegation, and representation/translation within the structure of self-organization.[116] In embracing electoral principles, Gramsci was not deviating as much from

Lenin, Marx, or Engels as one might think. Lenin's *State and Revolution* refused bourgeois modes of representation but argued that the 'way out of parliamentarianism is not, of course, the elimination of representative institutions and electivity'.[117] Marx embraced (at least in the 1870s) a kind of social republicanism, including popular delegation constrained by imperative mandates, the right to recall, and short terms of office—the forms of popular democracy at work in the Paris Commune.[118]

Autonomous organization, in Gramsci, then, is a form of popular democracy. Such forms of internal democracy have been considered vital to self-organization in Gramscian research. The Zapatista Army of National Liberation (EZLN), for instance, which has represented indigenous forces and their allies in a popular struggle against neoliberalism and the Mexican state in Chiapas since 1994, is said to have a thriving internal democracy, involving elected representatives, their close supervision, and removability at the community level.[119] The question, the challenge, and limit, for the EZLN, for Gramsci, and for the phase of democratic self-activity in general, is how to scale up such forms of democracy, how to write them into the national and even the transnational stage.

SELF-ACTIVITY IN SEXUALITY AND PRACTICES OF CARE

Since Gramsci's time, attention to self-activity has been broadened beyond economy and polity in vital ways. Gramsci raised questions of gender and sexuality in relation to hegemony, but these issues are developed with Marxist and Black feminism. Since the 1960s, when relations of reproduction; the household (both as drudgery and as revolution); and eventually practices of care, including queer forms of homosociality and care of the self as a political act—and all of the relations of gender and sexuality involved—new forms of autonomism in and out of the Gramscian tradition have received more attention, as part and parcel of subaltern struggles in general and studies of self-activity in particular.[120]

Queer activism and thinking has fundamentally reconceived relations of love, kinship, and household, opening up new possibilities for understanding autonomy beyond reproduction or heteronormative hegemony and discursive domination. This book has already broached the possibility that one can think Foucault within Gramscian perspectives, rather than the other way around. One can, indeed, draw on significant readings such as that by Eribon to understand how Foucault developed his ideas as part of 'the history of people coming to speak for themselves'.[121] In the first phase, we find a Foucault working out the ways in which sexuality is constructed in civil and political society, how it produces subjects. Here we find governmentality, discipline and surveillance, marginalizing spaces (asylums, hospitals, prisons, and so on), biopolitics, capillary power, and so on. In this phase of Foucault's thought, there is a grappling with sexual hegemony and its forms of domination, normalization, and discursive power. In this phase, even gay voices, speaking out for the first time, are seen as merely those 'incited to speak' by the dominant discourse:[122] coming out, gay pride, and gay identity politics can be interpreted within the same optic, which is redoubled when combined with a critique of Eurocentrism and Orientalism.[123]

Eventually, however, there is a change of emphasis, a new phase. Foucault starts to see the value in gay pride, in these expressions of autonomy, in the shifts brought about amid the popular self-activity of the 1960s. *Autonomia* comes to the fore in the rhythm of his thinking. In one interview, for instance, he emphasizes that 'political innovation, political creation, and political experimentation outside the great political parties and outside the normal or ordinary program' and at work in 'social movements' has 'really changed our whole lives, our mentality, our attitudes, and the attitudes and mentality of other people—people who do not belong to these movements. And that is something very important and positive.'[124] Foucault starts to follow up new thinking about counter-conduct (a kind of productive autonomy which is not reducible to the dominant discourse), care of the self, the ethics of care, homosociality, and the like. He starts to think of new spaces and places in which liberated gay practice and life-activity can take place. He writes, with great brilliance, 'We have to devote ourselves seriously to becoming homosexuals and not stubbornly limit ourselves to discovering that that is what we are.'[125] The homology with Gramsci's dialectics of social becoming is evident.

In other words, Foucault's own *leitmotiv*, the rhythm of thinking as it develops, arguably expresses and elaborates a history of subaltern social groups, a move from *dominazione* to *autonomia*, from subalternity to self-activity. As a gay man, Foucault was no traditional intellectual of sexuality.

He wrestled with his own lived experience and 'tormenting dramas' as Eribon has shown.[126] Perhaps we can read Foucault as the organic intellectual of subaltern queer sexuality who charted a course from *dominazione* to *autonomia*. Perhaps, instead of only arguing against Foucault in relation to Gramsci, we can see the forms of a Gramscian theory of popular mobilization in the life and works of Foucault. Homosexuality can be seen as a way of life, as a 'way out of an unbearable "positional suffering"'.[127]

We do not just see a pale echo of these forms, because Foucault vastly developed the theme of sexuality, a question which Gramsci only broaches. On the other hand, in a Gramscian perspective, Foucault stops short of fulfilling the sexual revolution: he does not move from *autonomia* to *consenso* or from *consenso* to *direzione*. In Foucault, we remain uncertain as to how queer liberation will enact itself in economic activity, civil and political society, and the wider culture. Queer *politics* remains underdeveloped. Care of the self, cannot, as many feminists have argued, devolve into individualism and the commodified care industry, but must remain a collective question. If Eribon is right with his powerful argument that there is no particular politics inherent or natural to gay existence, then political and ideological cultivation becomes all the more pressing.

If this reading has any merit, then 'coming out' can be read in a Gramscian perspective as signalling a powerful qualitative shift: the moment of transition from the subaltern phase of domination, marginality, social insult, and dispersal to an autonomous phase in which new forms of being, life-activity, and collectivity are constructed. Coming out, as Eribon underlines,[128] is always a heavily charged, high-stakes moment in relation to an entire life; it signals a real qualitative change, one that cannot be undone. It is a historical act par excellence —that is, one that cannot be reverse engineered, one that proves, as it were, the arrow of time. Gay self-activity, the construction of new spaces, new forms of leisure, and new social relations can also include considerable effervescence and expressions of pride (a spirit of *scissione*). One recalls Mr Loverman's expression in Bernadine Evaristo's novel of the same name: this Caribbean British man's gayness is generally closeted and unspoken, although he has same-sex relations and a long-standing partner. As a much older man he makes a rare trip to a gay bar in Soho: 'Amid all this gayness, boldness comes in leaps and bounds.'

The Wellsprings of Autonomy

Queer research and activism has also thought the limitations of queer autonomy, spaces, places, and practices of care. Eribon offers a very rich discussion of the potential and political limits of gay autonomy, while rejecting the deeply problematic republican critique that such spaces segment the nation on communitarian lines. More categorical, perhaps, is Duggan's critique of what she calls 'homonormativity', a 'neoliberal gayness' centred on domesticity and consumption, which does not fundamentally challenge heteronormativity, but instead develops a new homonormativity alongside it.[129] This criticism illustrates, in ways congruent with a Gramscian perspective, the limits of self-activity: the ways in which new spheres of autonomy and self-activity in cultural and sexual practice—in this case homonormativity— for all their importance and meaning in finding new ways of life against forms of social domination, wind up leaving the wider culture and its structures of consent and *direzione*—here, heteronormativity—intact. As elsewhere, autonomy and group consciousness are not enough.

COUNTERCULTURE

Gramsci attended also to cultural self-activity, autonomous cultural expression and what Gramscians (and others) have analyzed as counterculture. For instance, unlike most of his Marxist comrades in the Italian Socialist Party (PSI), in futurism Gramsci saw 'an ideological-cultural or aesthetic subversion of conventional values that, while not explicitly "Marxist", was nevertheless "preparing new ground in the class struggle" with revolutionary claims'. Gramsci paid attention to such 'embryonic but imperfect currents of cultural protest and revolt'.[130] Indeed, Gramsci came to criticize futurism's eventual detachment from any determinate politics.

Stuart Hall's Gramscian studies of popular culture considered the cultural potential and value of libertarianism on the Left among post-1968 youth in Britain, who outside of 'corporate capital' and 'statist provision' independently created choice and diversity in music, clothes, style, reading, and independent publications through 'local or "grass roots" initiatives' and 'direct self-activity'.[131] He was also sensitive to the ways in which these forms of autonomy 'were in constant danger of being regulated out of existence by the state or ripped off by the big commercial providers'.[132] Graeber captures the 'direct action' countercultural spirit of punk, as a stripped down 'anyone-can-do-it music of the people'.[133] Bayat offers a positive view of post-2011 graffiti and street art in Tunisia, as well as '[t]he public display of . . . counternormal ideas—whether deveiling, alternative sexuality, atheism, or anarchism' in North Africa in the 2010s.[134] Strikingly, he situates such forms of display as a development beyond non-movements—that is, beyond the subaltern phase.

These are salient directions indeed, while there is a critique, in a Gramscian perspective, of the problem of the impermanence and evanescence of such counter-hegemonic forms of culture. Tarlau suggests that in the face of this problem, the 'goal of a radical educational project is to create a stronger link between these diverse forms of cultural production, and a larger political intervention'.[135] The limits of counterculture herald the question of popular education.

SELF-ORGANIZATION

A further theme at work in the Councils is the question of relations of association and organization themselves—the existing institutions of civil society—which self-organization puts in question. Collectives, grassroots organizations, and the like start to raise the question of how voluntarily to associate, coordinate, organize, and relate. Against 'a reliance on large-scale organizational forms, professional leaders, and institutional hierarchies. . . . Gramsci opposed his prefigurative and molecular conception which, despite the catastrophe of the Turin council movement, he would carry forward into his later political thinking'.[136] The context for Gramsci's practical and to a lesser extent, theoretical, route into self-organization is very clearly described by Merrington: 'The emergence of reformist tendencies in the socialist parties in the pre-war period, the subsequent capitulation of the German SPD, the failure of the socialist leaderships to combat factional tendencies within their parties and their fatal inaction in the face of events immediately following the war, created a situation in which only radical new departures could create [renewal].'[137]

Indeed, Gramsci and his comrades in the *L'Ordine Nuovo* developed a swingeing critique of the bureaucratic, unresponsive, disorganic, reformist civil society organizations—the Italian Socialist Party and bureaucratic and co-opted trade unions: 'In most European countries, Gramsci observed, the unions came into being as radical mechanisms of working-class struggles but eventually ended up as bargaining components within the capital managerial structure.'[138] Unions may have started out as qualitatively new organizations, a step up from informal subaltern formations of wage-workers, and a vital component in the self-organization of workers' struggles. There is no reason why certain unions cannot be seen in this light in a Gramscian perspective, as not all unions inevitably follow the early twentieth-century Italian pattern of change.[139] Indeed, Gramsci roots the valorization of union organization in Marx's *Poverty of Philosophy*, where Marx writes that 'an important phase in the development of a social group born on the terrain of industry is the phase in which the individual members of an economic-corporate organization no longer struggle solely for their own corporate economic interests, but for the development of the organization itself, per se'.[140]

The trade union, therefore, can exist as the focus of loyalty, in a distinct, positive phase—a qualitative development beyond the informal and partial subaltern formations and combinations. At a certain threshold, loyalty to the organization as such comes into being. This is a vital advance. However, unions can also degenerate, in a Gramscian perspective, in various ways, and this was Gramsci's dominant experience and context: he had a developed criticism of Italian trade unions as bourgeois; integrated into capitalist relations; contractors of the commodity labour power; complicit in liberal, parliamentary politics; formalistic and bureaucratic; and as merely economic-corporate.

Self-organization raises all the questions of how voluntary association is to work and how loyalty is to be managed and constructed; it challenges existing modalities in civil society. It is intertwined with the existence of 'the self-conscious initiatives of the masses themselves'—that is, activity which did not come about 'through the directives of a vanguard party acting in their name'.[141] Gramsci noted that the factory councils would bring workers 'priceless gains in terms of autonomy and initiative'.[142] Loyalty to an organization—in theory and practice—is not the same as fetishizing organization per se or becoming an apparatchik loyal only to the furtherance of the bureaucracy. What matters in the living Gramscian tradition is how self-organization effects an organic link to, and more importantly, an organic passage from, subaltern activity at the margins.

There is a complex dialectic between autonomous self-activity and self-organization here. Rosa Luxemburg argued in her 1906 tract 'The Mass Strike' against the bureaucratic, corporate notion that large, well-financed unions were the precondition for successful mass mobilization. She maintained that in Russia of 1905 the new organizations were born from the 'apparently "chaotic" . . . revolutionary action' which became 'the starting point of a feverish *work of organization* [emphasis in original]'.[143] On the one hand, mass action does not depend on organization from above. On the other, such action does not remain in an uncoordinated state—lest it dissipate like steam. In the Gramscian view, which appears here to be very close to Rosa Luxemburg's, mass, 'spontaneous', autonomous activity is in fact the start point of organizational activity. Unlike some readings of Luxemburg, self-organization here, as such, is being specifically enjoined. It is the debt to strikes and insurrection and the organic relationship to subaltern social groups that matters—and here Luxemburg and Gramsci are surprisingly close together.

Loyalty to new forms of self-organization is intertwined with ties of solidarity to the subaltern social groups getting organized and to the conceptions for which they stand. Self-organization, then, is seen as tied into the development of forms of group and class consciousness, although conceptions and ideologies can vary greatly. As workers self-organized in Detroit in the 1930s, they started to see and interact with each other in new ways, as part of a distinct group, a distinct social class, with shared interests and purposes.[144] Class consciousness is greatly reinforced through rounds of strikes and confrontations with employers, managers, and their state backers. What matters here is the way that self-organization is organically rooted in social being and social consciousness, the way it intersects with the progressive acquisition of the historical personality. It is part and parcel of an organic passage from the phase of subaltern activity at the margins—common sense, contradictory consciousness, raising complaints in corridors, limited subaltern formations, and so on—to a qualitatively different phase: one of self-organization, the spirit of cleavage, and the strike, which together, amid confrontation, reinforce and develop a sense of class belonging. This view is consistent with E. P. Thompson's classical account of the making of the English working class—in which workers are very much present culturally and organizationally at their own making.[145] Conceptions of the world—whether visions of the people in the positive sense or visions characterized by xenophobia, racism, Orientalism, misogyny, and homophobia—can operate to colour and shape these forms of class consciousness in powerful ways. This immediately signals a vital limit, one necessitating a critique of ideology.

Self-organization is not limited to what workers do in factories. Trade unions are relevant, of course, to a very wide variety of non-factory workers, including teachers, nurses, cleaners, migrants, and the like. Self-organization also encompasses a very wide variety of groupings: popular committees, popular tribunals, grassroots organizations, community, group and neighbourhood organizations, campaign groups, and feminist collectives are all relevant here. For example, the popular committees formed in Egypt during and after the uprising of 2011. Or the wide variety of new collectives keyed into the self-activity of those emerging from histories of domination, like the feminist collective 'Feminism Attack'.[146] Or the Basic Ecclesial Communities formed in the Philippines after the 'people power' uprising that ousted Marcos.[147] Or the popular committees that were formed during the great Arab-Palestinian uprising against British colonialism and Zionism 1936-39.[148] Organic forms of self-organization can sometimes involve the emergence from a popular ferment of new organizations, or they can involve the takeover and transformation of existing organizations or a secession from them.

There are limits to self-organization, nonetheless. This is where the Gramscian perspective becomes most distinctive. What remains to be cultivated in the phase of self-organization is the sense of the wider civil society—and how it can be conquered and reorganized. Without a larger war of position—a way of transforming civil and political society beyond pockets of self-organization—self-organization can be quite vulnerable to co-optation. And the war of position cannot operate, furthermore, without a critique of ideology.

Chodor draws our attention, for example, to the co-optation of the *piqueteros*. The latter emerged in Argentina in the mid-1990s, especially among workers and women. They acquired their name by blocking streets, in protest against unemployment and other social problems in particular. They have formed the popular basis for the 'Unemployed Workers Movements'

(*Movimientos de Trabajadores Desempleados*, MTDs). They have also engaged in various forms of self-organization in social, economic, and community fields—such as sewing workshops and barter-markets. Chodor cautions against the autonom*ist* understanding of the movement in terms of a multitude seeking autonomy without ideology, arguing that careful note should be taken of the ways in which the Néstor Kirchner government and existing forms of civil and political society were able to absorb them, defanging their revolutionary potential.[149] The implication, arguably, is not that the piqueteros were wrong or fatally flawed—a far too vanguardist view—but that without a more developed set of organizational and political structures and alliances of their own, the piqueteros are threatened by neoformation, by absorption within structures that pre-existed them.

PLACE AND ITS LIMITS

During the subaltern phase, as we have seen, subaltern social groups find themselves in spaces and places built and controlled by others. They live at the margins in this sense. Self-activity forges new places; new, intensive spatial connections; new localities. Such place-making is intertwined inseparably with the exercise and enjoyment of autonomy.

An important illustration of the relationship between place-making and popular self-activity emerges in the work of Karriem on the MST in Brazil. Here, land is literally seized by occupation; each territory seized becomes a new camp, which then trains and socializes inhabitants, planning for the conquest of more land:

> A key factor that drives the territorialisation of the MST is the organizational praxis that is diffused in an acampamento or assentamento, which, once established, becomes a space for self-organization, political socialisation, solidarity, forging global ambition, and the making of a popular common sense. The MST's organizational structure draws on the ecclesiastical base communities (CEBs) promoted by liberation theologians. The CEBs are spaces where small groups or nucleos of individuals and families study, debate, and reflect on their social realities and organize to change them. Liberation theologians did not see the poor as victims who needed charity, but as actors who, through organization and struggle, can become the protagonists of their own liberation. Based on the CEB model, an acampamento or assentamento of 100 families is divided into 10 nucleos of 10 families, with two

coordinators—a man and a woman. Other members of the nucleo participate in the health, education, communication, political education, or mass front sectors.[150]

New forms of space and place are carved out by popular self-activity as against existing hegemonic constructions. The gains in relation to autonomy, livelihood, and even security should not be underestimated. These 'hot places' are not purely local: they have translocal dimensions—organizations that can link them, ideas that can form part of their inner cohesion, and temporal links to past such experiments and to ideas about the destiny of such bubbles of autonomy.

On the other hand, places have their limits. One of the problems with the factory councils and the Biennio Rosso were forms of 'localism'.[151] This is much of the point of Harvey's spatial Marxism, when he assesses the limits of 'militant particularism' above all in terms of its limitedness on the spatial plane.[152] There is a need for a wider construction of social space beyond 'hot' localities of belonging. The other point is that such a wider construction is *already in view*—new spaces can become sites where new forms of 'global ambition' are conceived.

THE CRISIS OF AUTHORITY

While the routes into the subaltern phase are defined by various forms of objective formation (objectification), the pathways into the phase of popular self-activity are defined in general by the antithesis of this: the crumbling of objective formation; the destabilization of the 'rigidified phase' of what was apparently solid; and a great subjective formation, in the positive sense, involving a passage from 'objective to subjective'.[153] Gramsci's major concept here is the 'crisis of authority'.

At the centre of the concept, as Gramsci explains, is the fact that '[a]t a certain point in their historical lives, social classes become detached from their traditional parties. In other words, the traditional parties in that particular organizational form, with the particular men who constitute, represent and lead them, are no longer recognised by their class (or fraction of a class) as its expression'.[154] Gramsci makes clear that these are situations of conflict between 'represented and representatives'. The crisis takes aim, therefore, at the passive or active adherence to dominant formations. It

The Wellsprings of Autonomy

heralds a new phase, in which such forms of adherence have reached their limits or are no longer operative, shaking the soil of subaltern quiescence and domination. It is important to underline that the question of sociology, of social being and social consciousness, of what Gramsci calls 'social content', is central to the notion of what Gramsci here calls 'organic crisis'. The situation, writes Gramsci, is

> connected to one of the most important questions concerning the political party—i.e. the party's capacity to react against force of habit, against the tendency to become mummified and anachronistic. Parties come into existence, and constitute themselves as organizations, in order to influence the situation at moments which are historically vital for their class; but they are not always capable of adapting themselves to new tasks and to new epochs, nor of evolving *pari passu* with the overall relations of force (and hence the relative position of their class) in the country in question, or in the international field.[155]

The party bureaucracy especially, writes Gramsci, can end up becoming anachronistic, and 'at moments of acute crisis it is voided of its social content and left as though suspended in mid-air.' Gramsci continues, 'French parties are a rich field for such research: they are all mummified and anachronistic—historico-political documents of the various phases of past French history, whose outdated terminology they continue to repeat.'[156]

The crisis of authority, the crisis in the relations between the representatives and the represented—another facet of the disunity of theory and practice—has a number of crucial features:

> When these crises occur, the immediate situation becomes delicate and dangerous because it opens the field to violent solutions, to the activities of dark forces represented by men who are charismatic or seem to be sent by providence. These conflicts between the represented and the representatives, which take place on the terrain of the parties (party organizations in the narrow sense, the electoral-parliamentary field, newspaper organization), have repercussions throughout the state organism, reinforcing the relative power of the bureaucracy (civil and military), high finance, the Church, and, generally, all the entities that are to a certain extent free from the fluctuations of public opinion.[157]

What is going on here, writes Gramsci, is nothing less than a 'crisis of the hegemony of the ruling class'.[158] The implication being that the ruling class can no longer effectively organize consent—through parties, intermediary groups and classes, and civil society—and the represented, the subaltern social groups, become unbound from the channels of passive and active adherence to the dominant political formation that had formerly contained and channelled their activity. The situation could be related to inter/transnational developments and forces: for instance, horizontalism might cross borders in ways that bolster the de-authorization of parties and give cohesion to new experiments. Far from seeing this is as an unalloyed aspect of the road to revolution, however, Gramsci emphasizes the short-run dangers of such a situation, noting with a powerful connective sense that such crises reinforce the entrenched powers—including those of high finance—and simultaneously pave the way for charismatic adventurers or providential deliverers.

Gramsci notes, in this regard, that the Lazzeretti popular religious movement 'showed the government the kind of subversive-popular-rudimentary tendency that could arise among the peasantry as a result of clerical-political abstentionism; it also showed that, in the absence of normal political parties, the rural masses sought local leaders who arose out of the same masses blending religion and fanaticism with a set of demands that, in basic form, had been brewing in the countryside.'[159] The implication is that such a popular movement, in this case following a charismatic leader, emerges not only in a situation where the gap between represented and representatives becomes incrementally wider but when the gap exists already, as a result of a prior process of 'clerical-political' 'absentionism' and in the 'absence of normal political parties'.

What is happening here, the larger sense, is that the ruling class is losing its consensus; it is ceasing to lead and becoming only dominant, exercising coercive force alone, offering police solutions only. The ruling strata lose prestige and are increasingly 'reduced to their initial economic-corporate stage',[160] meaning they pursue only private or private-group interests. 'The old intellectual and moral leaders of society', writes Gramsci, 'feel the ground slipping from under their feet; they perceive that their "sermons" have become precisely mere sermons, i.e. external to reality, pure form without any content, shades without a spirit.'[161] The implication is that the ruling classes will increasingly turn to their own narrow material interests, start calling for repressive measures, and fail to maintain the precise stream of concessions to subordinated groups which is required to secure adherence.

Guha's vivid explanation of the origins of the Naxalbari peasant movement in India traces this pattern very clearly:

> The rural and urban poor, including the impoverished middle classes, had expected [after independence] the newly formed government of Independent India to bring them relief. But the ruling elite represented by the Congress Party was far too busy consolidating its grip over the estate it had inherited from the British. It took for granted the consent of the people who had constituted the nonviolent armies of the nation in anti-imperialist struggles . . . [and] turned immediately to the task of manipulating the state apparatus in order to secure the interests of the classes and communities they represented. Initially, the communists and some of the other political groups on the left sought to resist this process, but without much success. The dominant elite broke up the resistance by a generous use of the army, police and draconian laws, and then persuaded its critics to be content with their role as a parliamentary opposition. The trick worked, but not well enough to silence the growing opposition outside the legislative chambers. By the late 1960s, the misery of the poor and the unemployed had driven them to such desperation as to require only a spark to set it ablaze. The Naxalbari peasant movement provided that spark. It started merely as a local uprising against landlords, but soon became the signal for small-scale insurgencies in some other rural parts as well. No less significant is the fact that it spread to urban areas too.[162]

Here new streams of popular mobilization are vividly inscribed within a developing crisis of authority.

There are also some distinctive spatialized ways of thinking a provocative marginalization process: 'we argue, like most scholars of postcolonial urban contexts, that the re-spatialisation of neoliberal powers by way of global governance is followed by a gradual displacement of politics itself from state institutions to marginal, interstitial and informal sites of society. Thus, the postcolonial city becomes a laboratory of new mobilizations.'[163] Here the spatial displacement of the site of politics from state and civil society is eventually a laboratory of new kinds of mobilization.

The crisis of authority can also be rapidly precipitated by the failure of the ruling classes in major undertakings, for which they have won or forcibly extracted consent. To the crisis in civil society (of representation) is added a crisis of the state, including in relation to the international stage. The great masses, in turn, are becoming detached from their traditional ideologies, shaking off the tissues of ideology that are no longer being proven in practice and can no longer be adequate to comprehend their current situations of objectification. In such a situation, the old is dying, but the new cannot be born, perhaps above all because the new has not yet found a way to organize a new structure of consent, a new organic relationship between represented and representatives.

Sara Motta gives a powerful description, an example of this process, in Venezuela. She writes:

> For large sections of Venezuela's urban poor, the experience of the Punto Fijo system (1958–99) was characterised by political, social, and economic exclusion. This exclusion occurred in a context of a party system and a democratically representative state and regime. It is from such experiences that the mistrust of political parties, political liberalism, and the state becomes both a rational and logical political response from those interested in progressive change. As Maria Teresa, the coordinator of Mission Ribas in La Vega Parroquia expressed it, 'We don't want to be politicos in the old sense . . . we want to create our own popular power from below.'[164]

In this case, the crisis of authority gives rise to a fundamental rethinking of the nature of politics and authority.

Stuart Hall describes a similar crisis of authority, this time in relation to a different history, place, and case—the riots on the Broadwater Farm Estate in Tottenham, England, in 1985. He speaks of a familiar pattern in Britain's 'history of urban and rural riot'. There is 'a long and gruelling period of deepening poverty and neglect', including social, political, economic, and cultural exclusion; racist policing; a Thatcherist insistence—in the case of Tottenham—that it is the rioters' fault for being poor; policies creating unemployment; defunding of community organizations and local authorities; increased police powers; use of the language of law and order; and wider forms of racism. Eventually, 'the fragile bonds . . . to the dominant society loosen. Those who have no stake in society, owe it nothing. . . . At that point, "the riots" have already begun, though no one has yet thrown a single brick. But everything that creates riots and disturbance, the spontaneous explosion of rage, anger and frustration that flows over like lava when things start, is already in place.'[165]

POPULAR UPRISINGS

Gramsci writes on popular uprisings when he refers to 'synthetic explosions' and to 'insurrection'. Gramsci's texts here, although not the topic in general, have been surprisingly neglected. The phrase 'synthetic explosion', for instance, although it refers to a kind of spontaneous popular revolt, is barely explored. Gramsci refers to 'popular intervention . . . in the concentrated and instantaneous form of an insurrection'.[166] Gramsci's framing strikes immediately against any overblown estimation of the popular uprising. He introduces the topic by writing that collective wills are forged and their strategic tasks defined only 'rarely', in 'sudden "synthetic" explosions. Synthetic "explosions" do occur, but if they are looked at closely it can be seen that they are more destructive than reconstructive; they remove mechanical and external obstacles in the way of an indigenous and spontaneous development.'[167]

This passage can be read to mean that a synthetic explosion, which implies a popular upsurge or insurrection, when many diverse strands rapidly come together as part of local causes and with a measure of spontaneity, is inevitably rather formless in terms of its own 'indigenous' and popular forms of collective will—that is, in terms of shared understandings, fundamental purposes, and hence shape, direction, application, strategy, and short- and long-term goals. Gramsci gives the example of the Sicilian Vespers as 'typical'.[168] On 31 March 1282, write the editors of the *Prison Notebooks*, 'the population of Palermo rose against the government of Charles of Anjou. The uprising, which came to be known as the Sicilian Vespers, spread rapidly throughout the island, and the French were expelled in less than a month. The throne was subsequently given to Frederick of Aragon. The rising had been the result of a combination of discontent and the plans of pro-Aragonese elements among the nobility.'[169]

Here and in homologous cases, writes Gramsci, 'an economic crisis, for instance, engenders on the one hand discontent among the subaltern classes and spontaneous mass movements, and on the other conspiracies among the reactionary groups, who take advantage of the objective weakening of the

The Wellsprings of Autonomy

government in order to attempt *coups d'état*.'[170] Gramsci adds that '[a]mong the effective causes of the *coups* must be included the failure of the responsible groups to give any conscious leadership to the spontaneous revolts or to make them into a positive political factor'.[171]

As a popular social force, Gramsci is saying, the popular insurrection is powerful and can blast away external structures. But it is often diffuse, and as such can be taken advantage of by more organized social forces. Gramsci argues, in an original manner, that the Vespers was *both* a 'spontaneous movement' and one 'planned in advance'. He writes: 'On the one hand, a spontaneous rising of the Sicilian people against their Provençal rulers which spread so rapidly that it gave the impression of simultaneity and hence of preconcertation; this rising was the result of an oppression which had become intolerable throughout the national territory. On the other hand, there was the conscious element, of varying importance and effectiveness, and the success of Giovanni da Procida's plot with the Aragonese.'[172]

Gramsci clearly believes that a popular insurrection of this kind is recurring. He writes: 'Other examples can be drawn from all past revolutions in which several subaltern classes were present, with a hierarchy determined by economic position and internal homogeneity. The "spontaneous" movements of the broader popular strata make possible the coming to power of the most progressive subaltern class as a result of the objective weakening of the State.'[173]

Here we learn the meaning of 'synthetic'. It contains the idea that 'several subaltern classes' are present but not necessarily formulated organically into a precise social force or a fully formed historical bloc. In other words, 'synthetic' carries the meaning of combining but not quite unifying. It also implies something not entirely naturalized, lacking a widely diffused new ideological formation, and somewhat artificial or fragile as a cohesive subject. The word 'explosion' conveys, furthermore, the powerful kinetic and energetic yet imprecisely directed nature of the social force in question. We also learn, crucially, that popular insurrection is often part and parcel of a revolution. Gramsci underlines indeterminacy in terms of nature and outcomes: we might find an example in which reactionary elements plot a coup or another in which the most progressive subaltern class comes to power. Gramsci also sees the Vespers as a 'progressive' example, while stating, intriguingly, that 'in the modern world, the regressive examples are more frequent'.[174] We can recall here that in September 1920—at the height of the popular upsurges—he had written, rather prophetically, of the danger of a *coup d'état* by regressive forces. 'The political power of capitalism' wrote Gramsci, 'can only be expressed today in a military *coup d'état* and the attempt to impose an iron nationalist dictatorship which will drive the brutalised Italian masses to revive the economy by sacking neighboring countries sword in hand.'[175] In this optic, the Biennio Rosso could be seen as a popular uprising which wound up in a fascist dictatorship. Contemporary examples are not hard to find. For instance, the trajectory of Egypt's two years of uprising, from 2011 to 2013, has been researched in this light.[176]

As always, a historicist (in this case meaning open-ended and dialectical) analysis, is Janus-faced. On the one hand, there is the danger of *coups* and formlessness. On the other hand, there is the possibility of progressive outcomes. Gramsci does not, it must be emphasized, succumb to a Jacobin or vanguardist criticism. He writes that we should *not* expect 'movements of revolt' such as the Vespers to be 'one hundred per cent conscious' or 'governed by plans worked out in advance to the last detail or in line with abstract theory', as 'reality produces a wealth of the most bizarre combinations [i.e. of spontaneity and planning]', which the theorist must 'unravel' in order not to press reality into 'abstract schema' but to '"translate" into theoretical language the elements of historical life'.[177] These last points are famous but rarely linked to the discussion of popular uprisings. Cleaving purely to abstract schema and refusing the elements of popular autonomy, writes Gramsci, insists on what 'will never happen', a point which implies that 'this conception is nothing but an expression of passivity'.[178] Gramsci here, in highly original fashion, links back the ways in which theories that fetishize either spontaneity or planning are in fact 'expressions of passivity'; they are not the expressions of a transformative, dialectical worldview. Most thinkers tend to link both positions (spontaneity/planning) to either voluntarism or agency. Instead, Gramsci's distinctive worldview associates these perspectives with passivity. It is easier to grasp here, then, the fact that the refusal of the extremes of spontaneity and planning in Gramsci's work are keyed fundamentally into Gramsci's insistence that the point is not just to

The Wellsprings of Autonomy

interpret but to change—the implication being that interpretations which themselves do not fertilize transformative activity are flawed.

Gramsci's writings on a year of European uprisings—1848-1849—deepen the analysis. In a discussion of particular aspects of the relation 'passive revolution / war of position' in the Italian Risorgimento, Gramsci writes that 'the regular, organic, traditional etc. political parties . . . at the moment of action (1848) revealed themselves inept or almost so, and . . . in 1848-49 were overtaken by the popular Mazzinian-democratic tidal wave'.[179] Gramsci explains that Mazzini was obsessed with the imperative necessity of a 'popular armed insurrection'.[180] Here, then, born of the ineptitude of the existing political parties, was a war of manoeuvre: as Gramsci writes, 'Cavour is the exponent of the passive revolution / war of position and Mazzini of popular initiative / war of manoeuvre.'[181] While the popular uprising need not be unarmed, Mazzini's war of manoeuvre was, nonetheless, lacking in various respects—as Mazzini was not a 'realistic politician' but a 'visionary apostle'.[182] Mazzini's insurrection 'was not preceded by long ideological and political preparation, organically devised in advance to reawaken popular passions and enable them to be concentrated and brought simultaneously to detonation point'.[183] Moreover, it lacked technical organization. Gramsci faults Mazzini for not organizing—and not wishing to organize— 'recruitment centres for an organic levy', which put him in conflict with Garibaldi (in 1859-60) and was 'the reason for his ineffectiveness in Milan'.[184]

These criticisms of Mazzini aside, Gramsci nonetheless granted the insurrection some effectivity: 'This tidal wave was chaotic, formless, "extempore" so to speak, but it nonetheless, under an improvised leadership (or nearly so—at any rate not one formed beforehand . . .) obtained successes which were indubitably greater than those obtained by the Moderates: the Roman Republic and Venice showed a very notable strength of resistance. In the period after '48 the relation between the two forces—the regular and the 'charismatic'—became organized around Cavour and Garibaldi and produced the greatest results (although these results were later confiscated by Cavour).'[185]

Gramsci's main point is to underline the ways in which Mazzini's forces were to succumb to the more detailed organizing of Cavour's war of position / passive revolution: '[A]lthough the course of events in the Risorgimento revealed the enormous importance of the "demagogic" mass movement, with its leaders thrown up by chance, improvised, etc., it was nevertheless in actual fact taken over by the traditional organic forces—in other words, by the parties of long standing, with rationally-formed leaders, etc.'[186] Gramsci found this to be quite widespread: 'identical results occurred in all similar political events. (Examples of this are the preponderance of the Orleanists over the radical-democratic popular forces in France in 1830; and, ultimately, the French Revolution of 1789 too—in which Napoleon represents in the last analysis the triumph of the organic bourgeois forces over the Jacobin petit-bourgeois forces).'[187] Gramsci's conclusion was that 'the absence among the radical-popular forces of any awareness of the role of the other side prevented them from being fully aware of their own role either; hence from weighing in the final balance of forces in proportion to their effective power of intervention; and hence from determining a more advanced result, on more progressive and modern lines'.[188]

Gramsci's writings on the crisis of authority echo these themes. The situation is indeterminate. There are progressive possibilities as the established order is shaken, but there are considerable dangers. On the one side, there are the dangers of military coups, Caesarism, adventurers, charismatic leaders. On the other hand, there is the danger that bureaucratic and military or religious-institutional powers will be reinforced, when public opinion radically fluctuates and systems of political representation and authority collapse. The ruling class, furthermore, Gramsci reminds us, has considerable resources and organizational capacity to manage the process, to retain power—even while making demagogic promises—and to reorganize, regroup, and eventually repress the newly activated subaltern social groups.

Chodor gives the example of the Caracazo in Venezuela—the anti-IMF, anti-austerity popular protest and crowd actions of February to March 1989, which were crushed by a massacre.[189] Ruling powers—including powers of repression—may be multiplied where dominant groups can acquire the support, in exchange for clientelist services, of international patrons. One might also think of Egypt after 2013, Bahrain in 2011 (in relation to Saudi Arabia), and Syria after 2015 (in relation to Russia).

Popular insurrectionary activity has a vast disruptive capacity. Part of the strategic strength of popular self-activity—often forgotten in vanguardism—is its very formlessness: it has 'no constant formation', just as 'water has no constant shape', and thus 'undercover espionage cannot find out anything, intelligence cannot form a strategy.'[190] But there are weaknesses too. Those who are suddenly activated may have unrealistic expectations (for instance as to economic gain) and are thus quickly disillusioned and disappointed when the millennium does not come. Furthermore, it is hard to keep reliving the dawn, the effervescence, the great feelings of communitas at work in the liminal subphase of coming together. These feelings subside over time because they are a product of the very process of formation, of the exit from domination, the immediate conquest of autonomy. They are by definition evanescent. This does not make them dispensable. It does mean that the energies of those who have gone through them will start, after a time, to subside or be redirected towards a search for a further development. Popular insurrection, indeed, requires intensive energies which can dissipate. After 1920, for instance: '[T]he unprecedented political energy that had sustained workers through their heroic actions over many months became rapidly dissipated.'[191]

Energies can run white hot and then dissipate, especially in the face of a grinding incarceration, torture, and repression over an extended period. In the case of the first Palestinian *intifada*, one of the longest running popular uprisings of modern times, many argue that the repressive Israeli response served initially to intensify and spread the process of popular mobilization. But eventually, even though it was sustained by a great depth of organization, the *intifada* was worn down by incarceration, beatings, and heavy personal costs, which fed into a pattern whereby solidarity started to break down.

The 'spirit of cleavage', moreover, is a blunt tool, and can lead to division between the different groups and classes involved. Popular uprisings may suffer from 'geographical dispersal'.[192] Autonomy, especially where street battles with security forces are involved, may be constructed in heroic, masculinist forms which are disabling for the wider unity of the movement, above all regarding gender and sexuality. There is also the fact that good sense is not a developed ideological conception of the world and can thus only organize the unification of theory and practice at a certain basic level and may not be widely diffused among all the newly active subaltern social groups. Popular revolt could even be 'mobilized in the direction of reactionary populism'.[193]

What, though, is the key to these forms of weakness? At one level, Gramscians are right to point to the ways in which Gramsci criticized spontaneity, lack of leadership, and lack of strategic direction.[194] There is a danger, however, that this can be interpreted in too vanguardist a way. Gramsci clearly recognizes the power of popular revolt. He valorizes the expression of subaltern autonomy. He grasps the powerful changes in social being and consciousness that popular insurrection can bring about. What is lacking? Certainly, strategic direction, but does this mean the lack of an all-seeing leader? Certainly not, as Gramsci criticizes sole leadership, charismatic delivers, and Caesarists of all stripes. Does it mean the lack of a fully developed plan and ideology? Not quite. As we have already seen, the popular insurrection involves bizarre combinations, and it is from such combinations that it draws social force and constitutes 'historical life'. Does it mean the lack of a large, bureaucratic organization? Not so, given the swingeing critique of such organizations and the partial valorization of self-organization. Above all, the problem identified by Gramsci has to do with the lack of consent (*consenso*). It is arguably *consenso* and the concomitant forms of conception and collective will that are lacking—or often lacking—and that constitute the main danger in the popular insurrection.

We can trace key aspects of this in Gramsci's discussions of crisis, Rosa Luxemburg, 1905, and Cadornism. In politics, writes Gramsci, in a critique of Luxemburg's over-valorization of spontaneity and economic causes in the insurrection of 1905, a major economic 'crisis cannot give the attacking forces the ability to organize with lightning speed in time and in space; still less can it endow them with fighting spirit. Similarly, the defenders are not demoralised, nor do they abandon their positions, even among the ruins, nor do they lose faith in their own strength or their own future.'[195] To assume that a crisis can endow the attacking forces with such things is to be guilty of 'political Cadornism'. Luigi Cadorna (d. 1928) was an Italian commander-in-chief at the famous defeat of Caporetto in 1917, for which he was held responsible. Cadorna 'was taken by Gramsci as the symbol of the authoritarian leader who makes no attempt to win the "consent" of those he is leading'.[196] In short, an economic crisis is not enough: what is also required, to head off dangers, is the organic formulation of popular consent over a longer temporality.[197]

Chodor captures the key point when he discusses more recent anarchist expressions in relation to the critique of post-hegemony and Hardt and Negri's concept of the multitude. It is no good, argues Chodor, to proclaim the death of ideology or celebrate the explosive nature of the multitude without offering 'a theory of politics that would enable this multitude to become a collective political actor'.[198] Without consent (and its underpinnings in conceptions and a collective will), the unity of the revolutionary bloc is constantly threatened, above all after initial gains are made, as there are forms of power to wield and 'spoils' to fight over. Recall the discussion above of the limits of myth in the construction of the collective will. It is the construction of consent, arguably, that enables a diverse rebellious formation to become a collective political actor, and it is this that is lacking in the popular insurrection. The implication is that a popular insurrection requires a subsequent—or a prior—phase of consent formation to give it direction.

Spontaneous revolts, the 'synthetic explosion', should not be neglected nor despised—nor glorified. Gramsci is neither a spontaneist nor given over to planning in this regard. He grasps the explosive power of the popular drive for autonomy, but he situates insurrections and evaluates them above all by reference to a broader passage from subordination to revolution.

THE BIRTH OF NEW PARTIES OF THE DOMINANT GROUPS

Gramsci includes as an important phase in the history of subaltern social groups 'the birth of new parties of the dominant groups to maintain the consent of the subaltern social groups and to keep them under control'.[199] Gramsci situates this phase as transpiring after the phase of passive and active adherence. The implication seems to be that such parties emerge when consent and control are starting to fail. In other words, there are challenges to the existing order and forms of popular self-activity which no longer conform to the grooves of objective formation, remnants of traditional ideology, or passive and active adherence. Here ruling groups start to organize in new ways in order to control and contain such challenges or to shore up forms of consent which are fraying. This dynamic is a major challenge in the phase of popular self-activity. Perhaps it is reasonable to link

The Wellsprings of Autonomy

such new parties to what Gramsci called the 'incessant and persistent efforts' by 'political forces which are struggling to conserve and defend the existing structure itself'.[200] If so, we can understand why this phase of ruling reorganization is so important for popular mobilization: because as Gramsci writes, 'it is upon this [conjunctural] terrain that the forces of opposition organize'.[201] The concept here is that an organic crisis is starting to appear—rather than just a more conjunctural and immediately rectifiable form of injustice and disunity. It is not that a single hoarder can be brought to book or that a greedy foreman can be removed from his position but that a whole new terrain has come into being—both over time, and to awareness—in which individual hoarders or exploitative foremen, for instance, are part of a new kind of arrangement of production and accumulation, a new kind of political economy. As Gramsci avers, in such a situation, the dominant classes do not simply give up or immediately lose heart. Instead, they seek to develop all the forms of life that are possible within the framework of the old—a process which includes reworking the conjunctural terrain (in civil and political society, in culture, and even in the economy and the international relation of forces) on which the forces of opposition inevitably have to fight.

The birth of new parties is one instance of this. Such parties are Janus-faced. They are a recognition that something is up, that the old parties and forms of control and consent are inadequate. They signal a certain disquiet among ruling groups. Certainly Bayat reminds us of the panic and opposition unleashed among ruling and conservative groups in Egypt in the face of the various manifestations of autonomous organizing, counterculture, and system rejection.[202] But these parties are also a real way in which new forms of popular mobilization can be contained (and even harnessed), as the new parties are designed to win consent and are thus not just controlling but potentially attractive. Good sense, the spirit of cleavage, and myth can be rearticulated in a reactionary and populist way. New parties can capture this, inducing a regression of such elements in the direction of common sense and subversivism.

Gramsci saw much of this last rearticulation in the 'nomadic' politics of the subversivist Mussolini. A contemporary example could be the emergence of populist, racist, and xenophobic (anti-immigrant) parties in Germany since the 2000s. Belina's analysis puts the accent on a changing political economy: there is a domestic situation in which wages are not keeping pace with productivity and an international situation in which Southern European countries are pushing back against the terms of their integration into a German-led system of financial and trade. Such a context is latent with potential challenge; old forms of passive and active adherence are not operative, and elements within ruling groups are seeking to shore up a changing structure. Belina argues that these populist parties emerge as solutions to a crisis of capitalist accumulation 'within the existing politico-economic order and under the leadership of the state'.[203]

ORGANIC INTELLECTUALS

Arguably, the lead note in popular self-activity regarding intellectuals is educating the educator. The irruption of new forces, self-organization in structure and superstructure, the emergence of good sense, and the changes in social being and social consciousness associated with the formation of new forms of solidarity and collectivity together make up a profound historical and political dynamic and a deep education for organic intellectuals. As Boggs has it, 'Thinking along much the same lines as Rosa Luxemburg, he [Gramsci] assumed that the initiative for revolutionary politics would have to grow out of popular self-activity, with leaders being no more than the "chorus" of the masses.'[204] Intellectuals discover new things: Marx regarding the Silesian weavers in the 1840s and the Commune in the 1870s; Trotsky, Lenin, and Luxemburg in relation to the Russian uprising of 1905.[205] Gramsci, Lukács, and others in relation to 1918–1920.

Traditional intellectuals, in the phase of popular self-activity, are shunted aside. At stake in the phase of popular self-activity is not a politics of representation (where intellectuals depict symbolically or leaders represent politically). Instead, there is a politics of presentation—in which new forces become present and bodies and forms of social being and newly forged elements of social consciousness impose themselves. It is not a politics of seeking inclusion, of expanding and making more inclusive an existing terrain, but a politics of creating a new terrain. It is not a politics of seeking respect and recognition, but of forging new kinds of self-respect. In Fanon, the anti-colonial protagonists do not seek to persuade Europe of their humanity, they seek to reconstruct their own humanity, to purge it of decades of oppression through violent revolution against the colonizer. This politics shunts aside traditional representatives of all kinds and demands to make new ones, reconstructing the forms and lines of authority and forging new kinds of organic intellectuals. Gramsci refers to 'the conditions under which a subordinate or rising class could generate its *own* intellectual stratum on the basis of its own self-activity'.[206]

For intellectuals, the humbling act of being educated can pave the way for the traps of autonom*ism*. The organic intellectuals of the phase of popular self-activity must not fall into the trap of fetishizing and romanticizing the spontaneity, the spirit of cleavage, the politics of presentation, the absence of representation, the self-activity, and autonomy that are so marked during this phase. This is Gramsci's critique of Sorel, Bergson, and others. This trap is especially open because the new forces, freshly aware of their newfound capacity, place all the emphasis on direct action, on the propaganda of the deed, and on doing not thinking: on transformation and not philosophy. Good sense is a powerful repudiator of the anachronistic schemes and ideologies of intellectuals. Nonetheless, those who succumb to this siren song will paradoxically end up playing the role of traditional intellectual, unless they are to resist this anti-intellectualism, as they hypostatize the conditions of a particular historical phase and turn its dynamics into an all-encompassing, deductive, purely continuous (timeless) theory. They fail, amid the need to defend the key value of the movement against its many detractors, to pose many of the vital and discriminating questions that will continue to foster dialectical unification. Indeed, while the intellectual during the phase of popular self-activity is above all educated, that intellectual continues (inevitably) to exist in the other phases and, in those other phases and via that wider history, will think back to popular self-activity and inform it, by making 'the conception implicit in human activity' explicit and by helping to develop 'a coherent and systematic ever-present awareness and a precise and decisive will'.[207]

Eventually, Gramsci argues, anarchism was politically underdeveloped. Its scorn for party politics, its total embrace of direct action, its inability (in the case of syndicalism) to see beyond the horizon of industrial struggle made it politically unstable. Indeed, as the editors of the critical edition of

The Wellsprings of Autonomy

Prison Notebook 25 remind us: the ranks of anarchists and syndicalists produced 'many nationalists and interventionists during the years leading to World War I, and quite a number of militant fascists in the post-war period'.[208] Indeed, some Southernists, erstwhile or actual Leftists, saw Italy as a 'great proletarian nation' teeming with emigrants needing land. They were in strong support of Italy's genocidal settler colonial project, a 'fourth shore' in Ottoman Tripolitania and Cyrenaica, what was to become Libya in 1951.[209] Colonialism, in these optics, was rewritten as a form of *opposition* to capitalism and plutocracy. Gramsci may not have grappled very much with popular mobilization in North Africa, and he read imperialism in terms of the placement of capital, especially to press a critique of Italian 'settlement colonies',[210] but his Southern Question and his national-popular were sharply opposed to any proletarian Southernism. The latter required the naturalization of profoundly oppressive racial and civilizational hierarchies, which Gramsci criticized. This is not to say that there is any necessary link between anarchism, syndicalism, and fascism and imperialism; but it is to underline the dangers of instability, indeterminacy, and shape-shifting attendant on theories purporting to reject politics. Grandiose rejections of politics may serve in some phases far more than in others, and they by definition can take on a great many different meanings.

Anarchists recognize problems besetting the autonomous phase. Graeber writes, 'Temporary bubbles of autonomy must gradually turn into permanent, free communities.' But, as he writes, isolation is not possible. Social relations are necessary, which generates vast problems: how much compromise is acceptable? 'For direct action-based groups, even working in alliance with radical NGOs or labor unions has often created what seem like insuperable problems.'[211]

The autonomist, revolutionary idea involves multiplying the spaces and bubbles of autonomy until the old order is so peppered with holes that it collapses, making way for the new. Gramsci came to realize the limits of such a strategy: how to coordinate the different bubbles of autonomy; how to deal with their internal forms of tension and leadership; how to ensure that different forms of autonomy are not working at cross-purposes; how to ensure that small bubbles of autonomy could acquire collective force and avoid encirclement and suppression by the powers of the state, capital, imperialism, and the ruling class; and, above all, how to develop the meaning and purpose of autonomy itself—which by definition loses its attraction the more the existing order collapses and the autonomous forces become the new leading forces.

Autonomists eschew the idea of a vanguard, of persuading others, of building up consent, which would imply some higher knowledge or leadership, with all the freight of authoritarianism and vanguardism that must be shunned. But anarchists do aim to set an example which others can imitate. The problem then becomes how to make others aware, given that '[w]hat participants experience as profound and transformative often looks, from the outside, as peculiar at best—at worst cult-like or insane'.[212] Graeber, perhaps true to his beliefs, does not offer explicit solutions to these autonomist dilemmas.

CONCLUSION

This Gramscian theory of popular mobilization valorizes the profound and transformative experiences associated with the wellsprings of autonomy. Gramsci cannot be read as dismissive of spontaneity. He does not dismiss the drive for autonomy as a 'youthful error'; in fact he valorizes rejuvenation, and he continuously repudiates any threatened regression towards middle-class reformism. For instance, his group seceded from the PSI, criticizing it for dismissing spontaneity, for 'failing to appreciate the *developmental* potential of "primitive" rebellion—e.g., populism, urban insurrection, utopianism, cultural revolt'.[213] He upheld the spontaneity of worker actions during the Biennio Rosso—aiming to show that the grievances were genuine and mobilization was not concocted by outside agitators. Moreover, Gramsci's early readings of the Bolshevik revolution defended it against the charge of Jacobinism, with its negative connotation of a minority seizure of power.[214] He depicted 1917 as a 'popular transformation based primarily in the local democratic organs (soviets, factory committees), with the party furnishing the essential coordination and strategic direction'.[215] He valorized the 'recovery of the subjective dimension, popular self-activity, democratisation'.[216] Gramsci, as we have seen throughout the chapter, saw the positive, indeed essential, aspects of popular self-activity. Gramsci's thinking here should not be dismissed as 'idealism' or 'voluntarism', but keyed into his valorization of a particular phase.

One should not miss how the subsequent travel, reading, and appropriation of Gramsci's thinking on popular self-activity has also followed an historical and political trajectory—that is, it has responded to specific contexts and phases of struggle. For instance, at certain periods 'Gramsci as builder of the Workers' Councils in Turin in 1919-20' has clearly been valorized. This was indeed the Gramsci of Alfred Rosmer, Pierre Monatte, Pierre Naville, and Alfonso Leonetti in France in the 1950s, who advanced a far-reaching critique of the fetishization of the Communist Party, at least in its Stalinist form.[217]

Nonetheless, the argument here is that the problem of building *consent* cannot be overcome within an autonomist framework. The establishment of a permanent, free community, the emancipation of the subaltern social groups, needs to progress beyond the phase of autonomy and popular self-activity. It needs to tackle head on problems of *consenso* and *direzione*—which are profoundly intertwined with hegemony. The lesson is vital in the present: however much Bayat, for example, positively evaluates new forms of autonomy and revolutionary life after 2011, he eventually makes some significant caveats. He makes clear that though these movements 'may form a new subjectivity', 'they still leave the *political question*—that is, a meaningful overhaul of the state institutions, ideology, and power block—unresolved. This crucial problem in current revolutionary movements remains to be tackled.'[218]

Gramsci reads anarchism against itself, counter-intuitively enough, by taking it seriously as an ideology that is intertwined with activism. He writes that '[t]he presence of a rudimentary element of conscious leadership, of discipline in every "spontaneous" movement is indirectly demonstrated by the fact that there exist currents and groups who uphold spontaneity as a method'.[219]

For Gramsci, then, protagonists of autonomy, of popular self-activity, contained those self-reflexive elements who start to see autonomy not just as a practice but also as a theory, a principled method to follow as against other principles (such as vanguardism or bourgeois electoralism). For Gramsci, the implication is that the very precepts of autonomism and spontaneism are thereby contradicted. This is because there are those in these very movements who uphold certain principles as against others (on the basis of an ideological elaboration); who impose discipline on this basis; or who seek to gather consent, engaging with civil society (e.g. in publishing), winning allies, or overcoming enemies. Such persons, for instance, might represent their views in a tract or publication or implement them in the rules of a popular assembly. As such, they are, by definition, engaged in the very politics of defending a particular representation of the world against others—a practice that they typically claim to refuse as the preserve of verticalists, leaders, and programmatic intellectuals. Indeed, the theory and practice of autonomy are always imbricated and situated within larger debates. There is no abstract universal space beyond such determinations. Thus, autonomists necessarily go beyond the very principles that they uphold; they go beyond autonomy in the very formulation and promotion of autonomism; they engage thereby not just in *autonomia* but in *direzione* and *consenso*. For those purists who never promote, publish, or persuade—who simply do—the Gramscian critique is that they will forfeit the levers required to acquire the popular force to enlarge their bubble.

Direct action, the politics of presentation, and the emphasis on deeds not words that suffuses the wellsprings of autonomy in the Gramscian theory put forward here is a vital phase, but it will be sublated. As Gramsci writes: 'The insistence on the element of "practice" in the theory-praxis nexus— after having not just distinguished but disconnected and separated the two elements (which is, in fact, just a mechanical and conventional operation)— means that one is going through a relatively primitive historical phase; it is still an economic-corporative phase in which the general "structural" framework is transformed and an adequate quality-superstructure is beginning to emerge but is not yet organically formed.'[220]

There is here a dialectical valorization of the turn to practice and the deed, but also a recognition of its limitations: namely, the failure to tackle consent and leadership, the forms of which are part and parcel of the old framework, which has not yet been overcome. There is a need for the development of a new phase beyond practice, which must undergo a fresh unification with theory, via further theoretical development. The denigration of theory fatally underestimates the fact that there *will be* disagreements as to how to organize, change, and engage as well as meaningful, sharp, and ongoing disagreements over interpretation and meaning itself. Consensus may not be achievable, and the attempt to achieve it may prove exhausting, if not fatal. One cannot then strive only for consensus, nor can one, in the major alternative, fetishize any 'ethic of dissensus'; agreements will have to be forged. But the whole process for achieving this needs to be scrutinized theoretically and taken into account. Autonomism, here, is lacking.

Autonomy is marked by fundamental forms of rehumanization; a discovering of immanent connections; an unfreezing of the dialectic, with dramatic forms of antithesis and negation; a birth of new forms of being posed against older forms of non-being; and a return of the subject and subjectivity as against objective formation.[221] The autonomous phase also involves the sense that a new unity of theory and practice is close at hand: a new world can be made and seized. For Gramsci, the reorganization entailed in the factory councils involved a 'spontaneous unity between theory and practice'.[222] This unification was based on a newly found 'freedom of initiative in industrial and agricultural production.'[223] Here we have a highly constructive use of the term 'spontaneous'. This, for Gramsci, was the great promise of the phase of popular self-activity. A way of registering its high effervescence. The meaning of its new dawn, its passionate spirit of renewal, its glimpse of liberation.

Hegel, from whom Gramsci took much, offers what can be read as a philosophical description of the phase of popular self-activity in his *Science of Logic*: 'In its first manifestation, a new creation usually behaves towards the entrenched systematisation of the earlier principle with fanatical hostility; in fear of losing itself in the expansion of the particular, it also shuns the labor that goes with scientific cultivation and, nevertheless in need of it, it grasps at first at an empty formalism. The demand for the elaboration and cultivation of the material becomes at that point all the more pressing.'[224]

Just as abstract particularity is overcome, as the subaltern phase is transcended, and autonomy established, just then a feeling of anxious defence takes over. The protagonists of popular self-activity, under attack from those who expand their categories of the particular to include what has just taken place (e.g. crowd actions, not just categories of persons, are condemned as irrational and violent). In response, they start to grasp at an empty formalism—that is, the consecration and formalization in hypostasized theory only of the autonomous activities in which they have just been

The Wellsprings of Autonomy

engaged. At the level of social consciousness, empty formalism (for instance, name calling in identity politics, the 'spirit of cleavage') risks a defensive relapse into the very genus-thinking that may have recently been partially transcended. It involves a shunning of the organic intellectual activity that goes with the development of good sense into ideology and the philosophy of praxis. Amid these aporias, we can certainly say with Hegel that just then the cultivation of the material (the development of consent and leadership) becomes all the more pressing.

The weaknesses and problems with the phase of popular self-activity do not mean that the whole phase should be discarded. This is too abstract and theoretical a move. It does not do justice to the value and indispensability of this lived history and its dialectics. This is a particularly hard lesson for the binary thinker or the logico-deductive thinker (i.e. the traditional rather than the organic intellectual) to learn. The latter remains embedded in the struggle. They do not ultimately choose from a menu of options like a consumer in a supermarket or a detached individual subject. The organic intellectual engages with life-activity in all its contradictions, acting through them and travelling with the movement. The constructive element is captured by Boggs. Even if the dialectically intertwined ideological and organizational problems 'were not soluble in the context of the Biennio Rosso, [they] yielded some important lessons for the future'.[225]

CHAPTER FIVE

The Expansive Search for Consent

Gramsci writes of a late phase in the history of subaltern social groups involving the 'formations that assert complete autonomy'.[1] The editors of the *Prison Notebooks* suggest that this is a reference to the Communist Party.[2] The party would surely have been among these formations, but given that a very broad reference to 'formation' (rather than, for instance, to 'organization' or 'party') is used and rendered in the plural, there is a provisional warrant to think beyond the Communist Party. The word 'assert' (rather than realize, for example) also suggests a phase prior to the culminating phases of the revolution. In 1924, Gramsci wrote, 'the phase we are passing through is not that of a direct struggle for power, but rather a preparatory phase, of transition to the struggle for power: in short, a phase of agitation, propaganda, and organization.'[3]

In Italy, the great uprisings of the Biennio Rosso had subsided, fascist power was on the rise, and communists realized that their journey to revolution was longer and harder than expected. Gramsci himself was no longer an ex-student journalist, critic, and organizer among a group of radical defectors from the Italian Socialist Party. He was in the top leadership of the newly founded (1921) Communist Party of Italy and of the Third International (the Comintern) with its core in the Soviet Union. In the new phase, the limits of the previous struggles were more clearly identified, while their potential and strengths were to be incorporated within new forms of concrete synthesis. Whereas in popular self-activity, autonomy (*autonomia*) is in the lead, the argument here is that there is a qualitatively distinct phase in which the search for consent (*consenso*) is central.

We discover in this phase the distinctions between autonomy within the old framework and assertions of integral autonomy; between the spontaneous and the in-depth unification of theory and practice; between group and class on the one hand and social bloc formation on the other; between the spirit of cleavage and the extended effort to construct; between counterculture and moral and intellectual reform; between *counter*hegemony and the struggle to hegemonize; between myth/good sense (and the struggle to draw good sense from common sense) on the one side and political ideology (and ideological competition) on the other; between the break of dawn and long preparation; between 'heroic' confrontation and underground warfare; between self-organization and extended organization in parties and civil society; between locality and wider spatial horizons; between the here and now and longer temporalities; between direct and indirect action; between the economic-corporate and the ethico-political; and between forceful, diffuse, and upwelling forces and an increasingly focused and strategic intervention. After a discovery of practice and the deed, a return to theory. After political will infused with impulse and generic voluntarism, political will as 'well thought-out conviction'.[4] After presentation (appearing, speaking *with*), representation (depicting culturally, speaking *for* politically).

BUILDING THE COLLECTIVE WILL

The emphasis is on 'conscious leadership' (*direzione consapevole*)[5] and its many dangers and problems and on the 'active and constructive' phase in the development of the collective will. At stake: 'the degree of ideological preparation, organizational cohesion and social unity ("homogeneity") of a revolutionary movement'.[6] Consent-winning chips away at the dominant hegemony, while developing a 'political hegemony' before taking governmental power.[7] Political ideologies compete, while one tends to prevail in the special hegemonic sense of making its assumptions and concepts apparently universal—that is, by achieving their internalization across the whole political field.[8] This can only be done through organization and therefore implicates (organic) intellectual and leaders, who both construct new forms of economy and do battle on the terrain of civil society and the integral state.[9] Such political development is important to prevent the danger posed when autonomists, demoralized and disappointed by the lack of force and success, drift away, perhaps eventually getting a regular job or moving to the suburbs.[10] It can also weigh against another danger: that posed by reactionary movements and coups d'état brewing in response to new assertions by subaltern social groups, popular uprisings, economic crisis, and the 'enfeeblement of the government'.[11]

The phase 'cultivates', draws on, is pushed forward by, grows out of, and eventually determinately negates popular self-activity. It is achieved *through*, and not in any simple way against, autonomy. It involves not disdain for but engagement with and in 'spontaneity' to connect to a wider political force. The motive force to generate a wider politics comes as much from within autonomous mobilization as from without, as newly minted leaderships seek to protect gains or translate them into wider fields, as popular and democratic capacities and ambitions expand, and as an understanding develops that strategies and tactics must adapt.[12]

The search for consent poses many hard questions: How to scale up and complexify—socially, politically, ideologically, spatially, and so on—without losing touch with popular elements and forces? How to avoid unacceptable compromises and the slide into reformism? How to organize without becoming authoritarian and remaining democratic? How to 'speak for' without speaking over? If there is a party to be organized, then what kind of party is in view? What is meant by the modern—or postmodern—Prince? Is there a parliamentary road in popular mobilization—and how does one engage with the extended state more generally? What is meant by popular education or by intellectual and moral reform, and how do these processes avoid elitism? Isn't the 'war of position'—the strategic centrepiece of the struggle for consent—with its heavy reliance on civil society, a fundamentally West-centric conception? How, practically, is social force developed in the face of asymmetries of power, opposition, and repression? All these questions resolve into one major question about whether it is possible to conceive of and practice a struggle for consent which is organic, democratic, revolutionary, and popular.

THE NEED FOR THEORETICAL RENEWAL

Not widely appreciated is Gramsci's still highly relevant argument that a new theory is required to answer these questions—nothing less than a development in the philosophy of praxis, beyond materialism and determinism. Mechanical determinism, Gramsci argues, can serve in the subaltern phase as a force of moral resistance and perseverance.

The Expansive Search for Consent

But when the subaltern becomes leader and is in charge, the mechanistic conception will sooner or later represent an imminent danger and there will be a revision of a whole mode of thinking because the mode of existence will have changed. The reach and ascendancy of the 'force of circumstance' will diminish. Why? Basically, because the 'subaltern' who yesterday was a 'thing' is now no longer a 'thing' but a 'historical person'; whereas yesterday he was not responsible because he was 'resisting' an extraneous will, he is now responsible, no longer a 'resister' but an active agent.[13]

Gramsci develops the sentences that follow the above paragraph more thoroughly and forcefully in a later notebook:

Although mechanical determinism [classical Marxism] is explainable as a naïve philosophy of the mass and, in this respect alone, an intrinsic element of strength, once it is accepted by intellectuals as a coherent and well-thought-out philosophy it becomes a cause of passivity, of stupid self-sufficiency—and this happens without any expectation that the subaltern will be a leader and director. There is always a segment of the mass, including the subaltern mass, that is in a position of leadership and responsibility, and the philosophy of that segment always precedes the philosophy of the whole, not only as a theoretical anticipation but as an actual necessity.[14]

Gramsci is making a powerful point about the development of the philosophy of praxis—that is, of 'an adequate quality superstructure'—beyond materialism and determinism. He is making the point that subaltern social groups will be present and contributing, both theoretically and practically, as part and parcel of their own collective transformation, imparting (new) meaning to the direction of change along the way. His is also making clear that the phase of conscious leadership builds very directly on popular self-activity. This is because the latter phase brings such leaders into being: certain persons find themselves in positions of responsibility and find themselves answerable to a group—in self-organization, in counterculture (even against every rejectionist wish), in describing myth, in acting together in the popular uprising, in protecting the group against the interruptions of new parties of dominant groups, and so on.

For Gramsci, the development of this phase required not only the rejection of classical Marxism but also of its main rival on the Left, theories of anarchism and syndicalism. Gramsci writes that the fundamental problem with 'theoretical syndicalism . . . has to do with a subaltern social group [the work-ing class] that is prevented by this theory from ever becoming dominant—prevented, that is, from leaving behind the economic-corporative phase in order to advance to the phase of politico-intellectual hegemony in civil soci-ety and become dominant in political society'.[15] Contrary to what is pro-claimed, 'the independence and the autonomy of the subaltern group that it claims to give voice to are in fact sacrificed to the intellectual hegemony of the dominant group.'[16] How so? '[B]ecause the transformation of the subordinate group into a dominant one is excluded, either by not raising the issue at all . . . or by asserting that one can jump directly from a social system of group divi-sions to a society of perfect equality'.[17]

Anarchists respond that they are well aware of the problems of getting from bubbles of autonomy to broader systemic forms of equality but whether they have a solution is another question. Certainly, contemporary currents are increasingly seeing the need to get beyond horizontalism or the eschewal of leadership. As Nunes has it, even the most horizontal forms of activity have their nodes, their points of maximum intersection, the strategic poten-tial of which needs to be developed[18] to avoid extremes of verticalism and horizontalism.[19] There are, one must confess, forms of leadership. In a Gramscian—and indeed in a powerful feminist—perspective, the more problematic position is not to admit this and to allow informal and unspoken elements (including race, class, gender and so on) to determine the course of events, bringing about the 'tyranny of structurelessness'.[20]

Gramscians have detected similar theoretical shifts in the past. For example, Sanbonmatsu notes that Marcuse's initial positive valorization of the autonomist 1960s turned to a more cautious attitude, evoking the dan-gers in expressivism. Marcuse started to sound 'a great deal like Antonio Gramsci', in searching for leadership in political education, to "translate" spontaneous protest into organized action, transcending immediate needs and aspirations, and aiming at broader radical reconstruction.[21]

AN ORGANIC FORMULATION

In the living Gramscian tradition, the search is on for an organic formula-tion. The interpretive criterion in the struggle for consent is the need for a 'unity between "spontaneity" and "conscious leadership" or "discipline" [which] is precisely the real political action of the subaltern classes, in so far as this is mass politics [i.e. popular mobilization] and not merely an adventure by groups claiming to represent the masses [i.e. populism]'.[22] It is a question of maintaining—against many odds—an organic connection to subaltern social groups; keeping one's feet on the ground, not closing off the organic passage into the new social force; cultivating the material currents and energies imparted by popular self-activity, partial subaltern formations, and contradictory consciousness; fortifying the sublation of these autonomous forms, preserving what is necessary among them while determinately negating their limits and dead ends, and overcoming abstract particularity. It is necessary to remember that the phase of consent-winning stems not from any great logical principle deduced from on high but from the discovery, in activity, in social becoming, of *both* the limitations and the potential of the phase of popular self-activity. In place of the way popular self-activity is galvanized rapidly in the crisis of authority, consent-winning arises on the slower basis of a constructive, organic formulation. Gramsci—between spontaneism and vanguardism—'sought to "democratise" the external element by giving it popular substance'.[23]

The Turin movement—that is, Gramsci's group within the PSI in November 1917—was accused by maximalists (who sought an immediate seizure of power) of being 'spontaneist', 'voluntarist', or Bergsonian. Gramsci argues that this was wrong:

> This was not an 'abstract' leadership; it did not consist in the mechanical repetition of scientific or theoretical formulas; it did not confuse politics, real action, with theoretical disquisition. It devoted itself to real people formed in specific historical relations, with specific sentiments, ways of life, fragments of world views, etc., which were the outcome of the 'spontaneous' combinations of a given environment of material production with the 'fortuitous' gathering of disparate social elements within that same environment. This element of 'spontaneity' was not neglected, much less disdained: it was *educated*, it was given a direction. . . . The leaders themselves [rightly] spoke of the 'spontaneity' of the movement . . . [T]his assertion was a stimulus, a tonic, an element of unification in depth; it was, above all, a denial that anything having to do with the movement might be reckless, fake. . . . It gave the masses a 'theoretical' consciousness of themselves as creators of historical and institutional values, as founders of states.[24]

Gramsci, we should note, far from defending any voluntarist millenarianism, is defending an organic praxis of leadership against a maximalism that sought immediate revolution. Between modern theory and the 'spontaneous' sentiments of the masses, he goes on, 'it should be possible to have a reciprocal "reduction", so to speak, a passage from one to the other, and vice versa.'[25]

THE WAR OF POSITION

The war of position is the strategic centrepiece of the struggle for consent, and one of Gramsci's most famous concepts. It is associated not with the immediate seizure of state power—typically the seizure of the means of coercion through the 'frontal assault' or 'war of manoeuvre'—but with a longer phase of preparation, typically linked to the organization of consent on a broad front, for a revolutionary project. It refers to 'the gradual, molecular process by which progressive socialist forces prepare the conditions for the conquest of power',[26] undertaking the groundwork for the unification of the subaltern social groups in the new state. The war of position is 'a long and arduous task to be carried out *before* the triumph of socialism, not after'.[27] The point 'is to conquer one after another all the agencies of civil society (e.g. the schools, the universities, the publishing houses, the mass media, the trade unions)'.[28] At stake is a 'genuine cultural confrontation with the bourgeoisie'.

Gramsci locates the war of position in terms of transformations taking place especially in Italy and France after 1870 by making an analogy to the changing art of war. He writes that

> [t]he same thing happens in the art of politics as happens in military art: war of movement increasingly becomes war of position, and it can be said that a State will win a war in so far as it prepares for it minutely and technically in peacetime. The massive structures of the modern democracies, both as State organizations, and as complexes of associations in civil society, constitute for the art of politics as it were the 'trenches' and the permanent fortifications of the front in the war of position: they render merely 'partial' the element of movement which before used to be 'the whole' of war.[29]

The war of position, therefore, is associated here very closely with 'minute' and 'technical' preparations for the frontal assault. In this sense it is *not* a simple substitute for the war of manoeuvre—but intertwined with it. Such preparations must involve activity in the state organizations as well as in civil society associations. Such activity puts the permanent fortifications—the strategic positions in civil and political society held by the existing hegemony—under siege, and then wins them, one by one, via incremental gains that eventually add up to more than the sum of their parts.

Gramsci makes the fundamental point that the war of position—unlike popular self-activity—does not stem most proximately from the crisis of authority. It becomes precisely a necessity because the crisis and the mass uprising (with its attendant popular self-activity) is insufficient. Gramsci makes this clear in his critique of Rosa Luxemburg and her overly 'economic' and 'spontaneist' understanding of 1905. Luxemburg, Gramsci writes, argues that

> [t]he immediate economic element (crises, etc.) is seen as the field artillery which in war opens a breach in the enemy's defences—a breach sufficient for one's own troops to rush in and obtain a definitive (strategic) victory. . . . [E]conomic factors . . . are held to . . . [throw the enemy] into disarray . . . causing him to lose faith in himself, his forces, and his future [and to] organize one's own troops and create the necessary cadres . . . [to organize] one's scattered forces . . . [and] in a flash they bring about the necessary ideological concentration on the common objective.[30]

Gramsci rejected this view of the uprising of 1905. He held it to suffer from 'a certain "economistic" and spontaneist prejudice' and to disregard 'the "voluntary" and organizational elements'.[31] He argued instead that 'in the case of the most advanced States, where "civil society" has become a very complex structure and one which is resistant to the catastrophic "incursions" of the immediate economic element (crises, depressions, etc.),' the 'war of manoeuvre' (here understood as a mass uprising involving a frontal assault on the state and its security forces) 'must be considered as reduced to more of a tactical than a strategic function'. Gramsci explains:

> The superstructures of civil society are like the trench systems of modern warfare. In war it would sometimes happen that a fierce artillery attack seemed to have destroyed the enemy's entire defensive system, whereas in fact it had only destroyed the outer perimeter; and at the moment of their advance and attack the assailants would find themselves confronted by a line

of defence which was still effective. The same thing happens in politics, during the great economic crises [i.e. a frontal assault, or uprising might only destroy the outer perimeter]. A crisis cannot give the attacking forces the ability to organize with lightning speed in time and in space; still less can it endow them with fighting spirit. Similarly, the defenders are not demoralised, nor do they abandon their positions, even among the ruins, nor do they lose faith in their own strength or their own future. Of course, things do not remain exactly as they were; but it is certain that one will not find the element of speed, of accelerated time, of the definitive forward march expected by the strategists of political Cadornism.[32]

The strategic function of the war of position, then, involves the ability to organize, the fighting spirit (including faith in the future), and the speed of action in time and space. The attacking forces are not granted these elements, nor the ruling groups robbed of them, simply because of an economic crisis or an uprising. Instead, these elements of strategic deployment, social force, collective will, and organizational capacity must be built up in the war of position, which in turn slowly eviscerates the strategic, ideological, and organizational depth of the existing hegemony. The war of position, then, is simultaneously organizational/practical and cultural/ideological—and cannot be reduced to politico-ideological rearticulation or, more vaguely, to a general effort to change 'the narrative'. One marks also that Gramsci developed the concept in a process of active learning from the lessons bequeathed by the insurrection of 1905 and the analyses of its organic intellectuals.

Developing the war of position strategically, writes Gramsci, 'is a question of studying "in depth" which elements of civil society correspond to the defensive systems in a war of position'.[33] In other words, strategic development means determining which elements of civil society are crucial in the defensive systems of the existing state apparatus and its ruling classes. Careful attention must also be paid 'to identifying the weakest points in that fortress against which pressure could be applied; among other things, these could be divisions or discontent within a fortress's population, inadequate supplies or flaws or shortcomings in the physical structure of the fortress or the organization of its defence.'[34]

Two further points are strategically potent. First, the strategy proceeds in increments, making specific achievable gains, quantitative additions which eventually bring about a qualitative shift. As the Gramscian Argentinian exile, Portantiero, underlined in an influential speech in Mexico in 1975: gradual and incremental changes are not necessarily reformist; cultural reform and renewal is eventually a revolutionary process; and insurgency, the frontal assault, the war of manoeuvre, has its place but it cannot be the only fulcrum around which a transformative politics turns.[35]

Second, a siege can enable a popular force that would lose in a frontal assault to wear down an enemy that has more powerful forces concentrated in a single point by encircling that enemy and cutting off their supplies (e.g. by boycott or divestment, including across national borders), eventually disabling by attrition their more powerful weapons. This does not make the war of position an easy business.[36] But it can mean that substantial asymmetries of kinetic power—in terms of technology, weaponry, and so on—can be challenged by attritional methods.

The rediscovery of democracy by the Left in many parts of the world since the 1970s—in the face of dictatorships in the Soviet Union, the Eastern Bloc, China, Latin America, and the Third World more generally, and of authoritarianism in Marxist-Leninist parties in Western Europe—has given the war of position, with its promise around consent, vital traction.[37] Interest in the possibilities of organizing in civil society was of key significance in relation to the appropriation of Gramsci in the Arab world in the 1980s and 1990s. The failure of guerrilla movements in Central America in the 1980s gave impetus to renewed interest in the war of position.[38] In Brazil in 2012, a national-level MST leader, spoke acutely of their war of position as involving 'the occupation of strategic positions within the hegemonic apparatus'.[39] In addition, feminist and queer critique, building on Gramsci's emphasis on collaboration and coalition rather than the 'immediate thrust for power',[40] has challenged the forms of hypermasculinism that can entangle the 'frontal assault'. The war of position has been thought not only in relation to domestic but also anti-colonial struggles. For example, a war of position has also been seen as relevant for the long temporality of China's independence struggle, which was in many ways at the same time a war of manoeuvre, against the fascist Japanese occupation.[41]

One of the great popular movements in the Americas in the 1990s was the EZLN, the Zapatistas under Subcomandante Marcos in Chiapas, Mexico.

Gramscians have understood the EZLN's primary strategy as a war of position. Some have given a strong affirmation of its effectivity as a revolutionary strategy, notably in part in relation to its transnational elements. For example, Subcomandante Marcos's Zapatista 'war of position' has been contrasted positively with the military focus of the Marxist-Leninist Ejercito Popular Revolucionario (EPR). The latter is a guerrilla group based in southern Mexico that has carried out attacks on military bases and oil pipelines since its emergence in 1996. Marcos emphasized language, civil society, organization (e.g. in congresses), and media strategy; engaged in alliance and bloc formation (ranging from indigenous to urban intellectuals to transnational organizations); made use of culture (such as poetry); and spoke a language of internationalism.[42] Morton explains that

> the EZLN represent a break with guerrilla movements of the past in many ways. The movement is distinct from the *foquista*-insurrection (*foco*) strategy of a small band of rebels launching a sporadic conflict of revolutionary warfare. Instead, the rebellion is a plan for a guerra *prolongada* involving the Indian population and a front in the international community. [It is a] . . . Gramscian war of position aimed at shifting the balance of forces in favour of popular and democratic movements, to penetrate and subvert the mechanisms of hegemonic diffusion on the cultural front within civil society.[43]

Morton thus concludes that the EZLN is a *counter*hegemonic force, engaging on the transnational terrain.

One of the great challenges to the war of position is state repression: 'When radical newspapers are closed, Marxist professors sacked and militant trade unionists arrested, the "war of position" must perforce grind to a halt.'[44] How to fight the war of position when the state repressive apparatuses—and their imperial backers—control civil society? How to cope with the 'escalating repression' that Kandil argues in his research on the Muslim Brotherhood's war of position in Egypt is a predictable response by the state to the emerging cultural counterhegemony attendant on the war of position.[45] Indeed, following the Muslim Brotherhood's electoral victories in 2005, the state moved to repress, and the electoral losses of 2010 proved to be a huge setback for the Muslim Brotherhood as a result.

Kandil's important article was published on the eve of the Arab uprisings of 2011, which provided an instructive, practical criticism of an important component of his argument. When the state moves to dismantle and repress terrain in civil society or in the extended state that has previously been ceded to oppositional forces, then there is a risk of provoking a crisis. Escalating repression is predictable indeed, but it can be destabilizing. There is the possibility of radicalization—that is, that those who were formerly positioned within the apparatus of consent will become more confrontational. Indeed, the Muslim Brotherhood, pushed by its youth, threw its hat in with the popular uprising two days after it began, a fact which made a significant difference on 28 January 2011, when Midan Tahrir was taken and held by the popular forces, partly thanks to the organization and numbers of the Muslim Brotherhood youth. The argument is *not* that the repression of the Muslim Brotherhood caused the uprising of 2011. The point is that it can be risky for rulers to repress gains made in the war of position as repression can provoke a switch from war of position to a more overtly confrontational stance. The general principle is the familiar one that hegemony requires some form of organized consent in civil and political society. Dismantling this terrain from above can upset the equilibrium in the balance of forces.

Is the war of position a fundamentally Eurocentric concept? Might the take-up of this theory around the globe only involve an essay in the 'coloniality of knowledge',[46] a process of Western intellectual colonization and non-Western mimicry? Gramsci made reference to the importance of the war of position in the West, as opposed to in the East, where civil society was 'primordial' and 'gelatinous'. This statement has been quoted thousands of times. He also states, at least once, that the far-reaching social transformations necessitating the war of position took place in modern states not 'backward' countries and colonies, where, he writes, 'anachronistic forms are still in vigour'.[47] This has been interpreted as a form of Eurocentrism—and some authors have suggested that the war of position is a strategy of lesser significance outside the West given the lack of a structured and independent civil society in many parts of the non-West. The implications are that Gramsci's thinking is somewhat parochial and even irrelevant to non-Western struggles. The implications also, arguably, involve smuggling in Orientalism by the back door. If strategies to win consent are irrelevant in the East/non-West, then the door is open to fundamental and still active Orientalist stereotypes about despotism and the efficacy of violence in the non-West.

It does not seem reasonable to defend Gramsci against all forms of Euro-centrism. He references the East in ways that could be misinterpreted and invokes 'anachronistic forms' in colonial settings on a questionable eviden-tial basis. Most of his examples are drawn from European history. Research and activism rooted in the non-West has come a very long way since Gram-sci's time—and Gramscian perspectives have especially developed in rela-tion to issues of race, Eurocentrism, and colonialism. Nonetheless, whatever Gramsci intended, the fact is that researchers and activists alike have made a great deal of the war of position concept in Latin America, the Middle East and North Africa, China, and beyond. Dismissing their lives and struggles as epistemologically colonized risks, not damping, but stoking the fires of the superpowered, armchair elitism of traditional intellectuals. Further, there is a surprising amount of evidence to cut against the irredeemably Eurocentric interpretation of the war of position. There is more support in Gramsci's texts for a non-binary, suitably historicized view of the concept than is generally appreciated. The main points are as follows:

First, in referring to the East, Gramsci was not referring to the Orient or the Slavic soul but to the 'Eastern front' in the European struggle for com-munism. It was a heuristic, thin, geographic, and military reference—functioning metonymically and rhetorically—with the analytical substance derived from the historicist analysis of determinate civil and political socie-ties.[48] That Russian civil society was 'primordial' and 'gelatinous'—that is, rooted in inherited rather than voluntary modes of association and merely jelly-like in relation to the overwhelming power of the state institutions—was a defensible, empirical proposition. That complex, sturdy, structures of civil society had emerged on a voluntary basis in countries like France and Italy is also defensible on a historical and non-Orientalist basis. Moreover, in Gramsci's single, but endlessly quoted reference to the East, the point of the passage is to underline that strategies need to be formed on a given *national* terrain. This is evident if one quotes the whole passage, not just an excerpt:

> [T]he fundamental task was a national one; that is to say it required a recon-naissance of the terrain and identification of the elements of trench and for-tress represented by the elements of civil society, etc. In the East the State was everything, civil society was primordial and gelatinous; in the West, there was a proper relation between State and civil society, and when the

State trembled a sturdy structure of civil society was at once revealed. The State was only an outer ditch, behind which there stood a powerful system of fortresses and earthworks: more or less numerous from one State to the next, it goes without saying—but this precisely necessitated an accurate reconnaissance of each individual country.[49]

The point here is not to make a vacuous, essentialist, detached, scholastic generalization about East and West. It seems to me that one conventional reading insists far too much on this point, reflecting more the Orientalist assumptions (inverted or not) of the readers than the actual text. Instead, the point is to think about how a revolution can be made to refine the collective will by following through with practical directives as to which parts of civil society and the state apparatuses need to be besieged and taken over through an accurate reconnaissance of the national terrain. Gramsci is insisting on this not to assert that the West is different to the East in general, but to affirm the importance of the national. Gramsci is involved here in a defence of Lenin, against Trotsky's cosmopolitanism, which occasionally lost touch with national realities, according to Gramsci.[50] The first point then, is that the references to East and West are properly understood in terms of what they imply about the importance of national terrain in deriving a strategy.

The second point is that Gramsci *does* envisage the importance of the war of position in Russia. Why else was Rosa Luxemburg's analysis of 1905 insufficient? The Russian 'revolution' of 1905 was incomplete because the war of position was lacking there—implying that the war of position is important in a country like Russia. Lenin's analysis, moreover, so appropriate and effective in Russia, also sensitized Gramsci to the long tactical and strategic struggles involved in the war of position, a point which Gramsci makes clear in his critiques of maximalism. Third, Gramsci did think, in one sense, that Russia suffered from the lack of a war of position after 1917. Here, an inspiration was Trotsky—another Russian from the 'Eastern front'—who Gramsci saw during his stay in the Soviet Union in the early 1920s. Trotsky had pointed out that difficulties arose in Russia because the rapid fall of the state power prevented a longer war of position. A longer, gruelling struggle for state power helps guarantee victory after the seizure of power.[51] Gramsci writes that: 'The [Eastern Front] had fallen at once, but unprecedented struggles had then ensued; in the case of [the Western front], the struggles would take place "beforehand". The question, therefore, was whether civil society resists before or after the attempt to seize power; where the latter takes place, etc. However, the question was outlined [by Trotsky] only in a brilliant, literary form, without directives of a practical character.'[52]

Gramsci is pointing out that even in Russia (where unprecedented struggles referred to the sacrifices of comrades in fighting and the civil war), civil society in whatever form would resist as it did after the seizure of power, absent a long war of position. Far from being in different epistemological and ontological spaces (a hallmark of Orientalism), the Eastern and Western fronts were intimately connected: not only in the Comintern or the exchange of ideas, the struggles among and between revolutionaries, but also in the connection between different revolutionary processes. Gramsci, for instance, took on Trotsky's point about how difficult the revolution would be in the West not only because of the balance between civil and political society but also because the Western bourgeoisie was 'forewarned'.

Third, it is sometimes forgotten that Gramsci *does* suggest a place for the war of position in anti-colonial struggles. The question is not only posed in the metropole or the 'West'. The point of departure here is that following conquest and occupation 'the defeated army is disarmed and dispersed, but the struggle continues on the terrain of politics and of military "preparation"'.[53] Gramsci references India and Ireland in the face of British colonialism and the Balkans in the face of the Ottoman empire. He suggests that 'India's political struggle against the British . . . knows three forms of war: war of movement, war of position, and underground warfare. Gandhi's passive resistance is a war of position, which at certain moments becomes a war of movement, and at others underground warfare.'[54] Gramsci goes on, referencing the Irish boycott of the 1880s, 'Boycotts are a form of war of position.' Here he suggests that strikes are part of a war of movement. Underground warfare involves 'the secret preparation of weapons and combat troops'.[55] The whole tenor of the surrounding discussion, including the insistence that frontal assaults are combined with the proper preparation of consent and that colonial authorities may seek to provoke underprepared attacks from the colonized in order to act swiftly to repress and decapitate them, implies that the strategic precepts of the war of position hold in a situation of anti-colonial struggle.

Fourth, it is arguable that there is no overburdening or fatal Orientalism (or nativism) in relation to the modern transformations that Gramsci mentions—they are neither celebrated nor condemned in and of themselves. He contrasts the modern forms with previous conditions where there was 'a relatively rudimentary state apparatus, and greater autonomy of civil society from State activity' as well as a 'greater autonomy of the national economies from the economic relations of the world market'.[56] He had in mind an expansion of the terrain of the political and of the extended state—accompanying the increasing growth of the state as an organization (the administration, the army, the judicial, executive, and legislative institutions) as a well as the complex of associations in civil society. Gramsci does *not* attach a teleology of Western freedom to these changes. We should note well that in fact, against the liberal conception, the process of modern transformation involves the *loss* of autonomy regarding civil society *and* regarding global capitalism. Gramsci, further, as we know, understands civil society to be intimately associated with 'private initiative', which often means ruling and middle classes—it is not an unsullied and 'naturally' sanctified space, therefore, even when sturdy, but a terrain of class struggle. Further, it was a staple of Marx, Engels, and Lenin to regard the modern state apparatus (not as some civilized advance) but as a tyrannical, parasitic structure that needed to be smashed. We should also attend to the fact that Gramsci read the most recent forms of dictatorship (notably fascist Italy) in terms of how they absorbed civil society within the state apparatus.

Gramsci knew less about non-European history—this is unquestionable—but the elements he associates with modern transformation have been attested in many non-European nineteenth- and twentieth-century settings in an overwhelming body of research. Such changes involved the expansion of the state apparatuses, the emergence of new complexes of associations in civil society, the abolition of older autonomous forms (e.g. guilds, Sufi orders, neighbourhood quarters, and tribes), varying relations between civil and political society, new hegemonic moral and social ideals associated with nationality, and the unequal incorporation into the periphery or semi-periphery of a global capitalist economy.[57] This research has in fact driven a coach and horses through Orientalist concepts, in which traditional state power ('despotism') is greatly exaggerated, premodern social autonomies are underestimated, global capitalism and local economic change underplayed, forms of culture romanticized, and a wide variety of popular and revolutionary struggles often left out of account. Contemporary research is not in any fundamental sense incompatible with the sorts of changes that Gramsci associated with modernity. Dictatorship in the Middle East and North Africa, for instance, among the single-party regimes was often a matter of the absorption of civil society within the state. Gramsci is a start point here in much research.[58] These dictatorships invented new 'massive state structures' in order to channel and contain new forms of popular politics; and the breakdown of such forms (the Ba'th Party, the Arab Socialist Union, the statist trade union federations and so on) has been associated with a prolonged crisis of authority.

Finally, we should note from Gramsci's texts that the war of position turns out *not* to be exclusively fought on the terrain of civil society. The massive state structures of the modern democracies, the educator state, and the mass organizations and institutions of the extended state (including for instance state schools, state media, and so on) are also legitimate terrain for the war of position. What matters is the organized struggle for consent that inhabits the hegemonic apparatus—which can vary in relation to political and civil society. Overall, then, it seems reasonable not to overdetermine and belabour Gramsci's references to East and West, and to work with a non-binary, historicized, and non-Eurocentric concept of the war of position. It is this sort of reading that has underpinned the uses of the concept by researchers and activists alike over decades in Asia, Africa, and Latin America.

THE PARTY

> The modern prince, the myth-prince, cannot be a real person, a concrete individual. It can only be an organism, a complex element of society in which a collective will, which has already been recognised and has to some extent asserted itself in action, begins to take concrete form. History has already provided this organism, and it is the political party—the first cell in which there come together germs of a collective will tending to become universal.[59]

The war of position involves a labour of collective organization on a much larger scale than was present in the previous phases. There is a qualitative shift from self-organization. What kinds of organization did Gramsci have in mind? The major question revolves around the meaning, form, and purpose of the party. The book has aimed to show that in Gramscian perspectives there are times and places—above all during the phase or subphases associated with domination and popular self-activity—when party organization is not the central answer to the dilemmas of popular mobilization. However, there are also phases when the question of the party is posed, above all the phase in which popular *consenso* is forged: 'it is undeniable that Gramsci underlined the councils in his *Ordine Nuovo* period, and the party thereafter.'[60] Boggs puts it more emphatically: 'the revolutionary party . . . was indispensable for taking the movement beyond its parochial, spontaneous, corporatist phase.'[61] To ignore or underestimate the party is to set aside a significant dimension of Gramsci's oeuvre and life-activity. Subversivist or individualist 'anti-politics' will not do.

Popular parties do not only arise because of this or that theory, as 'an arbitrary voluntarist construction',[62] but because at a certain point significant numbers of activists come to see them, perhaps for the first time, or after many years of finding nothing of value in the party form, as something worth trying, as against both opposition and the limits of autonomous forms of organization. The Indignados of Spain, for instance, decided to form a party, Podemos in January 2014.[63] Similar subjectivities were at work among the hundreds of thousands who joined the British Labour Party for the first time as Jeremy Corbyn ascended to the leadership in 2015. Likewise, some who joined the Italian Communist Party in January 1921 when it was founded, had spent much of the previous few years deserting or criticizing the existing parties of Italy, especially the timid and ineffective socialist party. In a historicized theory, at certain points parties become relevant, alongside controversies around timing, form, and purpose. Indeed, the different kinds of organization continue to develop over time, and they must prove their 'this-sidedness' in practice.

An historicizing and dialectical approach implies that there is no blueprint and we should not be searching for one. Gramsci's studies of organization, moreover, are always intertwined with all the other moments of hegemony, which gives a strong warrant for not abstracting out and fetishizing organizational structures alone. The dangers of proceduralism have shown themselves in various forms of activism past and present, including, more recently, in horizontalist forms. Indeed, as elsewhere, the central criterion for understanding and evaluating the party is the process of popular mobilization itself, how such forms of organization are situated in the long journey from subordination to revolution, in the line of renewal and unification, in the construction of a new hegemony. Gramsci's thinking on party organization is perhaps richer and more varied than many assume.

The Vanguardist Party

The first sort of party that has been read into Gramsci's work, not without foundation, is the tightly organized 'Leninist' vanguardist party of highly disciplined, committed, professional revolutionaries—a modern Prince that supplies consciousness to the masses or defines from on high who is and is not a true proletarian,[64] seizes state power, establishes the dictatorship of the proletariat and single-party rule, and eventually brings about communism, causing the state, in theory, to wither away.

Gramsci reportedly repeated the Communist Party line to comrades in prison: 'The aim of the party was the violent conquest of power and establishment of the dictatorship of the proletariat, to be achieved by tactical adjustment to its historical situation and the balance of class forces in successive phases of the struggle.'[65] One interpretation is that this was a reasonably accurate reflection of Gramsci's views, albeit stated rather baldly; here is a Marxist-Leninist Gramsci, in which demands such as the constituent assembly were merely tactical adjustments on the way towards the seizure of power by a single party. A contrary interpretation is contextual: Gramsci did not want to sow divisions among the faithful or demoralize and confuse loyal supporters; nor did he wish to appear disloyal at a time when his statements were being reported to USSR intelligence. So, he repeated the party line, while developing a less authoritarian conception in his *Prison Notebooks*.

Yet, there is other evidence for the single party. As Rosengarten writes:

[D]uring the years 1924 to 1926, above all in his official writings as head of the Communist Party of Italy, Gramsci was . . . a loyal adherent to . . . a 'Leninist stabilisation' of Communist practice. . . . The Communist Party, Gramsci wrote in a report of May 1925 . . . must improve its organization and raise the intellectual level of its members who 'will guide the revolution and administer the proletarian State'. The Party, he said, 'represents' the interests of the entire working class but 'carries out' the will of only a particular part of the masses, of the most advanced part, the proletariat, 'that wants to overthrow the existing régime with revolutionary means to found communism'.[66]

This picture is corroborated in Gramsci's pre-prison letters. 'Gramsci was firmly convinced', writes Boothman, 'that a communist State in the foreseeable future would be characterised by a single Party . . . represent[ing] the interests of the "working masses."'[67] Gramsci indeed rejected, in the early 1920s, the 'right wing' of the Italian Communist Party (PCI) led by Angelo Tasca. Gramsci argued that a workers' and peasants' government cannot be established via a bourgeois parliament; social democracy cannot be the right wing of proletariat but only the left wing of bourgeoisie. He resisted for a time—with Amadeo Bordiga—the idea of the United Front, lacerating petty bourgeois elements with criticism.

Here then, is the Gramsci of Bolshevik stabilization, seeking to establish the dictatorship of the proletariat, which may, as he admitted, involve a period of 'statolatry'. Criticisms of Trotsky, whose Mensheviks were generally seen as more democratic than Lenin's Bolsheviks, appear to receive more emphasis in this phase. Gramsci's newly discovered tolerance to oppositional forces (in 1923) contrasted with the views he expressed in 1924–26 when he denounced factions as 'incompatible with the essence of the proletarian party'.[68]

'Marxism-Leninism' is 'a category that emerged after Lenin's death'[69] and bears a highly contested relationship to Lenin's actual doctrine and practice.[70] Lenin had lived a revolutionary life full of debate and contest, he argued against bureaucratic-centralism, defended democratic-centralism, and only banned factions in the party under the duress of real politik. Zinoviev, argues Geier, not Lenin, played the leading role in the post-1917 emergence of bureaucratic despotism in the Soviet Union. Nonetheless, the impress on the twentieth century of Marxism-Leninism, caricatured and statist as it became post-1917, can hardly be denied. In the 1980s, more than a third of the world's population—in the USSR, Eastern Europe, China, Southeast Asia, and the Caribbean—was ruled by Communist Parties who made explicit appeals to Marxist-Leninism. There were significant

Communist Parties in Europe (Italy and France, for instance), the Middle East (in Iraq, for example). But the collapse of these parties since the 1980s has been just as dramatic. This sole party form, stripped of its hegemony, appears intimately linked with domination and oppression, what C. L. R. James called 'monstrous tyranny'. It is a history that 'weighs like a nightmare' on the present. Gramsci was formed in a different epoch. In his world, dominated above all by British and French liberal imperialist capitalism—almost none of this history had yet transpired.

It is easy to forget, however, that the vanguardist model of party organization continues in powerful forms in the twenty-first century. This time it is overladen with a new ideology, worldview, and myth. A distinctive subset of Islamist parties and groups—originating in Europe, Asia, the Middle East, and North and West Africa—have sometimes explicitly and sometimes implicitly borrowed from Leninist practice.[71] These parties are often understood in racist, Orientalist terms as inherently Muslim, Arab, or Eastern. In fact, their dynamics bear significant comparison to the parties of Marxism-Leninism. They are usually staffed by small, 'revolutionary' minorities; they are often committed to the violent conquest of state power; they exert an intense ideological discipline (in espousing one or other often highly developed form of Islamism, often associated with Salafi-Wahhabism); they demand full commitment to the group (e.g. the oath of allegiance); they wield an extremely powerful myth (the enactment of the true Islam of the pious ancestors); they are capable of diffusing a new common sense; they are quite sure who is and who is not a true Muslim (i.e. a true revolutionary subject) and what the best interests of Muslims are; they are organized along authoritarian lines internally, are usually statist, and are sectarian in various ways, above all against other 'deviant' Muslims and rivals; and they often split.[72] The culture and ideology may be completely different, but the modality of organization is vanguardist,[73] along the lines of the Leninist caricature. And the model has demonstrated a certain amount of this-sidedness in practice—drawing recruits from across the world, establishing a short-lived state in Iraq-Syria, and so on. Few would safely argue that world politics has not been impacted since the 1980s by such groups. Just as Marxism-Leninism was collapsing in world politics, one might say, in spite of all the talk about globalization and the internet (or perhaps because of it),

'Islamism-Leninism' appeared to replace it. On the other hand, in making this comparison, one is reminded of Marx: the first time as tragedy, the second time as farce. Certainly social justice and democratic socialism has suffered, and imperialism, petro-dollar rentierism, Zionism, and absolutism—not to mention racism and Orientalism—have thrived on what Timothy Mitchell calls McJihad.[74] 'Islamism-Leninism' is held back by the fact that the overwhelming majority of Muslims neither accept it nor its purported monopoly on the correct interpretation of the faith.

Vanguardist organizations live on in relation to the degree to which they hegemonize rather than purely in relation to abstracted organizational features. In 1933, Trotsky offered a profound insight: 'Naïve minds think that the office of kingship lodges in the king himself, in his ermine cloak and his crown, in his flesh and bones. As a matter of fact, the office of kingship is an interrelation between people. The king is king only because the interests and prejudices of millions of people are refracted through his person.'[75] This can be rewritten for the vanguardist party: 'Naïve minds think that the office of the modern Prince lodges in the modern Prince himself, in his centralized structure, his discipline, his strategic capacity. As a matter of fact, the modern Prince is an interrelation between people. The modern Prince is only Prince because the interests and prejudices of millions of people are refracted through his structure.' A formulation like this captures the relationship between hegemony and organization well. In the present, the vanguardist party, in the wake of the failures of its communist and Islamist forms, is perhaps just like Trotsky's king, a 'washed-out old man with a flabby lower lip'.

The vanguardist Gramsci, at a time when Marxism-Leninism is often seen as authoritarian and 'Islamism-Leninism' essentialist and sectarian, can perhaps serve only as a negative foil in the present. It can assist in conceiving contrasting forms of political renewal in matters of organization; it can be a guide to staying with the trouble, working through what went wrong, studying the traces, and acting collectively to figure out how alternative, more democratic organizational forms can be established. One does not escape the 'dustbin of history' by ignoring what is in it. In a Gramscian perspective, all the moments of hegemony are at stake—not just organizational questions but also issues relating to culture, ideology, social bloc, political society and so on. But regarding organization, the basic argument here is that Gramsci's Bolshevik phase in relation to the party was relatively brief and keyed into a particular context in which discipline and centralization, paradoxically, may also have been part and parcel of doing battle with what Togliatti called 'extreme infantile sectarianism'.[76] In fact, Gramscian perspectives offer a rich spring of more democratic possibilities and have been drawn on in the formulation and rethinking of more expansive and democratic forms of organization from China to Latin America.[77]

The Mass, Democratic Party

Many argue strongly that Gramsci's rigid, Bolshevized party was very much an artefact of his official writings of 1924-26, when he was Party Secretary and later 'transcended'.[78] 'Gramsci's "adherence" to Bordiga's positions' in the early 1920s, writes Coutinho, 'did not last very long'.[79] Femia concludes that Gramsci's party is 'more democratic than those of the Leninist model'.[80] The vision of the party in the *Prison Notebooks*, indeed, alongside other evidence from the early 1920s, can suggest a mass, democratic, revolutionary party. This was not so much the Leninist Gramsci, but the Gramsci of one of his closest comrades, Palmiro Togliatti, from the 1940s to the 1960s, and later of Eurocommunism and the hopes held out especially in Europe in the 1970s, and Latin America since, for a democratic and even parliamentary road to socialism.

After the turmoil and defeats of the early 1920s involving the fascist seizure of power, the splits between the Left (e.g. Gramsci, Bordiga) and Right (e.g. Tasca) of the PCI, the struggles with the Comintern (which was seeking to impose a United Front policy on the PCI), and the growing division among the top leadership between Gramsci and Bordiga, Gramsci wrote some significant lines assessing where things had gone wrong in the struggle for popular consent, putting forward in various letters what the editors of the *Prison Notebooks* call 'a new conception of the party'. In a key letter of 9 February 1924, Gramsci wrote:

> The error of the party has been to have accorded priority in an abstract fashion to the problem of organization, which in practice has simply meant creating an apparatus of functionaries who could be depended on for their orthodoxy towards the official view . . . The communist party has even been against the formation of factory cells. Any participation of the masses in the

activity and internal life of the party, other than on big occasions and following a formal decree from the centre, has been seen as a danger to unity and centralism. The party has not been seen as the result of a dialectical process in which the spontaneous movement of the revolutionary masses and the organizing and directing will of the centre converge.[81]

Gramsci believed that this situation, in which the party is 'suspended in air', meant a disconnection from the masses, who could not then be expected to show up suddenly and join 'when the situation is right' and 'at the crest of the revolutionary wave'. Moreover, it was a situation in which 'areas of opportunistic infection have formed without the centre knowing'.[82] In other words, Gramsci understood that a crucial error of the PCI in the early 1920s in Italy was not its revolutionary ambition but its bureaucratic centralism. Mass participation, far from being a threat to unity and direction, Gramsci was arguing, is the only way to make it live. A democratically centralist party must coordinate a convergence of spontaneous movement and the directing will to avoid being suspended in air—that is, severed from an organic connection to subaltern social groups—and thus ineffective. Gramsci wished 'to extend the sort of relationship Lenin considered appropriate only within a small élite . . . to the entire movement'.[83] Regarding bureaucratic centralism and the tendency of political parties 'to become mummified and anachronistic', Gramsci mustered a particularly strong criticism, writing that the party 'bureaucracy is the most dangerous customary and conservative force'.[84]

The guiding organizational principle is democratic centralism: '[a] "centralism" in movement—i.e. in a continual adaptation of the organization to the real movement, a matching of thrusts from below with orders from above, a continuous insertion of elements thrown up from the depths of the rank and file into the solid framework of the leadership apparatus which ensures continuity and the regular accumulation of experience'.[85] Gramsci writes, 'Democratic centralism is an elastic form that lends itself to many "incarnations." It subsists insofar as it is interpreted continuously and adapted continually to necessity. It consists in the critical pursuit of what is identical in apparent diversity and of what is distinct or contrary in apparent uniformity, as well as in the ability to organize and closely connect that which is similar.'[86]

This quotation dials up the power and significance of democratic central-ism, as the latter is the mode of coordination that allows the dialectic to oper-ate. In democratic centralism, social actors can find what is distinct or opposed in the apparent uniformity and what is equal and in common in the apparent diversity—the very process that subtends overcoming, sublation, and organic synthesis. There is thus an intimate connection to organic intellectual activity. Organization and connection 'have the semblance of an experimental, "induc-tive" practical necessity, rather than a rationalistic, deductive, abstract process—that is, something that typifies "pure" intellectuals'.[87] The relation-ship between the intellectual, party strata, and the experiences of the popular masses must be analogous to that between theory and practice.[88]

A non-Leninist reading of Gramsci on the party, has 'solid philosophical foundations'.[89] It is fully aligned with the lodestar of the philosophy of praxis—that is, a search for the unification of theory and practice. 'One must', wrote Gramsci,

> highlight the importance and significance that political parties in the mod-ern world have in the elaboration and dissemination of conceptions of the world insofar as they basically develop the ethics and the politics that go hand in hand with these conceptions; in other words, they function almost as the 'testing grounds' of these conceptions. The parties select individuals from the active mass and the selection occurs jointly in both fields, the prac-tical and the theoretical. The relation between theory and practice becomes even tighter the more the conception is vitally and radically innovative and opposed to old ways of thinking. One can, therefore, say that the parties are the elaborators of the new integral and all-encompassing intellectual corps; that is, the parties are the crucibles of the unification of theory and practice, understood as a real historical process.[90]

A mass, democratic party such as this would avoid vanguardist and sponta-neist extremes.[91]

Gramsci sought 'a communist party that is not a collection of dogmatists or little Machiavellis . . . in other words, a party of the masses who, through their own efforts, are striving to liberate themselves autonomously from political and industrial servitude through the organization of the social economy, and not a party which makes use of the masses for its own heroic attempts to imitate the French Jacobins'.[92]

In other words, in this interpretation, Gramsci favoured 'a mass party rooted in everyday social life and local democratic structures'.[93] The new, revolutionary party is a 'collective intellectual' because in it the clergy-lay distinction—also common in modern political formations—tends to disappear and mass participation is enjoined.[94] Here, coalition politics is not rejected.[95] About this, Gramsci was eventually a staunch opponent of Amadeo Bordiga, who sought a high degree of centralization, rejected spontaneity of any sort, and bent too far towards a narrow concern with state power.

The Organic Party

What is striking about Gramsci's democratic centralism, unlike Lenin's formulation, is its elasticity as an organizational form. Gramsci writes that it must be the *result* of the unity of spontaneity and conscious direction. This implies a junction with popular self-activity—a way to preserve while sublating autonomy. This is particularly important given the diversity of rhythms and temporalities and phases in the history of popular mobilization. Hence both partial subaltern formations and self-organization (in all their diversity) are bound to coincide in the same national or transnational space with much larger and more mediated forms of organization. No single top-down bureaucracy would be able to direct such a social diversity without splitting up or applying excessive discipline, holding back rather than fostering a new collective will. The implication is the refusal of a single, organizational blueprint; a wide field for experimentation; and a wide variety of 'incarnations' or organizational forms.

Suggestive in this regard is Gramsci's concept of the 'organic party'. The 'revolutionary party' is not so much a single, named, organization, with an HQ, central committee, heavy directive functions, and so on. In some sense it is 'the complex of cultural, social and political institutions that serve a particular class and worldview'.[96] Revolutionary organization is tied here usefully to the transformation and leading activities of the subaltern social group or bloc of groups, above all, rather than to a specific, organizational form. 'It is observable', writes Gramsci, 'that . . . organic and fundamental parties have . . . split into fractions [separate, named parties]. . . . Hence the intellectual General Staff of the organic party does not belong to any of these fractions, but operates as if it were a directive force standing on its own . . . a newspaper too . . . a review . . . is a "party" or "fraction of a party". . . . Think of the role of *The Times* in England.'[97]

It is hard to imagine that Gramsci was not also thinking of his own newspaper, *L'Ordine Nuovo*, whose journalists, including Gramsci, had sometimes operated in a directive fashion. Gramsci does indicate, in relation to questions of party organization, the important 'possibilities of socialist publications, which could provide not only an alternative [to the party] means of socialization but also a forum for the exchange of opinions and the airing of mass grievances'.[98] Gramsci also speaks of the liberal party in Italy after 1876, as referring to 'a general ideology, superior to the various, more immediate groupings' among which he includes the Popular Party, nationalism, 'a great part of socialism', the democratic radicals, and the conservatives.[99] Even in 'countries where there is a single, totalitarian governing party. . . . [where] no other legal parties exist, other parties [and tendencies] in fact always do exist'.[100] Relevant actors also include 'great, particularly active, intellectual figures'.[101] The implication is that the organic party is not just 'an organ (1) subject to tight, single-minded discipline, admitting of no opposition, and (2) geared solely to the over-arching goal of conquering power'.[102] Instead, it is a broadly defined 'grouping of those with similar interests and a similar ideology'.[103] It has been noted how Gramsci speaks of a phase when 'previously germinated ideologies become "party"'.[104] Here the overlap between party and ideology is at its most pronounced. A party here is also a political force, a 'great, historical collective movement', promoting a given ideology.

Such a usage of the term 'party' can be read into Marx's own lexicon. The 1848 *Communist Manifesto*, for instance, was originally entitled, the 'Manifesto of the Communist Party'. But no such party as organization existed. There were instead a variety of groupings, societies, committees, newspapers, leagues, and tendencies, often divided on significant issues, not least the distinction between Christian and scientific socialism. Official and so-named Communist Parties were creatures of the twentieth century, established after Lenin's (Bolshevik) Russian Social Democratic Labour Party seized power in October 1917. What did exist was a 'spectre haunting Europe', various ideologies, and a general movement of movements, an anticipated

The Expansive Search for Consent

social force that was not expressed in a single organization. This did not stop Marx calling it a party. As Dunayevskaya puts it with dramatic effect, 'Marx kept referring to "the Party" when all that was involved was himself and Engels.'[105] Marx's assertion may have been a monopolizing and aggrandizing gesture, but it may also reference an organic party form.[106]

An organic party comprises a variety of organizational types and activities, including international associations, popular schools, cultural societies, radical media, study groups, autonomous and grassroots collectives, popular committees, clubs, forum organizers, trade unions, cells, community organizations, campaign groups, inter alia. In 1917, Gramsci himself, against the denunciations of comrades such as Serrati or Bordiga, 'founded, outside the PSI, the 'Club of Moral Life', an association for the promotion of intellectual debates [providing] . . . education to young socialists'.[107] Gramsci was sharply critical of a party that opposed the formation of factory cells. Thomas writes suggestively of the modern Prince as 'an active organizational synthesis of various levels and instances of the struggles of subaltern social groups'.[108]

The centralized organizational structure may be minimal. It could look like the First International (est. 1864), for instance, which was merely a coordinating association, with few powers, at least initially, to direct or discipline the activities of the various member movements.[109] Marx was not the 'great leader and founder' of the First International: indeed, he sat without speaking in the inaugural meeting. The *prestige* of the international, in Gramsci's writing, operating transnationally, could hold together a party established at the national level. The 'centre' might be even 'thinner' than a coordinating association; it may act above all like a deliberative forum, a square, midan, *encuentro*, or plaza, like the World Social Forum, an organized encounter of diverse forces. The organic party operating transnationally, then, can comprise a network of different organizations, platforms, and structures.

Gramsci valorized internal democracy. The 'Party maintains decision-making power and has co-ordinating and directive functions, but its power is *ultimately based on and must ultimately respond to* the network of councils'.[110] Coordination in the formal sense may come from on high, but the powers to coordinate come from below. Here there is an organic passage from one form of organization (self-activity) into another (party activity). Here the party's 'leadership activities would be largely "indirect", structured around the tasks of guiding and educating in the broadest counter-hegemonic sense; spontaneity would be redirected through ideological as well as organizational methods.'[111] This means not policing but channelling and sublation.

An interesting example of such a dialectical unification comes from Podemos: 'Plaza Podemos inherits from [the] Indignados movement a participatory method for developing the electoral program, which is then elaborated by a team of intellectuals defined as "synthesisers," the ones who try to sublate common sense into argumentative logos.'[112] Briziarelli goes on: 'Such a democratic centralist [approach] confirms Podemos's will to sublate rather than rejecting the "real movement" originating from Indignados' through synthesizers and a forum.[113] Thus the 'energy of the masses' is not rejected or substituted but sublated, included within the larger organization.

Perhaps the anti-apartheid movement in South Africa is an example of a relatively successful movement which combined various forms of organization, including at the transnational level. Steve Biko, for instance, extensively and powerfully justified all-Black student unions by arguing for the need for autonomous Black consciousness-raising in the early 1970s.[114] On the other hand, the ANC put in place a vision of interracial organization, built out of an organic process of consultation and representation in the 1950s and 1960s.[115] Some old-established—and previously rather conservative organizations—were involved as well, after having been radicalized.[116] Indeed, some subaltern social groups may be finding each other for the first time. Others may have spent years in organized struggle. Regarding the former, autonomous self-organization is arguably necessary—not least to educate the educator. For this reason, the autonomous phase is bound to coincide temporally with the consent-winning phase. Perhaps the relationship which Bukharin extended from the Communist Party of the Soviet Union (CPSU) to American Black activists, calling them a 'fighting division of the proletariat' is just not adequate to the transnational struggle against white hegemony.[117] The Anti-Apartheid Movement sought to engage transnationally with calls for boycotts, divestment, and sanctions against the South African regime to be undertaken by a wide variety of social groups.

An interesting example regarding the functioning and effectiveness of Gramsci's democratic centralism, arguably, comes from research on the MST in Brazil. To begin with, the rapid growth of the movement, and the 'political crudity' of the new recruits, meant that from the 1990s onward 'eager militants' at the local level adopted a top-down, vanguardist approach, which caused excluded families to leave. The MST leadership intervened by sending a skilled organizer, who reintroduced participatory approaches at the local level.[118] Thus, autonomy and leadership, the horizontal and the vertical, were combined to solve problems attendant on both. The organization was restored to vitality by the accumulated experience of a more permanently established centre, which sent a more experienced activist, who taught the virtues of a more autonomous and democratic style of leadership, and the alienated sectors were reabsorbed. Autonomy turns out to be learned by experience—but also integrated and safeguarded by a larger organization. Autonomy, on the other hand, has the weakness of involving thin socialization processes—which admitted the vanguardist militants in the first place. Arguably, this example illustrates the salience of democratic centralism—avoiding centripetal and overly hierarchical forces at the same time. The MST's word for this, strikingly, is *organicidade* ('organicity').[119] Here it would appear that a longer socialization process is also envisaged, whereby there is a slower rearticulation of new elements, a question of not moving too fast too soon, a process, we note, which does not by any means forgo the necessity of having an overall *direzione*, albeit a slower and more careful one than envisaged by vanguardists.

Rehmann, drawing on recent experiences in the United States and on Haug's concept of 'activating arrangement', suggests a useful focus on the specific tasks of a party—namely, its *function* in building and educating a larger bloc, elaborating ideology, and transcending narrow corporate or group interests and linking subordinate groups together, all aimed at increasing the capacity of each element of organization to act.[120]

In keeping with Rehmann's focus on bloc formation, Gramscians have investigated the importance of how a political party can form an organic component of the life of a larger community. Here social 'underpinnings' matter as much as functions. For example, Cassidy's comparison of the Social Democratic and Labour Party (SDLP)—a social-democratic and Irish nationalist political party in the north of Ireland—and Sinn Féin (an Irish republican and democratic socialist party) argues that the latter was organically embedded in the community while the former was not. These were in some sense, therefore, different kinds of political parties—in spite of their formal similarity.[121] Cassidy draws attention to individuals working in community centres in leadership roles, who both organize and persuade, likening them to organic intellectuals. They disseminate conceptions of equality, republicanism, and rights while organizing—beyond economic-corporate service provision—as part of a larger bloc which includes Sinn Féin; sometimes they do so together, sometimes separately. Such community activity is a vital part of the electoral success of Sinn Féin. One such organizer stated that 'street rioting' and 'community provision' were all part of the same overall purpose and cause and that he engaged in the former when he was younger and the latter when he was older.[122] Here is an interesting example affirming a diachronic relationship between the phase of fleeting confrontations and popular self-activity (street rioting) and the phase of organized struggle over consent (community provision, organizing, and party activity). One notes also that a temporal juxtaposition is also being affirmed: several distinct phases are included together (where younger and older join hands in a larger bloc), a juxtaposition that is effected here in relation to a developed and diffused ideology, bloc formation and an in-depth organization, social becoming, and community connection. There is more than a hint here at how, in a Gramscian perspective, an organic passage between domination, popular self-activity, and the struggle for consent can be effected. Self-organization independent of party (popular self-activity) and party organization become operative together in a larger bloc. In the living Gramscian tradition, organic intellectuals 'who arise out of the proletariat, who are connected to it by familial and institutional attachments, who express its way of life—it is these individuals who will keep the party in touch with its roots'.[123]

There is at least a temporal contrast here, then, with Egan's view that the war of position requires a 'centralised political organization'. His argument is that 'specific movement organizations', even when they 'identify their specific terrains of struggle with the war of position', remain only 'tactical' for two key reasons: they lack the capacity—unlike a 'strategic political organization'—to identify precisely where and when the key weak points in the overall capitalist hegemony are; and second, they cannot by themselves, given how many and different they are, coordinate 'in a coherent manner'.[124] There is undoubtedly a pressing need to identify the weakest points, and the need to coordinate action to that end. Such strategizing is often born of a depth of continuous organization and experience. Gramsci, for instance, cautioned communist comrades not to move straight to revolution if they hadn't figured out how to neutralize Mussolini's armoured trains.[125]

The danger, however, is of a disorganic formulation—that is, an instrumentalization of peripheral actors, an ossification of the centre—and a shift to bureaucratic centralism and vanguardism. This might be particularly marked in relation to trans/international organization. Strategic effectiveness does not operate in a vacuum, at least not in the philosophy of praxis and the theory of hegemony, but is combined with other factors; culture, ideology, social being / social consciousness, organic intellectual activity, feeling, the depth and cohesion of the social bloc, and so on. The implication is that for Egan's point to hold at the scale of global capitalist hegemony, the struggle for consent would have to have reached a very advanced stage indeed. Given the temporally uneven and diverse trajectories in the histories of subaltern social groups and the diversity of social domination, such a compactness, simultaneity, and homogeneity seems unlikely. Those wrestling with contradictory consciousness, those searching for autonomy, those with highly diverse histories and forms of identification, are unlikely to take kindly to all-seeing strategists instructing them from another country which electricity substation they must sabotage. There would have to be a complete sublation of all forms of contradictory and autonomous activity. The danger, then, is of a premature and thus oppressive and ineffective centralization. The danger, after the assumption of state power, is of dictatorship. The future cannot be parachuted into the present. One does not want to be, like Ferrari, a latecomer because he was already too far into the future.

In the meantime, and one cannot really escape historicity, organic parties are a fruitful modality. The EZLN, for instance, maintains an anti-vanguardist style, does not assert itself as the sole organization, believes that there will be other valid organizations, and even states that the EZLN won't be desirable to many.[126] The EZLN rejects political parties and prefers civil society, commensurate with a strong sense in Mexico of corruption in the political parties.[127] Gramscians, as we saw above, have tended to be positive about the EZLN's capacities in building consent, locally and transnationally, against neoliberal hegemony, including in comparison with more monopolistic and vanguardist organizations. Still, they pose questions about scaling up, including about how local democracy can be scaled up to the national stage. The EZLN is a revolutionary, not a reformist, organization—and one conducting an armed struggle. However, the EZLN aims 'not to take state power in the name of revolution, along traditional Leninist lines, but to activate a mass movement throughout the civil society of Mexico'.[128]

Whereas many historical materialists have claimed to know objectively, scientifically, and correctly the laws and motions of capitalism, in the Gramscian tradition, 'complete knowledge' only comes after the fact and is incapable of rejuvenating the world. Predicting the future is part and parcel of creating a collective will. The anti-vanguardist implication is that no single organization can claim an interpretive monopoly on the revolution.

This section has described two kinds of modern Prince—the vanguardist, single party and the mass, democratic party. It has also argued for the contemporary historicity of a postmodern Prince—an organic, democratic party that finds organizational 'activating arrangements' amid diverse temporalities, to enable an organic engagement with plural subaltern formations and forms of popular self-organizing. Such arrangements, in line with Nunes's valorization of a diverse ecology of different initiatives and organizational forms,[129] will have many incarnations, on both the domestic and international stage. Shapelessness, nonetheless, is avoided: Gramsci's favoured political parties have something in common. They are all revolutionary organizations; they are all voluntary associations rooted in civil society; and they are organically associated with popular mobilization. Gramsci's position shows up in his criticism of inorganic political parties in late nineteenth-century Italy: 'the parties were not an organic fraction (a vanguard, an elite) of the popular classes; they were, rather, an ensemble of electoral canvassers and operators, an assemblage of minor provincial intellectuals that were the opposite of a representative selection.'[130]

In short, Gramsci conceived of and measured party organization—of whatever kind—in relation to the ascendant transformation of subaltern social groups. As Chen Yue, a leading Chinese interpreter of Gramsci, asserts, 'the "popular nature of the modern prince" (that is, the Jacobin vanguard party) is nothing but the "revolutionary potential of the people." [131] In conceiving of party organization in this way, Gramsci's oeuvre can think the renewal of the party beyond vanguardism, parliamentary reformism and post-1968 refusal.[132] The 'organic party' refers above all not to this or that specific organization or organism, but to a series of organisms or organizations, a movement of movements, including organisms that are not political parties but are grouped together in a larger organic party—a collective force and its many fractions aimed at forming a social and political bloc, prefiguring and eventually becoming the new civil society.

IDEOLOGICAL ELABORATION AND DIFFUSION

The struggle for consent involves an extensive ideological elaboration that goes well beyond good sense and plays a vital role in the development of new forms of popular consciousness, collective will, force, and the construction of alliance and bloc. This is the phase 'in which previously germinated ideologies become "party", come into confrontation and conflict'.[133] At stake is the development of ideology, not as mystification, but in part as constructive: 'on the level of ideology . . . man [sic] becomes conscious of social conflict. Consequently, ideologies have an historical value; they represent a tool for the understanding of socio-historical processes and a practical guide for the realisation of a given political program [and] . . . they are capable of organizing human masses.'[134] In his notes on the philosophy of Benedetto Croce, Gramsci writes: 'For the philosophy of praxis, ideologies are anything but arbitrary; they are real historical facts that one must fight against and unmask as instruments of domination—not as a matter of morality etc., but as a matter, precisely, of political struggle in order to make the ruled intellectually independent of the rulers, to destroy a hegemony and create another as a necessary moment of revolutionising praxis.'[135] At stake is the cultivation of the shared consciousness, language, and a system of ideas associated with conviction, with the collective will: 'no mass action is possible if the masses in question are not convinced of the ends they wish to attain or the methods to be applied.'[136]

Such ideological development prepares the ground for revolution. '[E]very revolution has been preceded by an intense critical effort of cultural penetration, of the infusion of ideas through groups of men who were initially unresponsive and thought only of resolving day by day, hour by hour, their own political and social problems, without creating links of solidarity with others who found themselves under the same conditions.'[137] The overthrow of the traditional order—in the Protestant Reformation or the French revolution—was not solely a dramatic event 'but rather [occurred] through a long and gradual phase of ideological-cultural ferment set in motion by subversive currents (Protestantism, the Enlightenment) linked to emergent social forces'.[138] One might argue the same for the Bolshevik revolution of 1917 (reaching back to the 1840s) or the Third World national liberation movements post-1945 (reaching back to the genesis of nationalism and pan-movements during the nineteenth century).[139]

Just as good sense is built not ex nihilo but out of fragments of common sense, so new ideologies are built out of a work of connecting in new ways fragments of the old ideologies and worldviews. 'What matters', writes Gramsci, 'is the criticism to which such an ideological complex is subjected by the first representatives of the new historical phase. This criticism makes possible a process of differentiation and change in the relative weight that the elements of the old ideologies used to possess. What was previously secondary and subordinate, or even incidental, is now taken to be primary—becomes the nucleus of a new ideological and theoretical complex. The old collective will dissolves into its contradictory elements since the subordinate ones develop socially.'[140] This is another stricture against (sometime modernist) ideological posturing as to revolutionary rupture, against proclaiming the new in an ahistorical and logico-deductive way. It has been shown, for example, how church, bible, and Christianity were reinterpreted (not simply opposed) in Black theology to challenge apartheid-supporting Christianity in South Africa.[141]

Ideological critique is linked to the social development of the subordinate elements. It guides the passages out of domination and autonomy. It offers, for example, a framework within which contradictory consciousness can be resolved and can respond to the urgings of good sense. It generates a new social force—and is responsible for undermining and fragmenting the old social force—that is, its form of collective will. It is also sensitive to different historical conditions. Gramsci states, 'After the formation of the party system—an historical phase linked to the standardisation of broad masses of the population (communications, newspapers, big cities, etc.)—the molecular processes [of collective will formation] take place more swiftly than in the past.'[142]

Critical self-understanding develops amid hegemonic ideological competition and aims to develop a more advanced conception of reality: 'Critical understanding of oneself, then, comes through a struggle of political "hegemonies", of opposing directions, first in the ethical and then in the political field, in order to arrive at a more advanced elaboration of one's conception of reality.'[143] In other words, the struggle for self-understanding is not only about the inventory of traces, which is but the 'start point' of critical consciousness—one that can give a sense of the social group or class. A deeper, more 'ethico-political' understanding of the group and the self involves a struggle of political hegemonies—where some politically salient theory of the subject, the group, the structure/superstructure, and so on—is at stake. In this struggle various ideologies, systems of ideas, must prove their this-sidedness.

The development of good sense into ideology involves 'the exercise of thought, the acquisition of general ideas, the habit of connecting cause and effect . . . enlivened by (political) organization'.[144] Just at the point when there are efforts to make good sense 'more unitary and coherent', a further problem of ideology is posed, that of 'preserving the ideological unity of the entire social bloc which that ideology serves to cement and unify.'[145] Gramsci is particularly concerned here with the *social* bloc, and references large, popular masses, and the ways in which they are integrated or not into activities in which an ideology is implicit. Only through organic contact with 'the simple' 'does a philosophy become "historical", purify itself of intellectualistic elements of an individual character and become "life"'.[146] Gramsci adds: 'It is a matter therefore of starting with a philosophy which already enjoys, or could enjoy, a certain diffusion, because it is connected to and implicit in practical life, and elaborating it so that it becomes a renewed common sense possessing the coherence and the sinew of individual philosophies. But this can only happen if the demands of cultural contact with the "simple" are continually felt.'[147]

A major problem in relation to ideological elaboration is not to reproduce the split between intellectuals and masses, leaders and led, but instead realize organic and dialectical relationships that do not preserve the 'simple' in their simplicity but 'lead them to a higher conception of life'.[148] One contrast here is with a dominant trend in the Catholic Church, whereby intellectuals are kept within certain limits by discipline, which shackles critical enquiry and serves to keep the masses in a world of passivity and superstition.[149] Another contrast involved Italian cosmopolitan intellectuals who are drawn to associate with each other horizontally, separated from the masses and social struggles.[150] Gramsci emphasized the need for active, direct participation of all members of the movement 'even if this creates an appearance of tumult and disintegration'; a collective consciousness, Gramsci suggests, 'is a living organism. It does not form until multiplicity is unified through the friction of individual atoms.'[151] Gramsci writes, 'an organic quality of thought and cultural strength would only have been possible if there were the same unity between intellectuals and the simple as there should be between theory and practice—if, in other words, the intellectuals had been organically the intellectuals of those masses and if they had developed and made coherent the principles and the problems raised by those masses in their practical activity, thus constituting a cultural and social bloc'.[152] Note again the intimate connection between intellectual and ideological elaboration and bloc formation. We are far here from the process of consciousness of social being and social domination alone and deep into the constructive phase of unifying a social bloc of diverse components.

The sorts of organic relationship between intellectual development and practical life envisaged by Gramsci overlaps more than one might expect with the more anarchist concept that 'the road is made by walking', as Bruhn puts it in her discussion of the EZLN. But the EZLN, Bruhn argues, take this lack of conception of the world and lack of a clear destination further than Gramsci would have allowed.[153]

Gramsci was occupied with questions of ideological diffusion and appropriation, above all among popular masses. Individual ideological elaboration—in ivory towers or behind closed doors—meant very little. He writes:

Creating a new culture does not just mean making 'original' discoveries on an individual level. It also, and especially, means the dissemination, critically, of truths that have already been discovered, 'socialising' them, so to speak, and thus making them the basis of vital action, an element of coordination, and of intellectual and moral order. Leading a mass of people to think coherently together about the present reality is a far more important and 'original' philosophical event than the discovery by some 'philosophical genius' of some new truth that remains the property of small groups of intellectuals.[154]

It was the problems of popular appropriation that he addressed. 'How and why do new conceptions of the world spread and become popular?' he asks, noting that the 'process of dissemination' is 'a replacement of the old and very often a combination of old and new'. Does diffusion stem from rationality, from authority, or from membership in the same organization? Gramsci suggests that the admixture of these factors varies according to group and to cultural level. He notes that the popular masses 'do not accept new concepts in their "pure" form but only and always in a more or less anomalous or bizarre combination'. He argues that reasoning is only occasionally decisive, for instance, when an individual is 'already in a state of intellectual crisis, wavering between the old and the new, having lost faith in the old but not having yet opted for new, etc.'[155]

Ideological elaboration guides the passage out of the crisis. Gramsci notes that constant repetition is necessary, as well as incessant work to 'elevate the intellectual level of the increasingly larger popular strata; that is, to give a personality to the amorphous mass element. This means working to generate elites of intellectuals of a new kind that emerge directly out of the masses while remaining in touch with them so that they become like the whalebone in the corset.'[156] Whalebones stiffen and smooth out the fabric, giving shape and structure to the corset, which in turn gives shape and structure to the (often female but also queer) body. Aesthetics and sexuality here mingle with ideological elaboration undertaken by organic intellectuals in relation to good sense—underlining the link between aesthetics and the 'mass of feelings' that Gramsci develops against Croce. Gramsci argues that these kinds of organic modes of dissemination would 'really change the "ideological panorama" of the age' and might emerge as a 'mass creation' by passing through 'many intermediate phases'.[157] Gramsci considers the concrete study of 'the cultural organization that keeps the ideological world in movement'. He wanted to examine how this organization 'functions in practice' in order to close the gaps between intellectuals and subalterns. He mentions the school and the church as being the two biggest organizations

The Expansive Search for Consent

in terms of the numbers employed, but then also refers to newspapers, periodicals, books, and private educational institutions and to doctors, military officers, and the legal profession.[158]

Ideological diffusion in relation to the development of popular mobilization does not depend on frame alignment or resonance with pre-existing cultural codes. Instead, it builds on good sense, helps to elucidate its more precise meaning, and connects powerfully with contradictory consciousness and its associated quest for new resolutions. Contradictory consciousness consists of a series of opposites—of theses and antitheses. It is discordant, a cacophony. In other words, the new ideology depends no more on resonance than a symphony on the cacophony of tuning up. At stake are new connections, qualitative shifts, and dialectical development.

Indeed, ideological development involves the discovery of new means of expression, new languages, new elements of articulation that bring with them altered conceptions of the world, redefinitions of the situation, and an altered sense of social being. Li's research on movement-oriented labour non-governmental organizations (MLNGOs) in China offers a good example.

> MLNGOs' patient coaching has transformed many otherwise timid migrant workers into worker leaders. . . . For example, a former worker representative HXJ described her change into an articulate worker leader . . .: 'Before . . . my Mandarin was awful. I could not articulate well. When I first came . . . I could not speak much. . . . Another major obstacle was fear. . . . Every time we came here, we expressed our concerns, what to do and how to say. They taught us many techniques, resolved some of our concerns and increased our confidence. . . . We asked them for copies of the labor laws, and they explained them to us well and answered our queries. Gradually, I was not so afraid.'[159]

A new language is developed. At one level this involves moving from a vernacular to a national language.[160] As elsewhere, the question then becomes one of understanding how such a process can unfold organically and thus join hands with a wider process of popular mobilization and social emancipation. Gramsci warns against the elite imposition of Piedmontese in Italy.[161] Instead, the development of language is a process of drawing out, of education—a process of overcoming and sublation. Vernacular can be associated with good sense, group rights and consciousness, and a national language with a new worldview and alternative social organization.[162]

Literature plays a role. Gramsci wrote on how French and Russian literature had generated genuinely national-popular forms. He criticized Italian literature with its patronizing sense of the 'humble', contrasting it with the more positive meaning contained in Dostoyevsky's 1861 novel, known in English as 'The Humiliated and Insulted'. Gramsci writes,

> In Dostoyevsky, there is a strong national-popular feeling, namely an awareness of a 'mission of the intellectuals' toward the people, who may be 'objectively' composed of the 'humble' but must be freed from this 'humility', transformed, regenerated. For the Italian intellectual, the expression the 'humble' indicates a relationship of paternal and divine protection, the 'self-sufficient' feeling of one's undisputed superiority; like the relationship between two races, one superior and the other inferior; like the relationship between adults and children in old schooling; or worse still, like the relationship of a 'society for the protection of animals', or like that of the Anglo-Saxon Salvation Army toward the cannibals of Guinea.[163]

Here bourgeois condescension, paternalism, racism, masculinism, and colonialism are all eschewed, while the humble (or subaltern) is specified in terms of an organically engaged mode of representation, diffused in rich literary forms, which evokes a language of transformation, regeneration, and freedom.

In *Prison Notebook* 25, Gramsci takes seriously, in a 'politico-historical' way, the nineteenth-century Italian 'religious-popular' movement of David Lazzaretti. Eschewing the thesis of simple 'spontaneity' while studying the ideas seriously, Gramsci finds the cultural structure of the religious revelation, so important to the movement, to have been worked out already in a previously published popular novel. He writes that 'the plot and episodes of the novel are transmitted intact in the "revelation" in the cave, and out of this revelation comes the beginning of Lazzaretti's religious propaganda'.[164] The point is that the apparently spontaneous and marginal also involves a cultural content.

New languages find footholds in practice, in organizations, in publishing houses, in community schools, in ecclesiastical base communities, in social media, in civil society—they are organized. As Rehmann writes: 'Without

The Expansive Search for Consent

some stable positions in civil society which allow us to spell out the critique of capitalism again and again, the "good sense" elements in common sense risk subsiding after a while, drowned out by the prevailing ideologies.'[165] Here, civil society organizations act also like 'whalebones' in the corset, giving strength and infrastructure to support good sense and continue the process of elaborating good sense into ideology. Schools built by subaltern activists, for example, played this role in reviving the Irish language against Anglophone hegemony in Ireland in the 1970s.[166] Gramsci also writes positively of 'integral journalism, which is not only intended to satisfy the immediate needs of its public but intended to create and develop those needs in order to extend gradually the area of interests of its public'.[167]

Note that Gramsci conceived—contra-Lenin—of the organic and democratic development of conceptions of the world: 'Certain theories camouflage a definite political program for real domination by one part over everything (whether the part consists of a particular stratum, such as the intellectuals, or of a privileged territorial group). Other theories are nothing more than a unilateral stance (which is also typical of intellectuals); they are, in other words, straightforwardly fanatical and sectarian, with a program for supremacy.'[168] This passage points to the democratic ways in which Gramsci thought theory should develop against domination. No wonder that Gramsci called for a 'democratic philosopher'.

In his pre-prison writings, Gramsci had made a point about certain popular, apparently spontaneous demonstrations and 'outbreaks'. He wrote of the 'invisible army of books and pamphlets that had swarmed out of Paris from the first half of the eighteenth century', which 'had prepared both men and institutions for the necessary renewal'. He went on, 'Later, after the French events had welded a unified consciousness, a demonstration in Paris was enough to provoke similar disturbances in Milan, Vienna and the smaller centres. All this seems natural and spontaneous to superficial observers, yet it would be incomprehensible if we were not aware of the cultural factors that helped to create a state of mental preparedness for those explosions.'[169] The point is that episodic, fragmented, 'spontaneous', and subaltern forms of mobilization, involve various forms of conscious leadership, even if partially 'invisible' or distant; these activities at the margins are embedded in cultural circuits, intellectual activity, and forms of diffusion, including on the transnational stage. In other words, although Gramsci's invocations of the national-popular regarding ideological elaboration were in part a critique of cosmopolitan intellectuals, there is also a vital place for transnational diffusion to fertilize the terrain and guide the tracks of passages out of domination. Consent-winning involves an extensive appropriation of models across national and popular boundaries.

The sheer efficacy of ideology and worldview needs, finally, to be underlined. For instance, the compelling idea—one might say myth—of the vanguard party or state was that it was working to bring about communism. As Lenin insisted throughout *State and Revolution*, the fundamental purpose of the party was to smash the state, destroy capitalism, and thus bring about a free society of producers in which the state no longer exists. A more complete historical irony could hardly be found: the 'really existing' (which is statist, dictatorial, and runs on a command economy) could not have been further from the ideal (which has no state, popular democracy, and is based on free production). The main point is that, in the Gramscian tradition, ideology/worldview and 'myth', in the positive sense, matter. Gramsci, indeed, wrote to Togliatti in 1926, accusing him of the taint of 'bureaucratism', asserting that 'today' what matters regarding revolutionizing the masses in Italy and elsewhere outside of Russia is not 'the fact of the seizure of power'. Instead, Gramsci writes: 'What is active today, ideologically and politically, is the conviction, if it exists that the proletariat, once power has been taken, can construct socialism.'[170]

As ever theory and practice are intertwined: the foregoing suggests that both idealist and materialist theories of ideological elaboration and dissemination are profoundly in contrast with a Gramscian perspective. As Badaloni has it, 'a great historical objective is not reached by returning to the automatism of facts, or even by claiming to guide them from the basis of an intellectual situation of exteriority in relation to those same facts, but on the contrary by giving to ideas this character of mass and unity which turns them into historical forces.'[171]

POPULAR EDUCATION

In the phase of popular self-activity, the principal accent is on educating the educator, as this book has argued. Good sense and feeling has the capacity to push back against intellectual sophistication and pedantry. In the struggle for consent, in which education of a new kind can be organized, the leading note is popular education. As conservatives and imperialists have long told each other, education can be dangerous. In the tradition of Gramsci; the Brazilian popular educator, Paulo Freire; Ambedkar (d. 1956), the Indian intellectual and activist of Dalit emancipation; and figures such as Henry Giroux in North America, popular education has a highly distinctive cast.[172] It can be sharply differentiated from liberal, paternalistic, colonial, civilizing, neoliberal, and 'banking' models, in which the masses are civilized or developed and packages of information are transferred. Gramsci writes critically of paternalist and colonial forms of education: 'The efforts of cultural movements "to go to the people"—the Popular Universities and the like—have always degenerated into forms of paternalism; besides, they utterly lacked coherence in philosophical thought as well as in organizational control. One got the impression that the efforts were like the contacts of English merchants with the negroes of Africa, offering trinkets in exchange for nuggets of gold.'[173] Education implies not the production of docile subjects for absorption within circuits of capitalist production, colonialism, and the state but an engagement with subaltern social groups in processes of critical development 'that will result in a more coherent, deeper, and realistic conception of the world.'[174]

Gramsci's popular education is not about registering the sense perceptions and crude sensation-feelings of subaltern social groups, taking these supposedly authentic experiences of the senses to be knowledge and then presenting such knowledge as a philosophy of life, substituting the low for the high. In Gramscian perspectives, this is populist education, 'flaunting the low', and it can only operate via a subterfuge in which the high certifies that the low is high, a ruse relying on the high cultural capital of the romancer who has ventured 'to the people'. It is an approach which will freeze popular culture in aspic, falling victim to mummification and essentialism. Instead, the sort of critical education animating the Gramscian tradition involves a critical engagement and a 'line of development'—neither the fetishization of subaltern knowledge; the abrogation of the role of the educator; nor the (liberal) glorification of the pedagogue as all-knowing, wise, virtuous, enlightened, scientific, and dispensing wisdom. Education is not about finding the truth ready-made in subaltern culture, nor is it about dispensing an elite-known monopoly of the truth, but instead it is a process of discovering the truth together—a critical and dialectical engagement, intertwined with passages out of domination and autonomy.

Gramsci and Freire's 'pedagogy of praxis', writes Mayo, 'is meant to connect with people's "common sense". Common sense, as conceived by Gramsci, contains elements of good sense that, however, need to be rendered more coherent, less contradictory. The "philosophy of praxis" must transcend "common sense" in a manner . . . that is neither doctrinaire (a definitive system of ideas) nor speculative.'[175] Popular education translates the elements of historical life into conceptions of the world and new forms of collective will. It involves both 'problematization' and 'intervention'.[176]

Popular educators are like midwives. They participate in and facilitate the birth of the new, in organic formation and in the qualitative leaps associated therewith. They *draw out* what is to begin with only latent—growing incrementally—or painfully contradictory. The method is sometimes referred to as a maieutic one. The term comes from 'maieutikos', the Greek word for 'of midwifery.' In one of Plato's dialogues, Socrates applies 'maieutikos' to his method of bringing forth new ideas by reasoning, probing questions, exposing hidden assumptions, and dialogue; he thought the technique analogous to those a midwife uses in delivering a baby—Socrates's mother was a midwife.

Gramscian themes have been shown to be operative in liberation theology in Latin America. In 1970s Brazil, drawing on Paulo Friere, 'the popular education project of the CEBs [Christian Ecclesiastical Base Communities] was directed towards drawing out the "good sense" perceptions of the base in order to develop a critical consciousness. [The CEBs were not] . . . simple bearers and transmitters of values which serve to radicalise the oppressed.'[177]

Popular education has also been tied directly to the reworking of capitalist relations of production and the development of eco-socialist alternatives. For instance, the MST in Brazil, in battling land inequality and building socialist agriculture, also develops an intertwined project of education and schooling.[178] It 'is linked to a vision of socialism in the countryside in which workers own their own means of production and are able to collectively produce the food and other products necessary for their communities' survival'.[179] In asserting 'seeds as a patrimony of humanity', for example, the MST contrasted seeds as a collective good that has been transferred and shared by peasants over centuries to the increased commodification and control over seeds by transnational corporations. The MST thus drew on a historical peasant consciousness and good sense to reinterpret the past in the present.[180]

In contrast to 'social education', writes Tarlau, 'the most important feature of popular education [in Latin America]—and the least understood in Europe and the United States—is the organic link between popular education and "popular movements." In other words, what makes popular education unique is its direct connection to collective action. . . . [It is used to] develop political consciousness and capacity for critical reflection, while also strategizing . . . about concrete actions communities can take to contest structural inequities and build a more just society.'[181] Popular education engages with and diagnoses social problems, elaborates a process of community participation for the analysis of these problems, and then implements proposals to take action to address these problems.[182] It is not a 'disconnected pedagogical intervention in schools that can magically contest the dominant ideology and create revolution'. Instead, it is connected to a 'political movement' and is a form of powerful knowledge that can be part of 'a slow and continual process of garnering consent for an alternative hegemonic project'.[183]

Popular working-class adult education was a key element in South Yorkshire working class culture, militancy, and experience from the 1950s to the 1980s. It included a range of intellectuals, associations, publications, and teachers with organic links to workers. Grayson contrasts such popular education with a more economic-corporate 'skills training' for trade unionists and the later domination under neoliberalism of a 'world of marketised "lifelong learning"'.[184]

MST critiques of agroecology and capital-intensive farming and support for small-scale family farming and the promotion of food sovereignty, as taught by graduate students teaching in primary schools, key into contradictory consciousness. They help students learn 'to perceive social, political, and economic contradictions, and to take action against the oppressive elements of reality'.[185] Here, 'contradictory moments, like Diana's [a student's]

recognition of the contradiction between mining and claims of environmental conservation, are when learning happens'.[186] Learning involves an
active process of generating new knowledge. Meek explains that these forms
of popular pedagogy involve a radically new integration of space and place
that changes conceptions and feelings about what is 'here' and what is
'there' and about how such things are related. Place is not discrete, 'here',
and environmental devastation distant and 'there'. Instead they are inter-
related: Amazonia is here, on the farm far from Amazonia.[187] Hegemonic
compartmentalization is contested. Consent-winning is an expansive work.
Popular education, in connecting to contradictory consciousness and good
sense, although never a magic wand in practice, can at best form a vital
organic passage between domination and autonomy and consent. It is part of
the 'intense labour of criticism and . . . the diffusion of culture and the
spread of ideas among masses' that builds for revolution.[188]

SOCIALIST ECONOMY

What happens to autonomous anti-capitalist economic activity—and the
social classes and groups associated with it—during the struggle for consent?
In a Gramscian perspective, arguably, such forms develop and scale up, taking their place in a larger social bloc. This is partly a matter of moving out of
factory production (the factory councils) into other spheres of production
(such as agriculture or artisanal or subsistence production), but it is also a
matter of developing anti-capitalist, eco-socialist commoning and communist forms in services, consumption, housing, credit, finance, pensions,
trade, retail, and so on. Cooperatives, non-profit production, free schools,
eco-agriculture, and so on are all at work: they break or interrupt from
below the extended reproduction of capital. They develop—as Holloway has
it—the powers of concrete labour as opposed to abstract labour. The idea is to
develop concretely the new forms of economic activity within the womb of
the old, so as not to rely too much on the powers of the state when the revolution comes. Such initiatives do not need to be organized from a sole central
point, and come in a huge variety of forms.

The MST in Brazil, for example, does not just seize and occupy land and
hand it to the landless; it develops new eco=socialist forms of agriculture.
The MST 'promotes practical alternatives by encouraging agro-ecological

methods of agriculture that respect the environment and the production of seeds that maintain biodiversity. Bionatur, the MST seed cooperative, markets 63 varieties of agro-ecological seeds with an annual output of 22 tons.'[189] Farmers are conceived here as guardians of the land, keying into long-standing elements of popular common sense and good sense. Karriem makes the point that MST built service, financial, and commercial cooperatives which brought economic benefits to land-settlers—just as various more Marxian collectivization experiments failed.[190]

In a Gramscian perspective these diverse new forms of economic activity are embedded in all the moving moments of a larger hegemony. They are mediated through civil society; they confront or engage the state; they form part of a larger social bloc (with alliances and enemies); they develop a certain kind of culture, and so on. While forms of autogestion can and have bubbled up, the larger embedding and expansion process, with its slower temporalities, involves a broader organization of consent, especially in and through civil society. The process of consent winning, and fundamental changes in social being and social consciousness within a larger social bloc, are vital if protagonists are not to lose heart, drift away, remain isolated, or allow capital to move in and appropriate the new, creative, and alternative forms.

ENGAGING THE STATE

Popular mobilization in the phase of consent-winning inevitably engages on the organizational terrain of the 'expanded state' and its hegemonic apparatus—this includes 'political society' (the executive government, the civil service, the military, the judiciary, the legislature)—as well as on an expanded terrain including a wide variety of state or semi-state organizations, including public schools and universities, state media, established religious institutions, ruling parties, nationalized companies or banks, public-private companies, social providers, and so on. New forms of popular self-activity and their organs of popular authority, forms of legality, and democratic self-rule do not remain purely autonomous, but expand in part by doing battle on the terrain of the extended state, which is also keyed into inter/transnational state relations and forces.

Gramsci, for instance, became a parliamentary deputy as part of the PCI, contesting elections and seeking votes, while challenging bourgeois parliamentarianism and, at least initially, rejecting electoral alliances. In the early 1930s, he supported, against the PCI party line, the demand for a constituent assembly (a parliament) aiming to generate broad alliances as part of the fight against fascism. Gramsci also spoke of underground warfare: 'the secret preparation of weapons and combat troops';[191] of implanting loyal elements in, or winning over the consent, of the military; and of evaluating interventions in state schools and language programmes.

Gramsci was neither an ideologue of extra-parliamentary politics nor a champion of the parliamentary road to socialism.[192] His view was more subtle, dialectical, and historical. Confrontation with the existing authorities is vital but not the whole of popular mobilization. At some point, the struggle on the state terrain takes place. There is no blanket purist, anarchist prohibition. Subsequent tendencies are not predetermined. There are perhaps three main lines. The first involves success in the development of the revolutionary social force in relation to the state-oriented war of position. The second involves a long process of *trasformismo* (reformism). The third involves the outright repression of the movement by the state. Gramsci had analyzed and encountered all these tendencies: the transformism of the Action Party during the Risorgimento and of the PSI in the 1910s; the revolutionary development, as he saw it, of the war of position, both in the PCI in the 1920s and in his position on the Constituent Assembly in the 1930s; and finally, in his own life, the outright repression he and many of his comrades faced at the hands of fascism.

Gramscian perspectives and research have developed our understandings of when to, when not to, and how to engage on the state terrain, and of the various subsequent possibilities and regressions. Arguably such an historical approach is helpful in thinking a present in various countries in which a generalized rejection of party politics in the autonomist, anarchist, and extra-parliamentary Left confronts a variety of progressive efforts to engage in such politics.

In historical terms, 'the parliamentary road' has been a familiar element in appropriations of Gramscian politics. On return from exile in 1944, Palmiro Togliatti, invoking the legacy of Gramsci—whom Togliatti described as '[t]he best of all of us'[193]—and Gramsci's aim of uniting anti-fascist forces and creating an alliance between the workers and the peasantry, made it clear that the PCI would become a legal parliamentary force, a mass party of the workers, the people, and the nation against fascism.[194] Togliatti's success in 'the growth of the PCI as the largest communist party in the whole of Western Europe' needs to be marked.[195]

Parliamentary engagements have been joined under the banners of Gramsci in Latin America. This was the view taken by left supporters, for instance, of the political project of the Argentinian radical social democrat Alfonsín (d. 2009)—who became the first democratically elected president of Argentina after the dictatorship in 1983. Some of this Argentinian Left had drawn on Gramsci via their time in exile in Mexico in the late 1970s and early 1980s. Reading Gramsci via Buci-Glucksmann, they believed that the fight had to be carried out on, among, and in the 'expanded state' including in 'electoral battles'.[196]

On the other hand, South Asian subaltern studies, largely an intellectual and academic current, looked at popular elements far beyond India's congress-dominated parliament and indeed turned to Gramsci to try to understand why parliamentary elites had repressed movements such as the Naxalbari movement.[197] Motta's appropriations of Gramsci in a Latin American context, at least during the early 2000s, are a strong counterpoint to the social democratic focus on the corrupted political parties of that period of neoliberal ascendancy.[198]

Gramsci's views have been criticized by Trotskyists or Bordigists as automatically reformist, as forsaking insurrection, as merely anti-fascist and not anti-capitalist, as eschewing rupture, as too national and (Italian) rather than internationalist. As Stefano Merli had it, in engaging the bourgeois state, 'one becomes imprisoned within the logic of the status quo, with the corollary that the fundamental objective fades from view and finally disappears into the distance.'[199] But Gramsci did not enjoin parliamentary engagement in all times and places, and in a Gramscian theory, *trasformismo* is neither automatic nor inevitable. Boggs argues that what went wrong with Togliatti's PCI is that it 'lost its revolutionary identity largely because it operated almost *exclusively* within the electoral and trade-union arenas, thus gradually submerging itself within the orbit of the bourgeois state. . . . Gramsci would have predicted as much.'[200] The weakness, then, was the loss of contact with subaltern and popular forces not with the effort to engage the

The Expansive Search for Consent

state on principle. Parliaments are part of the expanded state, and they mediate the relationship between parties and the military, fiscal, executive, and administrative parts of the state apparatus. They cannot be wholly ignored. What matters, above all, is how the engagement is carried out,[201] when it is undertaken, and how such protagonism is situated in relation to the phases of hegemony and popular mobilization.

Engels proposed, in 1895, that the defeat of the Paris Commune had paved the way for a turn from armed insurrection to parliamentarism: 'We, the "revolutionists", the "overthrowers"—we are thriving far better on legal methods than on illegal methods and overthrow. The parties of Order, as they call themselves, are perishing under the legal conditions created by themselves.'[202] Engels's insight captures the complex possibilities that attend on the use of legal or illegal methods—rather than setting up a binary in which legal methods are only ever associated with reformism and illegal methods only ever associated with revolution. The Gramscian approach is more subtle. There is a historicized sense of the ways in which it may be possible to work incremental changes on structures from within in molecular ways associated with the war of position, which might eventually bring about, by eating away at the woody integument and by generating new sites of articulation, a qualitative shift—without turning such 'legal methods' into any sort of panacea.

There is no blueprint for how the successful war of position unfolds. Perhaps one can infer the presence of a scaling up process in relation to forms of popular democracy, a passage from the developing social bloc, and new forms of civil society and economy into the extended state and vice versa, including the diffusion of the new legality. The main organizational vehicle for this is the organic party. The main principle at work was to be democratic centralism, allowing for autonomous activities among the peripheral forces (both within and without the party) or in the relations between the party as organization and all the other parts of the 'organic party'.

BUILDING THE SOCIAL BLOC

At a certain point in the development of popular mobilization, the question of the bloc starts to be posed. Bloc formation involves the sublation of the social being and consciousness associated with class and group and the formation of a new forms of popular and collective consciousness. There is a unification and further politicization of 'various local and sectoral struggles' into a revolutionary popular bloc, 'a counter-hegemonic convergence of forces still grounded in civil society but seeking expression on the terrain of state power'.[203] The popular social bloc is 'an historically crystallised formation of popular groupings or movements built around a common ideology— around a subjective sense of political identity—in contrast to the "objective" sociological categories (class, social position) employed by orthodox Marxism'.[204] The social bloc 'designates the ensemble of forces necessary for attaining determinate conjunctural political goals: governmental conquest, the realisation of a shared programme and so on'.[205]

In the popular social bloc, otherwise divergent interests converge around a certain vision and purpose:

> Rooted in Gramsci's critique of economism, this concept [of bloc] draws attention to a dialectic of mass mobilization within civil society around themes which transcend an exclusive class basis: nationalism, anti-authoritarianism, anti-clericalism, regional separatism, ethnicity, and so forth. While these supra-class issues might be antagonistic to socialist movements during periods of stability, or in the early stages of mass struggles, they can be sources of radicalisation at times of crisis, when strata previously in conflict sometimes join forces to fight a common battle—as in the development of a multi-class alliance around nationalist objectives.[206]

The accent on bloc formation taking place in a historically developed phase of popular struggle is unmistakable.

We can see, in the question of the popular bloc, the outlines of a united front strategy—one which Gramsci rejected in the early 1920s but eventually came to accept. In Gramsci's trajectory we can surely trace a painful process of learning. That rigid class affiliation; dogmatic vanguardism; the tight-knit revolutionary party; the purity of communist doctrine; the coruscating, masculinist critique of everything and everyone outside of the Communist Party; the rejection of the United Front—all of which were more or less associated with Bordiga but in which Gramsci participated in the early 1920s[207]— had to be overcome and a new, wider, and more effective social force established. In this trajectory, the learning process did not emerge from victory but from defeat in the fascist seizure of power; it did not come from a cumulative, linear, or smooth expansion of the struggle but out of dramatic setbacks and a period of regrouping and painful internal ructions. By the 1930s, Gramsci was arguing that without gaining the support of allied classes, such as the peasantry, 'the proletariat had no chance of building any serious revolutionary movement'.[208] Thus 'the party needed a line of action that, by unfolding in stages, became comprehensible and accessible to these social layers.'[209] Against vanguardism, and intellectuals removed from the masses, Gramsci argued '[i]n favor of homogeneous formations made up of compact social blocs and in favor of intellectuals, vanguards and commandos that work in order to give rise to such blocs rather than to perpetuate their own . . . domination'.[210] The organic party helps to build the bloc.

In the 1930s, disagreeing with the maximalist line of immediate revolution led by a vanguardist party and dictated internationally by Stalin, Gramsci 'was advocating solidarity not only with the impoverished peasants and the alienated intellectuals, but also with the brooding, restless petit-bourgeoisie'.[211] Gramsci went so far as to include in this system of alliances, in his own words, 'the lower ranks of the army officer stratum, discontented about lack of promotion, precarious conditions of existence, etc.'[212] The contrast with Gramsci's scathing and even at times sectarian criticism of the petty bourgeoisie in the early 1920s is striking. Here the popular road, deeply rooted in domestic space, contrasted with the dictats of an over-centralized, statist, and authoritarian 'international'. Far from being petty bourgeois, social bloc building is characterized by the *dissolution* of the petty bourgeois aspects of popular self-activity—its naïvety; its spontaneism; its effervescence; its boundless youth; its jealous guarding of new-found spheres of autonomy; its belief that all wrongs can be righted quickly; its rather Manichean division of the world into good and evil; and its lack of a larger politics, ideology, and economics.

In the development of the relations of political force, Gramsci speaks of a 'third moment' beyond trade solidarity and class interest, '[i]n which one becomes aware that one's own corporate interests, in their present and future development, transcend the corporate limits of the purely economic class, and can and must become the interests of the other subordinate groups too. This is the most purely political phase, and marks the decisive passage from the structure to the sphere of the complex superstructures.'[213] This

The Expansive Search for Consent

journey from the corporate or class consciousness towards the construction of a revolutionary social bloc is central to the struggle for popular consent. Arguably, and in the light of the diversity of subaltern social groups and radical and progressive activity since Gramsci, we must think of this moment or subphase not just in relation to economic interests and class formations but also in terms of the ways in which group consciousness in relation to gender, sexuality, race, nation, and anti-imperialism starts to 'transcend the corporate limits' of identity and group and 'can and must become the interests of the other subordinate groups'.[214] There is reciprocal passage or passages, from structure to superstructure and vice versa, in which social bloc formation and new forms of popular consciousness are central.

Gramsci, who had been a Sardinian nationalist in his youth, took on a leadership role in Italian communism. In what sense did such a role 'express' his social being and his class location? Certainly, the Gramsci family were not wealthy, but nor were they factory wage-workers or landless or small-holding peasantry. Gramsci was from the South, but he was also an activist in the North. His social being in terms of inheritance was, in a sense, that of a peripheral/Southern petty bourgeoisie. What he became was quite likely the most significant Italian communist of his generation. It is vital not to gloss over—for fear of inauthenticity—the passage from class and group to social and revolutionary bloc that is arguably at stake in this shift. Gramsci as a communist was both deeply connected to the struggles of the Italian working class and to the Southern question. His position in the oppositional bloc did not automatically 'reflect' nor completely disconnect from his background. In going beyond Sardinian nationalism, Gramsci came to weave two key questions—the Southern Question and the class question— together. His consciousness of group (the racialized South) and class (the proletariat) was, arguably, woven together in his search for a new, revolutionary bloc: 'an alliance [of Northern workers] with the Southern peasants, a policy of free trade, universal suffrage, administrative decentralisation and low prices for industrial products'.[215] Gramsci understood that such a bloc stood against a ruling historical bloc comprised in this case of a 'capitalist/ worker industrial bloc, without universal suffrage, with tariff barriers, with the maintenance of a highly centralised state (the expression of bourgeois dominion over the peasants, especially in the South and the Islands), and with a reformist policy on wages and trade-union freedoms'. The construction of the new bloc involved a complexus of class and group alliances, an ideology, a new culture, civil society and party organizing, democratic elections, certain kinds of state policy, and a markedly popular consciousness. Such a consciousness does not necessarily entail cultural, linguistic, or identitarian homogenization: for instance, in Gramsci it included but did not abolish Sardinian dialect and autonomy, while connecting the South more generally to the North across a colonial divide.

Reaching beyond the economic-corporate and the confines of economic class in bloc building can be a difficult process. Roberts has argued for the limitations of Liberation Theology in Brazil, which was wedded to a view in which the fundamental contradiction was between capital (foreign capital + state) and labour. This view 'precluded an understanding by the subaltern of how factions of labour may in fact be active in supporting and reproducing the domination of the capitalist class, something which prevents understanding of the need to form a counter-hegemonic project between the subaltern class fractions before opposing the leading group directly'.[216] Roberts' formulation captures the important sense in which social bloc formation precedes a culminating confrontation with the ruling groups.

Mouffe's reading of Gramsci arguably could have gone in a different direction after 1979. A richer appreciation of the history of subaltern social groups and popular mobilization and a lesser focus on the abstract critique of economism, instead of demoting practice, would have diversified a sense of the forces that made up the new social bloc, while greatly amplifying the role that democracy would have to play in securing its internal relations. This, indeed, would be the implication of a bloc in which no single group or class was naturally entitled to hegemonize—and where the (never inevitable) universalization process involved a *new* synthesis (all syntheses are new) proven through democracy, delegation, and popular assemblies. A revolutionary, popular, and democratic socialism, therefore, operates *through* the integration of a new, revolutionary social bloc. Here there will be a diversity of organizations and currents in civil and political society (revolutionary parties; mass, democratic parties; and organic parties, alongside coalitions of parties, and so on). This is neither the democracy of a proletariat-led bloc[217] nor is it the radical democracy of politico-ideological articulation which dissolves material relations and says little about the transformation of social being / social consciousness.[218] Popular consciousness and democratic politics are instead connected in working ways to the organic formation of a new social bloc. Black feminists have argued with great force that feminism and Black liberation can be linked.[219] Feminist and queer sensibilities, insofar as they promote practices of care and challenge masculinist pride, posturing, and monopolizing, are also powerfully operative in weaving together alliances. LGBTQ+ consciousness, with its profound sensitivity to the dialectics of social being (as in body), social consciousness (as in gender identity), and questions of 'becoming' is well-equipped to think the transformations and non-binary modes operative in new forms of social bloc. The fact that at points certain elements among or between subaltern social groups will tend to be leading—the proletariat in Italy in the 1920s and the Kurds in Türkiye in the 2010s, for instance—does not naturalize the domination of any single people, group, or class. This is because the proletariat in 1920s Italy and the Kurds in Türkiye in the 2020s mean much more than a given group or class. They come to stand for the consciousness of a whole social bloc of forces and can even be a potentially rather misleading and even essentialist shorthand for that bloc, which can connect whole peoples or 'ethnicities' (Kurds, Assyrians, Turkmen, Yezidis, and so on in Rojava or Sardinians in Gramsci's Italy). The popular social bloc is not above all led by a given social being, class, or group; it is based on the ways in which diverse forms of social being and social consciousness combine to create a new popular social force.

The concept combines democracy with strategic force. There is plenty of evidence for the force of the social bloc in processes of popular mobilization and consent-winning. Well before the electoral victory of the Left in Chile in 2021, Chodor was accounting for the success of the student movement there in the early 2010s in terms of its capacities in bloc formation. He writes that the

> student movement has used counter-hegemonic strategies to forge links with other social forces, transforming its assault on neoliberal education into a wider offensive against the hegemony of neoliberalism per se. This has involved alliances with indigenous and environmental groups, social movements, and unions, leading to a national strike in August 2011 that agitated

for a broad reform of Chilean society, including constitutional change, a new workers' code, tax reform, and free public education. In doing so, the student movement has had a significant impact on Chilean politics, with the newly elected Bachelet government committed to implementing much of its programme, including free education and constitutional reform.[220]

The emphasis here is on the way in which ideological struggle plays a vital role in the integration and cohesion of the system of alliances.[221]

Conversely, it has been argued that the miners' struggle in 1984-5 Britain suffered from economist unionism, when a broad democratic alliance would have been more effective.[222] Stuart Hall's criticism of the narrow, inadequate, corporatist, and top-down posture of British Labour in the age of Thatcherism is in the same vein. Hall gives the example of the Labour leader, Neil Kinnock, whose image 'carried not a single echo or trace of feminist struggles over two decades'.[223] Gramscians have criticized the communists of India for a narrow class vision that failed to see that the primary contradiction was between imperialism and the Indian people and thus failed to build a bloc.[224]

VANGUARDISM

Gramsci arguably stands against neither leadership nor the existence of a vanguard as such, but against various kinds of vanguardism: chiefly, political Cadornism, adventurism, volunteerism, maximalism, sole leadership, and voluntarism. These are major dangers during the expansive search for consent.

Political Cadornism—sometimes referred to as commando tactics and occasionally as volunteerism—means frontal assaults which are too easily defeated as they are insufficiently prepared. One example comes from anticolonial struggle: 'A kind of commando tactics is also to be found, but it can only be utilised with great circumspection' because there is a risk of adventurism (frontal assault without proper preparation of consent) and of premature attacks provoked by the occupier. These can then suit the occupiers' strategy, which relies on 'their ability to manoeuvre through control of the internal lines of communication, and to concentrate their forces at the "sporadically" most dangerous spot'. In such cases it would 'suit them [colonialists] to *provoke* a premature outbreak of the Indian fighting forces, in order to identify them and decapitate the general movement'.[225] Mass action, on the other hand, was a viable response[226] —presumably because it would create dispersed fronts, causing the colonial forces to be diluted.

Gramsci's criticism of maximalism—the insistence on revolution and nothing but revolution and, in the immediate present, the gospel of the immediate frontal assault—crops up at various points in his pre-prison writings. He wrote in *L'Unità*, in July 1925:

> Comrade Lenin has taught us that in order to defeat our class enemy, who is strong, who has many means and reserves at his disposal, we must exploit every crack in his front and must use every possible ally, even if he is uncertain, vacillating or provisional. He has taught us that in a war of armies you can't attain the strategic goal, which is the destruction of the enemy and the occupation of his territory, without having first attained a series of tactical objectives—which aim at breaking up the enemy—and then confronting him in the field.[227]

Tactical activity, then, aimed at immediate objectives, exploiting even minor 'cracks' in the ruling bloc, and making use of even provisional or uncertain alliances, are part and parcel of the expansive search for consent. Gramsci goes on:

> The entire pre-revolutionary period [in Russia in 1917, and in general] presents itself as one of primarily tactical activity, directed at acquiring new allies for the proletariat, breaking up the enemy's offensive and defensive organizational apparatus, and detecting and exhausting his reserves. Not taking account of this teaching of Lenin's, or only taking account of it theoretically without putting it in practice, without making it become daily activity, means being a maximalist, that is, speaking grand revolutionary words while being incapable of taking a step along the road of revolution.[228]

Grandiose expressions of revolutionary purity and intent, then, are not as valuable as small, incremental steps.

Gramsci also cautions against voluntarism. Here a narrow clique or elite unilaterally takes the movement in new, adventurous directions, either practically or theoretically, without any organic relationship to the masses or the membership. Gramsci distinguished between voluntarist 'intellectual *elites* separated from the masses' and 'intellectuals who are conscious of being linked organically to a national-popular mass'. The former fail in terms of 'organic collectivity' and the capacity to form a 'social bloc' and to elicit participation. They are vanguards without armies, commandos without infantry or artillery. Volunteerism is a form of vanguardism: it represents a decomposition of popular force.[229]

A final key danger involves the sole leader or the charismatic deliverer. Gramsci argued strongly against the idea that the *modern* Prince could be a single individual. The modern Prince would have to be 'an organism, a complex element of society'.[230] A sole leader may be a temptation in situations of great danger or when lightning speed and improvisation is required—here fanatical adherence can outweigh 'corrosive irony' regarding this or that leader. But such leadership cannot have a long-term or organic character by its very nature.[231] It will not be creative or state- or nation-founding, but merely defensive or restorative; it would act as the 'saviour' of a dispersed, largely collapsed, and 'nerveless' collective will rather than as a force capable of bringing new and as-yet-untested forms of collective will into existence. Charismatic leaders, and more generally oligarchical tendencies, prevail where a static equilibrium exists; where the relationship between leadership, intellectuals, and masses is no longer 'organic and dialectical'; and where, above all, there is an 'immaturity of the progressive forces'.[232]

Vanguardism, then, refers to disorganic leadership in various forms and is a danger that threatens to undermine and fragment the expansive search for consent. One interesting hypothesis in the above states that 'immature' forms of popular mobilization themselves are responsible for the ascendancy of a charismatic leader. This is contrary to a conventional picture in which the analysis unwittingly slights the powers of popular mobilization by reproducing the focus on the 'sovereign', agency-laden individual so admired by the crowds.

TRASFORMISMO

Trasformismo refers to the opposite major danger during the expansive search for consent. At work, over a period of several years and perhaps decades, are: the convergence of party programmes (from Left and Right) in the electoral arena; the loss of popular, socialist, and revolutionary content of a party programme; the disintegration of such parties into 'personal cliques and factions';[233] the absorption of radicals into middling or high positions in the state apparatus; the formation of 'an ever more extensive ruling class';[234] and the severance of any organic connection with popular classes, who are thus 'decapitated' and excluded from the state. In *trasformismo*, renewal morphs into neoformation.

For Gramsci, transformism took place among subordinate challengers, such as the Action Party in Italy after 1848: here it was a 'parliamentary expression' of the ways the Action Party were, in the larger sense, subjected to the 'action of intellectual, moral and political hegemony'.[235] This meant 'the gradual but continuous absorption, achieved by methods which varied in their effectiveness, of the active elements produced by allied groups—and even of those which came from antagonistic groups and seemed irreconcilably hostile. In this sense political leadership became merely an aspect of the function of domination—in as much as the absorption of the enemies' *élites* means their decapitation, and annihilation often for a very long time.'[236]

We note the intimate intertwining here of force and consent—the point being that leadership merges into domination when it decapitates social groups by 'transforming', absorbing, and neutralizing their leaderships. The Action Party should have counterposed to the 'spontaneous' attraction of the Moderates—'an "organized" attraction, according to a plan'.[237] Instead it was itself attracted, partly 'because of the atmosphere of intimidation that made it hesitant to incorporate certain popular demands into its program' and partly because some of its major figures (e.g. Garibaldi) had personal relations with the Moderates. This meant oscillations. Its critical task was to stamp the Risorgimento 'with a more markedly popular and democratic character'. It should have set out 'an organic program of government that embraced the essential demands of the popular masses and of the peasants in the first place'.[238] This popular content, however, was eviscerated, placing the Action Party in a subordinate position and creating ruling groups averse to popular intervention.[239] Transformism, then, can involve 'a strategy of assimilating and domesticating potentially dangerous ideas by adjusting them to the policies of the dominant coalition',[240] eviscerating their meaningful content and deploying them in way that does not challenge the status quo.

Gramsci also related transformism to colonialism. He wrote of the 'transformism [after 1900] of entire groups of leftists who pass over to the

The Expansive Search for Consent

moderate camp', a process involving first the 'the formation of the national-ist party, with ex-syndicalist and anarchist groups' and subsequently 'the Libyan war' and 'interventionism'.[241] Here the accent is on a shift in ideo-logical and political colour and affiliation, whereby a certain kind of Left opposition was drawn into settler colonial politics.

Transformism takes place in relation to economic power, as well as to the state and ideology. Trade unions, for instance, can decline through *trasform-ismo* into more purely economic-corporate forms of intermediary organiza-tion. Gramsci writes: 'The unions' normal course of development is marked by a continuous decline in the revolutionary spirit of the masses. The union increases their material strength, but weakens or completely destroys their appetite for conquest . . . heroic intransigence is succeeded by the practice of opportunism—"bread and butter" demands. An increase in quantity results in a decrease in quality, and a facile accommodation to capitalist forms; it results in the workers acquiring a stingy, narrow petty- and middle-bourgeois mentality.'[242] Trade unions' quality as vehicles of revolu-tionary class identity is dissipated into quantity: there is a reduction to the economic-corporate; there is no challenge to capitalist logics in which workers are commodities, wage-earners, and consumers. Capitalist legality predominates. Unions mediate between labour and industrial management, rather than fundamentally challenging capitalism. Unions gravitate towards bureaucratic centralism: 'hierarchical, specialised, rigidly disciplined, and (over time) remote from the everyday struggles of the majority of workers'.[243]

Gramsci argues that in Italian history up until the 1920s 'it was precisely the workers who brought into being newer and more modern industrial requirements and in their own way upheld these strenuously. It could also be said that some industrialists understood this movement and tried to appro-priate it to themselves. This explains Agnelli's attempt to absorb *L'Ordine Nuovo* and its school into the FIAT complex and thus to institute a school of workers and technicians qualified for industrial change and for work with "rationalised" systems.'[244] In the present one might think of corporate transformism in relation to efforts to own the 'grassroots' or queer, antira-cist, or ecological issues, subsuming them via astroturfing or under policies of socially responsible, green, or ethical investing.

Overall, *trasformismo* can be seen as an ineffective, or failed, translation and sublation of popular self-activity. It is not a simple matter of the collapse of popular self-activity itself or of repression alone. Transformism offers no martyrs, only sell-outs. Transformism is thus the failure to develop and expand on such forms of popular self-activity. It is the deformation of popular mobilization in relation to its internal morphology. It involves the failure of new popular forms of representation to retain an organic link to their grassroots. It is the negative twin of vanguardism.

RADICALIZATION

Gramsci's comparison between the Jacobins and the Action Party makes clear that the former 'struggled valiantly to secure the links between city and country', reaching out across social divides in a way mirrored and 'strongly felt' in 'French political literature'. Gramsci also writes that '[t]he history of the Communes is rich with experiences in this respect: the emerging bourgeoisie seeks allies among the peasants against the Empire and against its own local feudalism'. He adds that Machiavelli had 'posed the problem' of 'the need to forge links with the peasants in order to have a national militia that could eliminate mercenary companies'.[245]

Gramsci took an interest in the changing position of militias during the wars during the wars between the Communes in Italy of the medieval period. The Communes mobilized men for battle, but '[t]he fighting men remained united even in peacetime, which enabled them to make their services available and later, as their solidarity intensified, to pursue their own goals as well.'[246] Gramsci writes that these militias not only provided protection against external threats 'but also . . . provide[d] all commoners with the protection they needed from the aggressions of the nobles and the powerful', as well as discharging other 'communal obligations', like 'assisting the poor'.[247] Operative in the popular reorientation of the militias—this positive form of Jacobinism—is a weakening of the link between civil society and the state, between intermediary groups (in this case militias) and ruling groups (in this case the nobles).

Li's study of movement-oriented labour non-governmental organizations (MLNGOs) in Guandong, China, illustrates a dynamic in which middle-class and intermediary groups start to engage in popular mobilization, joining forces with the popular bloc. MLNGOs provided 'legal assistance or cultural and recreational activities to individual workers, shunning strikes. Since 2011, however, a subset of them in Guangdong Province have gradually changed to promote WLCB [worker-led collective bargaining] and to facilitate collective protest.'[248] MLNGOs raised consciousness about rights, interpreted rights / constitutional provisions in worker-friendly ways, countered legal atomization by encouraging workers to bypass the dispute resolution procedure, and encouraged strike action and worker-led collective bargaining.[249] Li's research attributes this to the proximity to Hong Kong, the 'offshore civil society of China'; the more developed market economy relative to other Chinese provinces; and more intensive labour conflicts.[250] The sense of a weakened link between civil society and the state is operative here: 'some stability maintenance officials categorised the MLNGOs as a faction that "loosens the soil"',[251] an expression which referred to the ways in which such organizations shook the mass foundations of the state. This attitude of the state was partly in response to the new forms of activism, but it also can be conceived as one of its causes and a reason why the more middle-class elements in the MLNGOs started to define themselves as in a situation of fundamental opposition to the state.

Another example, this time turning on sexual politics, involves rural, low caste, female, development rights' workers in twenty-first-century Rajasthan in India. Some had been drawn into programmes based around rights, development, and empowerment linked to the state and organized in civil society to seek state guarantees of rights through the constitution, citizenship, and legal instruments. They were, as Madhok writes, in some important sense the agents of statist development. In Gramscian terms, they operated a link between the state and civil society. What then happened, however, in the case Madhok studies, was a crisis in the relationship with the state over the sexual assault of Bhanwari Devi, one of their leading figures. The forces of law and order, as things transpired, failed to recognize, investigate, and bring to justice the perpetrators, and even abused the victims. The process led sections of development rights workers into a 'crisis of reflection over the nature of their relationship with the state, and subsequently, into open conflict with it over the question of rights, which they had thus far identified with the state'.[252] A radically more confrontational

The Expansive Search for Consent

view of the state was formed, in which the state was 'classist, casteist and masculinist, and radically estranged from any real commitment to social justice'.[253] Here we see the ways in which, when an aspect of civil society is repressed—this time in relation to sexual violence—the juridical language of rights drops out, the state becomes a tyrannical regime, and intermediary classes pass over to confrontation or become available for a potential joining of hands with forms of popular mobilization.

Other examples of processes of radicalization have been researched. For instance, the development of Black theology as a form of counterhegemony against apartheid: 'three student organizations were indisputably pivotal to the history of Black Theology: the Student Christian Association, established in 1896, the University Christian Movement, organized in 1966, and the South African Students Organization, founded in 1968. Remarkably, the political and social history of these three groups demonstrates a gradual shift from liberalism to radicalism and from interracial cooperation to racial separation.'[254] Here elements of civil society, previously acting to engineer consent in relation to the state and accommodating political and civil society to one another, now came into conflict with aspects of the state apparatus, forging new forms of 'intensified' solidarity with Black subaltern social groups.

Domingo's research traces a homologous shift from reformist union and community organization to more revolutionary forms among Filipino-Americans in Seattle in the late 1960s and early 1970s. Part of the background to this was transnational: it was the result of fractures going on in the Philippines—including the imposition of martial law, which brought about a confrontation with the state in the United States.[255]

A further example, in cultural, Marxist optics, involves the emergence of class and national consciousness and popular mobilization in Egypt before 1914. Middle-class nationalists, having given up hope in French diplomacy on the international stage, and in confronting the British in new ways, and in searching for constituencies to represent on the domestic stage, increasingly conceived of workers and the working class as a fundamental component of the Egyptian nation. These moves were part of the background to Egypt's revolutionary uprising of 1919.[256] Here we see how forms of national-popular consciousness came to be elaborated not just from the ensemble of subaltern social groups but also among middle classes defecting from their position as intermediaries of monarchy and colonial rule and joining hands with popular constituencies in a broader fight against the despotic colonial state.[257]

Unlike transformism, in which representatives are increasingly severed from represented, in relation to positive forms of leadership, the reverse situation applies: new representatives mobilize and start to find and join with the represented in new ways. New translations emerge. At stake is the defection of middle and intermediary groups and classes from the ruling bloc, the dissolution of their false universalism, the repurposing of their forms of civil society, and the increasingly organic formulation of their engagement with popular mobilization. For ruling groups, repression can be dangerous, as it can fuel this dynamic of reverse *trasformismo* and popular bloc formation. Overall, at stake here is a positive Jacobin move, a tendency of renewal, radicalization, and transformism in reverse. It is a salient meaning of 'radicalization' at a time when the term has been co-opted by security studies, conservatives, and forms of imperialism.

CONCLUSION

This chapter has shown how the expansive search for consent can be productively understood as a phase of popular mobilization in the long journey from subordination to revolution. The search for consent expands the new collective will, growing out of but sublating autonomy and posing many of the problems of responsible leadership *before* the revolution—as an adequate preparation for it. The phase transforms practice. But as this chapter has also shown, it requires a *theoretical* renewal—beyond both classical Marxism and anarchism—both of which fall short in relation to thinking the politics of consent and leadership: the former because it expects consent for socialist revolution to form automatically among subaltern social groups due to the grave-digging motions of capitalism and so fails to raise adequately the question of the collective will; the latter because consent is equated with spontaneity and leadership is disavowed. Marxism-Leninism is no solution because of the tendencies towards vanguardism while the reformism of the Second International (and the Risorgimento) presents other dangers—those of neoformation and *trasformismo*. This chapter sheds light on how Gramsci launched a new way of thinking, allowing us to theorize the search for consent in organic, popular, and democratic ways. Such theorization is renewed through engagements with anti-colonial, Black, feminist, and queer thinking. The phase, like the others, is understood in relation to transformations in spatio-temporality, the dialectics of social being and social consciousness, structures (civil society, culture, economy, and state), and the balance and relation of forces.

The chapter has elaborated on these four 'faces', while making three main arguments. The first claims that it is vital to study not just *trasformismo*, but its antithesis, radicalization, which involves defections from the historical bloc; the takeover of parts of civil society by popular forces; new forms of economy; ideological elaboration and popular education; and the mobilization of new representatives, who form new connections with the represented. The second argument claims that we can fruitfully think in terms of the formation of a social bloc, stitched together practically through modalities learned from intersectional sensibilities and culturally through ideological elaboration and the development of a popular consciousness which transcends proletarian and group consciousness. The third main argument has to do with the importance of the organic party, as opposed to the mass democratic party or the vanguardist party, as the key organizational modality for the expansion of consent. As we have seen, the organic party prefigures the new civil society; it is diverse, democratic, and transnational; it does not have a sole organizational command centre; and it takes shape amid the disputes and contests attendant on bloc formation, consciousness, and ideology. Overall, the theory proposes important criteria through which a line of organic development in consent-winning can be understood.

At a certain point, a more decisive confrontation, with new challenges, is in the making. The limits of the 'consensual revolution' start to be exposed. There is a crisis in the relations between civil and political society, a confrontation between the popular social bloc and the increasingly repressive forces of the ruling classes.

CHAPTER SIX

The Roiling Ferment of Revolution

In the previous chapter, we found Gramsci contrasting a preparatory phase, the struggle for consent, with a phase of 'the direct struggle for power'.[1] There is a warrant here for seeing the direct struggle over power as the 'actively revolutionary' phase in a theory of popular mobilization 'dense with successive [sub]phases', a culminating phase in which the subaltern social groups eventually put forward the basis of the new 'state'. In the revolutionary phase, there are, in Lenin's memorable phrase, weeks when decades happen. A new historical bloc comes together. The 'entire "logical" argument' put forward by revolutionaries during the struggle for consent now finally 'appears as nothing other than autoreflection on the part of the people'.[2] Structure and superstructure, class and group, space and time are remade. In this phase, the 'collective, social will', constructed by living people 'becomes the driving force of the economy and moulds objective reality, which lives and moves and comes to resemble a current of volcanic lava that can be channelled wherever and in whatever way men's [people's] will determines'.[3]

There is no millennium. The revolution is not complete. The subaltern social groups may still find themselves in a state of 'anxious defence' just as the French bourgeoisie did in the 1830s. The 'long revolution' is ongoing and encounters many coeval and subsequent dangers. But when the history of subaltern social groups is 'unified' in a new state, a strategic conjuncture of great magnitude and significance unfolds; there is a passage from *consenso* to *direzione*, a revolutionary rupture in the balance of forces,[4] a final act in the decomposition of the old hegemony, and the dynamics of a new form of hegemony are set in train.

This chapter takes up the roiling ferment of popular mobilization in the revolutionary phase, aiming to unpack some of its salient forms and dynamics. A Gramscian perspective is fruitful and distinctive. It takes aim at the mechanical determinism of conventional social science, which has either carried on a billiard-ball-like search for causes, shifting between structure and agency,[5] or it has overstressed relational interactionism[6]—or even 'anti-explanation'[7]—views which in Gramscian perspectives go too far in their embrace of indeterminacy and end in passivity. A Gramscian approach also offers a corrective to revolution-lite that has become conventional in political science in which revolution is often equated with large demonstrations or passing popular risings.[8] The importance of the war of manoeuvre, further, precludes a reading of revolution wholly in terms of non-violent or civil resistance.[9] Gramscian perspectives also strike against materialist Marxism, in which revolution is above all a seizure and transformation of the means of production, and 'Marxism-Leninism', in which the seizure of state power by an organized vanguard takes the lead. Marx, after all, invoked the importance of a 'real people's revolution' and Lenin cited him approvingly.[10] It is arguably a Gramscian perspective that can help us understand what this involves.

Studying popular mobilization in the revolutionary phase, far from being a matter of dreamy idealism, draws our attention to very practical questions and dynamics—helping us to identify what the revolutionary phase involves in concrete political terms, how it unfolds, and when and where it happens. It can help us understand dangers, such as Caesarism. These concrete political questions can go missing in idealist or post-Marxist readings, in which revolution is above all a matter of politico-ideological rearticulation, culture, and cultural hegemony, as various Gramscians have pointed out.[11] Mass revolutionary dynamics and strategies have been scarce indeed in Europe since the days of Luxemburg, Lenin, Lukács, Gramsci, Bordiga or Trotsky.[12] Popular revolutionary dynamics, on the other hand, have had a significant history outside of the West during the whole period since 1918, from China 1949 to Cuba 1959, from Algeria 1962 to Iran 1979, and from Chiapas in the 1990s to Rojava in the 2010s. The study of revolution is far from being a Eurocentric proposition. It is not a matter of taking a European model and generalizing it to the rest of the world. It is a matter of thinking in the terms of popular revolutionary experiences of many kinds from the eighteenth century to the present. The concept of the 'popular revolution' has some pedigree in Gramsci. For example, the PCI, under Gramsci, adopted the strategy of the 'popular revolution' from the Lyon Congress (January 1926) until June 1929, when 'the Comintern forced the party to renounce it'.[13]

Gramscian perspectives on revolution have often been vivified at moments of crisis in existing forms of hegemony. The sharpening crises and decomposition of neoliberalism in the present, along with the weakness of social democracy, and the false 'comforts' (racism, exclusion, masculinism, Orientalism, essentialism, and genus-thinking) of right-wing populism—is another such moment. Gramscian perspectives can play a part in a political renewal by helping us conceive, against both authoritarianism and anarchist incapacity, of a popular, democratic revolution. The search for such a conception was very much part of Gramsci's own life story—between the coopted social democracy of the PSI, the strategic weakness of the anarchists and revolutionary syndicalists, the maximalism and bureaucratic centralism of Stalinist tendencies, and the fascism of those who imprisoned him.

THE CULMINATING PHASE(S) OF THE WAR OF POSITION

It is conventional to read the war of position as paving the way for the final frontal attack on the state—i.e. a war of manoeuvre. This is certainly the overarching temporality. But there are two significant caveats. One is that the subaltern, autonomous, and consent-winning phases are peppered with forms of frontal assault—elements of war of manoeuvre, ranging from covert preparation for attack (underground warfare) to overt popular insurrections to strike action to the physical defense of autonomous spaces to scattered attacks 'on the town hall'. These considerations should already suggest a dialectical and temporally diverse approach to the war of position / war of manoeuvre, rather than a too linear, taxonomic view in which the whole of the 'frontal assault' is reserved for the revolutionary phase. But there is a further major caveat, which is that the war of position takes on different and distinctive forms of importance in the revolutionary phase itself, and revolutionary strategy must tack between frontal assault and war of position, sometimes emphasizing the latter.

In the revolutionary phase, Gramsci states that a frontal attack can give way to a war of position, which is in turn decisive. Here the war of position seems to involve a new intensity: a more forceful, arduous, and painful set of activities (siege warfare) than are sometimes associated with the 'gradual', organizing, and cultural 'trench warfare' of the war position. This is the thrust of an important passage in the *Prison Notebooks* entitled 'The transition from the war of manoeuvre (frontal attack) to the war of position'.[14] Gramsci writes that this is 'the most important question of political theory that the post-war period [i.e. since 1918] has posed, and the most difficult to solve correctly'. Trotsky, writes Gramsci, 'can be considered the political theorist of frontal attack in a period in which it only leads to defeats'.[15] Vacca suggests that this is rather a reference to 'Stalin's policy and the Comintern's strategy after the Sixth Congress (1928)'.[16] Gramsci goes on: 'The war of position demands enormous sacrifices by infinite masses of people. So an unprecedented concentration of hegemony is necessary, and hence a more "interventionist" government, which will take the offensive more openly against the oppositionists and organize permanently the "impossibility" of internal disintegration—with controls of every kind, political, administrative, etc., reinforcement of the hegemonic "positions" of the dominant group, etc. All this indicates that we have entered a culminating phase in the political-historical situation, since in politics the "war of position", once won, is decisive definitively.'[17]

Here there is a 'concentration of hegemony', referring to the intensive and extensive construction of consent among the revolutionary forces (and even, perhaps, on narrower bases) among ruling groups threatened by revolution. These latter groups become even more offensive and coercive against the revolutionaries, while aiming to shore up their own hegemony, and imposing a plethora of new controls, even on their own side. This polarizing situation is diagnostic of a culminating phase in the political-historical situation—an indication that we have now entered a revolutionary phase. Under such conditions, Gramsci sees great value in the war of position—when the revolutionaries put the ruling positions under siege. One reason for this has to do with coercion, the other with consent. As for coercion: 'In politics, in other words, the war of manoeuvre subsists so long as it is a question of winning positions which are not decisive, so that all the resources of the State's hegemony cannot be mobilized. But when, for one reason or another, these positions have lost their value and only the decisive positions are at stake, then one passes over to siege warfare; this is concentrated, difficult, and requires exceptional qualities of patience and inventiveness.'[18]

The assumption seems to be that ruling, coercive institutions, reduced to their hard core, must still be militarily stronger than those of the revolutionaries, in terms of resources, personnel, organization, and sheer firepower. This means that the frontal assault from below, on its own, can only succeed in taking over positions that are not absolutely central to the power of the ruling class. Even in the face of popular insurrection and attacks on state institutions, the hard core of coercion remains (the security forces; the army; or some subset thereof, such as the praetorian guard). The organs of repression remain 'the final arbiter of political power'.[19] One is reminded of toppled Tunisian President Ben Ali's final conversations with the security forces, taking place after he had departed the country on 14 January 2011. Eventually it came down to one question: whether the army could guarantee his safety. It is at this point, Gramsci is suggesting, when the organs of repression remain in a state of maximum mobilization, that they must be put once again under siege and thereby drained of their external and indirect supports—including in relation to culture, personnel and organization. At this point, a situation of 'reciprocal siege' comes to the fore. As Gramsci writes, 'In politics, the siege is a reciprocal one, despite all appearances, and the mere fact that the ruler has to muster all his resources demonstrates how seriously he takes his adversary.'[20] Engaging the war of position here is immensely arduous and requires exceptional patience. But we can understand that victory here is crucial—'decisive indefinitely'—because the coercive institutions, denuded of all support, would then be dismantled and thus be much less able to remain or reemerge in a counterrevolutionary form. Read in this way, the return to the war of position during the revolutionary phase is part and parcel of a strategy that would break up, rather than simply seize the state and its repressive organs. The message is that even in the revolutionary phase, frontal assault is not the only strategy and must be interwoven with the war of position. As Gramsci writes in reference to the achievements of the Risorgimento, Cavour (representing the war of position) and Garibaldi (representing the war of manoeuvre) were indispensable in equal measure.

The Roiling Ferment of Revolution

THE DANGER OF THE VIOLENT REVOLUTIONARY MINORITY

Indeed, it is arguably the case that a key danger during the war of position in the revolutionary phase is that of maximalism in another form: the weakness of the violent revolutionary minority, taking premature action without an organic connection to organized mass action. This kind of maximalism is consistently criticized by Gramsci—even in his supposedly 'voluntarist' period and in the midst of the Biennio Rosso. In November 1919, for instance, Gramsci wrote that '[e]ven if a revolutionary minority succeeded in seizing power violently, that minority would be overthrown the next day by the backlash of capitalism's mercenary forces. . . . The revolution finds the great popular masses of Italy still amorphous, still fragmented.'[21]

The editors continue: 'In Gramsci's view, it was only through the creation of organisms capable of uniting the masses and channelling their spontaneity, that the revolution could command majority assent and hence overcome definitively the power of the capitalist State.'[22] Arguably, it is the strategic function of the war of position and its detailed forms of organization, consent formation, and ideological dissemination which connect the revolutionary leadership in an organic way to organized mass action. If this is true then the bid to break and remake the state, the crucial move in the revolutionary phase, cannot possibly take place before consent-winning has progressed significantly—perhaps to the point where it can command the support of the majority. We can only, therefore, speak genuinely of a revolutionary phase once such a social force is in play. We should also expect *golpismo* (the seizure of state power by armed force), Blanquism, and so on to fail, and perhaps even to play into the hands of counterrevolutionary forces. This position translates, as we have seen, into a critique of vanguardism, whereby the latter involves a 'maximalist' position asserting, regardless of the actual capacities of the revolutionary bloc, that the time for a revolution is nigh. As Gramsci was said to have underlined when in prison (at a time when the USSR was urging maximalism), there was 'often talk about revolution without any precise idea of what would be needed to bring it about'.[23] Here there is also the danger of civil war, which both Trotsky and Gramsci attributed to the too rapid and insufficiently prepared seizure of power in the war of position.

THE WAR OF MANOEUVRE

We note, however, that the war of manoeuvre (sometimes called the 'war of movement') as 'the conquest of power through direct confrontation'[24] does not by any means drop out of this Gramscian scheme—just as the military war of manoeuvre should not, Gramsci writes, even in the 1920s and 1930s, be 'expunged from military science'.[25] As Egan has it: 'there can be no separation of the war of position from the war of manoeuvre. Among other things, a major condition for a successful siege was the threat, whether real or perceived, of an effective assault against a besieged fortress.'[26] There also has to be a strategy for confronting the power of the state as a coercive apparatus: '[T]he failure to adequately address the coercive power of the state places the left at a critical disadvantage, as the subordinate classes out of which the left arises are the principal targets of such power. A counter-hegemonic strategy that does not prepare to challenge and defend itself against state repression will come to naught.'[27]

The problem is posed most acutely during the revolutionary phase. In the Gramscian scheme, it is difficult to envisage a revolutionary phase without force and without a forceful, frontal challenge to the powers of the ruling groups. As Morera puts it, in the context of wrestling with the dilemma that this poses for democracy: '[T]he split between the dominant class, interested in preserving the status quo, and the progressive coalition, bent on changing it, presents a limit to consensus. It is not to be expected that those with power will relinquish it voluntarily, and hence methods other than consensual ones, what Gramsci refers to as force, may become necessary at some point.'[28]

Boggs lays a heavy stress on the argument that Gramsci presented a 'consensual' revolution. Eurocommunism, furthermore, came close to proposing an entirely peaceful route to revolution via elections, marking a clear distinction from a 'Leninist' obsession with a minority that seizes power. Nonetheless, forceful, frontal attack remains an important aspect of the forms of revolutionary popular mobilization envisaged in Gramsci. Femia's reading is aligned with the one presented here. Femia, indeed, writes that armed struggle is never repudiated in Gramsci, and there is no entirely peaceful road to revolution: 'scattered throughout his notebooks are passages that, in one way or another, indicate his acceptance of a violent, coercive phase of the revolutionary battle, when a fundamental and conclusive break with the past is effected.'[29]

While much can be done to bring rivals within civil society into an emerging historical bloc, it cannot really be expected that ruling groups and state powers will be handed over without some form of effective frontal assault—backed up, of course, by an effective war of position. Democratic and autonomous forms must be woven into the morphology of the attacking forces—perhaps as in the Rojava Revolution—but it does not mean that armed capacity is therefore expected to melt into a world of dialogue, consensus-building, and persuasion.

Kandil's research on the Muslim Brotherhood's war of position in Egypt in the 1990s and 2000s is instructive. Kandil argues that the war of position and the development of cultural hegemony in general is important but predictably generates escalating repression. When the Muslim Brotherhood really threatened the centre of power in Egypt's history—such as in 1954—they were repressed and largely dismantled. Kandil was writing before 2013, but 2013 was a powerful illustration of his point. After holding the presidency, the Muslim Brotherhood were heavily repressed and dispersed (in perhaps the largest civilian massacre in Egypt's modern history) in 2013. Kandil argues that more 'successful' Islamist movements—such as in Iran in 1979 or Palestine in 2006—either benefited from the paralysis or alienation of coercive institutions or developed strategies to neutralize them. The point is that, in a Gramscian perspective, at some point the war of manoeuvre comes into play.[30]

The Athos Manuscript, compiled by a Communist on the basis of what he heard Gramsci say in prison, is an important source—given the existence of prison censorship—for the war of manoeuvre. Here 'the military problem and the party' were addressed. Gramsci was reported to have said that 'the violent conquest of power necessitates the creation by the party of an organization of a military type, pervasively implanted within every branch of the bourgeois state apparatus, and capable of wounding and inflicting heavy blows on it at the decisive moment of struggle'.[31] He reportedly said that 'military relations of force' mean not just the 'possession of weapons or combat units, but the ability of the party to paralyse the nerve centres of the bourgeois state apparatus. For example: a general strike can shift the military relations of force in favour of the working class.'[32]

Certainly, this last point does appear in Gramsci's *Prison Notebooks*, where the general strike is integrated into a strategic and tactical analysis which encompasses both the war of manoeuvre and the war of position. Here the idea is that a ruler's superior resources will be concentrated in the defence of certain vital and decisive strategic positions—which the revolutionaries will put under siege. The siege's chances of successes can be mightily enhanced when a general strike intervenes, which then paralyzes the capacity of the ruler to continue to marshall and organize their strategic and material capabilities. As Gramsci wrote earlier, 'strikes [are a form] of war of movement'.[33] It is hard not to think of Iran in late 1978, when the strike action of millions—including oil-workers—quite literally paralyzed the regime. Could the army still have been deployed, without splitting up, against the millions on the streets, as some of the Shah's generals urged?

In the Athos Manuscript, Gramsci was said to have mentioned the 'armoured trains' at the disposal of the Italian ruling classes, noting that the party would have to create a 'military organization capable in some measure of paralysing the operation of these powerful instruments of bourgeois action'.[34]

The need for a people's militia, and the lack of one to defend the factory councils, was part of Gramsci's analysis. Without what Gramsci called 'coercive means' and 'lacking a people's militia, the council movement was more easily encircled and crushed than otherwise would have been the case'.[35] Gramsci wondered, 'how could the workers at the same time be in the factory and on the streets to defend their conquests, if there is not a State organization to train a loyal and well-positioned armed force, ready in all circumstances?'[36] Gramsci's position here was part of his generally positive assessment of the *arditi del popolo* (anti-fascist volunteer militias), frowned on as doctrinally impure by the Communist Party itself.[37] Gramsci also paid some attention to the realm of military-political combat and the battle for control of the state, including the role of fortunà (contingency and unpredictability).[38]

Femia points out convincingly that the war of position and war of manoeuvre are not mutually exclusive alternatives, that support for intermediate objectives and class alliances does not signal 'an acceptance of historical continuity and an exclusion of revolutionary rupture'.[39] Underlining the temporal dimension, Femia notes that '[t]he "military" aspect of the struggle becomes especially important when the proletariat has at last conquered the institutions of civil society and solidified a new counter-hegemony. At this point there remains the climactic attack on the state fortress.'[40] As we have seen, this is not the only temporality, but it captures key elements of the overarching rhythm. Femia notes that unlike Sorel—and one might add Fanon—Gramsci attributes no mythic, therapeutic, or humanizing content to violence, but 'his theory did not shrink from it' either. Indeed, 'physical confrontation and other militant tactics, while subordinate to the [war of position] . . . must always be kept in reserve, to be used as the situation demands.'[41]

In certain times and places, numerous progressive and popular mobilizers have felt it necessary to put frontal assault to one side and to concentrate on the war of position. Coutinho was one such figure. There has been much inspiration from Gramsci here. Other movements, however, drawing on Gramsci, have consciously combined the two strategies at least for a period. As Roberts argues, 'Instead of hypostatising and counterpoising the concepts of "war of position" and "war of movement", the leadership of the Landless Workers Movement view one as a necessary pre-requisite to the other. The possibility of revolutionary politics has not been closed off by modernisation in Brazil, according to the MST. Instead, by applying these categories as two moments of class struggle, the Landless Workers Movement articulate a strategy which is more than simply Eurocommunism or *golpismo* [a coup d'état mentality].'[42]

THE DANGER OF CAESARISM

Caesarism, in which a strong or charismatic leader seizes power and imposes autocratic or statist domination, is understood in the living Gramscian tradition as a major danger in the revolutionary phase. A key example was Napoleon III. Marx calls Caesarism Bonapartism in order to avoid analogy with pre-capitalist Rome.[43] Gramsci warned against its uses as 'polemical-ideological formula'; it is not a rigid scheme or category to be applied but a 'practical criteria of historical and political interpretation'.[44] Gramsci did not read Caesarism wholly in terms of brutal coercion. There is also some limited degree of consent formation (*consenso*). There is such a thing as both progressive Caesarism (e.g. Napoleon I, Caesar himself) and regressive Caesarism (e.g. Napoleon III and Bismarck). An example in the present is Al-Sisi of Egypt post-2013.[45]

While in classical Marxism the concept seems to be of a leader who appears amid the ruin of the contending classes, the routes into Caesarism/ Bonapartism in a Gramscian perspective are not determined in the last instance by economy and class. Caesarism can stem from flaws in the construction of the revolutionary project: excessive reliance on the war of manoeuvre;[46] a popular insurrection lacking consent; vanguardism and adventurism among minority groups detached from the masses; divisions in the revolutionary historical bloc; a crisis of authority which tilts the balance of power in favour of civil or military elites; and reformism and vacillation among supposedly revolutionary parties. Into the wreckage of *consenso* and *direzione*—the decomposition of the senate, the parliament, and the congress and the weakness and break up of civil society, ideology, consent, and effective leadership in relation to popular mobilization—and amid the insufficiencies of *autonomia* (popular self-activity) and the cries of chaos that surround it steps the 'strong man' in order to 'impose order'. The Caesarist is an embodiment of *dominazione* in new forms. In Boggs's summary analysis, Gramsci criticized volunteerism as 'an impatient military strategy oriented to rapid success but which in the end opens to the door to . . . Bonapartism, which is a "surrogate for popular intervention" and indulges the passivity of the masses. The strictly "conjunctural" focus was far too crisis-bound, too prone to look for organizational solutions where the issue of mass consciousness had yet to be posed. The result would likely be a form of detached vanguardism.'[47] Caesarism, then, is also a tendency that emerges when consciousness, ideology, and the collective will are insufficiently developed.

There is a less grandiose version, another tendency in case of revolutionary failure: not so much a Caesar as a series of adventurers, manipulators, and intriguers. Gramsci suggests that a revolution which destroyed capitalist power but which failed to produce a new proletarian governing class would likely fall 'into the hands of adventurers and political intriguers'. Gramsci writes therefore of the importance of prior training, education in the management of society, and a pedagogical network operating 'through its own channels and its own systems—meetings, congresses, discussions, mutual education'.[48]

PASSIVE REVOLUTION

A further danger in the revolutionary phase is passive revolution. Gramsci introduces the fundamental idea in his discussion of *trasformismo*. Gramsci writes: 'It was precisely the brilliant solution of these problems which made the Risorgimento possible, in the form in which it was achieved (and with its limitations)—as "revolution" without a "revolution" or as "passive revolution" to use an expression of Cuoco's in a slightly different sense from that which Cuoco intended.'[49]

What had Cuoco intended by 'passive revolution'? Vincenzo Cuoco (1770–1823) was an Italian thinker who had studied law in Naples and acted as an administrator in the short-lived republican government in Naples in 1799 after the overthrow there of the Bourbon monarchy.[50] Cuoco studied the Neapolitan revolution to relieve the tedium of his subsequent exile. He was at times a committed republican (although apparently also 'flexible' in practice). He opposed Jacobin radicalism and rationalism imported from France into the Italian South. The excellent here, he believed, was the enemy of the good, as such radicalism could never succeed, as it was too detached from the masses. On the other hand, Cuoco remained optimistic about the overall progress of the republican revolution, once a proper dose of moderation was applied. One could institute Napoleonic reforms from above, Cuoco was saying, while avoiding the tumults and terror of the Jacobins. The concept of passive revolution, therefore, described a moderate, long-term path towards revolution, as Furse has it, 'moderation as a revolutionary act'; the concept was invented by a figure who wished to play a role in administrating and governing such a moderate transition.

Gramsci's use of the concept is certainly 'slightly different'. It incorporates the sense of elites who seek—including skilfully—to resolve the problems thrown up by revolutionary activity. Such elites may be liberal or 'enlightened' but are not necessarily so. Gramsci also adopts the long temporality and broad spatial scale associated with the concept. But passive revolution is identified negatively with elite engineering and reorganization that tame popular mobilization and prevent genuine revolution.[51] It

The Roiling Ferment of Revolution

represents a deformation of popular mobilization from above. It thus formed part of Gramsci's critique of Croce's history of 1815–1871, which excluded the fire and thunder of the revolutionary explosion and concentrated 'placidly' on cultural and ethico-political expansion.[52] In passive revolution, '[t]he thesis alone . . . develops . . . to the point where it absorbs even the so-called representatives of the antithesis: it is precisely in this that the passive revolution or revolution/restoration consists.'[53] In passive revolution, 'a shifting equilibrium of forces . . . integrates opposition into the state apparatus while postponing real structural change and denying full entry of the masses into the political system.'[54]

Gramsci suggests a very broad application to the basic idea. He wondered whether the history of nineteenth- and twentieth-century Europe could be conceived in terms of passive revolution. 'Does Italy have the same relation vis-à-vis the USSR that the Germany (and Europe) of Kant and Hegel had vis-à-vis the France of Robespierre and Napoleon?'[55] Assimilating the French Revolution into an abstract liberalism (as in Kant) or incorporating the concept of freedom into a Hegelian ethical state (i.e. a state which actualizes the ethical ideal) are understood here as two different elite-engineered, passively revolutionary appropriations of French revolutionary politics. Gramsci here also considers the very different idea that the 1917 revolution and the 'threat' of the USSR led to a passive revolutionary solution in Italy. The rise of fascism acted, including through economic-corporate means, to contain the popular demands unleashed by the workers' revolution. In other words, liberalism as an intellectual current, German and Italian idealism—as well as the politics of Bismarck on the one side, and the politics of Mussolini on the other—could be interpreted in relation to the concept of passive revolution. Gramsci wondered: 'is not "fascism" precisely . . . the form of "passive revolution" proper to the twentieth century as liberalism was to the nineteenth?'[56]

Ruling class engineering of the passive revolutionary kind is intertwined with attempts to shore up capitalist (and state capitalist) profit and accumulation, especially in the face of forms of crisis, whether directly in the structure or in relation to 'politics' (including the significant challenges to profit posed by revolutionary popular mobilization). 'One way in which Gramsci uses this notion', writes Belina, 'describes the search for and pushing through of solutions for evident crisis of capitalist accumulation within the existing politico-economic order and under the leadership of the state.'[57] This line of thinking has involved a rich and various seam of research.[58]

An early example in relation to the post-independence Third World was Fatton's research on the way the ruling class in Senegal responded in the 1960s and 1970s to the 'organic crisis' generated by dependent capitalist underdevelopment. Potentially revolutionary forces were decapitated through the co-optation of their leading cadres in a reformed framework of political representation. Fatton argues that because this new hegemony was founded on passive revolution, it never reached the masses, generating widespread popular scepticism and cynicism.[59]

The concept has shed light on twentieth-century Mexico, where 'the state plays the leading role in fundamentally reorganizing social relations so as maintain or restore class dominance, while diffusing subaltern pressure'.[60] It has helped make sense of Japan's Meiji restoration.[61] It has been used, too, to understand post-2005 accommodation with neoliberalism in Bolivia.[62] Evan's usage—in relation to Welsh devolution—puts the accent on the incorporation of a national group in the United Kingdom.[63] Mallick considers various phases of passive revolution in Pakistan, putting emphasis on the incorporation of middle and intermediary classes.[64] Tuğal draws on the concept to understand the absorption of Islamism within neoliberal secularism in Turkey in the 1990s and 2000s, an absorption that relied significantly on the capacity of leading Islamist actors to put together an extensive ruling coalition in contrast with Islamist actors elsewhere in the region.[65] Mouffe went as far as to argue that passive revolution was often used by Gramsci 'to qualify the most usual form of hegemony of the bourgeoisie involving a mode of articulation whose aim is to neutralise the other social forces'.[66] It should perhaps be no surprise that strong arguments have been made against the overextension of the concept,[67] while Callinicos's own formulation—'socio-political processes in which revolution-inducing strains are at once displaced and at least partially fulfilled'—is a powerful and itself still quite a broad definition.

There is a useful contrast with *trasformismo*: the latter term throws the spotlight on qualitative degeneration and dissipation among the popular forces and their erstwhile middle-class allies and 'representatives', while the term 'passive revolution' throws the spotlight on the actions of ruling groups aiming to engineer absorption in terms of broader scales and longer temporalities. The passive revolution then represents the response of elites—including in relation to the international and transnational stage—to the forces of revolutionary popular mobilization: it is the widest canon of interpretation for understanding how even revolutionary forces can be derailed and absorbed without a fundamental rupture in the balance of forces, avoiding the formation of new historical bloc. It is a criterion for understanding one of the dangers in the phase of revolution.

THE HISTORICAL BLOC

Gramsci's analysis of the war of position and the war of manoeuvre has a very marked strategic dimension—these problematics are pursued not just in terms of theory, narrative, performance, symbols, and so on but in relation to practical questions about the balance and relation of forces. It seems reasonable to accept that part of what is distinctive about the revolutionary phase in Gramsci is not the mere presence of the war of manoeuvre or position but the fact that there is a 'rupture in the equilibrium of forces', as Gramsci puts it in a discussion of the French Revolution—the main point of which is to oppose a 'vulgar' economism, which 'aprioristically "discovers" [an economic] crisis coinciding with every major rupture of the social equilibrium'.[68] The rupture is not just a matter of economic crisis, nor is it permanent; but it gives rise to a new balance and relation of forces—the nature of which is not preordained. Setbacks and negative trajectories include *golpismo*/counterrevolution, intrigue, Caesarism, and civil war, especially in contexts where international and imperial actors weigh heavily. To think of rupture, however, is to grasp a crucial distinction between revolution and passive revolution. In the latter no fundamental rupture in the relations of forces takes place, and challenges are absorbed. But what is going on that can bring such a rupture about?

While few have seen Gramsci as a straightforward advocate of the 'dictatorship of the proletariat', there is a quite widely held perspective in which the proletariat is the fundamental class which brings about a revolution by abandoning particularistic and economistic interests, hegemonizing the other social classes (above all the petty bourgeoisie, the peasantry, and the lumpenproletariat), and forming a historical bloc in the name of the nation.[69]

Here the history of subaltern social groups is understood to involve first the ascendancy of the bourgeoisie and second the ascendancy of the proletariat. Each has a special characteristic—as fundamental class—under capitalist development. The new form of hegemony involves 'the conquest of cultural and political hegemony, that concrete historical moment when a given social group becomes the unifying and directing force of all other social groups'.[70] Such, writes Salamini, was the Jacobin experience in the French Revolution, when the bourgeoisie became the directing force.[71] It was, furthermore, the fundamental intent behind 1917: the idea that the proletariat as a class (not a party, a bureaucracy, or a sole leader) would lead the rest of the society through a fundamental transformation—that is, the true meaning of the 'dictatorship of the proletariat'.

Mouffe—alongside others associated with Eurocommunism in the 1970s—gave this what was then an exciting democratic interpretation: that the historical bloc under the leadership of the proletariat could only be constructed on a democratic basis. Hegemony here is the 'political, intellectual and moral leadership of the working class over all anti-capitalist sectors'.[72] This was a 'leadership which demands a real democratic relationship within the hegemonic system and which therefore implies a democratisation of the institutions through which it is exercised'. Mouffe continues, 'it provides us with the basis for a strategy of democratic transition to socialism: a "possible" eurocommunism which avoids both the perils of Stalinism and of social-democracy.'[73] An anti-passive revolution, which 'far from being limited to the developed capitalist countries, provides the basis for any real struggle for a democratic socialism'.[74] Here was an important Gramscian—if rather Eurocentric—route towards a democratic socialist revolution. As is well known, Mouffe and Laclau's subsequent turn towards politico-ideological articulation, which, rooted in a critique of economism, thus involved a fundamental demotion of the proletariat as the central revolutionary subject, led into a culturalist interpretation in which a bloc—the people—is formed almost entirely on ideology, representation, and discursive rearticulation. In this later reading, the problematics of economy and class, as well as the wider dialectics of social being and social consciousness, fall from view. It was arguably a problematic turn that forestalled a more interesting development of this very line of thinking.

It seems that one can indeed develop Laclau and Mouffe's earlier emphasis on the democratic, composite historical bloc by rooting it in the history of subaltern social groups and the dynamics of popular mobilization. The argument has been so far, against Eurocommunism, that no single group or class is naturally entitled to lead or hegemonize. In Gramsci's historico-political analysis, the subaltern social groups are unified when they coalesce to form the new state or community. While some subaltern social groups may be more marginal than others at certain points, while certain forces advance further along the line of development than others, at no point is the line of development propelled by the facts of social being themselves; by a wooden position in the relations of production (e.g. the fact of being doubly free wage-labour); or for instance, by epidermis, ovaries, or genitalia. Neither the often leaden and oppressive facts of objective formation, commodification, and the infinity of traces, nor embodied stigma, nor genus-thinking lead. It is these elements of subalternity, on the contrary, that must be overcome. Social being is always intertwined with social consciousness. Laclau and Mouffe's critique of Gramsci's so-called economism is powerful but misplaced. Gramsci's whole oeuvre was oriented against economism, as we have seen. Chapter 5 traced a process of bloc formation whereby diverse subaltern social groups and classes, including some formerly middle-class and intermediary groups via transformism in reverse, weld together a social bloc and forge a popular consciousness. This applies to workers, who may now be working in (and directing) an enormously diverse array of non-capitalist co-operatives and institutions, but also to Black activists, feminists, migrants, queer communities, and others bearing the traces of subalternity who are involved in such institutions—but also in their own and wider forms of cultural, political, and associational life. All the subaltern social groups will be organizing in civil society, which mediates between the new socialist economics, culture, and the state.

At a Gramsci seminar in Mexico in 1980 at the University of Morelia, Aricó sought a 'contextualisation of Marxism in the Latin American context—characterised by the lack of the proletariat as revolutionary class—by using the Gramscian concept of hegemony. This concept proposed a construction of social subjects through an intellectual and moral reform; this way the revolutionary subject was not conceived of as an a priori entity but as a historical bloc to be built.'[75] At a certain point, when the war of position has advanced in civil society—in trade unions, popular education, community organizations, campaign groups, international associations, alternative media, 'integral' journalism, and so on; when the war of position has also advanced on the terrain of the expanded state (e.g. in parliaments, the civil service, even the armed forces); when diverse subaltern social groups have already formed a social bloc with a strong popular consciousness; where there is an 'organic party'; where there are movements and campaigns that start to cluster around a developed and fertile ideology; where there are diverse streams of culture (songs, poems, films, novels, artworks, plays) expressing and working through the struggles of these elements, the question of the revolutionary historical bloc is posed. As Vacca has it, 'the concept of the "historical bloc" designates the fusion between structure and superstructures, which marks the birth of the new state.'[76]

Gramsci worried that passive revolution would be seen as inevitable and suggested otherwise:

> The thesis of the 'passive revolution' as an interpretation of the Risorgimento period, and of every epoch characterised by complex historical upheavals. Utility and dangers of this thesis. Danger of historical defeatism, i.e. of indifferentism, since the whole way of posing the question may induce a belief in some kind of fatalism, etc. Yet the conception remains a dialectical one—in other words, presupposes, indeed postulates as necessary, a vigorous antithesis which can present intransigently all its potentialities for development. Hence [the] theory of the 'passive revolution' [is] not [offered] as a programme, as it was for the Italian liberals of the Risorgimento, but as a criterion of interpretation.[77]

Gramsci was interested in the ways in which a war of position could develop, sought a 'vigorous antithesis' to the passive revolution, and 'present[ed] intransigently all its potentialities for development'.[78] While passive revolution has been richly explored in Gramsci studies, the meaning of this vital 'vigorous antithesis' has arguably been underexplored. We have already seen some part of this antithesis in the radicalization processes associated with transformism in reverse. At a more macrological level, this antithesis is operative in the revolutionizing, qualitative shift from the popular social bloc to the new historical bloc.

Several features combine. On the one hand, the revolution is organically formulated. In existence is a new popular social bloc which has won consent on a broad scale, perhaps even of the popular majority, through organic relationships between represented and representatives. On the other, the crisis in the old, now crumbling and contracted hegemony is much deeper, partly because the revolution itself has a much more developed content and a more developed and cohesive collective will. The crisis is also deeper, though, because of the new relationships at work in civil and political society. Instead of popular self-activity flinging itself against a rather exclusionary civil and political society mostly controlled by the ruling classes and their intermediaries and 'deputies', in the revolutionary phase, the coercive state apparatus, or even relatively narrow sections of it, stand pitted against organized and broadly disaffected elements in civil society and the extended state. This can add up to a qualitatively new situation. It involves the 'people / power bloc contradiction' invoked in Laclau's early writings[79]—the first caveat in relation to Laclau's early writings being that such a distinction has to come into existence in activity, in revolutionizing praxis. The second caveat, in relation to Laclau's later writings, is that the making of this distinction is as much practical as theoretical. Whole sections of middle and intermediary classes and groups break with previous forms of conformism and combine forces with the popular bloc. Previously 'respectable', middle-class- and status quo-oriented organizations start reaching out in larger numbers towards, and even help to organize forms of, popular self-activity and subaltern confrontation. The impetus comes from revolutionizing interactions and confrontations which pit the 'intermediary' middle-classes, civil society, and extended state elements on the one hand, against the coercive state and the ruling classes on the other.

The war of position itself exposes and confirms for these intermediary groups the ways in which civil society and the dominant culture is not a site of freedom but of struggle, of hegemonic discipline, linked instrumentally to state power and the ruling class. Middle-class verities are shaken; their worldview, bound up with false universality, is put in doubt. When the authorities use their powers of repression, especially against groups not accustomed to such repression, as is common in the face of a meaningful war of position, the violence of the ruling order is exposed and underlined, and intermediary groups are further shaken and alienated. The grievances and languages of ascendant subaltern social groups then start to make more sense to ever larger groups. The confrontation becomes wider, and civil society may turn to popular support to protect itself against a fiercer state engaged in repression in sections of civil society. It is a fertile terrain for forging organic connections. The centre cannot hold.[80] Increasingly, a stark and binary choice is presented: is one for or against the revolution? Sewell, for example, offers a highly eventful and compelling account of the ways in which those who led the fall of the Bastille came to be characterized—in the space of a few weeks—not as an unruly mob provoking disorder, but as a nation rising up against tyranny. Middle-class and intermediary elements, especially those staffing the representative institutions, which were under threat from and increasingly confrontational with the monarchy, were heavily involved in articulating such a national popular consciousness, which in turn was capable of enabling new conceptions, new bonds between social classes. It was a cultural shift long in the making but one which embodied, during a relatively short period, a powerful revolutionizing dynamic.

The crisis cascades down to the petty bourgeoisie (inhabiting authorized sites of autonomy), who have long taken their cue from middle-class definitions of the situation. The existing hegemony contracts, and social groups and classes increasingly form a new historical bloc. The 'vigorous antithesis' to passive revolution—a revolutionizing dynamic—attains a new threshold. For the first time, the coercive apparatus loses its hegemony among intermediary strata and its capacity to organize consent among them, a sign that the revolutionary phase has begun.

As Filippini has it, the historical bloc is 'formed through an organic movement, within the context of the decline of a social form, by means of political action based on realism that can be deployed in political relations of force in particular, taking advantage of the crisis as a terrain of political struggle'.[81] In the argument presented here, there is no dictatorship of the proletariat, and there is no literal leadership by a specific social class. There is, instead, a powerful new historical bloc comprised of a wide variety of formerly subaltern social groups and significant elements from defecting intermediary and middle classes. The popular social bloc had been in opposition, building consent; now it becomes a leading force, nothing less than a historical bloc.

The proletariat, as one of the elements of the historical bloc, has to be carefully redefined—and indeed, is in the process of redefining itself. It no longer consists of all of those dispossessed by or working for wages under or socially reproducing capitalism. One should not just trace the separation of a force from the dominant forces but grasp how that force is related to leadership.[82] The proletariat has gone through quite a few phases of development. Only in the subaltern phase can it be defined in terms of objectification, commodification, and marginalization. By the time these diverse groups reach the revolutionary phase as a proletariat, they are not only factory workers organized (or not) into unions or precarious or survivalist workers. They 'must not only think as proletarians, and no longer [think only] as metal-worker, joiner, building-worker, etc.'[83] They have become instead all of those who are working in ways that are socialist or eco-socialist or nearly so, all of those whose livelihoods interrupt the organogram of the extended reproduction of capital amid concrete, alternative forms, however discordant and diverse. Such workers are a living, organizing 'proletariat', a social class which is no longer subaltern in the original sense but active, a protagonist, and making history. This can mean various kinds of public service; household labour outside of wage-capital relations; care work; independent income-generation; creative labour; unpaid work; mutual aid; commoning; cooperative activity; non-profit provision; eco-socialist agriculture; communal living; or supporting family through remittances. A whole variety of classes emerge; they appear on the scene as constructing economic activities that refuse capitalist logics—that are in fact economic activities structured by alternate logics (including of love, of kin, of community, of hospitality, and so on). These diverse proletarians, in the positive sense, those who feel the pulse of the future city, will not 'change the world' without confronting capital or passing through the ruins of the former state. Instead, in the living Gramscian tradition, they take their place in the construction of the new hegemony. A socialist structure is accompanied by a new superstructure— that is, a new culture, a new state, and a new civil society. In this reading, then, the word 'proletariat' changes its meaning fundamentally as part and parcel of the history of subaltern social groups—as the class formations of capitalism are overcome in processes of popular mobilization. A proletariat is under formation: not the proletariat as the wage workers of capitalism (seeking to gain independence in the face of subordination and exploitation) but the proletariat which has become a set of crucial class and socialist forces, which can take its place in a larger popular historical bloc.

Morera writes of various kinds of coalition, including an intellectual-moral bloc and a social bloc, that '[t]his coalition, however, finds its limits in the long-term determining role of the class structure, limits that cannot be transcended without changing that class structure itself through the creation of a new historical bloc'.[84] Indeed, whatever else revolution involves, it involves a fundamental transformation in the ruling historical bloc. After 1789, the monarchy, nobility, and the clergy were fundamentally dispossessed—they were never to recover. After 1917, the Romanovs, the nobility, the clergy, and the bourgeoisie were shunted aside. In the revolutionary post-independence 'intermediary regimes' of the Middle East and North Africa (in Egypt, Algeria, Tunisia, Libya, Iraq, Syria, Yemen, and so on)monarchs, notables, large landowners, wealthy merchants, and certain religious authorities—the 'possessing classes' and faces (*wujaha*) of the region during the colonial period down to the 1950s and 1960s—were defeated. In their place came what Kalecki describes—referring to Egypt, India, and Bolivia—as intermediate regimes comprised of a rich peasantry, a lower middle class, and new state managers (who continued to suppress the poor peasantry, the rural proletariat, and urban workers). These are fundamental changes in the class structure.[85] A contemporary revolution in the Euro-American world, for instance, would fundamentally marginalize the financial capitalists, the 'noblesse managériale publique-privé', and other establishment groups that network with, surround, and service them.[86] One cannot think the revolutionary phase from a Gramscian perspective without the fundamental reconstruction of the historical bloc.

There are, further, significant historical and 'empirical' objections to the thesis that revolutionary transformation is led by a fundamental social class or group. Even Marx did not argue that the French revolution was led by the bourgeoisie—he saw the French revolution more as the *midwife* of the bourgeoisie. The French bourgeoisie in the 1780s and 1790s was a diverse group indeed—ranging from the maritime and commercial slaving interests to the old nobility-oriented bourgeoisie to liberals such as Barnave who frowned on popular and revolutionary activities to figures like Robespierre who encouraged them. It would be a brave historian who argued that the Bolshevik revolution of 1917 was literally led and implemented by the industrial wage workers of Tsarist Russia, who comprised a tiny fraction of the population. The same can be said of the class forces that made up the great anti-colonial revolutions. Forcing them into the model of nationalist bourgeoisie (e.g. in the case of Egypt) or proletarian revolutions (e.g. in the case of Dhufar, 1965–1975) is in fact an extremely difficult thing to do. Which social class led the Iranian revolution of 1978–79? Class readings have been undertaken, of course, and they capture an important part of the picture, but their explanatory limits have been extensively exposed. Using the word 'bourgeoisie' in relation to 1789, or 'proletariat' in 1917, or the 'nationalist bourgeoisie' in relation to 1919 in Egypt is arguably a way of summing up a whole hegemony or alternative hegemony—with a variety of complex moments—including a complex sociology. There is a vast storehouse of historical evidence to support the thesis that revolutions do not rest sociologically on the leadership of a single social class or group. Gramsci's interest in the historical bloc therefore carries a great deal of weight. Arguably it can fare well also against more recent possibilities in relation to 'the revolutionary subject': the intelligent multitude of Hardt and Negri, the precariat, and so on.

A historical bloc conceived this way has the democratic advantage of not being under the control or natural hegemony of any particular social group or class. Its economic dimensions, furthermore, far from involving a central plan or a command economy, involve a good deal of bottom-up experimentation—that is, experimentation with non-capitalist and eco-socialist relations of production and ways of life. There may be a way that democracy here combines (rather than conflicts) with strategic advantage: how else can a popular revolution muster the necessary social force, while engaging all the progressive forces in the history of subaltern social groups— feminism against patriarchy, Black liberation against white supremacy, queer struggle against masculinism and heteronormativity, and democracy and the plurinational against statism and colonialism? Only through such a broad-based historical bloc, arguably, can the popular force required for the overthrow of hegemony and the building of the new one be mustered.

Gramsci goes as far as to write that 'only the social group that poses the end of the State and its own end as the target to be achieved can create an ethical State'.[87] One can interpret this as Gramsci's answer to Hegel. Instead of imagining an ethical state to come into existence under the control of a particular group—for example, the German professional classes—through the perfection of an existing apparatus, Gramsci is suggesting that the state can only be completely broken down and replaced. Subsequently its minimal, democratic forms would not be under the control of any group, class or representative thereof. Such a reading, we note, opposes not only Hegel but 'Marxism-Leninism' and the thesis of the dictatorship of the proletariat, which implies a conception of the state that Gramsci arguably refused.[88]

THE TRANSNATIONAL POPULAR

In the roiling ferment of revolution, a new consciousness of emancipated community, long in gestation in translocal and popular forms, takes the lead. Gramsci understood the importance of the 'ideological bond between elites and popular strata embodied in Machiavelli's dream of a national community'.[89] This national-popular vision remained unrealized in Italy, especially in relation to Piedmont's domination without hegemony over the South. For Gramsci the Risorgimento was a failed revolution in this sense. Popular consciousness can weld together the diverse subaltern social groups—but the national popular consciousness was lacking. Here was where the Action Party fell short.

As a youth, Gramsci was an ardent Sardinian nationalist. He eventually came to see such a position as too limited to overcome the problems of the exploited periphery, the problem of North and South. The emancipation of the South was not to be achieved by nationalism and secession, Gramsci believed, but by the formation of a new all-Italian socialist historical bloc anchored in a national-popular consciousness. The national-popular was a work unrealized, a 'live work', and a positive 'myth' in both Machiavelli's and Gramsci's Italy.

In the 1920s, the positive myth of national liberation had already had an extraordinarily rich history. It was in the name of the nation that French revolutionary politics had gathered a plural ensemble of the subordinate and overthrown the monarchy, nobility, and church of the ancien régime and that Italy had struggled against various forms of Austro-Hungarian and French imperialism, aristocracy, and Catholicism. Nationalism had declared independence from European empires across the Americas from the late eighteenth to the mid-nineteenth centuries. It was under the banners of nationalism that popular mobilization developed in leaps and bounds across the colonized world in the wake of the First World War. It was in the name of the nation that Palmiro Togliatti was to argue against fascism and turn the decimated Italian Communist Party into a mass, democratic party after 1944. And the Third World national liberation movements were to be heavily involved in the 'mighty storm' that brought down the European empires and redrew the map of the Tricontinental world in the revolutionary decades following the Second World War.

Yet, half a century has passed since the high-water mark of the national popular. National liberation may have been a vital phase in the long history of popular mobilization, but a Gramscian theory in the 2020s is more likely to see the *national* popular as comparable to how Gramsci came to see Sardinian nationalism in the 1920s—too narrowly drawn to overcome the multiple problems and questions of imperialism, capitalism, nationalism, and statism to unleash new cultural riches and form the animating consciousness of a new and diverse historical bloc. Gramsci did not leave timeless blueprints. Phases eventually pass and are no longer of interest. Once leading as a concept of emancipated community, the national popular, although valuable in signalling autonomy, seems less able to serve as a horizon. Like other vital phases, it must be sublated and overcome.

So many of the great, progressive movements and their organic intellectuals in world politics, especially since the 1970s, including those studied by Gramscians, have rejected, downplayed, or sought to go beyond nationalism. Subaltern studies, and many accomplished historians besides, have long criticized bourgeois nationalism as a Eurocentric 'derivative discourse'. Indigenous organizing; decolonial and transnational thematics; deterritorial thinking; Marxist and Black internationalism; revolutionary feminism; subaltern cosmopolitanism; indigenous movements; the one-state and binational intellectuals of the Palestinian cause; the Zapatistas; the Palestinian Boycott, Divestment, and Sanctions movement; the Rojava Revolution have all pointed in postnationalist directions.[90] Nationalism has become much less as a positive element in popular mobilization, and too often a collaborator in inequality, statism, authoritarianism, right wing populism, xenophobia and the fragmentation and exclusion of subaltern social groups, who are diverse in terms of nationality, peoplehood, religion, ethnicity, minority status, and so on and may be migrants, non-citizens, stateless, indigenous, or liminal subjects or those accused of being alien, subversive, inauthentic, and the like.

Nationalism and statism was the off-spring of settler colonialism in the Americas at the genocidal expense of the indigenous. It had much to do with two twentieth-century world wars and their horrors and catastrophes, and it continues to fuel the increasingly genocidal anachronism of Israeli settler colonialism in the present or to exclude those without citizenship in Kuwait.[91] And historians and thinkers are discovering much more of the transnational and the non-nationalized in anti-colonialism, including in the various pan-Asian, pan-African, pan-Arab, and other anti-colonial movements, which are not fully assimilable to the national model.[92] The emancipated community, the *popolo*, can no longer be thought as a *national* entity, with all of its unduly homogenizing, carceral connotations and policing practices. As Cornel West writes, "I believed in Black peoplehood, but not Black nationhood."[93] Perhaps there comes a moment in world history when there is a qualitative shift and nationalism is no longer leading. Certainly, the nationalization of the popular uprising of 2011-13 in Egypt, for example, was a key element in the passive revolutionary components of the repressive and conservative trajectory of the Al-Sisi regime.

Nationalism, arguably, has had its day, and the *popolo* of the present and the future, then, is more likely to be searching for new forms of transnational popular consciousness. Here, state, territory, and border are released from a hidebound fusion with a single national group. The transnational popular is a social consciousness that expects a variety of peoples or nations bearing the histories and traces of domination to (be)come together in translation in a diverse (plurinational) emancipated community and that redraws a world map based on national flags. We recall that Gramsci believed that national languages could be translated into one another. We also recall Gramsci's view that eventually national and state politics in Europe may become merely municipal—in a larger federal or confederal arrangement.

Finally, one notes that Gramsci, although leaving Sardinian nationalist behind, did not adopt a superior or dismissive attitude to Sardinian autonomy, culture, or the Sard people. On the contrary he considered returning to Sardinia if he ever escaped his jailors and illness, and he urged that his sons be taught the Sardinian dialect. The transnational builds on the ways in which popular mobilization has already built up its powers, though by no means straightforwardly, against nationalism and statism by making translocal connections. It emphasizes the ways in which there can be an organic unification, a constantly enriching *translation*, across diversity. Translation is not lack; it doesn't produce bastards and half-castes but learning, education, and a deeper cultural life. One recalls the Qur'anic verse (49:13) in which peoples (*shuʿub*) are made to know one another. Moreover, 'trans' carries the positive connotation of a queer strike against binary thinking and static essentialism in matters of identity, favouring a flourishing sensibility of social becoming. The aim in transnational popular consciousness, pace Edward Said, is to get beyond the totalizing enclosures of flag, anthem, and central bank, all of which belong in the museum.

THE ASCENDANCY OF CIVIL SOCIETY

The driving force in the revolutionary phase in relation to the state is civil society, and the sorts of private, social, and voluntary initiatives that civil society organizes. Far from the massive accretion of power to a new state apparatus which then becomes the central social agency, in the revolutionary phase, civil society is in the ascendancy. The state, on the contrary, loses control—a crucial hallmark of the revolutionary phase. This in itself is a great galvanizer of organization from below, as popular committees and the like spring up to fill the vacuum. There is an 'electromagnetic' ferment of organization, catalyzed further by the fact that all of the parties, organizations, and associations that have been involved in one way or another in the ascendant social bloc are in the process of organizational, associational, and coordinating combination with organizations that had been more oriented to the status quo. There is an unleashing of pluripopular energies, a 'feverish work' of organization in civil society. At stake is not just the organic party of the revolution but of civil society at large. Civil society is thus not only a kinetic force (via the war of position and the war of manoeuvre) directed outwards in relation to the state, it is also gravitational, drawing the state into its orbit, subjecting parts of it to greater degrees of control, and completely absorbing other parts of the state, transforming them into civil society—that is, transforming coercive into voluntary association. Gramsci's 'concept of revolution was grounded in the historic effort of oppressed classes to reconquer civil society against the authoritarian state'.[94] The qualitative shift is not thus ascent to the state but the descent of the state and the transformation of civil society by the revolutionary historical bloc.

Some have pointed to the way this revolutionary view inverts the Hegelian scheme. Instead of the absorption of civil society into the state, the state is absorbed into civil society.[95] As Bobbio has it, 'Progress no longer moves from society to the state, but on the contrary, from the state to society.'[96] Society, as opposed to the state, is in the lead. We should recall that Gramsci sees political parties as aspects of civil society and never seems to alter or contradict this view. The enlargement of the state is not about Stalinist state reinforcement and suppression of civil society but is instead 'the grounds for a "socialisation" of politics'.[97] The process does not involve 'the consolidation of the state' but 'the self-regulation and expansion of civil society to the detriment of political society'.[98] Morera reached a similar conclusion.[99] In Coutinho's thinking, under socialism, the political institutions of the state are absorbed into the workers' organizations of civil society.[100] Gramscian research has taken note of how Subcomandante Marcos, for instance, appeals not to the proletariat but to civil society.[101]

It may be useful to recall the passages in Gramsci that give a decisive role to civil society in hegemony: perhaps this is something that is most significant during the revolutionary phase. Salamini underlines the importance of 'the reabsorption of political society into civil society'.[102] During the revolutionary phase, the state, indeed, is merely an 'outer ditch', as Gramsci calls it on one occasion. The real business of collective organization in the new society, the pulse of the future city, is to be found in civil society, in all its diversity. Gramsci considers the merit of the 'assertion' that the state becomes merely an 'element of active culture', part of a 'movement' to create a new society. This principle, he writes, 'must serve to generate the will to construct within the shell of political society a complex and well-articulated civil society, in which the single individual governs himself [or herself] [and where] . . . self-government [is the] . . . organic complement [of political society]'.[103] Tamburrano and Bobbio have argued that the agent of hegemony is not only the party 'but all the institutions of the civil society in charge of the elaboration and diffusion of culture'.[104] Salamini criticizes this formulation. But perhaps in the revolutionary phase, it is precisely this conception that holds sway—as long as it is understood that civil society also mediates organizationally between state and economic activity (it is not just about cultural diffusion). How else can we interpret the fact that Gramsci conceives of processes which 'make State life become "spontaneous"'?[105] Certainly, contemporary Gramscian research has written in a positive vein of the vast number of popular and grassroots organizations—health, land, and water committees; communal councils; and social missions—in Chavez's national-democratic transformation—organizations which have brought about reduction in overall inequality.[106]

Stuart Hall's reading of Gramsci captures many of the central themes of this general interpretation of the ascendancy of civil society in the revolutionary phase. He takes aim at both the 'gigantic expansion of the state complex within modern capitalism'[107] as well as the 'dictatorship of the proletariat' in existing socialism, in which the state, instead of withering away, 'has become a gigantic, swollen, bureaucratic and directive force, swallowing up almost the whole of civil society, and imposing itself (sometimes with tanks), in the name of the people, on the backs of the people'.[108] Hall also takes on socially democratic statism, writing of the 1880s–1920s as a 'formative period' during which 'the statist conception of socialism became rivetted in place as the dominant current within Labourism and the British left'.[109] He writes that 'the state has to be dismantled, and another conception of the state put in its place'.[110] Part of the appeal of Thatcherism, argues Hall, was the way it harnessed understandable opposition to bureaucratic forms of statism.[111] The Left found this very difficult to counter because of its own statism. Islamists, one might note, have had similar advantages against the statist Left in the Arab world.[112] Stuart Hall captures the point about civil society with great force: 'Once the logic of capital, property and the market are broken, it is the diversity of social forms, the taking of popular initiatives, the recovery of popular control, *the passage of power from the state into society*, which marks out the advance towards socialism.'[113] Hall adds that 'perhaps the most important lesson of all is the absolute centrality to all socialist thinking today of the deepening of democracy. . . . the real passage of power to the powerless, the empowerment of the excluded'.[114] Hall makes the crucial point that the shift from the 'ever-expanding state to a more diversified "civil society" state (and a "withering" state)' is a profound advance on the Left, not only in relation to democratic institutions, but also regarding thinking 'socialism anew from the perspective of some of the major themes of the agenda of feminism and sexual politics'.[115] Hegemony is constituted by the 'multiple centres of civil society', thus 'an alternative conception of socialism must embrace this struggle to democratise power across all the centres of social activity.'[116] Coutinho suggestively gives credit to Togliatti's formulations of 'progressive democracy', understood as 'a democratic-republican régime that, thanks to the dialectical articulation between the traditional organisms of democratic representation (for instance, parliaments) and the new institutions of direct democracy (for instance, factory- and district-councils), would allow for the progressive advance towards profound social and economic transformations'.[117] In short, liberal hegemony regarding the concept of civil society will not do: eventually the Gramscian concept of civil society comes to form a centrepiece of his understanding of popular revolution. In the revolutionary phase, it is civil society that comes to the fore, and the political society which recedes, a process given a strong impetus by the nature of the organic crisis (between the regime and civil society) and the revolutionizing tendencies mentioned above.

W(H)ITHER THE STATE?

The roiling ascendancy of civil society in the revolutionary phase raises core questions in relation to the place of the party, the place of the subaltern social groups, but also about the meaning of the new state. As we have seen: 'The subaltern classes, by definition, are not—and cannot be—unified until they are able to become a "state".'[118]

What sort of state? Why, in particular, is the word 'state' in inverted commas? In the revolutionary phase, the state stands stripped of its hegemony. It becomes a mere 'husk'—an 'outer ditch'. The resort to ever more intensive coercive measures is on the one hand felt to be necessary by increasingly fearful and uncertain ruling groups, but it is on the other hand a great accelerator of the alienation of civil society, of the vigorous antithesis to passive revolution. The velvet glove drops from the proverbial fist. The state becomes—in theory and practice—the very incarnation of revolutionary critique: a tyranny, perhaps propped up by external machination, which needs to be broken up and completely reconstructed. Ruling divisions, including over the use of coercion, may exacerbate the situation. Marx in the *Eighteenth Brumaire* spoke of the French state as an 'appalling parasitic organism'; Engels called it 'at *best* an evil inherited by the proletariat after its victory', 'rubbish' due to be 'sloughed off' and thrown away by a new generation.[119] The state should be smashed, Lenin wrote, on the eve of revolution in Russia, along with its 'filthy and bloody morass of bureaucratic-military institutions which subordinate everything to themselves and trample everything underfoot'.[120] Lenin even approved of Engels' idea in 1875 that the German workers' party should strike out the word 'state' from its programme and replace it with the word 'community' (*Gemeinwesen*), corresponding to the French word 'commune'.[121] The implication is the end of the state, and its replacement with community. Bobbio argues that Gramsci's theory of the state is similar to that of Marx and Engels—namely, the state is only an apparatus not an end in itself, only representative of particular interests, subject to society, not permanent but particular, and destined 'to disappear'.[122]

This revolutionary view of the state has also made sense to many translating Gramscian perspectives in the Third World, especially as the post-independence and single-party regimes were losing their lustre from the 1970s onwards. Gramsci became a key figure in the renewal of political thinking around the state, in particular as national independence states started to reveal a dictatorial face. Ranajit Guha, for example, explained in relation to the origins and inspiration for subaltern studies that, in South Asia, 'the end of colonial rule had done nothing to replace or substantially alter the main apparatus of colonial domination—that is, the state. It was transferred intact to the successor regime. . . . [P]ower was handed over to the Indian rulers and . . . the misery experienced under the previous regime continued undiminished.'[123]

Such criticisms—unthinkable to most people in ordinary times when the state form is hegemonic—were extraordinarily powerful among great masses of people in Russia, and to a lesser extent in Italy, after a war, prosecuted by the state, which had brought such failure, death, and misery to millions. In the revolutionary phase, this radical, revolutionary criticism of the state, then, becomes popular. Such a popularization is, from a Gramscian perspective, just as significant as the existence of the critique by this or that intellectual in the first place. The meaning of all this ferment against the state is not the seizure of state power and the reproduction of its tyranny but the break-up of the existing state. This meaning is not purely theoretical or wishful but also practical. During the revolutionary phase the state *is* breaking up in the practical sense: the security forces are pushed to breaking point; ordinary soldiers vote with their feet; the ruling party headquarters might be burned down; ministries are sacked; parliament and courts are not sitting; the trains are not running; the internet is down; communications are uncertain; officials are not showing up for work; salaries are unpaid; chains of command collapse; towns and regions find themselves ungoverned; and parts of the ruling group, seeing the writing on the wall, start to defect or to head for the border, sending funding overseas, faking their own death, shredding documents. The international scene is not just the enemy of the revolution, poised to invade it, but also an escape route, like Saudi Arabia was for Idi Amin or Ben Ali, a retirement home for dictators. There is a palpable sense, even among ruling groups, of state breakdown—the rupture in the balance of forces, a dramatic melting away of the very ground underfoot.

In such a phase, the reconstruction of the state is no longer a matter of normative political theory: it is a real possibility and, in some sense, a necessity. One possibility, grasped at by remnants of the old regime, is counterrevolution, restoration, coups d'état, and the like. But another is more transformative. Kingdoms and dynasties can become republics or communist societies; colonies, national states; neocolonial monarchies, Islamic republics. In considering this phase, Gramsci puts the word 'state' in inverted commas, suggesting a distance from it, a new kind of political community. What does this community, this commune, this unrealized communism, look like? Do the coercive, juridical state institutions wither away? Gramscian perspectives do not offer a complete blueprint, but there are plenty of indications.

First, the new state 'superstructure', at least in the revolutionary phase, is much more minimal than the history of twentieth-century socialism would lead us to expect. Gramsci refers to a minimal 'night-watch' state structure. Gramsci writes:

> In the theory of state -> regulated society (from a phase in which state equals government to a phase in which state is identified with civil society), there must be a transition phase of state as night watchman, that is of a coercive organization which will protect the development of those elements of regulated society that are continually on the rise and, precisely because they are on the rise, will gradually reduce the state's authoritarian and coercive interventions. This is not to say that one should think of a new 'liberalism', even if the beginning of an era of organic freedom were at hand.[124]

The 'night-watch state' is not a liberal right-hand state but, in the revolutionary phase, a minimal coercive organization designed to protect the functioning of a self-regulating civil society. The state, then, is thin. But in one interpretation of the above, it continues to exist in order to protect the revolutionary civil society, at least in the revolutionary phase. Gramsci's views here on the minimal state overlapped strongly with those of Lenin. Contrary to the stereotype, Lenin also invoked the night-watch state and believed that the state should wither away or at least be reduced to an absolute minimum.

Second, regarding centralization, Gramsci appears to argue that what matters is democratic centralism. He writes that if unity at the level of the state is enacted through bureaucratic centralism, then unity just means a 'superficially calm, "mute", stagnant swamp and a sack of potatoes rather than a federation'.[125] It is not a matter, Gramsci suggests, of deciding on a blueprint of a centralized, unified state; a federal arrangement; or even secession in advance and deeming one particular state organization superior to all the others.[126] What matters, above all, is that the state structure in question can act in a democratically centralist way, under given historical conditions.

How might such a theory translate into present history? Perhaps movements such as the Rojava Revolution are showing the way, with its theme of decentralized confederal democratic autonomy, in which sovereignty is layered; identities (including national, ethnic, religious, and minority identi-

The Roiling Ferment of Revolution

ties) are plural and overlap; territorialism is dismantled in whole regions; and minimal central authorities, complete with coercive protection and forming 'inter-state' relations with other confederal regions, are accountable to and based organically on local forms of government. Comparable plurinational and confederal visions of the state have been put forward in indigenous struggles in Latin America. Perhaps democratic confederalism is not that far from Gramsci's comments about how national states in the Europe of his day might eventually be transformed into the equivalent of municipalities in a future European confederacy.

Third, regarding how such structures will be put in the service of civil society, themes of democratic centralism and popular democracy are most prominent in Gramsci's writings. Gramsci was impressed by Lenin's own warning—in a speech to the Comintern in late 1922—against the power of state bureaucrats.[127] Gramsci's strictures against bureaucratic centralism and his embrace of democratic centralism drew from Lenin and are explicitly related to state life.[128] Gramsci associated bureaucratic centralism with privilege, overweening control, and suppression: 'Within states, bureaucratic centralism is indicative of the formation of a small, privileged group that seeks to perpetuate its privileges by controlling and even stifling the emergence of oppositional forces at the base, even if those forces have the same interests as the dominant group (for example, the struggle of protectionism against liberalism).'[129]

Gramsci's example refers to liberalism, but the same principles could have been used as a critique of Stalinist tendencies in the USSR. Gramsci's criticism of the CPSU, the Soviet state, and Soviet power and communism eventually became 'very harsh'.[130] Gramsci opposed the bourgeois parliament not because it was democratic but because it was an undemocratic 'talking shop' and because real power lay elsewhere. Indeed, the sense is of the democratization of the legislature—a 'new legality'—not its subordination or elimination. While details are not worked out, the intention to democratize the state's institutions is the leading theme.[131] Gramsci offers strictures against certain criticisms of 'all representative systems'. He notes instead the merit of a representative system where 'the people's consent does not end at the moment of voting', where 'self-government' is in play, and where 'elections are held on the basis not of vague, generic programmes, but of programmes of immediate, concrete work;' in such a system, he continues, 'anyone who gives his consent commits himself to do something more than the simple, juridical citizen towards [the programmes'] realisation . . . [they commit themselves to] active and responsible work.'[132] He seeks a 'new representative system, in which the will of the people and the new ideals of liberty and equality are asserted'.[133] He contrasts 'the rotation in governmental power of different fractions of the same dominant group . . . [with] a new type of civil society'.[134] In a critique of vocational schools, which affirm rather than transcend class divisions, Gramsci seems to contrast the illusion of 'political democracy' with a positive use of the word 'democracy'. He writes that 'democracy, by definition, cannot mean merely that an unskilled worker can become skilled. It must mean that every "citizen" can "govern" and that society places him, even if only abstractly, in a general condition to achieve this.'[135]

If Gramsci's views were in line with those sometimes expressed by Marx and Lenin, then popular control was modelled on the Paris Commune and meant a series of popular democratic mechanisms, including a popular militia, elections, short terms of office, recallability, specific mandates, accountability, 'workmen's wages' for officials, and deprofessionalization.[136] Indeed, in so far as the factory councils were the nucleus of the new state,[137] it would seem to make sense that the model of popular democracy at work in the factory councils was the model that Gramsci envisaged to be scaled up to mediate the state. Economic activity—finance, production, services, and trade—would come not under centralized state ownership, but decentralized social ownership.[138] All of the organisms of popular democracy would act as the new civil society— mediating between thin state institutions on the one side and cultural and economic activity on the other. As Gramsci wrote, 'it is time that events should be seen as the intelligent work of men [and women], and not the products of chance, of fatality.'[139] As Vacca writes, unlike much of the communist movement, 'Gramsci cannot . . . be considered hostile or indifferent to democracy.'[140] A popular, democratic, and non-statist reading of Gramsci, such as is found in a number of authors regarding new forms of the state is clearly defensible,[141] even if, as Coutinho and others caution, all the details of a democratic socialism are not worked out.[142] The state does not wither away; it is remade.

WORLDVIEW, CULTURE, AND LANGUAGE

As we have seen, in the struggle for consent, the leading question is the elaboration and dissemination of ideology and the development of new forms of language and culture—as well as the competition between different ideologies. The qualitative shift at the heart of the revolutionary phase has to do with the way in which a particular ideology is concretely universalized. It is preserved and yet transcended—preserved in a new common sense: 'this is how we do things,' 'this goes without saying'—and transcended in a larger worldview, the philosophy of an epoch. At stake is a new culture, a new concrete activity, dispersed into a new, enlightened common sense.[143]

The philosophy of the epoch is not the ideology of a particular group or philosopher. As Gramsci writes, 'The philosophy of an age is not the philosophy of this or that philosopher, of this or that group of intellectuals, of this or that broad section of the popular masses. It is a process of combination of all these elements, which culminates in an overall trend, in which the culmination becomes a norm of collective action and becomes concrete and complete (integral) "history".'[144] The process, in keeping with Gramsci's view of ideology and culture, cannot be seen as merely the instrumental imposition of a sole ideologue, a party, a class, or a state. It can only be a great dialectical working out—a philosophico-historical unification and translation, containing all the contradictions of the epoch—in which culture, ideology, language, and philosophy can make meaning and sense on the broadest scale. In this vital sense, the revolution *cannot* be monopolized, a crucial defence against vanguardism. As Boggs has it, 'philosophy became an emancipatory force—the basis of a theoretical "organizing principle" for an emergent moral-political (socialist) order, the source of a new community, world-view, and language for "subaltern" groups opposing capitalist domination.'[145] As Gramsci wrote, 'philosophical activity is not to be conceived solely as the "individual" elaboration of systematically coherent concepts, but also and above all as a cultural battle to transform the popular "mentality" and to diffuse the philosophical innovations which will . . . become concretely—i.e. historically and socially—universal.'[146]

The new worldview, then, is not really decided in advance. It is worked out, including under the pressure of necessity, amid the erosion of the old culture and the process of cultural reform. Amid the revolution and the new form of state and new form of hegemony there is the 'concrete birth of the need to construct a new intellectual and moral order'.[147] Stuart Hall goes as far as to say that the period of 'socialist construction might be the moment of greatest intensity in the battle for socialist ideas'.[148] The new worldview becomes the way in which a new historical bloc can make sense of itself. At stake also is catharsis—new translations between structure and superstructure, the working through of tormenting dramas of a whole community in cultural forms.[149] In the new order, 'all citizens should be able to develop their own, human personality to the full.'[150] The concept involves many clashing ideas but on a transformed basic cultural terrain.

In turn, the new culture is part of what makes the historical bloc 'directive': this, in a sense, was Gramsci's interpretation of Marx's statement that 'the German proletariat is the heir of classical German philosophy'.[151] The organized collective will is at the basis of the philosophy of praxis, while the creation of a philosophy, new speech, and new language undergirds a new collective will at the broadest level.[152] This new culture is a kind of positive conformism in which '[c]onformism is a concerted effort to attain a practical end spontaneously and not by coercion'.[153]

Intellectual and moral reform, the 'long revolution' at the level of feeling and culture envisaged by figures like Buey and Williams, is a crucial component of revolution in Gramscian perspectives, in which revolution cannot be reduced to the rupture in the balance of forces—and certainly not to the so-called 'seizure of state power'. The temporalities of cultural transformation are also much longer than the revolutionary phase—but then so are all the temporalities of the long journey from subordination to revolution. Indeed, in relation to culture, we can think of weeks when decades happen as being weeks that require decades to have happened before they can. The philosophy of praxis develops alongside the history of subaltern social groups and only becomes a concrete universal in and after the revolutionary phase. The revolutionary phase is not an end in itself: the horizon of Gramsci's popular revolution is a new way of living together.

> The books and newspapers that arrive here for me have already brought about a certain struggle between me and Bordiga, who wrongly maintains that I'm very untidy; behind my back he creates disorder among my things, with the excuse of symmetry and architecture: but in reality I can no longer find anything in the symmetrical mess that he arranges for me.[154]

What is the role, finally, in the revolutionary phase, of the party / modern Prince or organic party / postmodern Prince? It is understood that Gramsci did not seek bourgeois party politics but wished for a state-founding party. But what did Gramsci mean? We have already seen Gramsci's criticism of the hasty and insufficiently prepared actions of political Cardornism, vanguardism, and maximalism. These were commandos without infantry or artillery: they were all strategy, plan, and 'vision', but lacked the means to realize their vision. Gramsci's criticism of the Italian Socialist Party during the Biennio Rosso also offers some insight into his criticism of the inverse problem—that is, of party weakness, vacillation, inaction, and timorousness just when a revolutionary, or potentially revolutionary phase, was unfolding. The editors of the *Prison Notebooks* summarize these criticisms as follows:

> [D]espite its revolutionary language, the P.S.I. neither organized itself for insurrection, nor sought allies for the industrial proletariat (four million strong at this time) among the peasants or agricultural labourers (each of whom represented a further four millions, approximately). Although the peasants were occupying feudal estates in the South throughout the revolutionary years, the party made no attempt to co-ordinate their struggles. It allowed the catholic Popular Party to organize the mass of small peasants in North and Central Italy. And it neither carried out any serious work in the army, nor organized the proletariat militarily. Finally, it alienated the urban petite bourgeoisie and the demobilized officers and failed to channel their resentments (caused by their critical economic and social position) against the ruling class.[155]

This passage reveals, by implication, what a revolutionary party *should* be doing: namely, coordinating for the war of position and the war of manoeuvre and organizing, coordinating, or elaborating on views that would speak to the different social groups and classes involved in the revolutionary bloc.

Such party interventions, Gramsci is implying, would at the very least play a role in catalyzing the revolutionary phase.

Does this make Gramsci a 'Marxist-Leninist', an Amadeo Bordiga, who expected the party to control the state, take over the economy, supply correct consciousness, use the state to take over civil society and culture, and generally to monopolize the revolution by creating a highroad to dictatorship?

Remarkably, perhaps, there is little or no direct or unequivocal textual evidence to suggest that Gramsci believed that the political party would take over the functions of the state apparatus. Gramsci never wavered in his view that the political party was part of civil society not political society. We have already seen that the minimal state was to be subjected to popular democratic control through organisms mediating between the state and civil society. We have seen the emphasis that Gramsci put on the autonomous activity of the factory councils, which were not under the control of the party. And while Gramsci thought that the party played a role in directing and coordinating the war of manoeuvre during the revolutionary phase, there is evidence to suggest that he did not think that it should monopolize even these powers of direction. Unlike the PCI, for instance, Gramsci did not oppose the formation of *arditi del popolo*, popular militias to defend socialists against fascist attacks, even if they were not ideologically thoroughly communist or under party direction. His main concern was that they would not be able to withstand assaults by fascists backed by the state, not that they were out of control or doctrinally unsound.[156]

Secondly, Gramsci does not expect that the party will take over the economy, either directly through its own organizations, or indirectly through its control of state ministries. Indeed, the centrepiece of Gramsci's interest and inspiration regarding revolutionary economic organization was the workers' Soviets. As Boggs argues, Gramsci interpreted 1917 'as a process grounded above all in the soviets (popular assemblies) and factory committees, with the centralised party carrying out only supportive and coordinating functions'.[157] Here, social ownership did not mean state or party ownership.

Third, Gramsci worked extensively in the *L'Ordine Nuovo* and as an independent cultural critic. He believed in integral journalism and that media organs could be independent and directive. He further conceived of an enriching and dialectical shift from ideology to worldview, appreciated the complexities of language formation, and the cathartic burdens of culture. It would be deeply contradictory, therefore, if Gramsci were to see the party qua organization as monopolizing and supplying correct consciousness, culture, worldview, and philosophy.

Finally, Gramsci's criticisms of bureaucratic centralism were directed not only at state life but also at party activity—and at the Comintern which was controlled by the Communist Party of the Soviet Union. Gramsci writes: 'what merits attention here is that when bureaucratic centralism manifests itself, the situation is often brought about by a lack of initiative, that is, by the political crudity of the peripheral forces, even when these forces and the hegemonic territorial group are homogenous. The creation of such situations is extremely harmful and dangerous, especially in territorial (international) organizations.'[158]

Gramsci may have been discussing here the relations between the Comintern, a territorial national organization, and Italian communism—whose interests were aligned with the hegemonic group (i.e. the Soviet leadership). Gramsci is not moralizing about the USSR: indeed, he proposes that political crudity in Italy may have played its own role in bringing about bureaucratic centralism. In other words, if the forces of the revolution are insufficient or insufficiently prepared, bureaucratic centralism is a major danger. But he nonetheless says that this is an 'extremely harmful' and 'dangerous' situation. Gramsci certainly resisted the Comintern regarding the United Front in the early 1920s and the maximalist line in the early 1930s. He clearly did not accept the CPSU's monopoly of civil society or of the revolution in general. Gramsci wished to avoid the party as 'a police organ'.[159] This may have been a veiled reference to the USSR.[160] The foregoing could imply that the party should remain in civil society, should continue to involve private initiative and voluntary association, and should not transform itself into a state apparatus, which would risk turning the party into a police organ, suppressing civil society, and imposing doctrine and culture.

While strategic Gramscians tend to wish for a centralized organization which would control the revolution to ensure its most effective and coherent execution, democrats of all kinds worry about the ways in which such centralized control leads ineluctably to dictatorship. One interpretation is that Gramsci's view of hegemony precisely joins the two aspects together: without hegemony, strategy is a species of maximalism—a commando without an infantry—and will either fail or lead into a coercive implementation. On the other hand, highly democratic, purely consensual, and decentralized social forces without any strategic orientation or directive capacity are doomed to dispersal and defeat. Another way of putting the same point is that organization is not the only directive and coordinating social force: worldview, culture, language, historical bloc, and transnational popular consciousness are powerful forces in their own right. They are not kinetic, but they are connective, an element in formation and cohesion. By the same token, without a strategic orientation, the collective will—however determined—will not be sufficiently refined and precise to carry out properly timed, directed, and coherent wars of position and manoeuvre. As Gramsci writes:

> An appropriate political initiative is always necessary to liberate the economic thrust from the dead weight of traditional policies—i.e. to change the political direction of certain forces which have to be absorbed if a new, homogeneous politicoeconomic historical bloc, without internal contradictions, is to be successfully formed. And . . . two 'similar' forces can only be welded into a new organism . . . [by] compromise. Force can be employed against enemies, but not against a part of one's own side which one wishes rapidly to assimilate, and whose 'good will' and enthusiasm one needs.[161]

A new hegemony comes about when these diverse aspects of revolutionary activity are brought together, when coercion and consent are combined. No single social agency is 'in control'. Combination does not happen through imposition alone. The collective will is to be fostered by the revolutionary party,[162] but this doesn't imply complete organizational control and likely required that such control was not present. Hegemony is never complete. History does not end. The implication is that the party and/or the organic party is an important catalyst in the revolutionary phase and has many important tasks, including the task of 'promoting and orienting' an unpredictable process of transformation 'so as to arrive at the formation of a new "historical bloc."'[163] But it is not the sole directive centre, and it does not monopolize the revolution.

Boggs' reading is that '[t]he developmental pattern of the Soviet party-state cannot be attributed to leadership "betrayal" or to bureaucratic deformation alone. . . . [T]he main authoritarian and socially-repressive structures did originate in the Jacobin strategy authored by Lenin. . . . [Gramsci's] theoretical orientation in the Notebooks . . . suggests such a critique.'[164] What was the flawed Jacobin strategy? Its 'preoccupation with the existing state apparatus as a set of structures to be taken over, administered, and transformed from above'.[165] The flaw, then, was that an element of civil society, the revolutionary party, strayed into political society, took over the state and the economy, and then used its political and economic powers to become a repressive police organ, monopolizing civil society (and thereby extinguishing it by definition), and suppressing alternative forms of belief and culture. A Gramscian critique of Maoism, for instance, follows a similar logic: even the mass line failed to 'abolish the separation from the people', concentrating power in the 'party organization'.[166] In Gramsci's view, the fascist dictatorship absorbed civil society into the state. A Gramscian critique of the Soviet dictatorship, would be the inverse: the state was absorbed into civil society. The outcome was the same in both cases: civil society was destroyed and the state deformed. The message, then, is that the organic party, at all costs, does not take over the state. Nor does it monopolize civil society or culture. Its diverse organizational components strategically connect the historical bloc and become the new civil society that, among other things, activates and helps build the popular democratic forms which do control the minimal state.

CONCLUSION

In the familiar, sometimes caricatured perspective associated with 'Marxism-Leninism', the revolution is dominated by class, party, and state. The class means doubly free wage-labour under capitalism, an exploited proletariat with nothing to lose but their chains, whose fundamental interests would be served by the overthrow of capitalism, which pits two ever more separated and hostile classes against each other. The proletariat as a social class is represented by a largely separate, close-knit vanguard party of professional revolutionaries, with a correct view of capitalism, who, representing the true proletariat against petty-bourgeois deviations, set out to make a revolution, which they do above all by seizing state power, primarily in a context of mass uprising. The party then inaugurates the dictatorship of the proletariat, whereby new instruments of state power (the workers' militia) are used to abolish capitalism and smash the old state apparatus. This in turn brings about the withering away of the state, because the state only exists because of capitalism. An era of organic liberty, of communism, built out of a society of free producers is established.

This chapter has identified some core problems with this vanguardist model, which after all most likely did not fully exist *before* 1917, and conceives of a different revolutionary process: a popular revolution which is neither statist nor purely cultural. Instead of the class, which is naturally entitled to hegemonize, we have a historical bloc: a great diversity of groups with considerable experience in a whole range of anti-capitalist and eco-socialist activity and livelihoods who have forged a system of alliances with a great variety of other subaltern social groups, all of whom have already gone through several vital phases in the development of their activities and are not merely searching for some external force to represent them. Instead of vanguardists, the anti-capitalist, queer, anti-racist, feminist builders of the future transnational popular are organized in the diverse organizations of the organic party (a movement of movements)—which represents this anti-capitalist and cultural diversity along with its many differences. In place of statolatry—the belief that the state will be used to smash capitalism—the focus is on breaking up existing forms of the repressive husk of the state (which is, in fact, the essential prop of capitalism) and on putting new state forms under the popular democratic control of a transformed civil society, which organizes the relationship between economy, culture, and a minimal state. The revolutionary phase is embedded in a much longer temporality of cultural renewal and transformation, reworking racism, sexism, nationalism, statism, and homophobia, and their attendant forms of genus-thinking, while building up a convivial, living culture and transnational popular consciousness, endowed with the riches necessary to work through the passage from feeling to knowing and vice versa. In place of a revolution heralding repression, economic failure, and authoritarianism, popular mobilization in the living Gramscian tradition heralds a popular, democratic socialist, culturally-enriching, non-statist, and transnational revolution.

Conclusion

This book has aimed to put forward a Gramscian theory of popular mobilization at a time when mass mobilization is widespread but progressive gains are few or eroded. It contributes an updated Gramscian answer to the fundamental question of how subordinated social groups rearrange their relationships to challenge and overcome social domination and build alternatives. Drawing heavily on the living Gramscian tradition, the goal has been to articulate thoroughly how this complex morphology can be understood and how its diverse elements can be identified, situated, and connected. The process of theoretical articulation carried out in the book has inevitably involved a distinctive interpretation of the material, while offering some key points of theoretical renovation. This conclusion summarizes the points of departure, key elements, and main arguments, before discussing the main theoretical and practical implications.

FUNDAMENTALS, FACES, AND PHASES

The goal has been to build on and secure gains in relation to critical theories ranging from Marxism to intersectionality and to offer an alternative to conservative, liberal, and rationalist theories (including social movements theory). The contribution aims at a thorough articulation and interpretation which I have not yet seen fully specified in the dominant readings of Gramsci, whether in cultural Marxism, theories of cultural hegemony, the 'Leninist' Gramsci, the 'deviationist' Gramsci, post-Marxism, or subaltern studies. The point of departure in this book is an emphasis on the profound fecundity and originality of Gramsci's intervention, seen here as not fully assimilable to either Marxism or to German and Italian idealism and thus particularly rich in potential for a genuinely connecting theory.

The theory presented is not positivist, objectivist, nomothetic, logico-deductive, or taxonomic but historicist, organic, interpretive, and engaged. This has meant an effort to translate elements of historical life into theoretical language, as part of an endeavour to form shared understandings, a collective will, and a positive myth and thus to contribute to the making of a new social force. The book draws as much as possible on the historicist and philological methods of the integral historian, passing on what I have understood, aiming to contribute to the living Gramscian tradition.

The book understands popular mobilization as the transformation of a scattered multitude into an emancipated people. This transformation is at one level a process of social becoming, involving the dialectics of social being and social consciousness; the emergence of group, class, popular, and transnational consciousness; and the formation of new forms of social and historical bloc. At the same time and in line with revolutionizing praxis, popular mobilization is a matter of the radical transformation of structures: civil society, culture, economy, and the state. Equally, it involves the remaking of spatio-temporality and the construction, especially thanks to collective will formation and the morale inhering in a positive myth, of new social and popular domestic and transnational forces, weighing in the wider balance and relation of forces. The positive myth posits a horizon of liberation, an end to oppression and alienation, through an organic unification of theory and practice and a revolution in the secular basis of social life. The positive myth of emancipated community in the present invokes a transnational popular. A Gramscian theory of popular mobilization takes equal account, then, of the problematics of social becoming, structural transformation, spatio-temporality, and the construction of new social forces, 'faces' which are intimately intertwined.

Three key elements remain. First, organic intellectuals are intimately connected with the historical life of groups, classes, and the bloc; they construct, persuade, organize, articulate, connect, translate, and direct. They are at work in all the faces and phases of popular mobilization—and operate to link them together. They are contrasted with traditional intellectuals, who are disconnected from popular mobilization and from the historical life of social becoming and linked to social domination.

Second, the whole 'live work' involves a line of renewal, which is in turn always threatened by decomposition and neoformation. Renewal here means making history: doing something worth remembering; connecting past, present, and future in new ways; and creating new combinations of opposites and distincts that bring new energies, new forms, and new times. It is a process of organic unification. It is particularly associated with destabilizing social domination and with radicalizing and revolutionizing dynamics. Decomposition refers to all the ways in which new connections and energies stagnate, decay, ossify, weaken, or fall apart, while neoformation refers to all the ways in which new initiatives are absorbed within existing forms of hegemony, especially in transformism and passive revolution.

Finally, a core part of this theory is that social domination cannot be overcome in isolation, as domination is intertwined with, and a result of, all the other moments of hegemony, a system of power relations combining coercion and consent. The book has argued throughout, therefore, that popular mobilization must not only overcome social domination but also construct new forms of autonomy, win consent, and eventually achieve leadership. Social domination is not natural, eternal, divinely appointed, or a result of individual failings but a phase socially constructed in relation to hegemony. The long journey in time and space from subordination to revolution, the making of a new hegemony, involves four major configurations of relationships: domination, autonomy, consent, and leadership. These phases are defined in relation to social becoming, spatio-temporality, structures, and the balance and relation of forces. They are not just sequential but also temporally reversible, juxtaposed, internally differentiated, and intertwined. The full import of these phases, as we have seen, has been obscured by the way they were narrowly interpreted by the editors of the *SPN*.

DOMINATION

Subaltern social groups are not *outside* of history, however much ruling groups and conservative and Eurocentric theories may assume, assert, or believe that they are, but *in the margins* of history. It may be that history is being made elsewhere at the expense of subaltern social groups and that official historiography, along with ceremonies of state and nation, tends to relegate subaltern social groups to the footnotes and margins, but such social groups are still present, even if spectrally and inconspicuously, and they have a historical life in fragments and episodes (in both the positive and negative senses of these terms). Subaltern bodies bear the marks of an infinity of traces deposited historically, but an inventory of these traces, as a start point of critical consciousness, is not excluded, even if many subalterns feel that even their own history and ancestry has little worth. The demands of the present are heavy; some are frozen in a perpetual present, battling for survival, and for many the future is bleak, at least on this earth. But there are myths of liberation, albeit in many forms, and usually in this phase at a great distance from daily life.

The colonized and racialized groups, sexual minorities, women, workers, the enslaved, migrants, non-citizens, and indigenous communities, inter alia, are objectified, instrumentalized, and made to suffer bodily, but they are not mere objects, practices (a sum of behaviours), or solely experiencers of 'crude' sensation. Everyone has thoughts (intellectual activity, spontaneous philosophy), language, and feelings; there are always attempts to make sense of the world. Sense-making can be resistant to carceral practices and temporal freezing. Contradictory consciousness is an expression of all sorts of gaps between things as they are supposed to be and things as they are experienced and felt in the life-activity of the plural ensemble of the subordinate. Forms of popular memory and popular culture, even amidst commodification and degradation, can define elements of continuity and 'historical personality', even when group and class consciousness is scarce and genuine allies are few and far between.

Subaltern social groups live variously amid exclusion from civil society, cultural stigma and hegemonic common sense, state violence, economic dispossession, and national exclusion. Spatial marginalization, fragmentation, and apartness are typical. Private interests and personalistic strategies abound, born of forcelessness. Some undergo catastrophes of character—contradictions pile up until the subject is broken; others exhibit a studied indifference; some form up into a whole subterranean world; others cultivate conspiracy theories or usually disempowering forms of subversivism (the diffuse and personalized hatred of 'the official'). Nonetheless, some part of the subaltern is directive and responsible: subaltern formations make limited and partial demands, albeit within existing frameworks, and a scaling-up process is not excluded; fleeting confrontations with authorities take place, and can develop in unexpected ways; and common sense is not seamless, but riddled with gaps and ambiguities, and even contains glimmers of good sense which can coalesce on new lines. Further, there are organic intellectuals, even in this phase, however marginal and as-yet 'undiscovered', formed on the terrain of class and group, who wrestle with domination, aiming to resolve its contradictions and formulate pathways of escape. Finally, there are vital elements of passive and active adherence to dominant formations. Such forms are crucial, including in shoring up and recolouring existing forms of authorized autonomy, consent, and leadership via 'protest politics' (the expression and redress of grievance under domination via appeals to authority). Passive and active adherence are also Janus-faced: in times of crisis, when faith in authority is shaken or when beliefs or needs change, passive and active adherence is rendered fragile and unstable, loosening the soil and generating important cracks and fissures in the overall fabric of social domination.

A Gramscian theory thinks its way into the torturous contradictions of social domination with a reconstructive purpose. The aim is not to produce a hypostasized theory of why and how the subaltern is subaltern but to think through where and how such forms of domination can be—and have been—overcome. Domination is clearly the lead note throughout, but the historical life of subaltern social groups contains contrapuntal themes. Social domination appears solid, unyielding, but contains various elements of contradiction, ambiguity, and instability and thus various latent possibilities for molecular rearrangement. These contradictions are the roots and seedbeds of popular mobilization. They are a phase of gestation, an indispensable premise for the organic passage out of social domination.

AUTONOMY

As this book has argued, out of the indispensable premise of the subaltern phase and its torturous contradictions, a new phase can arise, involving a subaltern drive for autonomy. At a certain threshold of anomaly, contradiction, instability, amid a build-up of certain kinds of confrontation and subaltern formation, there is a qualitative shift; relationships are re-configured, old clusters of bonds are broken, new ones forged, and new forms of social activity emerge—some in leaps and bounds, and others more slowly. The vertical bonds, for example, underpinning unstable equilibria in relation to passive and active adherence, can finally snap: adherence is broken and there is a crisis of authority, pregnant with possibilities. Those long tortured by social domination, often joining hands with other alienated groups and individuals, become engaged in declaring and building up new forms and attachments. Forms near-at-hand seem broken and unattractive, and so invention and autonomy, fuelled by time-space compression, comes to the fore.

In this phase, the major forms of group and class consciousness are forged: gays, lesbians, bisexuals, and others come out, finding each other in public, shedding shame, asserting pride and confronting homophobia; women start to combine with other women and speak out on the layers of misogyny and patriarchy; racialized Others of all kinds come together to reject dehumanization and genus-thinking and to assert beauty and worth; workers start to see themselves not as improvident and 'riotous' or taken care of but as a class, exploited and dispossessed by capital. In the popular uprising, there is a synthetic explosion; the streets are filled with a diverse ensemble of the subordinate, who, under no single actor's control, are united in their strenuous rejection of the existing system. Among the colonized, demands for self-determination and independence take hold at the popular level.

Among those newly activated, there is abundance of good sense, identifying and rejecting in broad brushes the systemic forms of domination and oppression faced by the subordinate, systemic forms which hegemonic common sense had previously dissimulated. Positive myths are suddenly close at hand, inspiring effervescence and great outpourings of energy, while 'the spirit of cleavage' acts to galvanize and unite a previously shattered collective will, conjuring up new elements of social force and intervening with unexpected power in the balance and relation of forces. Social confrontation abounds. Strategic calculations are remade. Educators are educated. Organic intellectuals are thrown up from below or scramble to catch up. New and 'hot' places of belonging are carved within hostile space; territories are liberated or occupied. Existing structures are shaken, while new and autonomous structures—forms of self-organization, counterculture, socialist self-management, and organisms of popular authority—are built up. Models are appropriated translocally. Many a middle-class voice complains that 'we should have seen it coming' or we should have undertaken reform before it came to all this—while conservatives look for the knout and the noose.

Yet, against autonomism, the drive for autonomy eventually encounters limits. Consciousness of class and group is insufficient: ways will have to be found to mediate the relationships between groups and classes. The popular rising, moreover, is insufficiently constructive: it can tear down, but it is a blunt force and lacks constructive power. Independence and self-determination can become a mere shell—but a flag, a central bank, and a national anthem—unless the inter/transnational system is transformed and a sense of emancipated community reworked. Good sense is not enough; ideological elaboration is required, while the spirit of cleavage needs to be refined and directed. Bubbles of autonomy may dissipate; work at cross-purposes; become isolated, outflanked, and repressed; or get de-fanged and incorporated into existing forms of hegemony. Like hot places of belonging, they need to find ways to scale up, building and reworking translocal flows already established. Effervescence is hard to sustain. Those who thought the millennium was nigh are bound to be disillusioned. New parties and formations appear among the ruling groups aiming to control new forms of popular self-activity. Horizontalism is eventually exhausting, self-contradictory (a theory that claims to be only a practice), and strategically ineffective. Organic intellectuals of autonomy must not fall into the trap of autonom*ism*—fetishizing autonomy—and need to find ways to transcend autonomy once its vitality, forms of renewal, and expansive potential are exhausted, lest they stifle the potential of popular mobilization. Overall, autonomy is understood to be a vital phase of popular mobilization, which ultimately must be transcended in search of wider forms of consent and leadership.

CONSENT

This book has argued in detail that the sublation of popular self-activity involves another qualitative shift. The emergence out of the limits of popular self-activity cannot be achieved without a third major phase of popular mobilization in which the leading note, amid all the diversity, is the struggle for new forms of consent. Popular mobilization develops beyond autonomy—in time and place—above all by winning consent and forming alliances. At stake in this phase are all the questions and debates around the war of position, the party, ideological elaboration and diffusion, the development of a popular consciousness, popular education, socialist economy, engaging on the terrain of the extended state, transformism in reverse (radicalization), and social bloc formation. Consent-winning draws and appropriates models circulating transnationally, and it builds connections of solidarity and association across national borders. A Gramscian theory also allows us to identify the main dangers in this phase: vanguardism on the one side and reformism (*trasformismo*) and passive revolution on the other. Indeed, the main argument is that a Gramscian theory enables us to conceive of consent-winning in a way that is popular, democratic, and convivial. Two key points are worth underlining.

The first has to do with the importance of the formation of a social bloc in the phase of consent. A Gramscian theory, as I have argued, places a heavy emphasis on the *plural* ensemble of the subordinate, and the theory put forward in this book refuses the monist concept that any single class or group has the right to hegemonize all the others—drawing on Gramsci to put forward this 'minority' case. The problem in relation to consent-winning is only partly the conventional one of how to win over the more marginal elements of class and group. The more pressing question relates, I have argued, to the formation of a popular, social bloc. How can the very diverse identities, groups, and struggles, with their different histories, feelings, and priorities, be woven together? The book has argued that only through the formation of a popular social bloc can the forces of renewal hope to build a force strong and broad enough to stand against the many forces arrayed against them.

In the difficult and patient work of bloc formation, popular democratic forms are constantly being discovered and put in place, a necessity in relation to the absence of a natural or objectively formed hegemon. The argument is also that masculinist posturing, phallocentric fantasies about hard power, authoritarianism, doctrinal polemicizing, white saviourism, and various forms of abstract rationalism, as well as the insistence on economic-corporate 'bread and butter', are the enemies of bloc formation. White saviours, for example, in their undue confidence about being able to solve everyone's problems, may rush to the offices of the powerful, fail to coordinate, and wind up co-opted, bolstering the problem of *trasformismo*. Or they may become vanguards without troops and wind up decapitated. Intersectionality serves in insisting on, recognizing, and thinking through the specificities involved in locations in power relations: its attentiveness to positionality can work all the better to eventually bring about meaningful connections. Meanwhile certain queer and feminist sensibilities, including a grasp of the importance of feeling and affect and the importance of practices of care, are vitally at work in weaving together alliances across difference, comprehending diversity, creating convivial formations, and allowing sustainable connecting work.

The second point has to do with the organization and coordination of consent. The book has presented three readings of the party in Gramsci: the tight-knit vanguardist party, the mass democratic party, and the organic party. It is the latter, minority reading, that takes the lead in the theory presented here. The organic party, or the 'postmodern Prince', is a highly distinctive organizational form. It unites spontaneity and conscious direction, preserving and sublating autonomy rather than imposing a line known objectively or scientistically in advance. And rather than having a single, controlling, organizational-bureaucratic centre, it comprises numerous distinct but related organizations. The organic party has more than one organizational headquarters and may have allies situated in the transnational space. No single organization monopolizes either the truth about the social world or absolute knowledge of the best strategy to follow. This organizational diversity reflects the fact that the task of the organic party is to connect a plurality, with various groups and classes each having their own temporalities, feelings, priorities and so on. In other words, the task of the organic party in this phase is to stitch together the popular social bloc and to expand the elements of a genuinely democratic civil society (not to police it). Here one finds again the importance of queer, non-binary, feminist, and intersectional sensibilities, affects, and practices of care. The numerous organizations of the organic party reflect the many fronts on which popular mobilization does battle—civil society, culture, economy, the state, and space at many scales, including the transnational. No single organization, it is held, can pursue all these struggles without over-centralization, bureaucratization, vanguardism, and authoritarianism on the one side or without factionalism, division, and eventual collapse on the other. Sabotaging a pumping station is not the same thing as running a cooperative, administering a social media platform, cooking for a sit-in, or staging a play. The organic party is not a free-for-all, however, and must endeavour to link together the various fronts of struggle in the realization of new democratic socialist forms—and powerful new social forces. The organic party must perforce, therefore, form a coalition, an organizational bloc, both domestically and transnationally. It is related, coordinated, and unified not by organizational dictat from above, but by social bloc, popular consciousness, language, shared culture, myth, and collective will—a determination to build a new kind of civil society. It is the organic party, therefore, not the hidebound, single vanguardist party so fundamental to twentieth-century communism, that takes the lead in the theory of popular mobilization presented here.

LEADERSHIP

The culminating phase considered in this book involves the roiling ferment of revolution. The argument has been that at a certain point amid all the processes of popular consent-winning and a deeper crisis of authority, a qualitative shift can come about. A variety of revolutionizing processes are unleashed, marking the onset of the revolution, a rupture in the balance of forces, and the beginning of the phase of leadership.

The war of position takes on a new, culminating form involving a very rapid temporality and new forms of 'siege warfare' (in place of trench warfare) capable of paralyzing the ruling apparatus; there is a vigorous antithesis to passive revolution, a revolutionizing vector in which the apparatus of consent breaks with ruling groups and starts to organize among popular forces; there is an ascendancy of new forms of civil society, as against the contracted, now merely coercive, disintegrating state. The revolutionary phase is made possible by the ways in which civil society and middle and intermediary classes come into contradiction with the coercive state (political society) and form revolutionizing combinations with popular forces. The state is reduced to a 'husk'—ineffective on the one side, and tyrannical on the other—and made available for radical transformation. The war of manoeuvre cracks the last hold-outs and military positions of the embattled ruling class, including as their dependency on imperial sponsors is laid bare for all to see. There is a rupture in the balance of forces and a final disintegration of the old collective will. The organic party becomes the new, diverse, civil society; the state is reorganized in a minimal, confederal, and popular democratic way, and socialist economic relations become dominant (capitalist property and profit ends). At the centre of the phase is the formation of a revolutionary historical bloc. The latter is infused with a transnational consciousness capable of connecting various nations within, across, and without the new state, queering rigid binaries and overcoming masculinist territorialism. The historical bloc weaves together new forms of space, plural civil society, enriched culture, eco-socialist economy, and the minimal (confederal, democratic) state. And it becomes the leading force in the social formation on an expanded (cross-national, cross-regional) scale. The historical bloc, then, is the hegemon forged in the crucible of the popular, socialist and democratic revolution, the fruit of the long and variegated labour of popular mobilization, and under the control of no one. Unsurprisingly, success amid such a ferment is in no way guaranteed. A Gramscian theory of popular mobilization suggests that the great dangers in this phase, supposing that the snares of passive revolution have been overcome, are those posed by the violent revolutionary minority on the one side and by the risk of a strong leader taking over (Caesarism) on the other.

THE ARTICULATION OF STRUGGLES

> Crowned heads, wealth and privilege may well tremble should ever again the Black and Red unite!
>
> Otto von Bismarck, after the anarchist-Marxist split in 1872

Popular mobilization, from unpromising origins in the frozen depths of subordination and objectification, eventually becomes like a great river formed by the convergence of four streams or phases: challenges to domination, assertions of autonomy, the construction of consent, and organic leadership. Multiple passages out of and against domination find new grounds on which to stand (autonomy); there is an expansive process of consent building and eventually a new, organic leadership. The four phases of the new hegemony are both sequential, reversible, and juxtaposed (spatial). They are also internally differentiated and intertwined—both temporally and spatially.

Conclusion

Gramsci's intervention is the organic intellectual headwater of this mighty, living tradition, which itself undergoes, in relation to history, a process of renovation and renewal.

The theory articulates an array of struggles: a plural ensemble of the subordinate, distinct dialectics of social being and social consciousness, and diverse processes of social becoming; battles in civil society, culture, economy, and state; a wide variety of activities, forms, and strategies, ranging from armed struggle (the war of manoeuvre) to passive and active adherence to dominant formations, from the war of position to autonomous action, from intellectual elaboration and party activity to popular uprisings, and from contradictory consciousness to practices of care. It depicts popular mobilization above all as culminating in the formation of a historical bloc—understood as a living social force driving forward and combining social becoming via a transnational popular consciousness of emancipated community and a new fusion of structure and superstructure.

There are multiple, interconnected scales and temporalities. Translocal and transnational connections and forces are built up against hegemonic time and space, including its nationalist, statist, and imperialist forms. Many diverse rhythms are in play: there are decades when nothing much happens, and weeks when decades happen; there are dramatic and often quite unexpected times of radicalization and revolutionizing marked by qualitative shifts, reciprocal translations, and phase changes. Here opposites are connected—unleashing and creating new social forces. Such unexpected developments are at work in the humble and scattered subaltern formations that start to scale up in the face of repression, in the work of searching for allies, and building new organizations; in the defections from passive/active adherence to dominant formations that come in numbers at moments of crisis; in the moments when the elements of contradictory consciousness resolve into the core components of a new language, new good sense, and new forms of ideology; in the wellsprings of popular self-activity when social groups, passing from 'passivity' to 'activity' can redefine themselves—for example, supposed criminals, layabouts, drug-addicts, and football 'hooligans' become suddenly the heroic defenders of bread, dignity, and freedom on the squares. Such qualitative shifts are in play, further, when formerly middle-class organizations, NGOs, parties, unions, educational institutions, and tendencies become radicalized, joining hands with more subaltern formations; when 'spontaneous' outbreaks connect with new and radical ideas, diffused across national and regional borders; when popular education serves as the midwife of new connections, new spaces, new identities, and new ways of knowing. The book has also referred to revolutionizing dynamics, when, for instance, in the vigorous antithesis to passive revolution, sections of the hegemonic apparatus break off and connect to the revolutionary historical bloc. The book has underlined the significance of these processes of radicalization and revolutionizing, especially at a time when the important word 'radicalization' has been hijacked by the political right and when passive revolution often seems to rule the roost (in theory as well as practice).

There are also long periods of stagnation and decomposition, as well as periods of absorption and neoformation. Phases that were once full of vitality become no longer inspiring, although they can leave important sediments—in new forms of common sense, for example. The analysis also permits us to grasp a great array of wrong turns and dangers. On the one side, maximalism, vanguardism, bureaucratic centralism, authoritarianism, Caesarism, and materialism (a failure to connect the economic-corporate to the ethico-political). On the other side, subversivism, autonomism, reformism, *trasformismo*, passive revolution, and idealism (a failure to connect the ethico-political to the economic-corporate). The main dangers, indeed, emerge from a failure to connect in the making of a new common good, a failure to articulate the faces and phases of popular mobilization, and the lack of an organic formulation—in theory and practice.

The book, overall, has aimed at just such an organic formulation. It has aimed to achieve this by several key points of theoretical renovation: first, the fertility of thinking in terms of phases and of how phases are transformed by revolutionizing and radicalizing processes; second, a key emphasis on the importance of social and historical bloc formation; third, the vitality of the organic party; and finally, the important part played by the translocal and the transnational. The goal has been to identify, situate, and connect the living diversity of popular mobilization; to offer a connecting theory that can subtend, in theory and practice, the articulation of struggles. The aim is to contribute thereby, amid right-wing ascendancies, revolutionary weakness, and ongoing crisis, to the realization of new democratic socialist forces.

THEORETICAL IMPLICATIONS

Centring the plural ensemble of subaltern social groups, their diverse histories, and the search for an emancipated transnational community clearly displaces and decentres readings, Gramscian and Marxist, which do not question the national or statist framework and which put the working class and its struggle to overthrow capitalism nationally and internationally at the centre of the overall process of mobilization and emancipation. The working classes and all those dispossessed, marginalized, and objectified by capitalist profit are a vital part of the analysis, but they are not its unique figure, and they are not fundamentally operating at a national or international, state or interstate level. The national working class are not the sole vanguard in the history of subaltern social groups. And the achievement of a socialist *economy*—at any scale—is not the only measure of change.

This contribution aims at synthesis, not negation. Capitalist objectification and oppression, and class consciousness, are vital components of the analysis, as is socialist self-management, socialist engagements in civil society and in economic relations beyond the factory, and the eco-socialist transformation of the economy. The theory aims to take the state and nation extremely seriously. But the objectification and oppression attendant on racism, sexism, colonialism, homophobia, statism, and nationalism are no less significant. The inter/transnational world is not just capitalism writ large but also a matter of interconnected formations of culture, civil society, and the state. Imperialism past and present has just as much to do with violence and culture as it has to do with capitalist profit. Hence, this book has regarded group consciousness with the same degree of seriousness as class consciousness. It has also considered cultural, organizational, and political forms of autonomy and engagements in civil society aimed at the transformation of culture and the state. Popular mobilization builds a new social force by weaving together a social bloc of subaltern social groups (including working classes), including across national borders, and eventually comes to form a historical bloc. The historical bloc is the hegemon. This theory thus strikes against all those Gramscian and Gramscian-Marxist theories in which either the class, the party, the state, or the sole leader (Stalin, Mao, Castro, etc.) becomes the hegemon.

Popular mobilization is not guaranteed by any law of capitalist development: no such objective laws exist. To imagine that they do is to place a burdensome shackle on what popular mobilization can achieve. What matters above all is how a new hegemony is constructed: how democratic socialism is keyed into an enriching culture. The theory also pushes against those who, out of resignation and despair born of decades of defeat, draw exclusively on hegemony to explain (often with an 'encrustation' of positivism) the lack of revolution or only ever see passive revolution. We must, perhaps *especially* in periods of defeat when ruling classes thrive on subaltern despair, leave room for the analysis of potentially vital dynamics of renewal, radicalization, and revolutionizing. Here the method has been to draw on the concept of hegemony to understand better the terrain to be transformed. The task is a new hegemony, one that is socialist, to be sure—and in the present one must say eco-socialist—but also one that is revolutionary in relation to the state, culture, and civil society. Worth mentioning is the lack of emphasis on the terms 'production' and 'reproduction'. The worry is that such language repeats the productivist (and modernist, planet-destroying) capitalist imaginary that one aims to oppose, while affirming (in the second case) a (gendered, biogenetic, and potentially heteronormative) passivity, which misses the fact that hegemony, practices of care, and popular mobilization are always in formation—renewal, decomposition, and neoformation (not reproduction) being the key terms.

In stark contrast with 'Marxism-Leninism', the organic party does not 'seize power' in political society. Its plural organizational instances become the new civil society, and thus become the key mediation between the new minimal, democratic state on the one side and economy and culture on the other. The main tasks of the organic party during the revolutionary phase are to subtend the formation of the historical bloc and to ensure that popular and democratic institutions, mediating between the transnational people and the state, are firmly established and that the new civil society will be able to organize consent (and define the ethical content of the state) in relation to the new historical bloc. There is a radical refusal, in this view, of the dictatorship of the proletariat, the single party, authoritarianism, and statism—along with its often-attendant forms of masculinism and phallocentrism. In the present, popular mobilization can be seen as a search, subtended by a non-monopolistic and organizationally decentred organic party, for eco-socialism; popular democracy; a minimal, confederal, and transnational state; and an expanded, diverse civil society. In this view, there is a definite break with twentieth century communism.

On the other hand, popular mobilization is not above all a cultural process, a politico-ideological rearticulation, a 'moral-therapeutic' reworking of feeling and affect; nor is it a process of discursive deconstruction; nor is it solely the expression of a single, oppressed, non-class group, identity, or community. This book has used culture to refer to a dramatic intersubjective universe and not, as Raymond Williams does, to refer to a whole way of life, however salient Williams's work was for the New Left in the 1970s. Culture and feeling, in other words, is a vital domain, but it is not the whole process. The ways in which right-wing, Orientalist, and neoliberal forces have in recent decades re-engineered and weaponized cultural and affective expressions originally pushed for and championed by the long cultural revolution on the Left are salient warnings and indicators that popular mobilization in the present is not just a matter of culture. One only thinks of pink-washing (from the rainbow flag flying atop the Bank of England to 'gay-friendly' Israeli apartheid), neoliberal feminism, green capitalism, corporate community organizing, and a wide variety of tokenistic diversity initiatives in many settings, not least within the managerialist, endowment-driven university. Popular mobilization must include culture and feeling, but it must also work on civil society, the economy, and the state. I take as highly salient in this regard Stuart Hall's frustration with the oft-depoliticizing impact of the very cultural studies that he did so much to found. Social being is not just a question of hermeneutics, and history is not just a 'metanarrative'. Popular mobilization involves bodies and class elements and constructs a social force, with all the relevant strategic and political dimensions that this implies. Popular and transnational popular mobilization embraces and affirms much about the idea of intersectionality as we have seen throughout, but it finds insufficient any version thereof which stops short of tackling the political questions of how diversity and plurality are woven together to form a social force and eventually a new, post-subaltern form of hegemony.

Popular mobilization, moreover, is not always doomed in the face of discursive normalization. The thesis that the subaltern 'cannot speak' has too often implied binary thinking and armchair dismissals. Language may be fraught and under construction, but to strike the subaltern dumb (unspeaking) is far too close to the conservative thesis of the subaltern as genus. Social consciousness is not just a discursive effect. The importance of passive and active adherence to dominant formations, for example, and of the moments when this adherence breaks down, cuts very much against this view of the unthinking and immobile subaltern. Even resistance 'at the margins', as we have seen, is not always a matter of a seamless complicity and an illusion of autonomy. The book agrees that such resistance is not a matter of meaningful autonomy and that it is not in and of itself as transformative. And the book agrees, as we have seen, with Timothy Mitchell's theoretical critique of James C. Scott's pragmatism, individualism, and anarchism. But recasting in Gramscian theory diffuse and capillary forms of popular intervention and thinking these forms in relation to the torturous contradictions and ambiguities of domination make them part of a set of processes that can (but do not necessarily) prepare the ground for a radicalization process by rendering social domination unstable. Lisa Wedeen showed how, in Syria in the 1990s and 2000s, the 'ambiguities of domination' could be torturous, could crush subjects and generate 'wooden conformity'.[1] But as the 2011 popular uprising in Syria amply demonstrated, the torturous experience of these ambiguities also prepared the ground.[2] Other discursive approaches see subalternity as merely a spectral discursive figure or reject the concept of autonomy in toto, thereby missing the ways in which new grounds on which to stand are socially and historically constructed and remaining oblivious to the fact that such constructions are messy and certainly not immaculate.

The theorization here clearly draws on the democratic, anti-statist, and anti-vanguardist tendencies in anarchism, such as in Carl Bogg's interpretation of Gramsci, but there also are implications that strike against anarchism (in keeping with Gramsci's own orientation). First, there is an acceptance of the need for leadership, albeit in an organic and popular-democratic formulation. And while the approach here gives a key value to autonomy, it carries on a sharp critique of the ideological and intellectual fetishization of autonomy, what I have called *autonomism*. Autonomism arguably seeks to relive again and again the awesome break of dawn, the sunburst, the 'scenes of dissensus'—little realizing that the fruit of the long gestation is still young and that there is need of further development and cultivation, especially in civil society. I have also argued for the limits of horizontalism. The book has aimed to push against any romanticization of weapons of the weak, the concept of a consensual revolution (enemies must be defeated, politics is antagonistic), and the idea of a revolution that can bypass or avoid the state. As I have argued, the revolution passes through the state, breaking it up and remaking it. The state does not wither away but is reconstructed in a popular-democratic, minimal, plurinational, and confederal form.

Finally, the theory advanced here has pushed against interpretations of Gramsci which have dialled up or left unexamined elements of Eurocentric modernism, Orientalism, and colonialism. Civil society and the war of position have been read in West-centric ways. Gramscians who centre the working class (and sometimes those which centre the nation and the state) have found it difficult to do justice to the diversity of popular mobilization among the colonized, the indigenous, the Third World, and the Global South. Elementary forms of resistance, for example, have been falsely assimilated to the primitive, the traditional, the backward, or the archaic. The book certainly follows and accepts many of the points made by those who demonstrate elements of modernity/coloniality in Gramsci's work. The book, for instance, like much of subaltern studies, does not centre the working class (in any traditional sense of the phrase). I have also noted many points of overlap with the decolonial, including in relation to praxis. Wynter's point that the human is both *mythoi* and *bios*, for example, provides a striking parallel to the dialectics of social being and social consciousness offered in this book, including its treatment of myth.[3] The book has also argued, however, that decolonial critiques risk reinstating the binaries they wish to contest, a product, I have argued, of an unsustainably seamless view of discourse or of a homogenizing view of the colonial West. Popular mobilization is syncretic, based on recombination and connection, and is inevitably transnational: it cannot be only ever authentically situated against, outside of colonial modernity. Popular mobilization does not involve a civilizational telos: the torturous contradictions of domination register oppression, disunity, and dilemma (not backwardness), can involve highly sophisticated subaltern

Conclusion

engagements, and are potentially (but not always) the start points of a live work. They are not remnants left over from a traditional past but vital in the present and future, as new forms of social domination—from modern slavery to asylum systems—are constantly being invented (including by the colonial modern). Chapter 5 demonstrated, furthermore, the plausibility of a non-Eurocentric reading of the war of position. It is against oppression and domination—not backwardness, primitiveness, or recalcitrance—that popular mobilization takes aim. Self and Other, 'East' and 'West' are never complete, but always under construction. The view here overall is that the living Gramscian tradition, especially when read in combination with organic intellectuals of new forms of progressive and transnational popular struggle, from Chiapas to Rojava, can be renovated in ways which point beyond colonial modernism, nativism, and Eurocentrism.

The foregoing has underlined the ways in which a renovated Gramscian theory of popular mobilization cannot be easily assimilated to Marxism, cultural studies, nationalism, discursivism, anarchism, feminism, intersectionality, or the decolonial—although it builds on all of them. This point heavily underscores the profound originality of the inevitably updating Gramscian tradition and the fertility of the philosophy of praxis, the politics of hegemony, and the history of subaltern social groups. It is also a strike against the way that Gramsci is usually treated as but a planet in someone else's solar system (chiefly Croce, Foucault, Hegel, Lacan, and Marx). But the Gramscian tradition is no subaltern. My sense is that the current Gramsci revival is bearing this out, and perhaps further engaged research on a variety of topics and themes beyond popular mobilization will deepen this fundamental line of thought.

PRACTICAL IMPLICATIONS

The foregoing has aimed to fertilize the soil, but how to plough? This book is not a detailed practical handbook: its purpose has been theoretical. There is little scope—or even an appropriate methodology (such as participatory action research)—then, for tackling practice adequately. It would be better, furthermore, to take detailed practical advice directly from organic intellectuals and popular educators. However, the translation from historical life into theoretical language is intertwined with a reciprocal translation from theory to historical life. Praxis means that theory informs practice and lines of collective action. One studies not as a detached or managerial observer but as an already implicated and intervening subject. Taking responsibility for the interpretation thus has practical implications. The practical content of theory is discoverable in the intention not just to learn but to intervene in the balance and relation of forces. In a deeply historicist and connecting approach, one-size-fits-all schemes are inadequate. The theory can be, however, an orienting and situating device, offering broad criteria for thinking how best to connect and articulate diverse struggles in ways that can contribute to building new, popular social forces.

We have seen how popular mobilization is fed from many streams each proceeding from particularities—one fights not 'in general', but from where one is located. Positionality can be understood in relation to the phases of popular mobilization. Is one undergoing and grappling with the painful ambiguities, contradictions, and forms of instability associated with domination? Or is one enmeshed in the business of asserting and constructing new autonomous forms? Or is one's activism about the long, expansive search for consent? Or is one in a position to engage in various forms of leadership? It is useful to ask how one's activity relates to these fundamental phases, and how it intervenes in them, separately or together.

The theory suggests how to break down these orienting questions in some detail. Is one searching for class/group consciousness where it is lacking, asserting the autonomy of the class or group, weaving together a social bloc, or in the very process of forming a new historical bloc and thinking the sorts of community consciousness that could stitch it together? Is one searching for the glimmers of good sense in common sense, the elements of ideology (in the positive sense) in good sense, elaborating and diffusing an ideology and new cultural forms, or building out from ideology towards a new philosophy and worldview? Is one battling in civil society, culture, economy, or the state, and what are the transnational dimensions of one's activity? How is one positioned spatially and temporally and what sorts of new spatiality and temporality are in view? How are one's actions contributing to the construction of the new popular social force, and where is that force being applied? Is the strategy to shake the soil of domination, build autonomy, fight a war of position or a war of manoeuvre, or to contribute to the formation of a social, organizational, or historical bloc? What sort of collective will is in view, where is one in relation to the process of collective will formation, and what are its fundamental, positive myths? What trajectories of renewal, radicalization, and revolutionizing are conceivable? Posing these questions, to oneself and in relation to allies, foes, supporters, and bystanders, can help in orientating and situating protagonism and in clarifying situations, lines of antagonism, and alliance in relation to hegemony. At all points, popular mobilizers will need to keep scanning the horizon for crises of authority, which are great catalysts of radicalization and revolutionizing dynamics.

The aim is to connect—to realize—an organic formulation. This is the fundamental criterion by which protagonists can assess and make sense of the (great) possibilities and (terrible) dangers that surround them, the strengths and weaknesses of lines of collective action, and the difference between success and failure. Is one romanticizing the torturous contradictions of social domination, or is one taking insufficient account of the possibilities therein? One needs to ask how instabilities and contradictions can best be mobilized; passive and active adherence best broken; and subaltern formations and fleeting confrontations scaled up and connected to assertions of autonomy, consent-building, or the ferment of revolution. Further, activists can draw on this book to ask whether they are fetishizing or dismissing autonomy. The productive questions will be: how can new forms of autonomy best be asserted and connected with each other translocally, and how can new forms of class and group consciousness reach their fullness? Protagonists can expect to learn from autonomy and to offer resources to it— not to teach the autonomous how to behave. This is the phase, one recalls, when existing theories are shunted aside and new forms and forces created. The question then becomes, now that we have found new grounds on which to stand, how do we eschew *autonomism*, win consent, and connect autonomy to new forms of leadership and even revolution?

Regarding consent, the question is whether the formulation is vanguardist, maximalist, or authoritarian or whether it is reformist (that is— subject to absorption in transformism and passive revolution). This book has argued that rather than a single vanguard party on the one hand or a mass, democratic party on the other, contemporary activists will most productively build an organic party—a 'postmodern Prince' (one might just as easily say 'princess' or even 'queen'), an organizational bloc, in domestic and transnational space. Consent-winning will need to figure out how best to connect to assertions of autonomy and the contradictions of domination. In relation to social bloc formation, activists will need to ask whether they are overstating or understating the history, demands and feelings of a given group or a class. The line of renewal here has to do with finding the best ways to build a popular social bloc—a highly sensitive and demanding work and one which does not thrive on moralizing, righteousness, posturing, or assertions of authenticity (qualities which might have been more productive in earlier phases). The demand for immaculate resistance, especially here, is out. More promising in the face of these challenges would be a historicizing consciousness, an awareness of context and diverse temporalities, revolutionary patience, and ways to socialize apparent opposites, including through convivial modalities of 'call and response', and through a deep engagement with culture and the forms of connection and catharsis it can afford.[4]

The work of connection, further, relies on an expansive perspective regarding lines of alliance and enmity. Potential allies and supporters must be engaged (which can mean difficult forms of dialogue), while enemies still must be overcome (which can imply disruption, boycott, and the like). The capacious and expansive capacity of the popular social bloc is in no way a lack of clear-sightedness about foes. In this phase, cultural and intellectual elaboration, including in relation to positive myth, however apparently marginal, still has a significant place, as it forms the consciousness which can stitch the bloc together. It can guide the tracks on which apparently 'spontaneous' forms and relatively sudden, radicalizing, and unplanned exits from domination run. One will need to keep an eye out for radicalizing tendencies more generally, especially in relation to transformism in reverse, when, often through rounds of antagonism, middle classes or formerly 'respectable' elements in civil society start to break with ruling groups and existing ideologies and join hands with popular forces.

Finally, in respect of the roiling ferment of revolution, the question will be how to avoid the snares of passive revolution on the one side and Caesarism, statism, imperialism, the violent revolutionary minority, or civil war on the other. The main tasks of revolutionaries are to act as a catalyst in relation to revolutionizing dynamics, build an organic party diverse enough to become the new civil society, and construct popular democratic institutions and a minimal, confederal state safeguarding an eco-socialist economy that puts an end to capitalism. The search will be on for a post-subaltern historical bloc, infused with a transnational popular consciousness of emancipated community and an enriching, convivial culture. The eventually disabling, millenarian, and materialist belief that ending capitalism will *automatically* right all wrongs and cause the state to wither away will be put aside. Popular revolutionaries, instead, will be deeply convinced that transnational democratic socialism can only be achieved when economic and political transformation is articulated with a constructive and deeply compelling social and cultural reformation. This book has offered a Gramscian theory of popular mobilization to contribute to this socialist renewal.

NOTES

ABBREVIATIONS

FSPN   Antonio Gramsci, *Further Selections from the Prison Notebooks*, ed. and trans. Derek Boothman (London: Lawrence & Wishart, 1995).

HPC   Antonio Gramsci, *History, Philosophy and Culture in the Young Gramsci*, ed. Pedro Cavalcanti and Paul Piccone (Saint Louis: Telos Press, 1975).

LP   Antonio Gramsci, *Letters from Prison*, 2 vols., ed. Frank Rosengarten, trans. Raymond Rosenthal (New York: Columbia University Press, 1994).

PN   Antonio Gramsci, *Prison Notebooks*, 3 vols., ed. and trans. Joseph A. Buttigieg (New York: Columbia University Press, 2011).

PPL   Antonio Gramsci, *A Great and Terrible World: The Pre-Prison Letters, 1908-1926*, ed. and trans. Derek Boothman (London: Lawrence & Wishart, 2014).

QC   Antonio Gramsci, *Quaderni del Carcere*, 4 vols., ed. Valentino Gerratana (Torino: Einaudi, 1975).

SCW   Antonio Gramsci, *Selections from Cultural Writings*, ed. David Forgacs and Geoffrey Nowell-Smith, trans. William Boelhower (London: Lawrence & Wishart, 1985).

SPN   Antonio Gramsci, *Selections from the Prison Notebooks of Antonio Gramsci*, ed. and trans. Quintin Hoare and Geoffrey Nowell Smith (London: Lawrence & Wishart, 1971).

SPW1   Antonio Gramsci, *Selections from Political Writings (1910-1920)*, ed. Quintin Hoare, trans. John Mathews (London: Lawrence & Wishart, 1977).

SPW2   Antonio Gramsci, *Selections from Political Writings (1921-1926)*, ed. and trans. Quintin Hoare (London: Lawrence & Wishart, 1978).

SSG   Antonio Gramsci, *Subaltern Social Groups: A Critical Edition of Prison Notebook 25*, ed. and trans. Joseph A. Buttigieg and Marcus E. Green (New York: Columbia University Press, 2021).

INTRODUCTION

1. Gramsci to his sister-in-law Tatiana Schucht, 19 February 1927, in Antonio Gramsci, *Letters from Prison*, ed. Frank Rosengarten, trans. Raymond Rosenthal (New York: Columbia University Press, 1994), vol. 1, 73–74. Hereafter *LP* + volume number (e.g. *LP1*).

2. Carl Boggs, *The Two Revolutions: Antonio Gramsci and the Dilemmas of Western Marxism* (Boston: South End Press, 1984), 261; Roberto M. Dainotto and Fredric Jameson, eds., *Gramsci in the World* (Durham, NC: Duke University Press, 2020), 3.

3. Giuseppe Vacca, *Alternative Modernities: Antonio Gramsci's Twentieth Century*, trans. Derek Boothman and Chris Dennis (Cham: Palgrave Macmillan, 2021), xi.

4. Chantal Mouffe, ed., *Gramsci and Marxist Theory* (London: Routledge, 1979), 1–18, 168–204.

5. Erich Fromm, ed., *Socialist Humanism* (New York: Doubleday, 1965); Mihailo Marković, *From Affluence to Praxis: Philosophy and Social Criticism*, foreword by Erich Fromm (Ann Arbor: University of Michigan, 1974).

6. Raymond Williams, *The Long Revolution* (London: Chatto & Windus, 1961), 79.

7. Stuart Hall, *The Hard Road to Renewal: Thatcherism and the Crisis of the Left* (London: Verso, 1988), 11.

8. Anthony Crézégut, 'An Imaginary Gramscianism? Early French Gramscianism and the Quest for "Marxist Humanism" (1947–65),' in *Revisiting Gramsci's Notebooks*, ed. Francesca Antonini, Aaron Bernstein, Lorenzo Fusaro, and Robert Jackson (Chicago: Haymarket Books, 2020), 432.

9. Valentina Cuppi, 'The Diffusion of Gramsci's Thought in the "Peripheral West" of Latin America', in Antonini et al., *Revisiting Gramsci's Notebooks*, 420, 413, 417, 427; Carlos Nelson Coutinho, *Gramsci's Political Thought* (Chicago: Haymarket Books, 2013), 163–188; Alvaro Bianchi, *Gramsci's Laboratory: Philosophy, History and Politics* (Chicago: Haymarket Books, 2021), 25–32.

10. Ernesto Laclau, *Politics and Ideology in Marxist Theory: Capitalism, Fascism, Populism* (London: Verso, 1979), 141.

11. Ibid., 68, 87.

12. Fonseca Sandoval and José Daniel, 'Colonialidad del saber jurídico y derecho neo-constitucional en Colombia', *Trans-pasando Fronteras* 12 (2018): 45–81.

13. Fadi A. Bardawil, *Revolution and Disenchantment: Arab Marxism and the Binds of Emancipation* (Durham, NC: Duke University Press, 2020); Michelle

Browers, 'Beginnings, Continuities and Revivals: An Inventory of the New Arab Left and an Ongoing Arab Left Tradition', *Middle East Critique* 30, no. 1 (2021): 25–40; Hicham Safieddine, 'Mahdi Amel: On Colonialism, Sectarianism and Hegemony', *Middle East Critique* 30, no. 1 (2021): 41–56.

14. Nazih N. Ayubi, *Over-Stating the Arab State: Politics and Society in the Middle East* (London: Bloomsbury Publishing, 1996); Patrizia Manduchi, 'Between Old and New Epistemological Paradigms: Gramscian Readings of Revolutionary Processes in Egypt and Tunisia', *Journal of North African Studies* 26, no. 6 (2021): 1057–1076.

15. Gilbert Achcar, *Morbid Symptoms: Relapse in the Arab Uprising* (London: Saqi Books, 2016); Benoît Challand, *Violence and Representation in the Arab Uprisings* (Cambridge: Cambridge University Press, 2023); Maria D'Aria, 'Subalternity and Counter-Revolution: The Social Drivers of the Egyptian State Transformation', PhD diss. (University of Edinburgh, 2020); Brecht De Smet, *A Dialectical Pedagogy of Revolt: Gramsci, Vygotsky, and the Egyptian Revolution* (Leiden: Brill, 2015); Brecht De Smet, *Gramsci on Tahrir: Revolution and Counter-Revolution in Egypt* (London: Pluto Press, 2016); Brecht De Smet, '"Authoritarian Resilience" as Passive Revolution: A Gramscian Interpretation of Counter-Revolution in Egypt', *Journal of North African Studies* 26, no. 6 (2021): 1077–1098; Gennaro Gervasio and Andrea Teti, 'Prelude to the Revolution: Independent Civic Activists in Mubarak's Egypt and the Quest for Hegemony', *Journal of North African Studies* 26, no. 6 (2021): 1099–1121; Patrizia Manduchi, Alessandra Marchi, and Giuseppe Vacca, *Gramsci nel mondo arabo* (Bologna: Il Mulino, 2017); Alessandra Marchi, 'Molecular Transformations: Reading the Arab Uprisings with and beyond Gramsci', *Middle East Critique* 30, no. 1 (2021): 67–85; Fabio Merone, 'Analysing Revolutionary Islamism: Ansar al-Sharia Tunisia according to Gramsci', *Journal of North African Studies* 26, no. 6 (2021): 1122–1143; Roberto Roccu, *The Political Economy of the Egyptian Revolution: Mubarak, Economic Reforms and Failed Hegemony* (Basingstoke: Palgrave Macmillan, 2013); Sara Salem, 'Critical Interventions in Debates on the Arab Revolutions: Centring Class', *Review of African Political Economy* 45, no. 155 (2018): 125–134; Sara Salem, *Anticolonial Afterlives in Egypt: The Politics of Hegemony* (Cambridge: Cambridge University Press, 2020).

16. Ranajit Guha, 'Gramsci in India: Homage to a Teacher', *Journal of Modern Italian Studies* 16, no. 2 (2011): 289.

17. Ibid., 295.

18. Pu Wang, 'Gramsci and the Chinese Left: Reappraising a Missed Encounter', in *Gramsci in the World*, ed. Roberto M. Dainotto and Fredric Jameson (Durham, NC: Duke University Press, 2020), 206.

19. Ibid., 223.

20. Stephen Gill, 'Toward a Postmodern Prince? The Battle in Seattle as a Moment in the New Politics of Globalisation', *Millennium* 29, no. 1 (2000): 131–140.

21. Guido Liguori, *Gramsci's Pathways* (Leiden: Brill, 2015); Marcos Del Roio, *The Prisms of Gramsci: The Political Formula of the United Front* (Leiden: Brill, 2015); Perry Anderson, *The Antinomies of Antonio Gramsci* (London: Verso, 2017).

22. Francesca Antonini, Aaron Bernstein, Lorenzo Fusaro, and Robert Jackson, eds., *Revisiting Gramsci's Notebooks* (Leiden: Brill, 2019; Chicago: Haymarket, 2020); Giuseppe Cospito, *The Rhythm of Thought in Gramsci: A Diachronic Interpretation of Prison Notebooks* (Chicago: Haymarket Books, 2017); Peter Thomas, *The Gramscian Moment* (Leiden: Brill, 2009).

23. Michele Filippini, 'The Forms of a Travelling Theory: A New Approach to Gramsci's Texts', *Middle East Critique* 30, no. 1 (2021): 9–24.

24. Gayatri Chakravorty Spivak, 'In Response: Looking Back, Looking Forward', in *Can the Subaltern Speak? Reflections on the History of an Idea*, ed. Rosalind C. Morris (New York: Columbia University Press, 2010), 230–232.

25. Michael Ekers, Gillian Hart, Stefan Kipfer, and Alex Loftus, eds., *Gramsci: Space, Nature, Politics* (Newark: Wiley, 2012); Alex Loftus, 'Gramsci as a Historical Geographical Materialist', in Antonini et al., *Revisiting Gramsci's Notebooks*, 9–22.

26. Neelam Srivastava and Baidik Bhattacharya, eds., *The Postcolonial Gramsci* (New York: Routledge, 2012). Connotative articulations are 'evocative' or affective links established between social and conceptual elements in 'custom', 'opinion', and hegemonic common sense. Laclau, *Politics and Ideology*, 7–8.

27. John Chalcraft and Alessandra Marchi, 'Guest Editors' Introduction: Gramsci in the Arab World', *Middle East Critique* 30, no. 1 (2021): 1–8; Michael Ekers, Stefan Kipfer, and Alex Loftus, 'On Articulation, Translation, and Populism: Gillian Hart's Postcolonial Marxism', *Annals of the American Association of Geographers* 110, no. 5 (2020): 1577–1593; Zachary Levenson, 'Make "Articulation" Gramscian Again', in *Ethnographies of Power: Working Radical Concepts with Gillian Hart*, ed. Sharad Chari, Mark Hunter, and Melanie Samson, 187–216 (Johannesburg: Wits University Press, 2022).

28. Michael Denning, 'Everyone a Legislator', *New Left Review*, 129 (2021): 31.

29. Peter Thomas, 'Toward the Modern Prince', in *Gramsci in the World*, ed. Fredric Jameson and Roberto M. Dainotto (Durham, NC: Duke University Press, 2020), 30.

30. Alaa Abd El-Fattah, *You Have Not Yet Been Defeated: Selected Works, 2011–2021*, trans. a collective (London: Fitzcarraldo Editions, 2021), 87.

31. Maha Abdelrahman, *Egypt's Long Revolution: Protest Movements and Uprisings* (London: Routledge, 2015).

32. Achcar, *Morbid Symptoms*.

33. Asef Bayat, *Revolution without Revolutionaries: Making Sense of the Arab Spring* (Stanford, CA: Stanford University Press, 2017).

34. Laurence Cox and Alf G. Nilsen, *We Make Our Own History: Marxism and Social Movements in the Twilight of Neoliberalism* (London: Pluto Press, 2014).

35. Divisive tendencies in this regard were given an arguably unproductive impulse after the sharp dismissal, in the name of Marxism and universalism, of postcolonial, subaltern, and cultural studies in Vivek Chibber, *Postcolonial Theory and the Specter of Capital* (London: Verso, 2013). Chibber's intervention, by pitting postcolonialism against presumed Enlightenment universalism, has contributed to the making of a new front in the culture war, whereby 'Marxists' are positioned as doubty defenders of 'the West'.

36. Owen Jones, *This Land: The Struggle for the Left* (London: Penguin, 2020).

37. Jack Shenker, *Now We Have Your Attention: The New Politics of the People* (New York: Random House, 2019).

38. David Graeber, *The Democracy Project: A History, a Crisis, a Movement* (New York: Random House, 2013).

39. Vincent Bevins, *If We Burn: The Mass Protest Decade and the Missing Revolution* (London: Hachette, 2023).

40. Aasim Sajjad Akhtar, *The Struggle for Hegemony in Pakistan: Fear, Desire and Revolutionary Horizons* (London: Pluto Press, 2022), 87-107.

41. Sa'ed Atshan, *Queer Palestine and the Empire of Critique* (Stanford, CA: Stanford University Press, 2020).

42. Franck Gaudichaud, Massimo Modonesi, and Jeffery R. Webber, *The Impasse of the Latin American Left* (Durham, NC: Duke University Press, 2022).

43. For a recent example, see the exchange in the *Boston Review* between Jodi Dean and Ayça Çubukçu, 'Leadership and Liberation', 14 June 2024, https://www.bostonreview.net/articles/leadership-and-liberation-an-exchange/.

44. Lukas Slothuus, 'Faith between Reason and Affect: Thinking with Antonio Gramsci', *Distinktion: Journal of Social Theory* 22, no. 3 (2021): 342. Honneth writes, similarly, of widespread contemporary 'discontent' and 'outrage', but one lacking 'any sense of direction, any historical sense of its ultimate aim'. Alex Honneth, *The Idea of Socialism* (Cambridge: Polity Press, 2018), 1.

45. El-Fattah, *Not Yet Been Defeated*.

46. Thomas, 'Modern Prince', 32.

47. Steven Marsh, 'Gramsci and Contemporary Spanish Politics', in *Language, Image and Power in Luso-Hispanic Cultural Studies*, ed. Susan Larson, 121-134 (London: Routledge, 2021); Jan Rehmann, 'Bernie Sanders and the Hegemonic Crisis of Neoliberal Capitalism: What Next?', *Socialism and Democracy* 30, no. 3 (2016): 1-11.

48. There is a curious affinity with Aristotle's constituent elements of reality—earth, water, air, and fire, as well with modern physics' fundamental states of matter—solid, liquid, gas, plasma.

49. These terms will be explained in detail in chapter 2.

CHAPTER ONE. THE ORIGINALITY OF THE LIVING
GRAMSCIAN TRADITION

1. Benjamin Barber, *Jihad vs McWorld* (New York: Random House, 2010); Ted Gurr, *Why Men Rebel* (London: Routledge, 2015); Samuel Huntington, 'The Clash of Civilisations', *Foreign Affairs* 72, no. 3 (1993): 22-49; Gustave Le Bon, *The Crowd: A Study of the Popular Mind* (London: T. F. Unwin, 1896); Douglas Murray, *The Madness of Crowds: Gender, Race and Identity* (London: Bloomsbury, 2019).

2. Antonio Gramsci, *Subaltern Social Groups: A Critical Edition of Prison Notebook 25*, trans. and ed. Joseph A. Buttigieg and Marcus E. Green (New York: Columbia University Press, 2021), 3; Q25, §1. Hereafter *SSG*.

3. Riccardo Ciavolella, 'The Changing Meanings of People's Politics: Gramsci and Anthropology from Subaltern Classes to Contemporary Struggles', in Antonini et al., *Revisiting Gramsci's Notebooks*, 268.

4. Hall, *Hard Road*, 7, 140, 153, 157, 191-192.

5. Ibid., 153.

6. Marco Fonseca, *Gramsci's Critique of Civil Society: Towards a New Concept of Hegemony* (London: Routledge, 2016), viii-ix.

7. David Held and Anthony McGrew, *Globalisation/Anti-Globalisation: Beyond the Great Divide* (Cambridge: Polity, 2007).

8. Margaret E. Keck and Kathryn Sikkink, *Activists beyond Borders: Advocacy Networks in International Politics* (Ithaca, NY: Cornell University Press, 1998).

9. Fonseca, *Civil Society*, xiii-ix.

10. Ibid., 178.

11. Srila Roy, 'Affective Politics and the Sexual Subaltern: Lesbian Activism in Eastern India', in Nilsen and Roy, *New Subaltern Politics: Reconceptualising Hegemony and Resistance in Contemporary India*, 155.

12. Slothuus, 'Reason and Affect', 8.

13. Gene Sharp, *From Dictatorship to Democracy: A Conceptual Framework for Liberation* (New York: The New Press, 2012).

14. *SSG*, 59; Q8, §59.

15. Charles Dickens, *Bleak House*, ed. and intro. Nicola Bradbury, pref. Terry Eagleton (London: Penguin, 1996), 124.

16. Jan Willem Duyvendak and James M. Jasper, *Players and Arenas: The Interactive Dynamics of Protest* (Amsterdam: Amsterdam University Press, 2015); Doug McAdam, Sidney Tarrow, and Charles Tilly, *Dynamics of Contention* (Cambridge: Cambridge University Press, 2001); Sidney Tarrow, *Power in Movement* (Cambridge: Cambridge University Press, 2022).

17. Sidney Tarrow, 'Transnational Politics: Contention and Institutions in International Politics', *Annual Review of Political Science* 4, no. 1 (2001): 1-20.

18. Jacquelien Van Stekelenburg and Bert Klandermans, 'The Social Psychology of Protest', *Current Sociology* 61, no. 5–6 (2013): 886–905.

19. Cox and Nilsen, *Our Own History*, 17–19.

20. Robert D. Benford and David A. Snow, 'Framing Processes and Social Movements: An Overview and Assessment', *Annual Review of Sociology* 26, no. 1 (2000): 611–639.

21. Erving Goffman, *Frame Analysis: An Essay on the Organization of Experience* (Cambridge, MA: Harvard University Press, 1974), 13–14.

22. Gramsci, cited in Joseph Femia, *Gramsci's Political Thought: Hegemony, Consciousness, and the Revolutionary Process* (Oxford: Clarendon Press, 1987), 212.

23. Colin Barker, Laurence Cox, John Krinsky, and Alf Gunvald Nilsen, *Marxism and Social Movements* (Leiden: Brill, 2013).

24. As Lenin reported to the Russian Social Democratic Labour Party in October 1917, 'The Party could not be guided by the temper of the masses because it was changeable and incalculable; the Party must be guided by an objective analysis.' Cited in Mario Tronti, *Workers and Capital* (London: Verso, 2019), 263.

25. Michel Foucault, *Discipline and Punish: The Birth of the Prison*, trans. Alan Sheridan (Harmondsworth: Penguin Books, 1979); Michel Foucault, *Archaeology of Knowledge*, trans. A. M. Sheridan Smith (London: Routledge, 2002); Michel Foucault, *The History of Sexuality, 1: The Will to Knowledge*, trans. Robert Hurley (London: Penguin, 2019).

26. Didier Eribon, *Insult and the Making of the Gay Self* (Durham, NC: Duke University Press, 2004), xii.

27. John Sanbonmatsu, *The Postmodern Prince: Critical Theory, Left Strategy, and the Making of a New Political Subject* (New York: New York University Press, 2004), 101–124.

28. Challand, *Violence and Representation*, 99.

29. Cf. S. M. Shamsul Alam, *Governmentality and Counter-Hegemony in Bangladesh* (London: Palgrave Macmillan, 2015).

30. Dennis K. Mumby, 'The Problem of Hegemony: Rereading Gramsci for Organizational Communication Studies', *Western Journal of Communication* 61, no. 4 (1997): 366.

31. Joseph Massad, 'Re-Orienting Desire: The Gay International and the Arab World', *Public Culture* 14, no. 2 (2002): 371ff.

32. Judith Butler, *Gender Trouble* (London: Routledge, 2002); Angela Y. Davis, *Women, Race and Class* (London: Penguin, 1981); Simone de Beauvoir, *The Second Sex*, trans. H. M. Parshley (London: Vintage, 1997); W. E. B. Du Bois, *The Souls of Black Folk* (London: Routledge, 2015); Eribon, *Insult*; Frantz Fanon, *The Wretched of the Earth*, trans. Constance Farrington, pref. by Jean-Paul Sartre (New York: Grove Press, 1965); C. L. R. James, *The Black Jacobins: Toussaint L'Ouverture and the San*

Domingo Revolution (London: Penguin, 2001); bell hooks, *Ain't I a Woman: Black Women and Feminism* (London: Routledge, 2015); Audre Lorde, *Sister Outsider* (London: Penguin, 2019); Edward Said, *Orientalism: Western Conceptions of the Orient* (New York: Pantheon, 1978); Michelle Wallace, *Black Macho and the Myth of the Superwoman* (London: Verso, 1990).

33. Walter D. Mignolo and C. E. Walsh, *On Decoloniality: Concepts, Analytics, Praxis* (Durham, NC: Duke University Press, 2018), 4.

34. Abdullah Öcalan, *The Political Thought of Abdullah Öcalan: Kurdistan, Woman's Revolution and Democratic Confederalism*, foreword by Nadje Al-Ali (London: Pluto Press, 2017); Omar Jabary Salamanca, 'The Madrid Conference: Translating the One-State Slogan into Research and Political Action Agendas', *Arab World Geographer* 10, no. 1 (2007): 57–80.

35. Srivastava and Bhattacharya, *Postcolonial Gramsci*.

36. Patrizia Manduchi, 'Antonio Gramsci in the Arab World: The Ongoing Debate', in *Gramsci in the World*, ed. Roberto M. Dainotto and Fredric Jameson (Durham, NC: Duke University Press, 2020), 226.

37. Frank Rosengarten, *The Revolutionary Marxism of Antonio Gramsci* (Leiden: Brill, 2013), 57–58, 61, 62.

38. Gramsci, in *L'Ordine Nuovo*, 9 June 1919, cited in Rosengarten, *Revolutionary Marxism*, 150.

39. For example, David Featherstone, *Solidarity: Hidden Histories and Geographies of Internationalism* (London: Zed, 2012), 24–29.

40. Kang Liu, 'Hegemony and Cultural Revolution', *New Literary History* 28, no. 1 (1997): 82.

41. Giuseppe Fiori, *Antonio Gramsci: Life of a Revolutionary* (London: Verso, 1990), 9–10; Gianni Fresu, *Antonio Gramsci: An Intellectual Biography* (Cham: Palgrave Macmillan, 2023), 9, ftn 10.

42. Robert Chrisman, 'Black Studies, the Talented Tenth, and the Organic Intellectual', *The Black Scholar* 43, no. 3 (2013): 64–70; Christopher Harris, 'The Black Organic Intellectual Tradition and the Challenges of Educating and Developing Organic Intellectuals in the 21st Century', *Journal of Intersectionality* 2, no. 1 (2018): 51–107; Cornel West and Christa Buschendorf, *Black Prophetic Fire* (Boston: Beacon Press, 2015).

43. Renate Holub, *Antonio Gramsci: Beyond Marxism and Postmodernism* (London: Routledge, 2005), 191–195; Rosengarten, *Revolutionary Marxism*, 73, 88–89.

44. Rosengarten, *Revolutionary Marxism*, 90.

45. Holub, *Antonio Gramsci*, 195.

46. Francisco Fernández Buey, *Reading Gramsci*, trans. Nicholas Gray (Chicago: Haymarket Books, 2014), 163–167.

47. Rosengarten, *Revolutionary Marxism*, 82.

48. *SSG*, 59, 60–61; Q8, §156, §159; Holub, *Antonio Gramsci*, 29, 195–198; Rosengarten, *Revolutionary Marxism*, 82, 90; Roy, 'Affective Politics', 155–157, 159.

49. Robert Carley, 'Agile Materialisms: Antonio Gramsci, Stuart Hall, Racialisation, and Modernity', *Journal of Historical Sociology* 26, no. 4 (2013); Joan Cocks, *The Oppositional Imagination: Feminism, Critique and Political Theory* (London: Routledge, 1989); Richard Howson, *Challenging Hegemonic Masculinity* (London: Routledge, 2006); Margaret Ledwith, 'Antonio Gramsci and Feminism: The Elusive Nature of Power', *Educational Philosophy and Theory* 41, no. 6 (2009); Yaseen Noorani, *Culture and Hegemony in the Colonial Middle East* (New York: Palgrave Macmillan, 2010), 11–15.

50. Said, *Orientalism*, 7.

51. Vinayak Chaturvedi, ed., *Mapping Subaltern Studies and the Postcolonial* (London: Verso, 2000); Alf Gunvald Nilsen and Srila Roy, *New Subaltern Politics: Reconceptualising Hegemony and Resistance in Contemporary India* (Delhi: Oxford University Press, 2015).

52. Frantz Fanon, *Black Skin, White Masks*, trans. Charles Markham (London: Pluto Press, 1986), 109; R. A. Judy, 'Gramsci on *la questione dei negri: Gli intelletuali* and the Poesis of Americanisation," in *Gramsci in the World*, ed. Dainotto and Jameson, 166.

53. Eribon, *Insult*, 16.

54. Patti Lather, 'Research as Praxis', *Harvard Educational Review* 56, no. 3 (1986): 257–278.

55. Katherine McKittrick, *Sylvia Wynter: On Being Human as Praxis* (Durham, NC: Duke University Press, 2015), 3–8; Sylvia Wynter, 'Beyond the Word of Man: Glissant and the New Discourse of the Antilles', *World Literature Today* 63, no. 4 (1989): 640.

56. Mignolo, *On Decoloniality*, 7, 50.

57. Gustavo E. Fischman and Peter McLaren, 'Rethinking Critical Pedagogy and the Gramscian and Freirean Legacies: From Organic to Committed Intellectuals or Critical Pedagogy, Commitment, and Praxis', *Cultural Studies <-> Critical Methodologies* 5, no. 4 (2005).

58. *SPN*, 448; Q11, §34; Femia, *Political Thought*, 135; Abdurazack Karriem, 'The Rise and Transformation of the Brazilian Landless Movement into a Counter-Hegemonic Political Actor: A Gramscian Analysis', *Geoforum* 40, no. 3 (2009): 318; Alex Loftus, 'A Time for Gramsci', in *The International Handbook of Political Ecology* (Cheltenham: Edward Elgar Publishing, 2015), 89–102; Rosengarten, *Revolutionary Marxism*, 81; Catherine E. Walsh, 'Thinking Andean Abya Yala with and against Gramsci: Notes on State, Nature, and *Buen Vivir*', in Dainotto and Jameson, *Gramsci in the World*, 199.

59. Hall, *Hard Road*, 169–170.

60. Ibid., 249–250.

61. Ibid., 14.

62. Laurence Cox, *Why Social Movements Matter: An Introduction* (London: Rowman & Littlefield, 2018), 101-103.

63. Kimberlé Williams Crenshaw, 'Mapping the Margins: Intersectionality, Identity Politics, and Violence against Women of Color', in *The Public Nature of Private Violence*, ed. Martha Albertson Fineman, 93-118 (London: Routledge, 2013); Patricia Hill Collins, *Intersectionality as Critical Social Theory* (Durham, NC: Duke University Press, 2019); Patricia Hill Collins and Sirma Bilge, *Intersectionality* 2nd edn (Cambridge: Polity, 2020).

64. Brenna Bhandar and Rafeef Ziadah, *Revolutionary Feminisms: Conversations on Collective Action and Radical Thought* (London: Verso Books, 2020); Chandra Talpade Mohanty and Linda Carty, eds., *Feminist Freedom Warriors: Genealogies, Justice, Politics, and Hope* (Chicago: Haymarket Books, 2018).

65. Michael Albert, *Liberating Theory* (Boston: South End Press, 1986), 6–11.

66. de Beauvoir, *Second Sex*, 88, 90, 91. Angela Davis, to give a more recent example, rejects the thesis that the 'housewife is actually a secret worker inside the capitalist production process.' Davis, *Women, Race and Class*, 211.

67. Wallace, *Black Macho*, xxiv and passim.

68. Antonio Gramsci, *Prison Notebooks*, 3 vols., ed. and trans. Joseph A. Buttigieg (New York: Columbia University Press, 2011), vol. 2, 176-177; Q4, §37. Hereafter *PN* + volume number (e.g. *PN1*).

69. Esteve Morera, 'Gramsci and Democracy', *Canadian Journal of Political Science/Revue canadienne de science politique* 23, no. 1 (1990): 34–35.

70. David Graeber, *Direct Action: An Ethnography* (Oakland, CA: AK Press, 2009); James C. Scott, *Weapons of the Weak: Everyday Forms of Peasant Resistance* (New Haven: Yale University Press, 1985); James C. Scott, *Domination and the Arts of Resistance: Hidden Transcripts* (New Haven: Yale University Press, 1990); James C. Scott, *The Art of Not Being Governed: An Anarchist History of Upland Southeast Asia* (New Haven: Yale University Press, 2009); Marina Sitrin, *Horizontalism: Voices of Popular Power in Argentina* (Oakland, CA: AK Press, 2006); Marianne Maeckelbergh, *The Will of the Many: How the Alterglobalisation Movement is Changing the Face of Democracy* (London: Pluto Press, 2009); Michael Hardt and Antonio Negri, *Multitude: War and Democracy in the Age of Empire* (London: Penguin, 2004).

71. Massimo Salvadori, 'Gramsci and the PCI: Two Conceptions of Hegemony', in Mouffe, *Gramsci and Marxist Theory*, 237-258.

72. Sara C. Motta, 'Old Tools and New Movements in Latin America: Political Science as Gatekeeper or Intellectual Illuminator?', *Latin American Politics and Society* 51, no. 1 (2009): 31–56.

73. Hall, *Hard Road*, 51.

74. Boggs, *Two Revolutions*, 16.

75. Hall, *Hard Road*, 244.

76. Ibid., 125.

77. Gramsci had an explicit and implicit influence here on Western Marxism, the Frankfurt School, British cultural studies, and international relations, especially after Robert W. Cox, 'Social Forces, States and World Orders: Beyond International Relations Theory', *Millennium* 10, no. 2 (1981): 126–155.

78. George Lipsitz, 'The Struggle for Hegemony', *Journal of American History* 75, no. 1 (1988): 146–147.

79. *SPN*, 113; Q15, §25.

80. Louis Althusser, Etienne Balibar, Pierre Macherey, Jacques Rancière, and Roger Establet, *Reading Capital: The Complete Edition* (London: Verso, 2016), 222, 269–270.

81. Salvadori, 'Gramsci and the PCI'.

82. Norberto Bobbio, 'Gramsci and the Conception of Civil Society', in Mouffe, *Gramsci and Marxist Theory*, 21–47; Giuseppe Tamburrano, *Antonio Gramsci* (Milano: SugarCo Edisioni, 1963).

83. Vacca, *Alternative Modernities*, xii, 37. Major interpreters include Femia, *Political Thought*; Fabio Frosini, *De Gramsci á Marx: Idéologie, verité et politique* (Paris: Éditions Critiques, 2019); Mouffe, *Gramsci and Marxist Theory*; Thomas, *Gramscian Moment*.

84. For a distinction between historical economism and historical materialism, see Palmiro Togliatti, *On Gramsci, and Other Writings* (London: Lawrence & Wishart, 1979), 169.

85. Cf. Ekers's key criticism of Thomas's work. Ekers et al., *Gramsci, Space, Nature*, 30.

86. Ernesto Laclau and Chantal Mouffe, *Hegemony and Socialist Strategy: Towards a Radical Democratic Politics* (London: Verso, 1985).

87. Hall, *Hard Road*, 157.

88. Chaturvedi, *Subaltern Studies*; Partha Chatterjee, *The Politics of the Governed: Reflections on Popular Politics in Most of the World* (New York: Columbia University Press, 2004).

89. Christine Buci-Glucksmann, *Gramsci and the State*, trans. David Fernbach (London: Lawrence & Wishart, 1980), 6.

90. *SSG*, 6; Q25, §2.

91. Marcus Green in *SSG*, xxii–xxiii.

92. Gayatri Chakravorty Spivak, 'Can the Subaltern Speak?', in *Marxism and the Interpretation of Culture*, ed. Cary Nelson and Lawrence Grossberg (Urbana: University of Illinois Press, 1988).

93. *SSG*, 7; Q25, §2.

94. 'Sati in the piece ['Can the Subaltern Speak?']', writes Spivak, 'was not given as a generalisable example of the subaltern not speaking, or rather not being able to speak—trying to, but not succeeding in being heard.' Spivak, 'Looking Back, Looking Forward', 228.

95. Eliah Bures, 'The Intellectual as Culture Warrior: Metapolitics and the European New Right', *Fascism* 12, no. 1 (2023): 1-26; Rob van Kranenburg, 'Whose Gramsci? Right-Wing Gramscism', *International Gramsci Society Newsletter* 9 (1999): 14-18.

96. Bures, 'Intellectual as Culture Warrior', 19.

97. Ibid., 8.

98. *SPN*, 396; Q16, §9.

99. These Gramscian readings are rich and creative and often accept or attract a broadly Marxist labelling, but they wear lightly such a labelling, which may only be serving as a protective cloak against heresy hunting. Cox and Nilsen, *We Make Our Own History*; Ekers et al., 'Hart's Postcolonial Marxism'; Nilsen and Roy, *Subaltern Politics*; Salem, *Anticolonial Afterlives*. Raymond Williams's 'You're a Marxist, Aren't You?' remains enduringly relevant in this regard. Raymond Williams, *Resources of Hope: Culture, Democracy, Socialism*, ed. Robin Gable, 65-76 (London: Verso, 1989).

100. For example, Antonini et al., *Revisiting Gramsci's Notebooks*.

101. *SPN*, 463; Q11, §27.

102. *PN3*, 354; Q8, §206.

103. *SPN*, 465; Q11, §27.

104. Vacca, *Alternative Modernities*, 246, ftn 248.

105. I take the formulation 'abandoning' from Frosini, *De Gramsci*, 8.

106. Vacca, *Alternative Modernities*, 43.

107. *SPN*, 165; Q13, §18; Anderson, *Antinomies*.

108. Buey, *Reading Gramsci*, 131.

109. Antonio Gramsci, *Selections from the Prison Notebooks of Antonio Gramsci*, ed. and trans. Quintin Hoare and Geoffrey Nowell Smith (London: Lawrence & Wishart, 1971), 125, 126-127; Q13, §1. Hereafter *SPN*.

110. *PN2*, 52; Q3, §48.

111. *PN3*, 175; Q7, §25.

112. *SSG*, 49; Q6, §125.

113. *SSG*, 93; Q11, §16; Femia, *Political Thought*, 23; Morera, 'Gramsci and Democracy', 32; Leonardo Salamini, *The Sociology of Political Praxis: An Introduction to Gramsci's Theory* (London: Routledge, 1981), 160.

114. *SPN*, 450; Q11, §28; Peter Ives, *Language and Hegemony in Gramsci* (London: Pluto Press, 2004).

115. Salamini, *Political Praxis*, 38.

116. *SPN*, 412; Q11, §52.

117. Fabio Frosini, 'Time and Revolution in Gramsci's *Prison Notebooks*', in Antonini et al., *Revisiting Gramsci's Notebooks*, 128.

118. *SPN*, 84 ftn; Q19, §28.

119. *SPN*, 85 ftn; Q19, §28.

120. *SPN*, 201; Q9, §63.

121. *PN2*, 137; Q4, §1.

122. Ibid.

123. Fiori, *Gramsci*, 75.

124. Ranajit Guha, 'The Prose of Counter-Insurgency 1', in *The Rise and Fall of Modern Empires*, ed. Saul Dubow (London: Routledge, 2013); Michel-Rolph Trouillot, *Silencing the Past: Power and the Production of History* (Boston: Beacon Press, 2015); Howard Zinn, *Howard Zinn on History* (New York: Seven Stories Press, 2011).

125. Antonio Gramsci, *Quaderni del Carcere*, 4 vols., ed. Valentino Gerratana (Torino: Einaudi, 1975). Hereafter *QC* + volume number (e.g. *QC1*).

126. *SPN*; Antonio Gramsci, *Further Selections from the Prison Notebooks*, ed. and trans. Derek Boothman (London: Lawrence & Wishart, 1995). Hereafter *FSPN*.

127. *PN1*, *PN2*, and *PN3*.

128. *SSG*.

129. Antonio Gramsci, *Selections from Cultural Writings*, ed. David Forgacs and Geoffrey Nowell-Smith, trans. William Boelhower (London: Lawrence & Wishart, 1985). Hereafter *SCW*.

130. Antonio Gramsci, *Selections from Political Writings (1910-1920)*, ed. Quintin Hoare, trans. John Mathews (London: Lawrence & Wishart, 1977). Hereafter *SPW1*; Antonio Gramsci, *Selections from Political Writings (1921-1926)*, ed. and trans. Quintin Hoare (London: Lawrence & Wishart, 1978). Hereafter *SPW2*.

131. Antonio Gramsci, *History, Philosophy and Culture in the Young Gramsci*, ed. Pedro Cavalcanti and Paul Piccone (Saint Louis: Telos Press, 1975). Hereafter *HPC*.

132. Antonio Gramsci, *A Great and Terrible World: The Pre-Prison Letters, 1908-1926*, ed. and trans. Derek Boothman (London: Lawrence & Wishart, 2014). Hereafter *PPL*.

133. *Dizionario Gramsci*, accessed 2 April 2024, http://disionario.gramsciproject.org/.

134. Anderson, *Antinomies*.

135. Antonini et al., *Revisiting*; Thomas, *Gramscian Moment*.

136. Bianchi, *Gramsci's Laboratory*; Buey, *Reading Gramsci*; Cospito, *Rhythm of Thought*; Coutinho, *Political Thought*; Del Roio, *Prisms*; Michele Filippini, *Using*

Gramsci: A New Approach (London: Pluto Press, 2016); Fresu, *Antonio Gramsci*; Liguori, *Pathways*; Vacca, *Alternative Modernities*.

137. Boggs, *Two Revolutions*; Femia, *Political Thought*; Salamini, *Political Praxis*.

138. Fiori, *Gramsci*.

139. John Chalcraft, *The Striking Cabbies of Cairo and Other Stories: Crafts and Guilds in Egypt, 1863-1914* (Albany: State University of New York Press, 2004); John Chalcraft, *The Invisible Cage: Syrian Migrant Workers in Lebanon* (Stanford, CA: Stanford University Press, 2009); John Chalcraft, *Popular Politics in the Making of the Modern Middle East* (Cambridge: Cambridge University Press, 2016).

140. Emanuele Saccarelli, 'The Intellectual in Question: Antonio Gramsci and the Crisis of Academia', *Cultural Studies* 25, no. 6 (2011); Cox, *Social Movements*, 83-105.

141. Ives, *Language and Hegemony*, 461.

142. *SPN*, 175-176; Q13, §2.

143. Emily Hauptmann, *Foundations and American Political Science: The Transformation of a Discipline, 1945-1970* (Lawrence: University Press of Kansas, 2022).

CHAPTER TWO. THE FACES AND PHASES OF POPULAR MOBILIZATION

1. *SSG*, 130; Q27, §1.

2. *Dizionario Gramsciano*, accessed 16 April 2022, https://www.gramscionline.org/2020/09/22/dizionario-gramsciano-gramsci-project.

3. Green in *SSG*, xxxvii.

4. Boggs, *Two Revolutions*, 133.

5. Fontana, paraphrased in Derek Boothman, 'The Sources for Gramsci's Concept of Hegemony', *Rethinking Marxism* 20, no. 2 (2008): 210.

6. In Arabic, a widely used term for a people is *sha'b*. It is rarely remarked that this noun derives from a verb which means *both* 'to disperse, to scatter' *and* 'to gather, to assemble, to rally'. In Arabic, then, we find in the very word for a people—a word with a pedigree predating the eighteenth century—a suggestion of the fundamental dialectical tension between dispersal and assembly considered central in the theory advanced here.

7. *SPN*, 351; Q10 II, §54.

8. Buey, *Reading Gramsci*, 15.

9. *SPN*, 353; Q10 II, §54.

10. *SSG*, 74; Q11, §12 I.

11. *SPN*, 353; Q10 II, §54.

12. James, *Black Jacobins*, xviii.

13. Green in *SSG*, xxxvii.

14. Ibid., xxxviii.

15. Green, citing Baratta in *SSG*, xl, xxxix.

16. Ibid., xl; see also Cospito, *Rhythm of Thought*, 70.

17. *SSG*, 21; Q12, §1.

18. Judy, 'Poesis', 176–177.

19. *SPN*, 294; Q22, §3.

20. *SPN*, 295; Q22, §3.

21. *SSG*, 9; Q25, §4.

22. *SPN*, 7; Q12, §1.

23. *SPN*, 453; Q11, §16.

24. Ibid.

25. *SPN*, 5; Q12, §1; cf. *PN3*, 328; Q8, §244; Salamini, *Political Praxis*, 106.

26. *SPN*, 10; Q12, §3.

27. *SSG*, 81; Q11, §12.

28. *SSG*, 81–82; Q11, §12.

29. *QC2*, 1403; Q11, §14.

30. *SPN*, 351; Q10 II, §54. Gramsci, like so many Western thinkers before the 1970s, used masculine pronouns and terms when discussing humanity in general. I have added [*sic*] here and subsequently in order to mark a critical distance from such forms of masculinism.

31. Ibid., 352.

32. *SSG*, 10; Q25, §5.

33. *SPN*, 208; *QC2*, 1253; Q10 II, §15.

34. Daniel Egan, 'Gramsci's War of Position as Siege Warfare: Some Lessons from History', *Critique* 44, no. 4 (2016): 436; Roger Simon, *Gramsci's Political Thought: An Introduction*, 3rd edn (London: Lawrence & Wishart, 2015), 12–13, 23–24, 71.

35. *SPN*, 208; *QC2*, 1253; Q10 II, §15.

36. Femia, *Political Thought*, 139.

37. Coutinho, *Political Thought*, 75.

38. *SPN*, 349; Q10, §44; Ives, *Language and Hegemony*, 455.

39. *SSG*, 70; Q10 II, §41.

40. *SPN*, 413; Q11, §52.

41. Vacca, *Alternative Modernities*, 85–149.

42. Cospito, *Rhythm of Thought*, 91–132.

43. Ibid., 61.

44. *SSG*, 66; Q9, §67.

45. Vacca, *Alternative Modernities*, 36, 52, 53.

46. *PN1*, 219; Q1, §134.

47. *SPN*, 12; Q12, §1.

48. Simon, *Political Thought*, 72.

49. Benedetto Fontana, 'Liberty and Domination: Civil Society in Gramsci', *boundary 2* 33, no. 2 (2006): 57.

50. *SPN*, 244; Q15, §10.

51. Morera, 'Gramsci and Democracy', 27–28.

52. Cospito, *Rhythm of Thought*, 136.

53. Referenced in Loftus, 'Historical Geographical Materialist', 11.

54. David McNally, 'Intersections and Dialectics: Critical Reconstructions in Social Reproduction Theory', in *Social Reproduction Theory*, ed. Tithi Bhattacharya (London: Pluto Press, 2017), 97–99.

55. Loftus, 'Historical Geographic Materialist', 8–10.

56. *SPN*, 176; Q13, §2.

57. 'The Eighteenth Brumaire of Louis Bonaparte. Karl Marx 1852', accessed 13 October 2021, https://www.marxists.org/archive/marx/works/1852/18th-brumaire/ch01.htm.

58. *SPN*, 438; *QC2*, 1403; Q11, §15.

59. *SPN*, 182; Q13, §17.

60. *SPN*, 235; Q13, §24.

61. *SPN*, 176, 185; Q13, §17, §2.

62. *SPN*, 176; Q13, §2.

63. *SPN*, 182; Q13, §17.

64. Ibid.

65. Gill, 'Postmodern Prince'.

66. Fred Judson, 'Sandinista Revolutionary Morale', *Latin American Perspectives* 14, no. 1 (1987): 24–38.

67. *PN3*, 381; Q8, §240.

68. *SSG*, 10; Q25, §5.

69. Robert Jackson, 'The "Mummification of Culture" in Gramsci's *Prison Notebooks*', in Antonini et al., *Revisiting Gramsci's Notebooks*, 312–335.

70. Leon Trotsky, *The History of the Russian Revolution* (London: Pluto, 1997), 19. Trotsky is referring here to the dissipation of the energy and driving force of mass activity when 'a guiding organization' is lacking.

71. Abdallah Laroui, *Les Origines Sociales et Culturelles de Nationalisme Marocain, 1830–1912* (Paris: Maspero, 1977), 160.

72. Anderson, *Antinomies*, 21.

73. Massimo Modonesi, *Subalternity, Antagonism, Autonomy: Constructing the Political Subject*, trans. Adriana V. Rendón Garrido and Philip Roberts, foreword by John Holloway (London: Pluto Press, 2013), 18–23; Cosimo Zene, 'Self-Consciousness of the Dalits as "Subalterns": Reflections on Gramsci in South Asia', *Rethinking Marxism* 23, no. 1 (2011): 84, 94–95.

74. Filippini, *Using Gramsci*, 42.

75. Karl Marx, *Critique of Hegel's Philosophy of Right* (1843), trans. Joseph O'Malley (Oxford: Oxford University Press, 1970), https://www.marxists.org/archive/marx/works/download/Marx_Critique_of_Hegels_Philosophy_of_Right.pdf.

76. *SSG*, 10; Q25, §5.

77. *SPN*, 97; Q13, §18.

78. *SPN*, 181; Q13, §17.

79. *SPN*, 181–182; Q13, §17.

80. *SSG*, 39; Q4, §38.

81. *SSG*, 11; Q25, §5.

82. Ibid.

83. Ibid.

84. Cf. Modonesi, *Subalternity*, 145–149.

85. Editors, drawing on Sorel, in *SSG*, 144, ftn 1 (§5).

86. *PN3*, 175; Q7, §25.

87. Charles Tripp, 'Battlefields of the Republic: The Struggle for Public Space in Tunisia', *LSE Middle East Centre Paper Series* 13 (2014).

88. Gramsci, cited in Salamini, *Political Praxis*, 211.

89. Boggs, *Two Revolutions*, xi, 8, 16.

90. *SSG*, 10; Q25, §5.

91. Ibid., 10–11.

92. Ibid.

93. *SPN*, 176; Q13, §2.

94. *SSG*, 10; Q25, §5.

95. Gramsci, 9 February 1924, cited in Rosengarten, *Revolutionary Marxism*, 115.

96. *SSG*, 73; Q11, §12.

CHAPTER THREE. THE TORTUROUS CONTRADICTIONS OF DOMINATION

Epigraph: Ralph Ellison, *Invisible Man* (1952; Random House, 1995), 3.

1. *SSG*, 13; Q25, §7.

2. Marchi, 'Molecular Transformations'.

3. SPN, 110; Q15, §11.

4. *SSG*, 32; Q3, §48.

5. Riccardo Ciavolella, 'Gramsci in and beyond Resistances: The Search for an Autonomous Political Initiative among a Subaltern Group in the Beninese Savanna', *Focaal*, no. 82 (2018): 49.

6. Chalcraft, *Invisible Cage*, 52.

7. *SPN*, 60; Q19, §24.

8. Sumi Madhok, *Rethinking Agency: Developmentalism, Gender and Rights* (Delhi: Routledge India, 2014).

9. Gurr, *Why Men Rebel*.

10. Uday Singh Mehta, *Liberalism and Empire: A Study in Nineteenth-Century British Liberal Thought* (Chicago: University of Chicago Press, 2018).

11. Eric Hobsbawm, *Primitive Rebels: Studies in Archaic Forms of Social Movement in the 19th and 20th Centuries* (Manchester: Manchester University Press, 1971); Eric Hobsbawm, *The Age of Extremes: The Short Twentieth Century, 1914–1991* (London: Abacus Books, 1994), 202.

12. Ciavolella, 'People's Politics', 279.

13. Ranajit Guha, *Elementary Aspects of Peasant Insurgency in Colonial India* (Durham, NC: Duke University Press, 1999).

14. For an example of such (satirical) sophistication and practical mastery in relation to codes, narratives, and limits see Michael Gilsenan, *Lords of the Lebanese Marches: Violence and Narrative in an Arab Society* (Berkeley: University of California Press, 1996), 241–243.

15. Dimitris Papadopoulos, Niamh Stephenson, and Vassilis Tsianos, *Escape Routes: Control and Subversion in the 21st Century* (London: Pluto Press, 2008).

16. Michel de Certeau, *The Practice of Everyday Life*, trans. Steven Rendall (Berkeley: University of California Press, 1984).

17. José Ciro Martínez, 'Site of Resistance or Apparatus of Acquiescence? Tactics at the Bakery', *Middle East Law and Governance* 10, no. 2 (2018): 160–184.

18. Scott, *Weapons of the Weak*.

19. Asef Bayat, *Street Politics: Poor People's Movements in Iran* (New York: Columbia University Press, 1997), 44.

20. Diane Singerman, *Avenues of Participation: Family, Politics, and Networks in Urban Quarters of Cairo* (Princeton, NJ: Princeton University Press, 2020).

21. Ranajit Guha and Gayatri Chakravorty Spivak, eds. *Selected Subaltern Studies* (Oxford: Oxford University Press, 1988).

22. Rosalind O'Hanlon, 'Recovering the Subject: Subaltern Studies and Histories of Resistance in Colonial South Asia', *Modern Asian Studies* 22, no. 1 (1988): 191.

23. Ciavolella, 'People's Politics', 272.

24. *L'Ordine Nuovo*, 2 August 1919, *SPW1*, 83–84.

25. Timothy Mitchell, 'Everyday Metaphors of Power', *Theory and Society* 19, no. 5 (1990): 545–577.

26. Paul Willis, *Learning to Labour: How Working Class Kids Get Working Class Jobs* (London: Routledge, 2017).

27. Michael Burawoy, *Manufacturing Consent: Changes in the Labor Process under Monopoly Capitalism* (Chicago: University of Chicago Press, 2012).

28. T. J. Jackson Lears, 'The Concept of Cultural Hegemony: Problems and Possibilities', *American Historical Review* 90, no. 3 (1985): 567–593, https://doi.org/10.2307/1860957.

29. Chalcraft, *Invisible Cage*, 165–170.

30. Lisa Wedeen, 'Acting "As If": Symbolic Politics and Social Control in Syria', *Comparative Studies in Society and History* 40, no. 3 (1998): 503–523.

31. Armelle Choplin and Riccardo Ciavolella, 'Gramsci and the African Città Futura: Urban Subaltern Politics from the Margins of Nouakchott, Mauritania', *Antipode* 49, no. 2 (2017): 315.

32. Gayatri Chakravorty Spivak, 'Can the Subaltern Speak?', in *Marxism and the Interpretation of Culture*, ed. Cary Nelson and Lawrence Grossberg, 271–313 (Urbana: University of Illinois Press, 1988).

33. Guha, 'Prose of Counter-Insurgency'.

34. Zene, 'Self-Consciousness of Dalits', 86.

35. Massad, 'Gay International'.

36. Atshan, *Queer Palestine*.

37. *SSG*, 10; Q25, §5.

38. de Beauvoir, *Second Sex*, 15.

39. Eribon, *Insult*, xxi.

40. Ibid., 55.

41. de Beauvoir, *Second Sex*, 29.

42. Zene, 'Self-Consciousness of Dalits', 88.

43. Ibid., 93.

44. Cf. Eribon, *Insult*, 54.

45. Wallace, *Black Macho*, 176.

46. Judy, 'Poesis', 165.

47. Ibid., 166.

48. *SSG*, 58; Q8, §151.

49. Gramsci, cited in Rosengarten, *Revolutionary Marxism*, 120.

50. Antonio Labriola, *Essays on the Materialistic Conception of History* (Chicago: Charles H. Kerr & Company, 1908), 63.

51. Eribon, *Insult*, 16.

52. Gramsci, cited in Rosengarten, *Revolutionary Marxism*, 97.

53. Karin Kapadia, '"Mirrored in God": Gramsci, Religion and Dalit Women Subalterns in South India', *Religions* 10, no. 12 (2019): 2.

54. Roy, 'Affective Politics', 151–153.

55. Peter Thomas, 'We Good Subalterns', in Antonini et al., *Revisiting Gramsci's Notebooks*, 182.

56. Ibid.

57. Femia, *Political Thought*, 210; Cf. Thomas, 'Good Subalterns', 182.

58. *SSG*, 9; Q25, §4.

59. Gramsci, November 1919, cited in editors' introduction, *SPN*, xl.

60. Gramsci, cited in Choplin and Ciavolella, 'Urban Subaltern', 317.

61. de Beauvoir, *Second Sex*, 23.

62. Liguori, *Pathways*, 98.

63. Machiavelli, cited in Boothman, 'Sources for Hegemony', 210.

64. de Beauvoir, *Second Sex*, 19.

65. Eribon, *Insult*; Édouard Louis, *The End of Eddy: A Novel*, trans. Michael Lucey (London: Vintage, 2017).

66. *SSG*, 32; Q3, §48.

67. Paul Apostolidis, *The Fight for Time: Migrant Day Laborers and the Politics of Precarity* (Oxford: Oxford University Press, 2018), 6.

68. *PN1*, 99.

69. *PN1*, 173; Q1, §65.

70. Ibid.

71. Salamini, *Political Praxis*, 101.

72. Ibid., 82.

73. *SPN*, 323; Q11, §12.

74. Liguori, *Pathways*, 99.

75. Ibid., 98.

76. Kate Crehan, *Gramsci's Common Sense: Inequality and Its Narratives* (Durham, NC: Duke University Press, 2016), x.

77. Liguori, *Pathways*, 89. Iman Dawood's rich ethnography has shown from a Gramscian perspective how transnational Salafi ideologues in the first decades of the twentieth century built up a new common sense among British Muslims, who acquired new, naturalized conceptions of themselves and their faith, which for them had no connection to Salafi ideology or politics. Iman Dawood, 'Reworking the Common Sense of British Muslims: Salafism, Culture, and Politics within London's Muslim Community', PhD diss. (London School of Economics and Political Science, 2021).

78. Salamini, *Political Praxis*, 83.

79. *SPN*, 324; Q11, §12.

80. *PN1*, 173; Q1, §65.

81. Liguori, *Pathways*, 91–92.

82. *SPN*, 420; Q11, §13.

83. *SPN*, 423–424; Q11, §13.

84. *SSG*, 58; Q8, §151

85. Liguori, *Pathways*, 92.

86. Thomas, *Gramscian Moment*, 359.

87. *SPN*, 295; Q22, §3.

88. Liguori, *Pathways*, 99.

89. *SPN*, 422; Q11, §13.

90. *SSG*, 74; Q11, §12 I.

91. *PN3*, 333; Q8, §173.

92. Ligouri, *Pathways*, 96.

93. Ibid., 101.

94. *SPN*, 326; Q11, §12.

95. *SSG*, 74; Q11, §12.

96. *SPN*, 327; Q11, §12.

97. Choplin and Ciavolella, 'Urban Subaltern', 318.

98. Hall, *Hard Road*, 8–9.

99. Ibid., 166.

100. Liguori, *Pathways*, 93.

101. *SPN*, 332; Q11, §12. See also Salamini, *Political Praxis*, 86.

102. Carl Levy, ' "Sovversivismo": The Radical Political Culture of Otherness in Liberal Italy', *Journal of Political Ideologies* 12, no. 2 (2007): 151.

103. *SPN*, 195; Q8, §195.

104. Betty Friedan, *The Feminine Mystique*, intro. Lionel Shriver (London: Penguin, 2010), 248.

105. Fanon, *Black Skin*, xvii.

106. Jean-Paul Sartre, *Saint Genet: Actor and Martyr*, trans. Bernard Frechtman (Minneapolis: University of Minnesota Press, 2012), 587.

107. de Beauvoir, *Second Sex*, 21.

108. Said, *Orientalism*, 25–26.

109. Ibid., 286.

110. Ibid., 306.

111. Ibid., 308.

112. Popular Memory Group, 'Popular Memory: Theory, Politics, Method', in *Making Histories: Studies in History-Writing and Politics*, ed. Richard Johnson et al. (London: Hutchinson, 1982).

113. Holub, *Antonio Gramsci*, 15.

114. Stuart Hall and David Morley, *Essential Essays, Volume 1: Foundations of Cultural Studies* (Durham, NC: Duke University Press, 2018), 20.

115. Ciavolella, 'People's Politics', 277.

116. Rosengarten, *Revolutionary Marxism*, 93–109.

117. Hall and Morley, *Cultural Studies*, 20.

118. de Martino, cited in Ciavolella, 'People's Politics', 273.

119. Robin D. G. Kelley, *Thelonious Monk: The Life and Times of an American Original* (New York: Free Press, 2009); Cedric J. Robinson, *Black Marxism: The Making of the Black Radical Tradition*, foreword by Robin D. G. Kelley (Chapel Hill: University of North Carolina Press, 2000).

120. Choplin and Ciavolella, 'Urban Subaltern', 318.

121. *SPN*, 405; Q11, §62.

122. *SPN*, 150; Q17, §37.

123. *SSG*, 61; Q8, §205.

124. *SPN*, 195; Q8, §195.

125. *SSG*,12; Q25, §7.

126. Ibid.

127. *SSG*, 13; Q25, §7.

128. *SSG*, 146; Q1, §62.

129. *SSG*, 61; Q8, §159.

130. Kapadia, 'Mirrored in God'.

131. Vacca, *Alternative Modernities*, 71.

132. Levy, 'Sovversivismo', 149.

133. Boggs, *Two Revolutions*, 210.

134. Levy, 'Sovversivismo', 149.

135. Ibid.

136. Ibid.

137. Ibid., 150.

138. Philip Proudfoot, *Rebel Populism: Revolution and Loss among Syrian Labourers in Beirut* (Manchester: Manchester University Press, 2022).

139. Jann Boeddeling, 'From Resistance to Revolutionary Praxis: Subaltern Politics in the Tunisian Revolution', PhD diss. (London School of Economics and Political Science, 2020).

140. Ibid., 119-124.

141. Ibid., 124.

142. Ibid., 136.

143. Ibid., 125.

144. Ibid., 133.

145. Ibid., 135.

146. Ibid., 136-138.

147. Gramsci, paraphrased in Buey, *Reading Gramsci*, 33.

148. Gramsci, cited in ibid., 33.

149. *SSG*, 10; Q25, §5.

150. Lila Abu-Lughod, 'The Romance of Resistance: Tracing Transformations of Power through Bedouin Women', *American Ethnologist* 17, no. 1 (1990).

151. Saba Mahmood, *Politics of Piety: The Islamic Revival and the Feminist Subject* (Princeton, NJ: Princeton University Press, 2011).

152. Anderson, *Antinomies*.

153. Edward P. Thompson, 'The Moral Economy of the English Crowd in the Eighteenth Century', *Past & Present* 50, no. 1 (1971); Peter King, 'Edward Thompson's Contribution to Eighteenth-Century Studies: The Patrician-Plebeian Model

Re-Examined', *Social History* 21, no. 2 (1996): 218, 220; Edward P. Thompson, *Customs in Common* (New York: New Press, 1993), 16-96.

154. John Chalcraft, 'Engaging the State: Peasants and Petitions in Egypt on the Eve of Colonial Rule', *International Journal of Middle East Studies* 37, no. 3 (2005): 303-325; John Chalcraft, 'Counterhegemonic Effects: Weighing, Measuring, Petitions and Bureaucracy in Nineteenth-Century Egypt', in *Counterhegemony in the Colony and Postcolony*, ed. John Chalcraft and Yaseen Noorani (New York: Palgrave Macmillan, 2007).

155. John K. Walton and David Seddon, *Free Markets and Food Riots: The Politics of Global Adjustment* (Hoboken, NJ: Wiley & Sons, 2008).

156. Maria P. Posusney, 'Irrational Workers: The Moral Economy of Labor Protest in Egypt', *World Politics* 46, no. 1 (1993).

157. Deniz Kandiyoti, 'Bargaining with Patriarchy', *Gender & Society* 2, no. 3 (1988): 274-290.

158. Chalcraft, *Popular Politics*, 125.

159. Zeinab Abul-Magd, *Imagined Empires: A History of Revolt in Egypt* (Berkeley: University of California Press, 2013), 93.

160. Paolo Drinot, 'Hegemony from Below: Print Workers, the State and the Communist Party in Peru, 1920-40', in Chalcraft and Noorani, *Counterhegemony in the Colony*, 204-227.

161. Jonathon Glassman, 'The Bondsman's New Clothes: The Contradictory Consciousness of Slave Resistance on the Swahili Coast', *Journal of African History* 32, no. 2 (1991): 289.

162. Posusney, 'Moral Economy'.

163. Glassman, 'Bondsman's New Clothes', 277.

164. Stephanie Cronin, ed., *Subalterns and Social Protest: History from below in the Middle East and North Africa* (London: Routledge, 2007), 4.

165. Alia Mossallam, '*Hikāyāt Sha'b*—Stories of Peoplehood: Nasserism, Popular Politics and Songs in Egypt, 1956-1973', PhD diss. (London School of Economics and Political Science, 2012).

166. Robert Malley, *The Call from Algeria: Third Worldism, Revolution, and the Turn to Islam* (Berkeley: University of California Press, 1996).

167. Hugh Roberts, 'Moral Economy or Moral Polity? The Political Anthropology of Algerian Riots' (Crisis States Research Centre, London School of Economics and Political Science, 2002).

168. Glassman, 'Bondsman's New Clothes', 289.

169. Chalcraft, 'Counterhegemonic Effects', 198-199.

170. Alan Knight, 'Hegemony, Counterhegemony and the Mexican Revolution', in Chalcraft and Noorani, *Counterhegemony in the Colony and Postcolony* (Houndmills: Palgrave Macmillan, 2007), 24ff.

171. *SPN*, 80 ftn49; Q13, §37.

172. Salamini, *Political Praxis*, 78.

173. *Avanti!*, 26 August 1916, *SPW1*, 17.

174. Gramsci, cited in Choplin and Ciavolella, 'Urban Subaltern', 317–318.

175. Salamini, *Political Praxis*, 79.

176. *Avanti!*, 26 August 1916, *SPW1*, 17.

177. Ibid.

178. Gramsci to Piero Sraffa, 21 December 1926, *LP1*, 52.

179. *SSG*, 10; Q25, §10.

180. *SPN*, 52, ftn 2.

181. *SPN*, 181; Q13, §17.

182. Ibid.

183. Hall, *Hard Road*, 171.

184. Cox, *Social Movements*, 1–3.

185. Eribon, *Insult*, 25.

186. Joel Beinin and Marie Duboc, 'A Workers' Social Movement on the Margin of the Global Neoliberal Order, Egypt 2004–2009', in *Social Movements, Mobilization, and Contestation in the Middle East and North Africa*, ed. Joel Beinin and Frédéric Vairel, 205–227 (Stanford, CA: Stanford University Press, 2013).

187. Lorenzo Feltrin, 'The Struggles of Precarious Youth in Tunisia: The Case of the Kerkennah Movement', *Review of African Political Economy* 45, no. 155 (2018): 44–63.

188. *SSG*, 11–12; Q25, §6.

189. *SSG*, 12; Q25, §6.

190. Margaret S. Chalcraft, 'Staging Atlantic Slavery: Figuring Theatricality, Performance and Resistance in Anglo-Caribbean Narratives of Slavery and Abolition', PhD diss. (University of East Anglia, 2020), 18–21, 48–71. (NB: this author is also known as Mags Chalcraft Islam.)

191. Eribon, *Insult*, 9.

192. Roy, 'Affective Politics', 163.

193. Ibid., 158.

194. Ibid., 144–148, and 75.

195. Cronin, *Social Protest*, 3–4.

196. Salwa Ismail, *Political Life in Cairo's New Quarters: Encountering the Everyday State* (Minneapolis: University of Minnesota Press, 2006), 161–166.

197. Choplin and Ciavolella, 'Urban Subaltern', 327.

198. Heba M. Khalil, 'Revolution in Parallel Times: An Egyptian Village's Lived Revolution' (LSE Middle East Centre, 2021), 10–11.

199. Yasmine Laveille, 'Contestation in Marginalised Spaces: Dynamics of Popular Mobilization and Demobilization in Upper Egypt since 25 January 2011', PhD diss. (London School of Economics and Political Science, 2016), 87–96.

200. Roy, 'Affective Politics', 166.

201. Kevin Gray, 'Labour and the State in China's Passive Revolution', *Capital & Class* 34, no. 3 (2010): 461.

202. Ibid., 465.

203. Chun Lin, *The Transformation of Chinese Socialism* (Durham, NC: Duke University Press, 2006); Chun Lin, 'The Language of Class in China', *Socialist Register* 51 (2015): 24–53.

204. Rick Fantasia, *Cultures of Solidarity* (Berkeley: University of California Press, 1989), 11.

205. Featherstone, *Solidarity*, 15–39.

206. Singerman, *Avenues of Participation*, 271.

207. Rosengarten, *Revolutionary Marxism*, 89.

208. *SPN*, 326, 333; Q11, §12.

209. SPN, 326; Q11, §12.

210. *SPN*, 327; Q11, §12.

211. Ngai-Ling Sum, 'The Makings of Subaltern Subjects: Embodiment, Contradictory Consciousness, and Re-Hegemonisation of the Diaosi in China', in *Chinese Labour in the Global Economy*, ed. Andreas Bieler and Chun-Yi Lee (London: Routledge, 2018), 120–134.

212. Femia, *Political Thought*, 185.

213. Gilsenan, *Lebanese Marches*, 303.

214. Rosengarten, *Revolutionary Marxism*, 97, 102–103.

215. *SSG*, 76; Q11, §12 IV.

216. Femia, *Political Thought*, 223.

217. Ibid., 225.

218. Manali Desai, 'Rethinking Hegemony: Caste, Class, and Political Subjectivities among Informal Workers in Ahmedabad', in Nilsen and Roy, *New Subaltern Politics*, 73.

219. *SSG*, 58–59; Q8, §153.

220. *SPN*, 342; Q11, §12.

221. Femia, *Political Thought*, 45.

222. Anouar Abdel-Malek, *Contemporary Arab Political Thought* (London: Zed, 1983), 90–92.

223. Michael G. Hanchard, *Orpheus and Power: The Movimento Negro of Rio de Janeiro and São Paulo, Brazil, 1945-1988* (Princeton, NJ: Princeton University Press, 1991).

224. Femia, *Political Thought*, 44.

225. Glassman, 'Bondsman's New Clothes', 283.

226. Desai, 'Rethinking Hegemony', 72.

227. *SPN*, 114; Q15, §62.

228. Gramsci, paraphrased in Buey, *Reading Gramsci*, 52.

229. Buey's phrase, ibid., 54.

230. Ibid.

231. Buey, *Reading Gramsci*, 140.

232. David Harvey and Raymond Williams, 'Militant Particularism and Global Ambition: The Conceptual Politics of Place, Space, and Environment in the Work of Raymond Williams', *Social Text*, no. 42 (1995): 89.

233. As the narrator puts it in Kate Elisabeth Russell, *My Dark Vanessa: A Novel* (New York: William Morrow, 2020).

234. Karl Marx, 'Theses on Feuerbach', in *Marx/Engels Selected Works*, vol. 1, trans. W. Lough (Moscow: Progress Publishers, 1969) https://www.marxists.org/archive/marx/works/1845/theses/theses.htm.

235. Salamini, *Political Praxis*, 59.

236. Ciavolella, 'Beyond Resistances', 49.

CHAPTER FOUR. THE WELLSPRINGS OF AUTONOMY

1. *SSG*, 10; Q25, §5.

2. *SPN*, 52, ftn 2.

3. Boggs, *Two Revolutions*, 2.

4. Robert J. Young, *Postcolonialism: An Historical Introduction* (Hoboken, NJ: John Wiley & Sons, 2016), 161–166.

5. George Katsiaficas, *Asia's Unknown Uprisings*, vol. 1 (New York: PM Press, 2012).

6. Asef Bayat, *Revolutionary Life: The Everyday of the Arab Spring* (Cambridge, MA: Harvard University Press, 2021).

7. Geoffrey Pleyers, *Alter-Globalisation: Becoming Actors in a Global Age* (Cambridge: Polity, 2010); Fonseca, *Civil Society*, 179.

8. Gaudichaud et al., *Latin American Left*, 12.

9. Ibid.

10. Boggs, *Two Revolutions*, 108.

11. Sanbonmatsu, *Postmodern Prince*, 21–37.

12. Boggs, *Two Revolutions*, 75.

13. Femia, *Political Thought*, 212.

14. Hall, *Hard Road*, 51.

15. Leon Trotsky, *The History of the Russian Revolution* (London: Pluto Press, 1997), 17.

16. *L'Ordine Nuovo*, 9 October 1920, *SPW1*, 351.

17. *L'Ordine Nuovo*, 5 June 1920, *SPW1*, 262.

18. Boggs, *Two Revolutions*, 207.

19. Lila Leontidou, 'Athens in the Mediterranean "Movement of the Piazzas"': Spontaneity in Material and Virtual Public Spaces', *City* 16, no. 3 (2012): 301–302.

20. Georges Sorel, *Reflections on Violence*, trans. T. E. Hulme (Miami, FL: Hard Press, n.d.), 41.

21. Hal Draper, *The Two Souls of Socialism* (Highland Park, MI: International Socialists, 1966).

22. Tronti, *Workers and Capital*, 338, 337–343.

23. Note that Althusser may have shifted away from this view towards the very end of his life, as he referred positively in the 1980s to the 'social and popular movements and the struggles of marginalized people . . . all over the planet', movements that 'followed the line of Rosa Luxemburg and not that of Lenin'. Paraphrased in Nick Henck, *Insurgent Marcos: The Political-Philosophical Formation of the Zapatista Subcommander* (Durham, NC: Editorial A Contracorriente, 2016), 126.

24. Martin Breaugh, *The Plebeian Experience: A Discontinuous History of Political Freedom*, trans. Lazer Lederhendler (New York: Columbia University Press, 2013), xv–xvi.

25. Bevins, *If We Burn*.

26. Michael Hardt and Antonio Negri, *Assembly* (Oxford: Oxford University Press, 2017).

27. Gaudichaud, *Latin American Left*, 7.

28. Bevins, *If We Burn*, 41–42.

29. Motta, 'New Movements', 51.

30. Francisco Panizza, 'Parties, Democracy and Grounded Utopias: A Reply to Sara Motta', *Political Studies* 55, no. 4 (2007): 885–892.

31. Gaudichaud, *Latin American Left*, 31.

32. Graeber, *Direct Action*; Graeber, *Democracy Project*; Jeffrey S. Juris and Alex Khasnabish, eds., *Insurgent Encounters: Transnational Activism, Ethnography, and the Political* (Durham, NC: Duke University Press, 2013); Jodi Dean, *Crowds and Party* (London: Verso Books, 2016).

33. Maeckelbergh, *Will of the Many*.

34. Pleyers, *Alter-globalisation*, 201–227.

35. Harvey and Williams, 'Militant Particularism'.

36. Bayat, *Revolutionary Life*, 227.

37. Barbara Epstein, *Political Protest and Cultural Revolution: Nonviolent Direct Action in the 1970s and 1980s* (Berkeley: University of California Press, 1991), 266.

38. Bevins, *If We Burn*.

39. Sanbonmatsu, *Postmodern Prince*, 23.

40. Ibid., 27.

41. Graeber, *Direct Action*, 259-260.

42. Salamini, *Political Praxis*, 108.

43. *SPN*, 181; Q13, §17.

44. Morera, 'Gramsci and Democracy', 35.

45. Cf. Eribon, *Insult*, 132.

46. *SSG*, 74; Q11, §12 I.

47. John Grayson, 'Developing the Politics of the Trade Union Movement: Popular Workers' Education in South Yorkshire, UK, 1955 to 1985', *International Labor and Working-Class History* 90 (2016): 118-119.

48. Steve Biko, *I Write What I Like: A Selection of His Writings*, ed. Aelred Stubbs (Harlow: Heinemann, 1987), 4.

49. Ibid., 15.

50. Marco Briziarelli, 'To "Feel" and to "Understand" Political Struggle: The National-Popular Rhetoric of Podemos', *Journal of Communication Inquiry* 40, no. 3 (2016): 295.

51. Ibid.

52. *SPN*, 181; Q13, §17.

53. Zene, 'Self-Consciousness of Dalits', 95.

54. Mumby, 'Problem of Hegemony', 351; Willis, *Learning to Labour*.

55. Ayyaz Mallick, 'Beyond "Domination without Hegemony": Passive Revolution(s) in Pakistan', *Studies in Political Economy* 98, no. 3 (2017): 246.

56. *SSG*, 117; Q15, §74.

57. Del Roio, *Prisms*, 186.

58. *SCW*, 390; Q3, §49.

59. Gramsci, cited in Femia, *Political Thought*, 211.

60. Eribon, *Insult*, 69.

61. Rosengarten, *Revolutionary Marxism*, 57.

62. Cf. Albert, *Liberating Theory*, 6.

63. *SSG*, 77; Q11, §12 IV.

64. *SSG*, 63; Q8, §220.

65. *SSG*, 63; Q8, §220.

66. Rehmann, 'Bernie Sanders', 7; *SPN*, 376-377; Q7, §19.

67. *SSG*, 58; Q8, §151.

68. I.e. 'common sense' in the English definition, combined with domination, cf. Crehan, *Common Sense*, 45.

69. *SPN*, 157-158; Q15, §6.

70. *PN3*, 333; Q8, §173.

71. Hall, *Hard Road*, 179.

72. Jan Rehmann, 'Occupy Wall Street and the Question of Hegemony: A Gramscian Analysis', *Socialism and Democracy* 27, no. 1 (2013): 10. Others have criticized Occupy Wall Street (OWS) in terms of racial exclusion: Konstantin Kilibarda, 'Lessons from# Occupy in Canada: Contesting Space, Settler Consciousness and Erasures within the 99%', *Journal of Critical Globalisation Studies* 5 (2012): 24–41.

73. Rehmann, 'Occupy Wall Street', 10–11.

74. Ibid., 11. A rich, critical, and educative engagement with common sense in relation to the 'hatred' of bureaucrats in France, aiming to build on elements of good sense and move the ideology leftward in confrontation with neoliberal managerial classes is in Julie Gervais, Claire Lemercier, and Willy Pelletier, *La haine des fonctionnaires* (Paris: Éditions Amsterdam, 2024), 36–38, 195–204.

75. Boggs, *Two Revolutions*, 102; *L'Ordine Nuovo*, 4, 9 September 1920, *SPW1*, 331–332.

76. Glassman, 'Bondsman's New Clothes', 305.

77. Cf. Rehmann's criticism of the social consciousness of OWS, in Rehmann, 'Occupy Wall Street', 15.

78. Robin D. G. Kelley, *Freedom Dreams: The Black Radical Imagination* (Boston: Beacon Press, 2002).

79. Sorel, *On Violence*, 22.

80. Ibid., 32.

81. Ibid., 26.

82. Ibid., 32.

83. *SPN*, 126; Q13, §1.

84. Ibid., 127; Q13, §1.

85. Ibid., 128–129; Q13, §1.

86. Ibid., 130; Q13, §1.

87. Ibid., 128; Q13, §1.

88. Boggs, *Two Revolutions*, 94.

89. Ibid., 171.

90. *L'Ordine Nuovo*, 3 July 1920, *SPW1*, 305.

91. *SSG*, 66; Q9, §67.

92. Cited in Crézégut, 'An Imaginary Gramscianism?', 445.

93. Nicola Badaloni, 'Gramsci and the Problem of the Revolution', in Mouffe, *Gramsci and Marxist Theory*, 90–91.

94. Boggs, *Two Revolutions*, 94.

95. Ibid., 83.

96. Sajjad Akhtar, *Struggle for Hegemony*, 32.

97. 'Miel orgánica en el Impenetrable', Tierra Viva, accessed 20 May 2024, https://agenciatierraviva.com.ar/miel-organica-en-el-impenetrable-la-alternativa-del-pueblo-qom-frente-al-desmonte/.

98. Rahmat Budiono, Bramasto Nugroho, and Dodik Ridho Nurrochmat, 'The Village Forest as a Counter Teritorialisation by Village Communities in Kampar Peninsula Riau', *Jurnal Manajemen Hutan Tropika* 24, no. 3 (2018): 115–125.

99. Boggs, *Two Revolutions*, 98.

100. Ibid., 177.

101. Asef Bayat, *Workers and Revolution in Iran: A Third World Experience of Workers' Control* (London: Zed, 1987); Ian Clegg, *Workers' Self-Management in Algeria* (London: Allen Lane, 1971).

102. *SSG*, 34; Q3, §48.

103. 'What is the MST?', Friends of the MST, accessed 27 April 2022, https://www.mstbrazil.org/content/what-mst.

104. Expressão Popular, accessed 9 May 2023, https://expressaopopular.com.br/.

105. David Meek, 'Learning as Territoriality: The Political Ecology of Education in the Brazilian Landless Workers' Movement', *Journal of Peasant Studies* 42, no. 6 (2015): 1191.

106. Boggs, *Two Revolutions*, 73.

107. *L'Ordine Nuovo*, with Togliatti, 21 June 1919, *SPW1*, 67.

108. Boggs, *Two Revolutions*, 108.

109. Ibid.

110. Ibid., 245.

111. Ibid., 15.

112. *SPN*, 265–266; Q14, §13.

113. *SPN*, 266; Q14, §13.

114. Motta, 'New Movements', 51.

115. *SPN*, 265–266; Q14, §13.

116. Salamini, *Political Praxis*, 2.

117. Vladimir I. Lenin, *The State and Revolution*, intro. and trans. Robert Service (London: Penguin, 1992), 42.

118. Bruno Leipold, 'Marx's Social Republic', in *Radical Republicanism: Recovering the Tradition's Popular Heritage*, ed. Bruno Leipold, Karma Nabulsi, and Stuart White (Oxford: Oxford University Press, 2020), 172–173. This view is expounded in full in Bruno Leipold, *Citizen Marx: Republicanism and the Formation of Karl Marx's Social and Political Thought* (Princeton University Press, 2024). Arguably, this work inadvertently underlines the changeability and instability of Marx's political theory.

119. Kathleen Bruhn, 'Antonio Gramsci and the Palabra Verdadera: The Political Discourse of Mexico's Guerrilla Forces', *Journal of Interamerican Studies and World Affairs* 41, no. 2 (1999): 47.

120. Nancy Fraser, 'Contradictions of Capital and Care', *New Left Review*, 100, no. 100 (2016): 99–117; Silvia Federici, *Revolution at Point Zero: Housework, Reproduction, and Feminist Struggle* (New York: PM Press, 2020); Davis, *Women, Race and Class*, 200–219; Melanie Marie Lindsay, 'An Exploratory Analysis of How Maya Angelou, Audre Lorde, and Patrisse Cullors Radicalized the Meaning and Practice of Self-Care', PhD diss. (Claremont Graduate University, 2022).

121. Eribon, *Insult*, xiv.

122. Ibid., 301–302.

123. Massad, 'Gay International'.

124. Foucault, cited in Sanbonmatsu, *Postmodern Prince*, 119.

125. Foucault, cited in Eribon, *Insult*, 117, 306, 323.

126. Eribon, *Insult*, 333.

127. Ibid., 40.

128. Ibid., 106.

129. Lisa Duggan, 'The New Homonormativity: The Sexual Politics of neoliberalism', in *Materializing Democracy: Toward a Revitalized Cultural Politics*, ed. Russ Castronovo and Dana Nelson (Durham, NC: Duke University Press, 2002), 175–194.

130. Boggs, *Two Revolutions*, 205.

131. Hall, *Hard Road*, 229.

132. Ibid.

133. Graeber, *Direct Action*, 259.

134. Bayat, *Revolutionary Life*, 216, 226–227.

135. Rebecca Tarlau, 'The Social(ist) Pedagogies of the MST: Towards New Relations of Production in the Brazilian Countryside', *Education Policy Analysis Archives* 21, no. 41 (2013): 14.

136. Boggs, *Two Revolutions*, 95.

137. John Merrington, 'Theory and Practice in Gramsci's Marxism', *The Socialist Register* 5 (1968): 145.

138. Boggs, *Two Revolutions*, 79.

139. Marcel van der Linden, *Workers of the World: Essays toward a Global Labor History* (Leiden: Brill, 2008), 219–258.

140. Cited in *SSG*, 43; Q3, §28.

141. Femia, *Political Praxis*, 143.

142. Gramsci, cited in Boggs, *Two Revolutions*, 86.

143. Rosa Luxemburg, *'Reform or Revolution' and 'The Mass Strike'* (Denver, CO: Frederic Ellis, n.d.), 39.

144. Fantasia, *Cultures of Solidarity*, 11.

145. Edward P. Thompson, *The Making of the English Working Class*, intro. Michael Kenny (London: Penguin, 2013).

146. Bayat, *Revolutionary Life*, 214–217, 226.

147. Christopher Moxham and Miriam Grant, 'Passive Revolution: A Church-Military Partnership in the Philippines', *Singapore Journal of Tropical Geography* 34, no. 3 (2013): 307.

148. Charles W. Anderson, 'From Petition to Confrontation: The Palestinian National Movement and the Rise of Mass Politics, 1929–1939', PhD diss. (New York University, 2013), 593, 596, 641–647.

149. Tom Chodor, 'Not Throwing The Baby Out With The Bathwater: A Gramscian Response to Post-Hegemony', *Contemporary Politics* 20, no. 4 (2014): 497.

150. Karriem, 'Brazilian Landless Movement', 320.

151. Boggs, *Two Revolutions*, 105.

152. Harvey, 'Militant Particularism'.

153. *SPN*, 367; Q10 II, §6i.

154. *SPN*, 210; Q13, §23.

155. *SPN*, 211; Q13, §23.

156. Ibid.

157. *SSG*, 103; Q13, §23.

158. Ibid.

159. *SSG*, 4; Q25, §1.

160. *SPN*, 270; Q6, §10.

161. *SPN*, 242, ftn 42.

162. Guha, 'Gramsci in India', 290.

163. Choplin and Ciavolella, 'Urban Subaltern', 315.

164. Motta, 'New Movements', 47.

165. Hall, *Hard Road*, 78–79.

166. *SPN*, 110; Q15, §11.

167. *SPN*, 194; Q8, §195.

168. Ibid.

169. *SPN*, 199, ftn 102.

170. *SPN*, 199; Q3, §48.

171. Ibid.

172. *SPN*, 199–200; Q3, §48.

173. Ibid.

174. Ibid.

175. *L'Ordine Nuovo*, 4 and 9 September 1920, *SPW1*, 336.

176. Jamie Allinson, 'Counter-Revolution as International Phenomenon: The Case of Egypt', *Review of International Studies* 45, no. 2 (2019): 320–344; De Smet, 'Passive Revolution'.

177. *SPN*, 200; Q3, §48.

178. Ibid.

179. *SPN*, 111; Q15, §11.

180. *SPN*, 110; Q15, §11.

181. *SPN*, 108; Q15, §11.

182. Ibid.

183. Ibid., 110.

184. *SPN*, 112; Q15, §15. Gramsci was a philosopher and historian, but he was also, as this example shows, a politician—intensely practical, organizational, and strategic.

185. *SPN*, 111; Q15, §11.

186. *SPN*, 112; Q15, §15.

187. Ibid.

188. *SPN*, 113; Q15, §15. In this example, 'awareness' or consciousness is clearly not just a matter of philosophy or culture, but is an operative factor in the relation and balance of forces, and thus in the politics of hegemony.

189. Chodor, 'Not Throwing the Baby', 497.

190. Sun Tzu, Chinese strategist, quoted in Sanbonmatsu, *Postmodern Prince*, 189.

191. Boggs, *Two Revolutions*, 105.

192. Susi Meret, 'What Can We Learn from Gramsci Today? Migrant Subalternity and the Refugee Movements: Perspectives from the Lampedusa in Hamburg', in Antonini et al., *Revisiting Gramsci's Notebooks*, 211.

193. Boggs, *Two Revolutions*, 209.

194. E.g. ibid., 175.

195. *SPN*, 235; Q13, §24.

196. The editors, *SPN*, 145, ftn 29.

197. Salamini, *Political Praxis*, 60.

198. Chodor, 'Not Throwing the Baby', 500.

199. *SSG*, 10; Q25, §5.

200. *SPN*, 178; Q13, §17.

201. Ibid.

202. Bayat, *Revolutionary Life*, 226.

203. Bernd Belina, 'Germany in Times of Crisis: Passive Revolution, Struggle over Hegemony and New Nationalism', *Geografiska Annaler Series B—Human Geography* 95, no. 3 (2013): 275.

204. Boggs, *Two Revolutions*, 15.

205. Raya Dunayevskya, *Rosa Luxemburg, Women's Liberation, and Marx's Philosophy of Revolution*, 2nd edn, foreword by Adrienne Rich (Urbana: University of Illinois Press, 1991), 5–9.

206. Boggs, *Two Revolutions*, 17.

207. *SPN*, 335; Q11, §12.

208. *SSG*, 159–160.

209. Ali Ahmida, 'When the Subaltern Speak: Memory of Genocide in Colonial Libya 1929 to 1933', *Italian Studies* 61, no. 2 (2006): 175–190.

210. Vacca, *Alternative Modernities*, 126.

211. Graeber, *Direct Action*, 210–211.

212. Ibid.

213. Boggs, *Two Revolutions*, 207.

214. Del Roio, *Prisms*, 188, ftn 1.

215. Boggs, *Two Revolutions*, 58.

216. Ibid., 59.

217. Crézégut, 'An Imaginary Gramscianism?', 431.

218. Bayat, *Revolutionary Life*, 246.

219. *SSG*, 33; Q3, §48.

220. *SSG*, 82; Q11, §12.

221. Salamini, *Political Praxis*, 69.

222. Femia, *Political Thought*, 143.

223. *L'Ordine Nuovo*, 3–10 April 1920, *SPW1*, 188.

224. Georg Wilhelm Friedrich Hegel, *The Science of Logic*, trans. and ed. George Di Giovanni (Cambridge: Cambridge University Press, 2010), 9.

225. Boggs, *Two Revolutions*, 105.

CHAPTER FIVE. THE EXPANSIVE SEARCH FOR CONSENT

1. *SSG*, 10; Q25, §5.

2. *SPN*, 52, ftn 2.

3. *L'Ordine Nuovo*, 1 September 1924, *SPW2*, 264.

4. A shift that Gramsci himself arguably underwent: Rosengarten, *Revolutionary Marxism*, 114.

5. Liguori, *Pathways*, 100–101.

6. Boggs, *Two Revolutions*, 166; Salamini, *Political Praxis*, 82.

7. *PN1*, 137; Q1, §44.

8. *SPN*, 181–182; Q13, §17.

9. *SSG*, 10; Q25, §5; *SSG*, 81; Q11, §12 IV.

10. Graeber, *Direct Action*. See also Sanbonmatsu, *Postmodern Prince*, 37.

11. Ibid.

12. Hall makes this point in *Hard Road*, 171. For an example in the MST, see Karriem, 'Brazilian Landless Movement', 319.

13. *SSG*, 61; Q8, §205.

14. *SSG*, 84; Q11, §12.

15. *SSG*, 42; Q4, §38.

16. Ibid.

17. Ibid.

18. Rodrigo Nunes, *Organisation of the Organisationless: Collective Action after Networks* (Lüneburg: Mute, 2014), 41–44.

19. Rodrigo Nunes, *Neither Vertical nor Horizontal: A Theory of Political Organisation* (London: Verso Books, 2021).

20. Jo Freeman, 'The Tyranny of Structurelessness', *Berkeley Journal of Sociology* (1972): 151–164.

21. Sanbonmatsu, *Postmodern Prince*, 45, see also 37.

22. *SPN*, 198; Q3, §48.

23. Boggs, *Two Revolutions*, 219.

24. *SSG*, 34; Q3, §48.

25. Ibid., 35; Q3, §48.

26. Salamini, *Political Praxis*, 128.

27. Rosengarten, *Revolutionary Marxism*, 112.

28. Femia, *Political Thought*, 52, 53.

29. *SPN*, 243; Q13, §7.

30. *SPN*, 233; Q13, §24.

31. Ibid.

32. *SPN*, 235; Q13, §24.

33. *SPN*, 235; Q13, §24.

34. Egan, 'War of Position', 448.

35. Cuppi, 'Diffusion', 427.

36. *SPN*, 239; Q6, §138.

37. Cuppi, 'Diffusion', 414.

38. Fonseca, *Civil Society*, viii.

39. Cited in Philip Roberts, 'Gramsci in Brazil: From the PCB to the MST', *Thesis Eleven* 147, no. 1 (2018): 71.

40. Rosengarten, *Revolutionary Marxism*, 122.

41. Liu, 'Cultural Revolution'.

42. Bruhn, 'Palabra Verdadera'.

43. Adam D. Morton, 'Mexico, Neoliberal Restructuring and the EZLN: A Neo-Gramscian Analysis', in *Globalisation and the Politics of Resistance*, ed. B. K. Gills (London: Palgrave Macmillan, 2000), 261.

44. Femia, *Political Thought*, 238; cf. Challand, *Violence and Representation*, 99–100, 323–357.

45. Hazem Kandil, 'Islamising Egypt? Testing the Limits of Gramscian Counterhegemonic Strategies', *Theory and Society* 40 (2011): 37–62.

46. Walter D. Mignolo, 'Mariátegui and Gramsci in "Latin" America: Between Revolution and Decoloniality', in Srivastava and Bhattacharya, *Postcolonial Gramsci*, 191–217.

47. *SPN*, 243; Q13, §7.

48. Bianchi, *Gramsci's Laboratory*, 188.

49. *SPN*, 238; Q7, §16.

50. *SPN*, 237; Q7, §16; Vacca, *Alternative Modernities*, 72.

51. *SPN*, 236, ftn 34.

52. *SPN*, 236; Q13, §24.

53. *SPN*, 229; Q1, §134.

54. Ibid.

55. *SPN*, 230; Q1, §134.

56. *SPN*, 243; Q13, §7.

57. For an example of one such account, along with references to the relevant historiography, see Chalcraft, *Striking Cabbies*, especially pp. 15–35. See also Noorani, *Culture and Hegemony*, 209–212.

58. Ayubi, *Over-Stating the Arab State*.

59. *SPN*, 129; Q13, §1.

60. Femia, *Political Thought*, 143.

61. Boggs, *Two Revolutions*, 19; see also Femia, *Political Thought*, 146.

62. Femia, *Political Thought*, 135.

63. Briziarelli, 'Rhetoric of Podemos'.

64. Robert Mayer, 'The Status of a Classic Text: Lenin's *What is to be Done?* after 1902', *History of European Ideas* 22, no. 4 (1996): 317.

65. Athos Manuscript, in Anderson, *Antinomies*, 161–162.

66. Rosengarten, *Revolutionary Marxism*, 116 and see 37–38.

67. *PPL*, 50.

68. Femia, *Political Thought*, 158.

69. Fresu, *Antonio Gramsci*, 14.

70. Joel Geier, 'Zinovievism and the Degeneration of World Communism', *International Socialist Review* 93 (2014): 41–73; Lars T. Lih, *Lenin Rediscovered: 'What is to be Done?' in Context* (Leiden: Brill, 2005); Lars T. Lih, *Lenin* (London: Reaktion Books, 2012); Robert Mayer, 'One Step Forward, Two Steps Back: On Lars Lih's Lenin', *Historical Materialism: Research in Critical Marxist Theory* 18, no. 3 (2010): 47–63.

71. Mohanad Hage Ali, *Nationalism, Transnationalism, and Political Islam: Hizbullah's Institutional Identity* (Cham: Palgrave Macmillan, 2017).

72. Tore Refslund Hamming, 'Jihadi Politics: Fitna within the Sunni Jihadi Movement, 2014–2019', PhD diss. (European University Institute, 2020).

73. Massimo Ramaioli, 'Salafism as Gramscian Informed Vanguardism', *Contemporary Islam* 17, no. 2 (2023): 297–318.

74. Timothy Mitchell, 'McJihad: Islam in the US Global Order', *Social Text* 20, no. 4 (2002): 1–18.

75. Leon Trotsky, 'What is National Socialism?', June 1933, accessed 16 September 2022, https://www.marxists.org/archive/trotsky/germany/1933/330610.htm.

76. Togliatti, *On Gramsci*, 162.

77. Wang, 'Chinese Left', 209; Gaudichaud, 'Latin American Left'.

78. Rosengarten, *Revolutionary Marxism*, 117.

79. Coutinho, *Political Thought*, 31.

80. Femia, *Political Thought*, 165.

81. *SPN*, lxii.

82. Ibid., lxiii.

83. Femia, *Political Thought*, 157.

84. *SSG*, 104; Q13, §23.

85. *SPN*, 188–189; Q13, §36.

86. *SSG*, 68; Q9, §68.

87. Ibid.

88. Femia, *Political Thought*, 161.

89. Ibid., 163.

90. *SSG*, 82; Q11, §12.

91. Boggs, *Two Revolutions*, 106.

92. *L'Ordine Nuovo*, 3 July 1920, *SPW1*, 309.

93. Boggs, *Two Revolutions*, 107.

94. Buey, *Reading Gramsci*, 126; Rosengarten, *Revolutionary Marxism*, 33.

95. *SPN*, 194; Q8, §195.

96. Femia, *Political Thought*, 155.

97. *SPN*, 148–149; Q17, §37.

98. Femia, *Political Thought*, 164.

99. Ibid., 155.

100. *SPN*, 149: Q17, §37.

101. Vacca, *Alternative Modernities*, 189.

102. Femia, *Political Thought*, 156.

103. Ibid., 155.

104. *SPN*, 181; Q13, §17.

105. Dunayevskaya, *Women's Liberation*, 155.

106. Cf. Femia, *Political Thought*, 136.

107. Coutinho, *Political Thought*, 10.

108. Thomas, 'Modern Prince', 31; cf. Boggs, *Two Revolutions*, 264.

109. Buey, *Reading Gramsci*, 157.

110. Martinelli, cited in Femia, *Political Thought*, 144.

111. Boggs, *Two Revolutions*, 264.

112. Briziarelli, 'Rhetoric of Podemos', 298.

113. Ibid.

114. Biko, *I Write*, 4.

115. El-Fattah, *Not Yet Defeated*, 59-61.

116. Rupe Simms, 'Black Theology, a Weapon in the Struggle for Freedom: A Gramscian Analysis', *Race and Society* 2, no.2 (2000): 176.

117. Cf. Jeffrey B. Perry, *Hubert Harrison: The Struggle for Equality, 1918-1927* (New York: Columbia University Press, 2020), 150-151, 152-154, and passim.

118. Karriem, 'Brazilian Landless Movement', 323.

119. Vincent Bevins, email message to author, May 2023.

120. Rehmann, 'Occupy Wall Street', 13.

121. Kevin J. Cassidy, 'Organic Intellectuals and the Committed Community: Irish Republicanism and Sinn Féin in the North', *Irish Political Studies* 20, no. 3 (2005): 341-356.

122. Ibid., 344-345.

123. Femia, *Political Thought*, 164.

124. Egan, 'War of Position', 448.

125. Athos Manuscript. in Anderson, *Antinomies*, 160.

126. Bruhn, 'Palabra Verdadera', 46.

127. Ibid., 49.

128. Morton, 'Neoliberal Restructuring', 265.

129. Nunes, *Neither Vertical Nor Horizontal*, 286-287.

130. *SSG*, 113; Q14, §10.

131. Cited in Wang, 'Chinese Left', 220.

132. Hall, *Hard Road*, 181.

133. *SPN*, 181; Q13, §17.

134. Salamini, *Political Praxis*, 44.

135. *SSG*, 70; Q10 II, §41.

136. 'Some Aspects of the Southern Question', 1927, *SPW2*, 448.

137. *Il Grido del Popolo*, 29 January 1916, *HPC*, 21.

138. Boggs' words, in *Two Revolutions*, 189.

139. Cemil Aydin, *The Politics of Anti-Westernism in Asia: Visions of World Order in Pan-Islamic and Pan-Asian Thought* (New York: Columbia University Press, 2007).

140. *SPN*, 195; Q8, §195.

141. Simms, 'Black Theology'.

142. *SPN*, 195; Q8, §195. Contrarywise, in the present, a Gramscian hypothesis is that the internet and social media fragment and dislocate the very process of collective will formation itself.

143. *SSG*, 81; Q11, §12.

144. Gramsci writing in 1917, cited in *HPC*, 44.

145. *SPN*, 328; Q11, §12.

146. *SPN*, 330; Q11, §12.

147. Ibid.

148. *SPN*, 332; Q11, §12.

149. *SPN*, 331; Q11, §12.

150. Salamini, *Political Praxis*, 107.

151. Gramsci, cited in Femia, *Political Thought*, 157.

152. *SSG*, 78; Q11, §12.

153. Bruhn, 'Palabra Verdadera'.

154. *SSG*, 75; Q11, §12 IV.

155. *SSG*, 85; Q11, §12 IV.

156. *SSG*, 86; Q11, §12 IV.

157. *SSG*, 86–87; Q11, §12 IV.

158. Ibid.

159. Chunyun Li, 'From Insurgency to Movement: An Embryonic Labor Movement Undermining Hegemony in South China', *Industrial and Labour Relations Review* 74, no. 4 (2021): 859–860.

160. Briziarelli, 'Rhetoric of Podemos', 295; Pravina Pillay, 'Gramsci on Language and Its Relevance to South Africa', *Journal of Gender, Information and Development in Africa (JGIDA)* 7, no. 1 (2018): 39–47.

161. Boothman, 'Sources for Hegemony'.

162. Briziarelli, 'Rhetoric of Podemos', 295.

163. *SSG*, 69; Q9, §135.

164. *SSG*, 5; Q25, §1.

165. Rehmann, 'Occupy Wall Street', 12.

166. Kerron Ó Luain, 'Gaelscoil Activists as a Postcolonial Subaltern and the Emergence of the Gaelscoileanna, ca. 1970', *Radical History Review* 2022, no. 143 (2022): 64–77.

167. Gramsci, cited in Briziarelli, 'Rhetoric of Podemos', 299.

168. *SSG*, 67; Q9, §68. The 'privileged territorial group' could have referred to the CPSU in the wider Comintern/transnational communist movement.

169. *Il Grido del Popolo*, 29 January 1916, *SPW1*, 12.

170. 26 October 1926, *SPW2*, 440.

171. Badaloni, 'The Revolution', 104.

172. Cosimo Zene, 'Justice for the Excluded and Education for Democracy in B. R. Ambedkar and A. Gramsci', *Rethinking Marxism* 30, no. 4 (2018): 494–524.

173. *SSG*, 62; Q8, §213.

174. Morera, 'Gramsci and Democracy', 24.

175. Peter Mayo, 'Antonio Gramsci's Impact on Critical Pedagogy', *Critical Sociology* 41, no. 7–8 (2015): 1130.

176. Meek, 'Learning as Territoriality', 1188.

177. Philip Roberts, 'Passive Revolution in Brazil: Struggles over Hegemony, Religion and Development, 1964–2007', *Third World Quarterly* 36, no. 9 (2015), 1673.

178. Tarlau, 'Social(ist) Pedagogies', 3–4.

179. Ibid., 6.

180. Karriem, 'Brazilian Landless Movement', 323.

181. Tarlau, 'Social(ist) Pedagogies', 4.

182. Ibid., 5.

183. Ibid., 8.

184. Grayson, 'Workers' Education', 129.

185. Freire, cited in Meek, 'Learning as Territoriality', 1180.

186. Ibid., 1187.

187. Ibid., 1187–1188.

188. Gramsci, cited in Mayo, 'Critical Pedagogy', 1125.

189. Karriem, 'Brazilian Landless Movement', 323.

190. Ibid.

191. *SPN*, 229; Q1, §134.

192. Femia, *Political Thought*, 196, 215.

193. Togliatti, *On Gramsci*, 33.

194. Ibid., 42, 69, 74, 83, 85.

195. Dainotto, 'Introduction', in *Gramsci in the World*, 3.

196. Cuppi, 'Diffusion', 428.

197. Guha, 'Gramsci in India'.

198. Motta, 'New Movements'.

199. Femia, *Political Thought*, 199.

200. Boggs, *Two Revolutions*, 231.

201. *SPN*, 155; Q14, §34.

202. Engels, cited in Dainotto, 'Introduction', 2.

203. Boggs, *Two Revolutions*, 228.

204. Ibid., 229. I refer to this as a social not historical bloc for reasons clarified in the next chapter.

205. Vacca, *Alternative Modernities*, 184.

206. Boggs, *Two Revolutions*, 229.

207. Coutinho, *Political Thought*, 26–31.

208. Athos Manuscript, in Anderson, *Antinomies*, 160.

209. Ibid., 161.

210. *PN3*, 382; Q8, §244.

211. Femia, *Political Thought*, 195.

212. Gramsci, cited in Femia, *Political Thought*, 195.

213. *SPN*, 181; Q13, §17.

214. Ibid.

215. Gramsci, cited in Bob Jessop, 'Gramsci as a Spatial Theorist', *Critical Review of International Social and Political Philosophy* 8, no. 4 (2005): 434.

216. Roberts, 'Passive Revolution in Brazil', 1674-1675.

217. Mouffe, *Marxist Theory*, 1-18, 168-204.

218. Laclau and Mouffe, *Socialist Strategy*.

219. hooks, *Ain't I a Woman*, 185-196; Wallace, *Black Macho*, 189-127.

220. Chodor, 'Not Throwing the Baby', 495.

221. Karriem notes how militant particularism was overcome in Brazil through bloc formation in 'Brazilian Landless Movement', 319.

222. Peter Ackers, 'Gramsci at the Miners' Strike: Remembering the 1984-1985 Eurocommunist Alternative Industrial Relations Strategy', *Labor History* 55, no. 2 (2014): 151-172.

223. Hall, *Hard Road*, 263.

224. Sanjay Joshi and B. Josh, *Struggle for Hegemony in India* (New Delhi: Sage, 2011).

225. *SPN*, 230; Q1, §134.

226. *SPN*, 230, ftn 25.

227. Gramsci, 'Maximalism and Extremism', *L'Unità*, 2 July 1925, accessed 12 November 2021, https://www.marxists.org/archive/gramsci/1925/07/maximalism.htm.

228. Ibid.

229. Boggs refers to degeneration in *Two Revolutions*, 265.

230. *QC3*, 1558; Q13, §1.

231. *SPN*, 129; Q13, §1.

232. Salamini, *Political Praxis*, 64-65.

233. *SPN*, 58, ftn 8.

234. *SPN*, 58; Q19, §24.

235. Ibid.

236. *SPN*, 59; Q19, §24.

237. *PN1*, 138; Q1, §44.

238. Ibid.

239. *SPN*, 58, ftn 8; Hesketh has understood early twentieth-century Mexico using similar optics. Chris Hesketh, 'From Passive Revolution to Silent Revolution: Class Forces and the Production of State, Space and Scale in Modern Mexico', *Capital & Class* 34, no. 3 (2010): 388.

240. Morton, 'Neoliberal Restructuring', 258.

241. *SPN*, 58, ftn 8.

242. *L'Ordine Nuovo*, 8 November 1919, *SPW1*, 109.

243. Boggs, *Two Revolutions*, 80-81.

244. *SPN*, 292; Q22, §6.

245. *PN1*, 139-140; Q1, §44.

246. *SSG*, 7; Q25, §4.

247. Ibid.

248. Li, 'Insurgency to Movement', 852.

249. Ibid., 854-857.

250. Ibid., 852.

251. Ibid., 866.

252. Sumi Madhok, *On Vernacular Rights Cultures: The Politics of Origins, Human Rights, and Gendered Struggles for Justice* (Cambridge: Cambridge University Press, 2022), 134.

253. Ibid.

254. Simms, 'Black Theology', 176.

255. Ligaya Rene Domingo, 'Building a Movement: Filipino American Union and Community Organizing in Seattle in the 1970s', PhD diss. (University of California, Berkeley, 2010).

256. Zachary Lockman, 'Imagining the Working Class: Culture, Nationalism, and Class Formation in Egypt, 1899-1914', *Poetics Today* (1994): 157-190.

257. A final example is Stuart Hall's analysis of how a municipal authority (Greater London Council), in moving to the left, started to 'positively identify itself with popular cultural life, and feed into itself some of the energy generated.' Hall, *Hard Road*, 235, 238.

CHAPTER SIX. THE ROILING FERMENT OF REVOLUTION

1. *L'Ordine Nuovo*, 1 September 1924, *SPW2*, 264.

2. *SPN*, 126-127; Q13, §1.

3. *Avanti!*, 24 December 1917, *SPW1*, 35.

4. Femia, *Political Thoughts*, 212.

5. Theda Skocpol, 'Rentier State and Shi'a Islam in the Iranian Revolution', *Theory and Society* 11, no. 3 (1982): 265-283; Jack A. Goldstone, 'Toward a Fourth Generation of Revolutionary Theory', *Annual Review of Political Science* 4, no. 1 (2001): 139-187; George Lawson, *Anatomies of Revolution* (Cambridge: Cambridge University Press, 2019).

6. Donatella Della Porta, *Where Did the Revolution Go? Contentious Politics and the Quality of Democracy* (Cambridge: Cambridge University Press, 2016); Neil Ketchley, *Egypt in a Time of Revolution* (Cambridge: Cambridge University Press, 2017); Frederick Volpi and James Jasper, eds., *Microfoundations of the Arab Uprisings: Mapping Interactions between Regimes and Protesters* (Amsterdam: Amsterdam University Press, 2018).

7. Charles Kurzman, *The Unthinkable Revolution in Iran* (Cambridge, MA: Harvard University Press, 2004).

8. Mark R. Beissinger, 'The Semblance of Democratic Revolution: Coalitions in Ukraine's Orange Revolution', *American Political Science Review* 107, no. 3 (2013): 574-592.

9. Peter Ackerman and Jack DuVall, *A Force More Powerful: A Century of Non-Violent Conflict* (London: Palgrave Macmillan, 2000); Erica Chenoweth and Maria. J. Stephan, *Why Civil Resistance Works: The Strategic Logic of Nonviolent Conflict* (New York: Columbia University Press, 2011).

10. Lenin, *State and Revolution*, 34.

11. Liu, 'Cultural Revolution', 69-73.

12. Anderson, *Antinomies*, 148.

13. Vacca, *Alternative Modernities*, 19.

14. *SPN*, 238; Q6, §138.

15. Ibid.

16. Vacca, *Alternative Modernities*, 47.

17. *SPN*, 238-239; Q6, §138.

18. Ibid.

19. Kandil, 'Islamising Egypt', 40.

20. *SPN*, 239; Q6, §138.

21. Cited by the editors, *SPN*, xl.

22. Ibid.

23. Anderson, *Antinomies*, 160.

24. Salamini, *Political Praxis*, 128.

25. *SPN*, 235; Q13, §24.

26. Egan, 'War of Position', 449.

27. Ibid., 450.

28. Morera, 'Gramsci and Democracy', 33.

29. Femia, *Political Thought*, 205.

30. Kandil, 'Islamising Egypt'.

31. Athos Manuscript, in Anderson, *Antinomies*,158.

32. Ibid., 159.

33. *SPN*, 229; Q1, §134.

34. Athos Manuscript, in Anderson, *Antinomies*, 160.

35. Boggs, *Two Revolutions*, 105.

36. *Avanti!*, 2 September 1920, *SPW1*, 328.

37. *SPN*, 230, ftn 25. Gramsci did point to the weakness of such *arditi* in the face of state power / state-backed militias.

38. Boggs, *Two Revolutions*, 262.

39. Femia, *Political Thought*, 205.

40. Ibid., 207.

41. Femia, *Political Thought*, 208.

42. Roberts, 'Gramsci in Brazil', 71. Roberts's analysis does not involve an uncritical celebration of the MST. He leaves open the question as to whether it will be a new 'modern Prince' (p. 73). Indeed, with Lula's return to the Presidency, as well as the MST and Brazilian government's new partnerships with the Chinese state in its agricultural projects, there is a debate as to whether this is socialist, anti-imperialist solidarity or whether such partnerships involve a Chinese state expansion of capitalism.

43. Francesca Antonini, 'Interpreting the Present from the Past: Gramsci, Marx and the Historical Analogy', in Antonini et al., *Revisiting Gramsci's Notebooks*, 165-166.

44. Ibid., 167-168; and see Cospito, *Rhythm of Thought*, 207-217.

45. De Smet, *Dialectical Pedagogy*, 354-358. Chavez has been criticized in Gramscian terms for charismatic, individualistic, and imposing leadership and for stifling grassroots institutional building and local initiative, while leaving behind an over-powerful bureaucracy. Efe Can Gürcan, 'Hugo Chávez's Unwritten Testament: National-Democratic Struggle and Contradictions of Socialism', *Dialectical Anthropology* 37, no. 3-4 (2013): 351.

46. Boggs, *Two Revolutions*, 263.

47. Ibid., 264.

48. *L'Ordine Nuovo*, 28 February-6 March 1920, *SPW1*, 171.

49. *SPN*, 59; Q19, §24.

50. Thomas Furse, 'Vincenzo Cuoco: Moderation as a Revolutionary Act', *Journal of the History of Ideas Blog*, accessed 21 September 2022, https://jhiblog.org/2019/10/28/vincenzo-cuoco-moderation-as-a-revolutionary-act/.

51. *SPN*, 118-119; Q10 I, §9.

52. Ibid.

53. *SPN*, 110; Q15, §11.

54. Boggs, *Two Revolutions*, 177.

55. *SPN*, 110; Q15, §11.

56. Ibid. See also, Coutinho, *Political Thought*, 100-105; Vacca, *Alternative Modernities*, 85-149.

57. Belina, 'Passive Revolution', 275.

58. Morton, 'Neoliberal Restructuring', 316-317.

59. Robert Fatton, 'Gramsci and the Legitimisation of the State: The Case of the Senegalese Passive Revolution', *Canadian Journal of Political Science/Revue canadienne de science politique* 19, no. 4 (1986): 729-750.

60. Hesketh, 'From Passive Revolution to Silent Revolution', 384.

61. Jamie Allinson and Alexander Anievas, 'The Uneven and Combined Development of the Meiji Restoration: A Passive Revolutionary Road to Capitalist Modernity', *Capital & Class* 34, no. 3 (2010): 469–490.

62. Chris Hesketh and Adam David Morton, 'Spaces of Uneven Development and Class Struggle in Bolivia: Transformation or Trasformismo?', *Antipode* 46, no. 1 (2014): 149–169.

63. Daniel John Evans, 'Welsh Devolution as Passive Revolution', *Capital & Class* 42, no. 3 (2018): 489–508.

64. Mallick, 'Passive Revolution(s)', 253–254.

65. Cihan Tuğal, *Passive Revolution: Absorbing the Islamic Challenge to Capitalism* (Stanford, CA: Stanford University Press, 2009).

66. Mouffe, *Marxist Theory*, 11.

67. Alex Callinicos, 'The Limits of Passive Revolution', *Capital & Class* 34, no.3 (2010): 491–507.

68. *SPN*, 184; Q13, §17.

69. Mouffe, *Marxist Theory*, 8–10, 13. See also Salamini, *Political Praxis*, 57; Egan, 'War of Position', 438.

70. Salamini, *Political Praxis*, 56.

71. Ibid.

72. Mouffe, *Marxist Theory*, 15.

73. Ibid.

74. Ibid.

75. Cuppi, 'Diffusion', 428.

76. Vacca, *Alternative Modernities*, 184.

77. *SPN*, 114; Q15, §62. Gramsci's text here is in note form.

78. Ibid.

79. Laclau, *Politics and Ideology*, 108.

80. William Sewell, 'Historical Events as Transformations of Structures: Inventing Revolution at the Bastille', *Theory and Society* 25, no. 6 (1996): 841–881.

81. Filippini, *Using Gramsci*, 12.

82. *SSG*, 11; Q25, §5.

83. 'Some Aspects of the Southern Question,' 1927, *SPW2*, 448.

84. Morera, 'Gramsci and Democracy', 32–33.

85. Michał Kalecki, 'Social and Economic Aspects of Intermediate Regimes', in *Selected Essays on the Economic Growth of the Socialist and the Mixed Economy*, ed. Zdislaw Sadowski (Cambridge: Cambridge University Press, 1972), 162–169.

86. Julie Gervais, Claire Lemercier, and Willy Pelletier, *La valeur du service public* (Paris: La Découverte, 2021), 135–140.

87. *SPN*, 259; Q8, §179.

88. Vacca, *Alternative Modernities*, 19.

89. Boggs, *Two Revolutions*, 172–173.

90. Henck, *Insurgent Marcos*; Michael Knapp, Anja Flach, and Ercan Ayboğa, *Revolution in Rojava: Democratic Autonomy and Women's Liberation in Syrian Kurdistan*, foreword by David Graeber, afterword by Asya Abdullah, trans. Janet Biehl (London, Pluto Press, 2016); Subcomandante Marcos, *Professionals of Hope: The Selected Writings of Subcomandante Marcos*, afterword Gabriela Jauregui (N.p.: The Song Cave, 2017); Öcalan, *Political Thought*; Salamanca, 'The Madrid Conference'; Gary Wilder, *Freedom Time: Negritude, Decolonisation, and the Future of the World* (Durham, NC: Duke University Press, 2015).

91. Nour Almazidi, 'Out of Politics, History, and Time: Stateless Subaltern Struggle, Resistance, and Refusal in the Arabian Peninsula', PhD diss. (London School of Economics and Political Science, 2025).

92. Marral Shamshiri-Fard, 'Challenging Empire in the Middle East: Revolutionary Transnationalism in the Iranian and Arab Lefts, 1963–1979', PhD diss. (London School of Economics and Political Science, 2025); Alicia Turner, Laurence Cox, and Brian Bocking, *The Irish Buddhist: The Forgotten Monk Who Faced Down the British Empire* (Oxford: Oxford University Press, 2020).

93. West and Buschendorf, *Black Prophetic Fire*, 133.

94. Boggs, *Two Revolutions*, 84.

95. Salamini, *Political Praxis*, 142.

96. Bobbio, 'Civil Society', 24.

97. Christine Buci-Glucksmann, 'State, Transition and Passive Revolution', in Mouffe, *Gramsci and Marxist Theory*, 219.

98. Ibid., 225.

99. Morera, 'Gramsci and Democracy', 32.

100. Roberts, 'Gramsci in Brazil', 66.

101. Bruhn, 'Palabra Verdadera', 51.

102. Salamini, *Political Praxis*, 22.

103. *PN3*, 310; Q8, §130.

104. Cited in Salamini, *Political Praxis*, 135.

105. Ibid., 141.

106. Gürcan, 'Chávez's Unwritten Testament', 342–343.

107. Hall, *Hard Road*, 221.

108. Ibid.

109. Ibid.

110. Ibid., 230.

111. Ibid., 227.

112. Gennaro Gervasio, 'Marxism or Left-Wing Nationalism? The New Left in Egypt in the 1970s', in *Arab Lefts: Histories and Legacies, 1950s-1970s*, ed. Laure Guirguis (Edinburgh: Edinburgh University Press, 2020), 148.

113. Hall, *Hard Road*, 231.

114. Ibid.

115. Ibid., 280.

116. Ibid., 232.

117. Coutinho, *Political Thought*, 108; cf. Vacca, *Alternative Modernities*, 233-234.

118. *SSG*, 10; Q25, §5.

119. Engels, cited in Lenin, *State and Revolution*, 71.

120. Lenin, *State and Revolution*, 35.

121. Ibid., 59.

122. Bobbio, cited in Alessio Panichi, 'Between Belonging and Originality: Norberto Bobbio's Interpretation of Gramsci', in Antonini et al., *Revisiting Gramsci's Notebooks*, 403.

123. Guha, 'Gramsci in India', 291.

124. *PN3*, 75-76; Q6, §88.

125. *SSG*, 68; Q9, §68.

126. *SSG*, 49; Q6, §125.

127. Lenin, cited in Buey, *Reading Gramsci*, 82.

128. *SSG*, 66; Q9, §68.

129. *SSG*, 67-68; Q9, §68.

130. Vacca, *Alternative Modernities*, 140; see also 31, 33, 137-143, 216-218.

131. Coutinho, *Political Thought*, 123-124.

132. *SPN*, 193-4; Q13, §30.

133. *L'Ordine Nuovo*, 21 April 1921, *SPW2*, 36.

134. *SSG*, 42; Q4, §38.

135. *SPN*, 40; Q12, §2.

136. Leipold, 'Marx's Social Republic'.

137. Boggs, *Two Revolutions*, 85.

138. Cf. Hall, *Hard Road*, 212.

139. *Avanti!*, 26 August 1916, *SPW1*, 18.

140. Vacca, *Alternative Modernities*, 208, 195-242.

141. Femia, *Political Thought*, 172-183; Boggs, *Two Revolutions*.

142. Coutinho, *Political Thought*, 119.

143. Buey, *Reading Gramsci*, 145.

144. *SPN*, 345; Q10 II, §17.

145. Boggs, *Two Revolutions*, 141.

146. *SPN*, 348; Q10 II; §44.

147. *SPN*, 388; Q11, §70.

148. Hall, *Hard Road*,184.

149. Thomas, *Gramscian Moment*, 297.

150. Gramsci writing in 1917, cited in Filippini, *Using Gramsci*, 13.

151. Salamini, *Political Thought*, 82.

152. Ibid., 175; Boothman, 'Sources for Hegemony', 211.

153. Salamini, *Political Praxis*, 214.

154. 15 January 1927, *LP1*, 68.

155. Editors, *SPN*, xxxvii.

156. *SPN*, 230, ftn 25.

157. Boggs, *Two Revolutions*, 18.

158. *SSG*, 68; Q9, §68.

159. *QC3*, 1692; Q14, §34.

160. Femia, *Political Thought*, 158.

161. *SPN*, 168; Q13, §23.

162. Vacca, *Alternative Modernities*, 190.

163. Ibid., 183.

164. Boggs, *Two Revolutions*, 266.

165. Ibid., 85.

166. Dirlik, cited in Wang, 'Chinese Left', 209.

CONCLUSION

1. Wedeen, 'Acting "As If"'.

2. Charles Tripp, *The Power and the People: Paths of Resistance in the Middle East* (Cambridge: Cambridge University Press, 2013), 15.

3. McKittrick, *Sylvia Wynter*, 29–33.

4. I take this to be a key lesson of Cornel West's inspiring discussion of an imaginary meeting between Malcolm X and Martin Luther King Jr. in West and Buschendorf, *Black Prophetic Fire*, 130–131.

Abdel-Malek, Anouar. *Contemporary Arab Political Thought*. London: Zed, 1983.

Abdelrahman, Maha. *Egypt's Long Revolution: Protest Movements and Uprisings*. London: Routledge, 2015.

Abrahamian, Ervand. 'Ali Shari'ati: Ideologue of the Iranian Revolution'. *MERIP Reports*, no. 102 (1982): 24–28. https://doi.org/10.2307/3010795.

Abd El-Fattah, Alaa. *You Have Not Yet Been Defeated: Selected Works, 2011–2021*. Translated by a collective. London: Fitzcarraldo Editions, 2021.

Abu-Lughod, Lila. 'The Romance of Resistance: Tracing Transformations of Power through Bedouin Women'. *American Ethnologist* 17, no. 1 (1990): 41–55.

Abul-Magd, Zeinab. *Imagined Empires: A History of Revolt in Egypt*. Berkeley: University of California Press, 2013.

Achcar, Gilbert. *Morbid Symptoms: Relapse in the Arab Uprising*. London: Saqi Books, 2016.

Ackerman, Peter, and Jack DuVall. *A Force More Powerful: A Century of Non-Violent Conflict*. London: Palgrave Macmillan, 2000.

Ackers, Peter. 'Gramsci at the Miners' Strike: Remembering the 1984–1985 Eurocommunist Alternative Industrial Relations Strategy'. *Labor History* 55, no. 2 (2014): 151–172.

Ahmida, Ali. 'When the Subaltern Speak: Memory of Genocide in Colonial Libya 1929 to 1933'. *Italian Studies* 61, no. 2 (2006): 175–190.

Akhtar, Aasim Sajjad. *The Struggle for Hegemony in Pakistan: Fear, Desire and Revolutionary Horizons*. London: Pluto Press, 2022.

Alam, S. M. Shamsul. *Governmentality and Counter-Hegemony in Bangladesh*. London: Palgrave Macmillan, 2015.

Albert, Michael. *Liberating Theory*. Boston: South End Press, 1986.

Ali, Mohanad Hage. *Nationalism, Transnationalism, and Political Islam: Hizbullah's Institutional Identity*. Cham: Springer, 2017.

Allinson, Jamie. 'Counter-Revolution as International Phenomenon: The Case of Egypt'. *Review of International Studies* 45, no. 2 (2019): 320–344.

Allinson, Jamie, and Alexander Anievas. 'The Uneven and Combined Development of the Meiji Restoration: A Passive Revolutionary Road to Capitalist Modernity'. *Capital & Class* 34, no. 3 (2010): 469–490.

Almazidi, Nour. 'Out of Politics, History, and Time: Stateless Subaltern Struggle, Resistance, and Refusal in the Arabian Peninsula'. PhD diss., London School of Economics and Political Science, 2025.

Althusser, Louis, Etienne Balibar, Pierre Macherey, Jacques Rancière, and Roger Establet. *Reading Capital: The Complete Edition*. London: Verso, 2016.

Anderson, Charles W. 'From Petition to Confrontation: The Palestinian National Movement and the Rise of Mass Politics, 1929–1939'. PhD diss., New York University, 2013.

Anderson, Perry. *The Antinomies of Antonio Gramsci*. London: Verso, 2017.

Antonini, Francesca. 'Interpreting the Present from the Past: Gramsci, Marx and the Historical Analogy'. In Antonini et al., *Revisiting Gramsci's Notebooks*, 160–174.

Antonini, Francesca, Aaron Bernstein, Lorenzo Fusaro, and Robert Jackson, eds. *Revisiting Gramsci's Notebooks*. Chicago: Haymarket, 2020.

Apostolidis, Paul. *The Fight for Time: Migrant Day Laborers and the Politics of Precarity*. Oxford: Oxford University Press, 2018.

Armbrust, Walter. *Martyrs and Tricksters: An Ethnography of the Egyptian Revolution*. Princeton, NJ: Princeton University Press, 2019.

Atshan, Sa'ed. *Queer Palestine and the Empire of Critique*. Stanford, CA: Stanford University Press, 2020.

Aydin, Cemil. *The Politics of Anti-Westernism in Asia: Visions of World Order in Pan-Islamic and Pan-Asian Thought*. New York: Columbia University Press, 2007.

Ayubi, Nazih N. *Over-Stating the Arab State: Politics and Society in the Middle East*. London: Bloomsbury Publishing, 1996.

Badaloni, Nicola. 'Gramsci and the Problem of the Revolution'. In Mouffe, *Gramsci and Marxist Theory*, 80–110.

Barber, Benjamin. *Jihad vs McWorld*. New York: Random House, 2010.

Bardawil, Fadi A. *Revolution and Disenchantment: Arab Marxism and the Binds of Emancipation*. Durham, NC: Duke University Press, 2020.

Barker, Colin, Laurence Cox, John Krinsky, and Alf Gunvald Nilsen. *Marxism and Social Movements*. Leiden: Brill, 2013.

Bayat, Asef. *Workers and Revolution in Iran: A Third World Experience of Workers' Control*. London: Zed, 1987.

———. *Street Politics: Poor People's Movements in Iran*. New York: Columbia University Press, 1997.

———. *Revolution without Revolutionaries: Making Sense of the Arab Spring*. Stanford, CA: Stanford University Press, 2017.

———. *Revolutionary Life: The Everyday of the Arab Spring*. Cambridge, MA: Harvard University Press, 2021.

Beinin, Joel, and Marie Duboc. 'A Workers' Social Movement on the Margin of the Global Neoliberal Order, Egypt 2004-2009'. In *Social Movements, Mobilization, and Contestation in the Middle East and North Africa*, edited by Joel Beinin and Frédéric Vairel, 205-227. Stanford, CA: Stanford University Press, 2013.

Beissinger, Mark R. 'The Semblance of Democratic Revolution: Coalitions in Ukraine's Orange Revolution'. *American Political Science Review* 107, no. 3 (2013): 574-592.

Belina, Bernd. 'Germany in Times of Crisis: Passive Revolution, Struggle over Hegemony and New Nationalism'. *Geografiska Annaler Series B–Human Geography* 95, no. 3 (2013): 275-285.

Benford, Robert D., and David A. Snow. 'Framing Processes and Social Movements: An Overview and Assessment'. *Annual Review of Sociology* 26, no. 1 (2000): 611-639.

Bevins, Vincent. *If We Burn: The Mass Protest Decade and the Missing Revolution*. London: Hachette, 2023.

Bhandar, Brenna, and Rafeef Ziadah. *Revolutionary Feminisms: Conversations on Collective Action and Radical Thought*. London: Verso Books, 2020.

Bianchi, Alvaro. *Gramsci's Laboratory: Philosophy, History and Politics*. Chicago: Haymarket Books, 2021.

Biko, Steve. *I Write What I Like: A Selection of His Writings*. Edited by Aelred Stubbs. Harlow: Heinemann, 1987.

Bobbio, Norberto. 'Gramsci and the Conception of Civil Society'. In Mouffe, *Gramsci and Marxist Theory*, 21-47.

Boeddeling, Jann. 'From Resistance to Revolutionary Praxis: Subaltern Politics in the Tunisian Revolution'. PhD diss., London School of Economics and Political Science, 2020.

Boggs, Carl. *The Two Revolutions: Antonio Gramsci and the Dilemmas of Western Marxism*. Boston: South End Press, 1984.

Boothman, Derek. 'The Sources for Gramsci's Concept of Hegemony'. *Rethinking Marxism* 20, no. 2 (2008): 201-215.

Breaugh, Martin. *The Plebeian Experience: A Discontinuous History of Political Freedom*. Translated by Lazer Lederhendler. New York: Columbia University Press, 2013.

Briziarelli, Marco. 'To "Feel" and to "Understand" Political Struggle: The National-Popular Rhetoric of Podemos'. *Journal of Communication Inquiry* 40, no. 3 (2016): 287–304.

Browers, Michelle. 'Beginnings, Continuities and Revivals: An Inventory of the New Arab Left and an Ongoing Arab Left Tradition'. *Middle East Critique* 30, no. 1 (2021): 25–40.

Bruhn, Kathleen. 'Antonio Gramsci and the Palabra Verdadera: The Political Discourse of Mexico's Guerrilla Forces'. *Journal of Interamerican Studies and World Affairs* 41, no. 2 (1999): 29–55.

Buci-Glucksmann, Christine. 'State, Transition and Passive Revolution'. In Mouffe, *Gramsci and Marxist Theory*, 207–236.

———. *Gramsci and the State*. Translated by David Fernbach. London: Lawrence & Wishart, 1980.

Budiono, Rahmat, Bramasto Nugroho, and Dodik Ridho Nurrochmat. 'The Village Forest as a Counter Teritorialisation by Village Communities in Kampar Peninsula Riau'. *Jurnal Manajemen Hutan Tropika* 24, no. 3 (2018): 115–125.

Buey, Francisco Fernández. *Reading Gramsci*. Translated by Nicholas Gray. Chicago: Haymarket Books, 2014.

Bukharin, Nicolai. *Historical Materialism: A System of Sociology*. Authorized translation from the 3rd Russian edn. New York: International Publishers, 1925.

Burawoy, Michael. *Manufacturing Consent: Changes in the Labor Process under Monopoly Capitalism*. Chicago: University of Chicago Press, 2012.

Bures, Eliah. 'The Intellectual as Culture Warrior: Metapolitics and the European New Right'. *Fascism* 12, no. 1 (2023): 1–26.

Butler, Judith. *Gender Trouble*. London: Routledge, 2002.

Callinicos, Alex. 'The Limits of Passive Revolution'. *Capital & Class* 34, no.3 (2010): 491–507.

Carley, Robert. 'Agile Materialisms: Antonio Gramsci, Stuart Hall, Racialisation, and Modernity'. *Journal of Historical Sociology* 26, no. 4 (2013): 413–441.

Cassidy, Kevin J. 'Organic Intellectuals and the Committed Community: Irish Republicanism and Sinn Féin in the North'. *Irish Political Studies* 20, no. 3 (2005): 341–356.

Chalcraft, John. *The Striking Cabbies of Cairo and Other Stories: Crafts and Guilds in Egypt, 1863-1914*. Albany: State University of New York Press, 2004.

———. 'Engaging the State: Peasants and Petitions in Egypt on the Eve of Colonial Rule'. *International Journal of Middle East Studies* 37, no. 3 (2005): 303–325.

———. 'Counterhegemonic Effects: Weighing, Measuring, Petitions and Bureaucracy in Nineteenth-Century Egypt'. In Chalcraft and Noorani, *Counterhegemony in the Colony and Postcolony*, 179–203.

———. *The Invisible Cage: Syrian Migrant Workers in Lebanon*. Stanford, CA: Stanford University Press, 2009.

———. *Popular Politics in the Making of the Modern Middle East*. Cambridge: Cambridge University Press, 2016.

Chalcraft, John, and Alessandra Marchi. 'Guest Editors' Introduction: Gramsci in the Arab World'. *Middle East Critique* 30, no. 1 (2021): 1–8.

Chalcraft, John, and Yaseen Noorani, eds. *Counterhegemony in the Colony and Postcolony*. New York: Palgrave Macmillan, 2007.

Chalcraft, Margaret S. 'Staging Atlantic Slavery: Figuring Theatricality, Performance and Resistance in Anglo-Caribbean Narratives of Slavery and Abolition'. PhD diss., University of East Anglia, 2020.

Challand, Benoît. *Violence and Representation in the Arab Uprisings*. Cambridge: Cambridge University Press, 2023.

Chatterjee, Partha. *The Politics of the Governed: Reflections on Popular Politics in Most of the World*. New York: Columbia University Press, 2004.

Chaturvedi, Vinayak, ed. *Mapping Subaltern Studies and the Postcolonial*. London: Verso, 2000.

Chenoweth, Erica, and Maria. J. Stephan. *Why Civil Resistance Works: The Strategic Logic of Nonviolent Conflict*. New York: Columbia University Press, 2011.

Chibber, Vivek. *Postcolonial Theory and the Specter of Capital*. London: Verso, 2013.

Chodor, Tom. 'Not Throwing the Baby Out with the Bathwater: A Gramscian Response to Post-Hegemony'. *Contemporary Politics* 20, no. 4 (2014): 489–502.

Choplin, Armelle, and Riccardo Ciavolella. 'Gramsci and the African Città Futura: Urban Subaltern Politics from the Margins of Nouakchott, Mauritania'. *Antipode* 49, no. 2 (2017): 314–334.

Chrisman, Robert. 'Black Studies, the Talented Tenth, and the Organic Intellectual'. *The Black Scholar* 43, no. 3 (2013): 64–70.

Ciavolella, Riccardo. 'Gramsci in and beyond Resistances: The Search for an Autonomous Political Initiative among a Subaltern Group in the Beninese Savanna'. *Focaal*, no. 82 (2018): 49–63.

———. 'The Changing Meanings of People's Politics: Gramsci and Anthropology from Subaltern Classes to Contemporary Struggles'. In Antonini et al., *Revisiting Gramsci's Notebooks*, 266–282.

Clegg, Ian. *Workers' Self-Management in Algeria*. London: Allen Lane, 1971.

Cocks, Joan. *The Oppositional Imagination: Feminism, Critique and Political Theory*. London: Routledge, 1989.

Collins, Patricia Hill. *Intersectionality as Critical Social Theory*. Durham, NC: Duke University Press, 2019.

Collins, Patricia Hill, and Sirma Bilge. *Intersectionality*. 2nd edn. Cambridge: Polity, 2020.

Cospito, Giuseppe. *The Rhythm of Thought in Gramsci: A Diachronic Interpretation of Prison Notebooks*. Chicago: Haymarket Books, 2017.

Coutinho, Carlos. N. *Gramsci's Political Thought*. Chicago: Haymarket Books, 2013.

Cox, Laurence. *Why Social Movements Matter: An Introduction*. London: Rowman & Littlefield, 2018.

Cox, Laurence, and Alf G. Nilsen. *We Make Our Own History: Marxism and Social Movements in the Twilight of Neoliberalism*. London: Pluto Press, 2014.

Cox, Robert W. 'Social Forces, States and World Orders: Beyond International Relations Theory'. *Millennium* 10, no. 2 (1981): 126–155.

Crehan, Kate. *Gramsci's Common Sense: Inequality and Its Narratives*. Durham, NC: Duke University Press, 2016.

Crenshaw, Kimberlé Williams. 'Mapping the Margins: Intersectionality, Identity Politics, and Violence against Women of Color'. In *The Public Nature of Private Violence*, edited by Martha Albertson Fineman, 93–118. London: Routledge, 2013.

Crézégut, Anthony. 'An Imaginary Gramscianism? Early French Gramscianism and the Quest for "Marxist Humanism" (1947–65)'. In Antonini et al., *Revisiting Gramsci's Notebooks*, 430–450.

Croce, Benedetto. *What is Living and What is Dead of the Philosophy of Hegel*. London: Macmillan and Company, 1915.

Cronin, Stephanie, ed. *Subalterns and Social Protest: History from Below in the Middle East and North Africa*. London: Routledge, 2007.

Cuppi, Valentina. 'The Diffusion of Gramsci's Thought in the "Peripheral West" of Latin America'. In Antonini et al., *Revisiting Gramsci's Notebooks*, 412–429.

Dainotto, Roberto M., and Fredric Jameson, eds. *Gramsci in the World*. Durham, NC: Duke University Press, 2020.

D'Aria, Maria. 'Subalternity and Counter-Revolution: The Social Drivers of the Egyptian State Transformation'. PhD diss., University of Edinburgh, 2020.

Davis, Angela Y. *Women, Race and Class*. London: Penguin, 1981.

Dawood, Iman. 'Reworking the Common Sense of British Muslims: Salafism, Culture, and Politics within London's Muslim Community'. PhD diss., London School of Economics and Political Science, 2021.

de Beauvoir, Simone. *The Second Sex*. Translated by H. M. Parshley. London: Vintage, 1997.

de Certeau, Michel. *The Practice of Everyday Life*. Translated by Steven Rendall. Berkeley: University of California Press, 1984.

De Smet, Brecht. *A Dialectical Pedagogy of Revolt: Gramsci, Vygotsky, and the Egyptian Revolution*. Leiden: Brill, 2015.

———. *Gramsci on Tahrir: Revolution and Counter-Revolution in Egypt*. London: Pluto Press, 2016.

———. ' "Authoritarian Resilience" as Passive Revolution: A Gramscian Interpretation of Counter-Revolution in Egypt'. *Journal of North African Studies* 26, no. 6 (2021): 1077-1098.

Dean, Jodi. *Crowds and Party*. London: Verso Books, 2016.

Del Roio, Marcus. *The Prisms of Gramsci: The Political Formula of the United Front*. Leiden: Brill, 2015.

Della Porta, Donatella. *Where Did the Revolution Go? Contentious Politics and the Quality of Democracy*. Cambridge: Cambridge University Press, 2016.

Denning, Michael. 'Everyone a Legislator'. *New Left Review*, 129 (2021): 29-44.

Desai, Manali. 'Rethinking Hegemony: Caste, Class, and Political Subjectivities among Informal Workers in Ahmedabad'. In Nilsen and Roy, *New Subaltern Politics*, 54-75.

Dickens, Charles. *Bleak House*. Edited and introduced by Nicola Bradbury. Preface by Terry Eagleton. London: Penguin, 1996.

Domingo, Ligaya Rene. 'Building a Movement: Filipino American Union and Community Organizing in Seattle in the 1970s'. PhD diss., University of California, Berkeley, 2010.

Draper, Hal. *The Two Souls of Socialism*. Highland Park, MI: International Socialists, 1966.

Drinot, Paolo. 'Hegemony from Below: Print Workers, the State and the Communist Party in Peru, 1920-40'. In Chalcraft and Noorani, *Counterhegemony in the Colony and Postcolony*, 204-227.

Du Bois, W. E. B. *The Souls of Black Folk*. London: Routledge, 2015.

Duggan, Lisa. 'The New Homonormativity: The Sexual Politics of Neoliberalism'. In *Materializing Democracy: Toward a Revitalized Cultural Politics*, edited by Russ Castronovo and Dana D. Nelson, 175-194. Durham, NC: Duke University Press, 2002.

Dunayevskaya, Raya. *Rosa Luxemburg, Women's Liberation, and Marx's Philosophy of Revolution*. 2nd edn. Foreword by Adrienne Rich. Urbana: University of Illinois Press, 1991.

Duyvendak, Jan Willem, and James M. Jasper. *Players and Arenas: The Interactive Dynamics of Protest*. Amsterdam: Amsterdam University Press, 2015.

Egan, Daniel. 'Gramsci's War of Position as Siege Warfare: Some Lessons from History'. *Critique* 44, no. 4 (2016): 435-450.

———. 'Rosa Luxemburg and the Mass Strike: Rethinking Gramsci's Critique'. *Socialism and Democracy* 33, no. 2 (2019): 46-66.

Ekers, Michael, Gillian Hart, Stefan Kipfer, and Alex Loftus, eds. *Gramsci: Space, Nature, Politics*. Newark: Wiley, 2012.

Ekers, Michael, Stefan Kipfer, and Alex Loftus. 'On Articulation, Translation, and Populism: Gillian Hart's Postcolonial Marxism'. *Annals of the American Association of Geographers* 110, no. 5 (2020): 1577–1593.

Epstein, Barbara. *Political Protest and Cultural Revolution: Nonviolent Direct Action in the 1970s and 1980s*. Berkeley: University of California Press, 1991.

Eribon, Didier. *Insult and the Making of the Gay Self*. Durham, NC: Duke University Press, 2004.

Evans, Daniel John. 'Welsh Devolution as Passive Revolution'. *Capital & Class* 42, no. 3 (2018): 489–508.

Fanon, Frantz. *The Wretched of the Earth*. Translated by Constance Farrington. Preface by Jean-Paul Sartre. New York: Grove Press, 1965.

———. *Black Skin, White Masks*. Translated by Charles Markham. London: Pluto Press, 1986.

Fantasia, Rick. *Cultures of Solidarity*. Berkeley: University of California Press, 1989.

Fatton, Robert. 'Gramsci and the Legitimisation of the State: The Case of the Senegalese Passive Revolution'. *Canadian Journal of Political Science/Revue canadienne de science politique* 19, no. 4 (1986): 729–750.

Featherstone, David. *Solidarity: Hidden Histories and Geographies of Internationalism*. London: Zed, 2012.

Federici, Silvia. *Revolution at Point Zero: Housework, Reproduction, and Feminist Struggle*. New York: PM Press, 2020.

Feltrin, Lorenzo. 'The Struggles of Precarious Youth in Tunisia: The Case of the Kerkennah Movement'. *Review of African Political Economy* 45, no. 155 (2018): 44–63.

Femia, Joseph. *Gramsci's Political Thought: Hegemony, Consciousness, and the Revolutionary Process*. Oxford: Clarendon Press, 1987.

Feuerbach, Ludwig. *The Essence of Christianity*. Translated by George Eliot. Milton Keynes: Digireads.com Publishing, 2012.

Filippini, Michele. *Using Gramsci: A New Approach*. London: Pluto Press, 2016.

———. 'The Forms of a Travelling Theory: A New Approach to Gramsci's Texts'. *Middle East Critique* 30, no. 1 (2021): 9–24.

Fiori, Giuseppe. *Antonio Gramsci: Life of a Revolutionary*. London: Verso, 1990.

Fischman, Gustavo E., and Peter McLaren. 'Rethinking Critical Pedagogy and the Gramscian and Freirean Legacies: From Organic to Committed Intellectuals or Critical Pedagogy, Commitment, and Praxis'. *Cultural Studies <-> Critical Methodologies* 5, no. 4 (2005): 425–446.

Fonseca, Marco. *Gramsci's Critique of Civil Society: Towards a New Concept of Hegemony*. London: Routledge, 2016.

Fontana, Benedetto. 'Liberty and Domination: Civil Society in Gramsci'. *boundary 2* 33, no. 2 (2006): 51–74.

Foucault, Michel. *Discipline and Punish: The Birth of the Prison*. Translated by Alan Sheridan. Harmondsworth: Penguin Books, 1979.

———. *Archaeology of Knowledge*. Translated by A. M. Sheridan Smith. London: Routledge, 2002.

———. *The History of Sexuality, 1: The Will to Knowledge*. Translated by Robert Hurley. London: Penguin, 2019.

Fraser, Nancy. 'Contradictions of Capital and Care'. *New Left Review* 100, no. 100 (2016): 99–117.

Freeman, Jo. 'The Tyranny of Structurelessness'. *Berkeley Journal of Sociology* (1972): 151–164.

Fresu, Gianni. *Antonio Gramsci: An Intellectual Biography*. Cham: Palgrave Macmillan, 2023.

Friedan, Betty. *The Feminine Mystique*. Introduction by Lionel Shriver. London: Penguin, 2010.

Fromm, Erich, ed. *Socialist Humanism*. New York: Doubleday, 1965.

Frosini, Fabio. *De Gramsci à Marx: Idéologie, verité et politique*. Paris: Éditions Critiques, 2019.

———. 'Time and Revolution in Gramsci's *Prison Notebooks*'. In Antonini et al., *Revisiting Gramsci's Notebooks*, 125–140.

Gaudichaud, Franck, Massimo Modonesi, and Jeffery R. Webber. *The Impasse of the Latin American Left*. Durham, NC: Duke University Press, 2022.

Geier, Joel. 'Zinovievism and the Degeneration of World Communism'. *International Socialist Review* 93 (2014): 41–73.

Gerges, Fawaz. *The Rise and Fall of Al-Qaeda*. Oxford: Oxford University Press, 2011.

Gervais, Julie, Claire Lemercier, and Willy Pelletier. *La valeur du service public*. Paris: La Découverte, 2021.

———. *La haine des fonctionnaires*. Paris: Éditions Amsterdam, 2024.

Gervasio, Gennaro. 'Marxism or Left-Wing Nationalism? The New Left in Egypt in the 1970s'. In *Arab Lefts: Histories and Legacies, 1950s–1970s*, edited by Laure Guirguis, 148–168. Edinburgh: Edinburgh University Press, 2020.

Gervasio, Gennaro, and Patrizia Manduchi. 'Introduction: Reading the Revolutionary Process in North Africa with Gramsci'. *Journal of North African Studies* 26, no. 6 (2021): 1051–1056, https://doi.org/10.1080/13629387.2020 .1801264.

Gervasio, Gennaro, and Andrea Teti. 'Prelude to the Revolution: Independent Civic Activists in Mubarak's Egypt and the Quest for Hegemony'. *Journal of North African Studies* 26, no. 6 (2021): 1099–1121.

Gill, Stephen. 'Toward a Postmodern Prince? The Battle in Seattle as a Moment in the New Politics of Globalisation'. *Millennium* 29, no. 1 (2000): 131–140.

Gilsenan, Michael. *Lords of the Lebanese Marches: Violence and Narrative in an Arab Society*. Berkeley: University of California Press, 1996.

Glassman, Jonathon. 'The Bondsman's New Clothes: The Contradictory Consciousness of Slave Resistance on the Swahili Coast'. *Journal of African History* 32, no. 2 (1991): 277–312.

Goffman, Erving. *Frame Analysis: An Essay on the Organization of Experience*. Cambridge, MA: Harvard University Press, 1974.

Goldstone, Jack A. 'Toward a Fourth Generation of Revolutionary Theory'. *Annual Review of Political Science* 4, no. 1 (2001): 139–187.

Graeber, David. *Direct Action: An Ethnography*. Oakland, CA: AK Press, 2009.

———. *The Democracy Project: A History, a Crisis, a Movement*. New York: Random House, 2013.

Gramsci, Antonio. *Selections from the Prison Notebooks of Antonio Gramsci*. Edited and translated by Quintin Hoare and Geoffrey Nowell Smith. London: Lawrence & Wishart, 1971.

———. *Quaderni del Carcere*. 4 vols. Edited by Valentino Gerratana. Torino: Einaudi, 1975.

———. *History, Philosophy and Culture in the Young Gramsci*. Edited by Pedro Cavalcanti and Paul Piccone. Saint Louis: Telos Press, 1975.

———. *Selections from Political Writings (1910-1920)*. Edited by Quintin Hoare. Translated by John Mathews. London: Lawrence & Wishart, 1977.

———. *Selections from Political Writings (1921-1926)*. Edited and translated by Quintin Hoare. London: Lawrence & Wishart, 1978.

———. *Selections from Cultural Writings*. Edited by David Forgacs and Geoffrey Nowell-Smith. Translated by William Boelhower. London: Lawrence & Wishart, 1985.

———. *Letters from Prison*. 2 vols. Edited by Frank Rosengarten. Translated by Raymond Rosenthal. New York: Columbia University Press, 1994.

———. *Further Selections from the Prison Notebooks*. Edited and translated by Derek Boothman. London: Lawrence & Wishart, 1995.

———. *Prison Notebooks*. 3 vols. Edited and translated by Joseph A. Buttigieg. New York: Columbia University Press, 2011.

———. *A Great and Terrible World: The Pre-Prison Letters, 1908-1926*. Edited and translated by Derek Boothman. London: Lawrence & Wishart, 2014.

———. *Subaltern Social Groups: A Critical Edition of Prison Notebook 25*. Edited and translated by Joseph A. Buttigieg and Marcus E. Green. New York: Columbia University Press, 2021.

Gray, Kevin. 'Labour and the State in China's Passive Revolution'. *Capital & Class* 34, no. 3 (2010): 449–467.

Grayson, John. 'Developing the Politics of the Trade Union Movement: Popular Workers' Education in South Yorkshire, UK, 1955 to 1985'. *International Labor and Working-Class History* 90 (2016): 111-132.

Guha, Ranajit. *Dominance without Hegemony: History and Power in Colonial India*. Cambridge, MA: Harvard University Press, 1997.

———. *Elementary Aspects of Peasant Insurgency in Colonial India*. Durham, NC: Duke University Press, 1999.

———. 'Gramsci in India: Homage to a Teacher'. *Journal of Modern Italian Studies* 16, no. 2 (2011): 288-295.

———. 'The Prose of Counter-Insurgency 1'. In *The Rise and Fall of Modern Empires*, edited by Saul Dubow, 145-186. London: Routledge, 2013.

Guha, Ranajit, and Gayatri Chakravorty Spivak, eds. *Selected Subaltern Studies*. Oxford: Oxford University Press, 1988.

Gürcan, Efe Can. 'Hugo Chávez's Unwritten Testament: National-Democratic Struggle and Contradictions of Socialism'. *Dialectical Anthropology* 37, no. 3-4 (2013): 341-356.

Gurr, Ted. *Why Men Rebel*. London: Routledge, 2015.

Hall, Stuart. *The Hard Road to Renewal: Thatcherism and the Crisis of the Left*. London: Verso, 1988.

Hall, Stuart, and David Morley. *Essential Essays, Volume 1: Foundations of Cultural Studies*. Durham, NC: Duke University Press, 2018.

Hamming, Tore Refslund. 'Jihadi Politics: Fitna within the Sunni Jihadi Movement, 2014-2019'. PhD diss., European University Institute, 2020.

Hanchard, Michael G. *Orpheus and Power: The Movimento Negro of Rio de Janeiro and São Paulo, Brazil, 1945-1988*. Princeton, NJ: Princeton University Press, 1991.

Hardt, Michael, and Antonio Negri. *Multitude: War and Democracy in the Age of Empire*. London: Penguin, 2004.

———. *Assembly*. Oxford: Oxford University Press, 2017.

Harris, Christopher. 'The Black Organic Intellectual Tradition and the Challenges of Educating and Developing Organic Intellectuals in the 21st Century'. *Journal of Intersectionality* 2, no. 1 (2018): 51-107.

Harvey, David, and Raymond Williams. 'Militant Particularism and Global Ambition: The Conceptual Politics of Place, Space, and Environment in the Work of Raymond Williams'. *Social Text*, no. 42 (1995): 69-98.

Hauptmann, Emily. *Foundations and American Political Science: The Transformation of a Discipline, 1945-1970*. Lawrence: University Press of Kansas, 2022.

Hegel, Georg Wilhelm Friedrich. *The Science of Logic*. Translated and edited by George Di Giovanni. Cambridge: Cambridge University Press, 2010.

Held, David, and Anthony McGrew. *Globalisation/Anti-Globalisation: Beyond the Great Divide*. Cambridge: Polity, 2007.

Henck, Nick. *Insurgent Marcos: The Political-Philosophical Formation of the Zapatista Subcommander*. Durham, NC: Editorial A Contracorriente, 2016.

Hesketh, Chris. 'From Passive Revolution to Silent Revolution: Class Forces and the Production of State, Space and Scale in Modern Mexico'. *Capital & Class* 34, no. 3 (2010): 383-407.

Hesketh, Chris, and Adam David Morton. 'Spaces of Uneven Development and Class Struggle in Bolivia: Transformation or Trasformismo?' *Antipode* 46, no. 1 (2014): 149-169.

Hobsbawm, Eric. *Primitive Rebels: Studies in Archaic Forms of Social Movement in the 19th and 20th Centuries*. Manchester: Manchester University Press, 1971.

———. *The Age of Extremes: The Short Twentieth Century, 1914-1991*. London: Abacus Books, 1994.

Holub, Renate. *Antonio Gramsci: Beyond Marxism and Postmodernism*. London: Routledge, 2005.

Honneth, Alex. *The Idea of Socialism*. Cambridge: Polity, 2018.

hooks, bell. *Ain't I a Woman: Black Women and Feminism*. London: Routledge, 2015.

Howson, Richard. *Challenging Hegemonic Masculinity*. London: Routledge, 2006.

Huntington, Samuel. 'The Clash of Civilisations'. *Foreign Affairs* 72, no. 3 (1993): 22-49.

Ismail, Salwa. *Political Life in Cairo's New Quarters: Encountering the Everyday State*. Minneapolis: University of Minnesota Press, 2006.

Ives, Peter. *Language and Hegemony in Gramsci*. London: Pluto Press, 2004.

Jackson, Robert. 'The "Mummification of Culture" in Gramsci's *Prison Notebooks*'. In Antonini et al., *Revisiting Gramsci's Notebooks*, 312-335.

James, C. L. R. *The Black Jacobins: Toussaint L'Ouverture and the San Domingo Revolution*. London: Penguin, 2001.

Jessop, Bob. 'Gramsci as a Spatial Theorist'. *Critical Review of International Social and Political Philosophy* 8, no. 4 (2005): 421-437.

Jones, Owen. *This Land: The Struggle for the Left*. London: Penguin, 2020.

Joshi, Sanjay, and Bhagwan Josh, *Struggle for Hegemony in India*. New Delhi: Sage, 2011.

Judson, Fred. 'Sandinista Revolutionary Morale'. *Latin American Perspectives* 14, no. 1 (1987): 19-42.

Judy, R. A. 'Gramsci on *la questione dei negri: Gli intelletuali* and the Poesis of Americanisation'. In Dainotto and Jameson, *Gramsci in the World*, 165-178.

Juris, Jeffrey S., and Alex Khasnabish, eds. *Insurgent Encounters: Transnational Activism, Ethnography, and the Political*. Durham, NC: Duke University Press, 2013.

Kalecki, Michał. 'Social and Economic Aspects of Intermediate Regimes'. In *Selected Essays on the Economic Growth of the Socialist and the Mixed Economy*, edited by Zdislaw Sadowski, 162–169. Cambridge: Cambridge University Press, 1972.

Kandil, Hazem. 'Islamising Egypt? Testing the Limits of Gramscian Counterhegemonic Strategies'. *Theory and Society* 40 (2011): 37–62.

Kandiyoti, Deniz. 'Bargaining with Patriarchy'. *Gender & Society* 2, no. 3 (1988): 274–290.

Kapadia, Karin. '"Mirrored in God": Gramsci, Religion and Dalit Women Subalterns in South India'. *Religions* 10, no. 12 (2019): 666. https://doi.org/10.3390/rel10120666.

Karriem, Abdurazack. 'The Rise and Transformation of the Brazilian Landless Movement into a Counter-Hegemonic Political Actor: A Gramscian Analysis'. *Geoforum* 40, no. 3 (2009): 316–325.

Katsiaficas, George. *Asia's Unknown Uprisings, Volume 1*. New York: PM Press, 2012.

Keck, Margaret E., and Kathryn Sikkink. *Activists beyond Borders: Advocacy Networks in International Politics*. Ithaca, NY: Cornell University Press, 1998.

Kelley, Robin D. G. *Freedom Dreams: The Black Radical Imagination*. Boston: Beacon Press, 2002.

———. *Thelonious Monk: The Life and Times of an American Original*. New York: Free Press, 2009.

Ketchley, Neil. *Egypt in a Time of Revolution*. Cambridge: Cambridge University Press, 2017.

Kilibarda, Konstantin. 'Lessons from #Occupy in Canada: Contesting Space, Settler Consciousness and Erasures within the 99%'. *Journal of Critical Globalisation Studies* 5 (2012): 24–41.

King, Peter. 'Edward Thompson's Contribution to Eighteenth-Century Studies: The Patrician–Plebeian Model Re-Examined'. *Social History* 21, no. 2 (1996): 215–228.

Khalil, Heba M. 'Revolution in Parallel Times: An Egyptian Village's Lived Revolution'. LSE Middle East Centre, 2021.

Knapp, Michael, Anja Flach, and Ercan Ayboğa. *Revolution in Rojava: Democratic Autonomy and Women's Liberation in Syrian Kurdistan*. Foreword by David Graeber, afterword by Asya Abdullah, and translated by Janet Biehl. London: Pluto Press, 2016.

Knight, Alan. 'Hegemony, Counterhegemony and the Mexican Revolution'. In Chalcraft and Noorani, *Counterhegemony in the Colony and Postcolony*, 23–48.

Kurzman, Charles. *The Unthinkable Revolution in Iran*. Cambridge, MA: Harvard University Press, 2004.

Labriola, Antonio. *Essays on the Materialistic Conception of History*. Chicago: Charles H. Kerr & Company, 1908.

Laclau, Ernesto. *Politics and Ideology in Marxist Theory: Capitalism, Fascism, Populism*. London: Verso, 1979.

Laclau, Ernesto, and Chantal Mouffe. *Hegemony and Socialist Strategy: Towards a Radical Democratic Politics*. London: Verso, 1985.

Laroui, Abdallah. *Les origines sociales et culturelles de nationalisme Marocain, 1830-1912*. Paris: Maspero, 1977.

Lather, Patti. 'Research as Praxis'. *Harvard Educational Review* 56, no. 3 (1986): 257-278.

Laveille, Yasmine. 'Contestation in Marginalised Spaces: Dynamics of Popular Mobilization and Demobilization in Upper Egypt since 25 January 2011'. PhD diss., London School of Economics and Political Science, 2016.

Lawson, George. *Anatomies of Revolution*. Cambridge: Cambridge University Press, 2019.

Le Bon, Gustave. *The Crowd: A Study of the Popular Mind*. London: T. F. Unwin, 1896.

Lears, T. J. Jackson. 'The Concept of Cultural Hegemony: Problems and Possibilities'. *American Historical Review* 90, no. 3 (1985): 567-593. https://doi.org/10.2307/1860957.

Ledwith, Margaret. 'Antonio Gramsci and Feminism: The Elusive Nature of Power'. *Educational Philosophy and Theory* 41, no. 6 (2009): 684-697.

Leipold, Bruno. 'Marx's Social Republic'. In *Radical Republicanism: Recovering the Tradition's Popular Heritage*, edited by Bruno Leipold, Karma Nabulsi, and Stuart White, 172-193. Oxford: Oxford University Press, 2020.

———. *Citizen Marx: Republicanism and the Formation of Karl Marx's Social and Political Thought*. Princeton, NJ: Princeton University Press, 2024.

Lenin, Vladimir I. *The State and Revolution*. Introduced and translated by Robert Service. London: Penguin, 1992.

Leontidou, Lila. 'Athens in the Mediterranean "Movement of the Piazzas": Spontaneity in Material and Virtual Public Spaces'. *City* 16, no. 3 (2012): 299-312.

Levenson, Zachary. 'Make "Articulation" Gramscian Again'. In *Ethnographies of Power: Working Radical Concepts with Gillian Hart*, edited by Sharad Chari, Mark Hunter, and Melanie Samson, 187-216. Johannesburg: Wits University Press, 2022.

Levy, Carl. '"Sovversivismo": The Radical Political Culture of Otherness in Liberal Italy'. *Journal of Political Ideologies* 12, no. 2 (2007): 147-161.

Li, Chunyun. 'From Insurgency to Movement: An Embryonic Labor Movement Undermining Hegemony in South China'. *Industrial and Labour Relations Review* 74, no. 4 (2021): 843-874.

Liguori, Guido. *Gramsci's Pathways*. Leiden: Brill, 2015.

Lih, Lars T. *Lenin Rediscovered: 'What is to be Done?' in Context*. Leiden: Brill, 2005.

———. *Lenin*. London: Reaktion Books, 2012.

Lin, Chun. *The Transformation of Chinese Socialism*. Durham, NC: Duke University Press, 2006.

———. 'The Language of Class in China'. *Socialist Register* 51 (2015): 24-53.

Lindsay, Melanie Marie. 'An Exploratory Analysis of How Maya Angelou, Audre Lorde, and Patrisse Cullors Radicalized the Meaning and Practice of Self-Care'. PhD diss., Claremont Graduate University, 2022.

Lipsitz, George. 'The Struggle for Hegemony'. *Journal of American History* 75, no. 1 (1988): 146-150.

Liu, Kang. 'Hegemony and Cultural Revolution'. *New Literary History* 28, no. 1 (1997): 69-86. https://doi.org/10.1353/nlh.1997.0010.

Lockman, Zachary. 'Imagining the Working Class: Culture, Nationalism, and Class Formation in Egypt, 1899-1914'. *Poetics Today* (1994): 157-190.

Loftus, Alex. 'A Time for Gramsci'. In *The International Handbook of Political Ecology*, edited by Raymond L. Bryant, 89-102. Cheltenham: Edward Elgar Publishing, 2015.

———. 'Gramsci as a Historical Geographical Materialist'. In Antonini et al., *Revisiting Gramsci's Notebooks*, 9-22.

Lorde, Audre. *Sister Outsider*. London: Penguin, 2019.

Louis, Édouard. *The End of Eddy: A Novel*. Translated by Michael Lucey. London: Vintage, 2017.

Luain, Kerron Ó. 'Gaelscoil Activists as a Postcolonial Subaltern and the Emergence of the Gaelscoileanna, ca. 1970'. *Radical History Review* 2022, no. 143 (2022): 64-77.

Luxemburg, Rosa. *'Reform or Revolution' and 'The Mass Strike'*. Denver, CO: Frederic Ellis, n.d.

Madhok, Sumi. *Rethinking Agency: Developmentalism, Gender and Rights*. Delhi: Routledge India, 2014.

———. *On Vernacular Rights Cultures: The Politics of Origins, Human Rights, and Gendered Struggles for Justice*. Cambridge: Cambridge University Press, 2022.

Maeckelbergh, Marianne. *The Will of the Many: How the Alterglobalisation Movement is Changing the Face of Democracy*. London: Pluto Press, 2009.

Mahmood, Saba. *Politics of Piety: The Islamic Revival and the Feminist Subject*. Princeton, NJ: Princeton University Press, 2011.

Malley, Robert. *The Call from Algeria: Third Worldism, Revolution, and the Turn to Islam*. Berkeley: University of California Press, 1996.

Mallick, Ayyaz. 'Beyond "Domination without Hegemony": Passive Revolution(s) in Pakistan'. *Studies in Political Economy* 98, no. 3 (2017): 239-262.

Manduchi, Patrizia. 'Antonio Gramsci in the Arab World: The Ongoing Debate'. In Dainotto and Jameson, *Gramsci in the World*, 224–239.

———. 'Between Old and New Epistemological Paradigms: Gramscian Readings of Revolutionary Processes in Egypt and Tunisia'. *Journal of North African Studies* 26, no. 6 (2021): 1057–1076.

Manduchi, Patrizia, Alessandra Marchi, and Giuseppe Vacca. *Gramsci nel mondo arabo*. Bologna: Il Mulino, 2017.

Marchi, Alessandra. 'Molecular Transformations: Reading the Arab Uprisings with and beyond Gramsci'. *Middle East Critique* 30, no. 1 (2021): 67–85.

Marcos, Subcomandante. *Professionals of Hope: The Selected Writings of Subcomandante Marcos*. Afterword by Gabriela Jauregui. N.p.: The Song Cave, 2017.

Marković, Mihailo. *From Affluence to Praxis: Philosophy and Social Criticism*. Foreword by Erich Fromm. Ann Arbor: University of Michigan, 1974.

Marsh, Steven. 'Gramsci and Contemporary Spanish Politics'. In *Language, Image and Power in Luso-Hispanic Cultural Studies*, edited by Susan Larson, 121–134. London: Routledge, 2021.

Martínez, José Ciro. 'Site of Resistance or Apparatus of Acquiescence? Tactics at the Bakery'. *Middle East Law and Governance* 10, no. 2 (2018): 160–184.

Marx, Karl. *Critique of Hegel's Philosophy of Right* (1843). Translated by Joseph O'Malley (Oxford: Oxford University Press, 1970), https://www.marxists.org/archive/marx/works/download/Marx_Critique_of_Hegels_Philosophy_of_Right.pdf.

———. 'Theses on Feuerbach'. In *Marx/Engels Selected Works, Volume 1*. Translated by W. Lough. Moscow: Progress Publishers, 1969. https://www.marxists.org/archive/marx/works/1845/theses/theses.htm

Massad, Joseph. 'Re-Orienting Desire: The Gay International and the Arab World'. *Public Culture* 14, no. 2 (2002): 361–386. https://doi.org/10.1215/08992363-14-2-361.

Mayer, Robert. 'The Status of a Classic Text: Lenin's *What is to be Done?* after 1902'. *History of European Ideas* 22, no. 4 (1996): 307–320.

———. 'One Step Forward, Two Steps Back: On Lars Lih's Lenin'. *Historical Materialism: Research in Critical Marxist Theory* 18, no. 3 (2010): 47–63.

Mayo, Peter. 'Antonio Gramsci's Impact on Critical Pedagogy'. *Critical Sociology* 41, no. 7–8 (2015): 1121–1136.

McAdam, Doug, Sidney Tarrow, and Charles Tilly. *Dynamics of Contention*. Cambridge: Cambridge University Press, 2001.

McKittrick, Katherine. *Sylvia Wynter: On Being Human as Praxis*. Durham, NC: Duke University Press, 2015.

McNally, David. 'Intersections and Dialectics: Critical Reconstructions in Social Reproduction Theory'. In *Social Reproduction Theory*, edited by Tithi Bhattacharya, foreword by Lise Vogel, 94–111. London: Pluto Press, 2017.

Meek, David. 'Learning as Territoriality: The Political Ecology of Education in the Brazilian Landless Workers' Movement'. *Journal of Peasant Studies* 42, no. 6 (2015): 1179–1200.

Mehta, Uday Singh. *Liberalism and Empire: A Study in Nineteenth-Century British Liberal Thought*. Chicago: University of Chicago Press, 2018.

Meret, Susi. 'What Can We Learn from Gramsci Today? Migrant Subalternity and the Refugee Movements: Perspectives from the Lampedusa in Hamburg'. In Antonini et al., *Revisiting Gramsci's Notebooks*, 209–230.

Merone, Fabio. 'Analysing Revolutionary Islamism: Ansar al-Sharia Tunisia according to Gramsci'. *Journal of North African Studies* 26, no. 6 (2021): 1122–1143.

Merrington, John. 'Theory and Practice in Gramsci's Marxism'. *The Socialist Register* 5 (1968): 145–176.

Mignolo, Walter D. 'Mariátegui and Gramsci in "Latin" America: Between Revolution and Decoloniality'. In Srivastava and Bhattacharya, *Postcolonial Gramsci*, 191–217.

Mignolo, Walter. D., and C. E. Walsh. *On Decoloniality: Concepts, Analytics, Praxis*. Durham, NC: Duke University Press, 2018.

Mitchell, Timothy. 'Everyday Metaphors of Power'. *Theory and Society* 19, no. 5 (1990): 545–577. https://doi.org/10.1007/BF00147026.

———. 'McJihad: Islam in the US Global Order'. *Social Text* 20, no. 4 (2002): 1–18.

Modonesi, Massimo. *Subalternity, Antagonism, Autonomy: Constructing the Political Subject*. Translated by Adriana V. Rendón Garrido and Philip Roberts. Foreword by John Holloway. London: Pluto Press, 2013.

Mohanty, Chandra Talpade, and Linda Carty, eds. *Feminist Freedom Warriors: Genealogies, Justice, Politics, and Hope*. Chicago: Haymarket Books, 2018.

Morera, Esteve. 'Gramsci and Democracy'. *Canadian Journal of Political Science/ Revue canadienne de science politique* 23, no. 1 (1990): 23–37.

Morton, Adam D. 'Mexico, Neoliberal Restructuring and the EZLN: A Neo-Gramscian Analysis'. In *Globalisation and the Politics of Resistance*, edited by B. K. Gills, 255–279. London: Palgrave Macmillan, 2000.

———. 'The Continuum of Passive Revolution'. *Capital & Class* 34, no. 3 (2010): 315–342.

Mossallam, Alia. '*Hikāyāt Sha'b*—Stories of Peoplehood: Nasserism, Popular Politics and Songs in Egypt, 1956-1973'. PhD diss., London School of Economics and Political Science, 2012.

Motta, Sara C. 'Old Tools and New Movements in Latin America: Political Science as Gatekeeper or Intellectual Illuminator?' *Latin American Politics and Society* 51, no. 1 (2009): 31–56.

Mouffe, Chantal, ed. *Gramsci and Marxist Theory*. London: Routledge, 1979.

Moxham, Christopher, and Miriam Grant. 'Passive Revolution: A Church-Military Partnership in the Philippines'. *Singapore Journal of Tropical Geography* 34, no. 3 (2013): 307–321.

Mumby, Dennis K. 'The Problem of Hegemony: Rereading Gramsci for Organizational Communication Studies'. *Western Journal of Communication* 61, no. 4 (1997): 343–375.

Murray, Douglas. *The Madness of Crowds: Gender, Race and Identity*. London: Bloomsbury, 2019.

Nilsen, Alf Gunvald, and Srila Roy. *New Subaltern Politics: Reconceptualising Hegemony and Resistance in Contemporary India*. Delhi: Oxford University Press, 2015.

Noorani, Yaseen. *Culture and Hegemony in the Colonial Middle East*. New York: Palgrave Macmillan, 2010.

Nunes, Rodrigo. *Organization of the Organizationless: Collective Action after Networks*. Lüneburg, Germany: Mute, 2014.

———. *Neither Vertical nor Horizontal: A Theory of Political Organization*. London: Verso Books, 2021.

O'Hanlon, Rosalind. 'Recovering the Subject: Subaltern Studies and Histories of Resistance in Colonial South Asia'. *Modern Asian Studies* 22, no. 1 (1988): 189–224. http://www.jstor.org/stable/312498.

Öcalan, Abdullah. *The Political Thought of Abdullah Öcalan: Kurdistan, Woman's Revolution and Democratic Confederalism*. Foreword by Nadje Al-Ali. London: Pluto Press, 2017.

Paggi, Leonardo. 'Gramsci's General Theory of Marxism'. In Mouffe, *Gramsci and Marxist Theory*, 113–167.

Panichi, Alessio. 'Between Belonging and Originality: Norberto Bobbio's Interpretation of Gramsci'. In Antonini et al., *Revisiting Gramsci's Notebooks*, 391–411.

Panizza, Francisco. 'Parties, Democracy and Grounded Utopias: A Reply to Sara Motta'. *Political Studies* 55, no. 4 (2007): 885–892.

Papadopoulos, Dimitris, Niamh Stephenson, and Vassilis Tsianos. *Escape Routes: Control and Subversion in the 21st century*. London: Pluto Press, 2008.

Perry, Jeffrey. B. *Hubert Harrison: The Struggle for Equality, 1918–1927*. New York: Columbia University Press, 2020.

Pillay, Pravina. 'Gramsci on Language and Its Relevance to South Africa'. *Journal of Gender, Information and Development in Africa (JGIDA)* 7, no. 1 (2018): 39–47.

Pleyers, Geoffrey. *Alter-Globalisation: Becoming Actors in a Global Age*. Cambridge: Polity, 2010.

Popular Memory Group. 'Popular Memory: Theory, Politics, Method'. In *Making Histories: Studies in History-Writing and Politics*. Edited by Richard Johnson, Gregor McLennan, Bill Schwarz, and David Sutton, 205-253. London: Hutchinson, 1982.

Posusney, Maria P. 'Irrational Workers: The Moral Economy of Labor Protest in Egypt'. *World Politics* 46, no. 1 (1993): 83-120.

Proudfoot, Philip. *Rebel Populism: Revolution and Loss among Syrian Labourers in Beirut*. Manchester: Manchester University Press, 2022.

Ramaioli, Massimo. 'Salafism as Gramscian Informed Vanguardism'. *Contemporary Islam* 17, no. 2 (2023): 297-318.

Rehmann, Jan. 'Occupy Wall Street and the Question of Hegemony: A Gramscian Analysis'. *Socialism and Democracy* 27, no. 1 (2013): 1-18.

———. 'Bernie Sanders and the Hegemonic Crisis of Neoliberal Capitalism: What Next?' *Socialism and Democracy* 30, no. 3 (2016): 1-11.

Roberts, Hugh. 'Moral Economy or Moral Polity? The Political Anthropology of Algerian Riots'. Crisis States Research Centre, London School of Economics and Political Science, 2002.

Roberts, Philip. 'Passive Revolution in Brazil: Struggles over Hegemony, Religion and Development, 1964-2007'. *Third World Quarterly* 36, no. 9 (2015): 1663-1681.

———. 'Gramsci in Brazil: From the PCB to the MST'. *Thesis Eleven* 147, no. 1 (2018): 62-75.

Robinson, Cedric J. *Black Marxism: The Making of the Black Radical Tradition*. Foreword by Robin D. G. Kelley. Chapel Hill: University of North Carolina Press, 2000.

———. *An Anthropology of Marxism*. Foreword by H. L. T. Quan. London: Pluto Press, 2019.

Roccu, Roberto. *The Political Economy of the Egyptian Revolution: Mubarak, Economic Reforms and Failed Hegemony*. Basingstoke: Palgrave Macmillan, 2013.

Rosengarten, Frank. *The Revolutionary Marxism of Antonio Gramsci*. Leiden: Brill, 2013.

Roy, Srila. 'Affective Politics and the Sexual Subaltern: Lesbian Activism in Eastern India'. In Nilsen and Roy, *New Subaltern Politics*, 149-175.

Russell, Kate Elisabeth. *My Dark Vanessa: A Novel*. New York: William Morrow, 2020.

Saccarelli, Emanuele. 'The Intellectual in Question: Antonio Gramsci and the Crisis of Academia'. *Cultural Studies* 25, no. 6 (2011): 757-782.

Safieddine, Hicham. 'Mahdi Amel: On Colonialism, Sectarianism and Hegemony'. *Middle East Critique* 30, no. 1 (2021): 41-56.

Said, Edward. *Orientalism: Western Conceptions of the Orient*. New York: Pantheon, 1978.

———. *The Politics of Dispossession: The Struggle for Palestinian Self-Determination, 1969-1994*. London: Chatto, 1994.

Salamanca, Omar Jabary. 'The Madrid Conference: Translating the One-State Slogan into Research and Political Action Agendas'. *Arab World Geographer* 10, no. 1 (2007): 57-80.

Salamini, Leonardo. *The Sociology of Political Praxis: An Introduction to Gramsci's Theory*. London: Routledge, 1981.

Salem, Sara. 'Critical Interventions in Debates on the Arab Revolutions: Centring Class'. *Review of African Political Economy* 45, no. 155 (2018): 125-134.

———. *Anticolonial Afterlives in Egypt: The Politics of Hegemony*. Cambridge: Cambridge University Press, 2020.

Salvadori, Massimo. 'Gramsci and the PCI: Two Conceptions of Hegemony'. In Mouffe, *Gramsci and Marxist Theory*, 237-258.

Sanbonmatsu, John. *The Postmodern Prince: Critical Theory, Left Strategy, and the Making of a New Political Subject*. New York: New York University Press, 2004.

Sandoval, Fonseca, and José Daniel. 'Colonialidad del saber jurídico y derecho neo-constitucional en Colombia'. *Trans-pasando Fronteras* 12 (2018): 45-81.

Sartre, Jean-Paul. *Saint Genet: Actor and Martyr*. Translated by Bernard Frechtman. Minneapolis: University of Minnesota Press, 2012.

Scott, James C. *Weapons of the Weak: Everyday Forms of Peasant Resistance*. New Haven: Yale University Press, 1985.

———. *Domination and the Arts of Resistance: Hidden Transcripts*. New Haven: Yale University Press, 1990.

———. *The Art of Not Being Governed: An Anarchist History of Upland Southeast Asia*. New Haven: Yale University Press, 2009.

Sewell, William. 'Historical Events as Transformations of Structures: Inventing Revolution at the Bastille'. *Theory and Society* 25, no. 6 (1996): 841-881.

Shamshiri-Fard, Marral. 'Challenging Empire in the Middle East: Revolutionary Transnationalism in the Iranian and Arab Lefts, 1963-1979'. PhD diss., London School of Economics and Political Science, 2025.

Sharp, Gene. *From Dictatorship to Democracy: A Conceptual Framework for Liberation*. New York: The New Press, 2012.

Shenker, Jack. *Now We Have Your Attention: The New Politics of the People*. New York: Random House, 2019.

Simms, Rupe. 'Black Theology, a Weapon in the Struggle for Freedom: A Gramscian Analysis'. *Race and Society* 2, no. 2 (2000): 165-193.

Simon, Roger. *Gramsci's Political Thought: An Introduction*. 3rd edn. London: Lawrence & Wishart, 2015.

Singerman, Diane. *Avenues of Participation: Family, Politics, and Networks in Urban Quarters of Cairo*. Princeton, NJ: Princeton University Press, 2020.

Sitrin, Marina. *Horizontalism: Voices of Popular Power in Argentina*. Oakland, CA: AK Press, 2006.

Skocpol, Theda. 'Rentier State and Shi'a Islam in the Iranian Revolution'. *Theory and Society* 11, no. 3 (1982): 265-283.

Slothuus, Lukas. 'Faith between Reason and Affect: Thinking with Antonio Gramsci'. *Distinktion: Journal of Social Theory* 22, no. 3 (2021): 340-357.

Sorel, Georges. *Reflections on Violence*. Translated by T. E. Hulme. Miami, FL: Hard Press, n.d.

Spivak, Gayatri Chakravorty. 'Can the Subaltern Speak?' In *Marxism and the Interpretation of Culture*, edited by Cary Nelson and Lawrence Grossberg, 271-313. Urbana: University of Illinois Press, 1988.

———. 'In Response: Looking Back, Looking Forward'. In *Can the Subaltern Speak? Reflections on the History of an Idea*, edited by Rosalind C. Morris, 225-236. New York: Columbia University Press, 2010.

Srivastava, Neelam, and Baidik Bhattacharya, eds. *The Postcolonial Gramsci*. New York: Routledge, 2012.

Sum, Ngai-Ling. 'The Makings of Subaltern Subjects: Embodiment, Contradictory Consciousness, and Re-Hegemonisation of the Diaosi in China'. In *Chinese Labour in the Global Economy*, edited by Andreas Bieler and Chun-Yi Lee, 120-134. London: Routledge, 2018.

Tamburrano, Giuseppe. *Antonio Gramsci*. Milano: SugarCo Edisioni, 1963.

Tarlau, Rebecca. 'The Social(ist) Pedagogies of the MST: Towards New Relations of Production in the Brazilian Countryside'. *Education Policy Analysis Archives* 21, no. 41 (2013): 1-22. https://doi.org/10.14507/epaa.v21n41.2013.

Tarrow, Sidney. 'Transnational Politics: Contention and Institutions in International Politics'. *Annual Review of Political Science* 4, no. 1 (2001): 1-20.

———. *Power in Movement*. Cambridge: Cambridge University Press, 2022.

Thomas, Peter. *The Gramscian Moment*. Leiden: Brill, 2009.

———. 'We Good Subalterns'. In Antonini et al., *Revisiting Gramsci's Notebooks*, 1-6.

———. 'Toward the Modern Prince'. In Dainotto and Jameson, *Gramsci in the World*, 17-37.

Thompson, Edward P. 'The Moral Economy of the English Crowd in the Eighteenth Century'. *Past & Present* 50, no. 1 (1971): 76-136.

———. *Customs in Common*. New York: The New Press, 1993.

———. *The Making of the English Working Class*. Introduction by Michael Kenny. London: Penguin, 2013.

Togliatti, Palmiro. *On Gramsci, and Other Writings*. London: Lawrence & Wishart, 1979.

Tripp, Charles. *The Power and the People: Paths of Resistance in the Middle East*. Cambridge: Cambridge University Press, 2013.

———. 'Battlefields of the Republic: The Struggle for Public Space in Tunisia'. *LSE Middle East Centre Paper Series* 13 (2014): 1–24.

Tronti, Mario. *Workers and Capital*. London: Verso, 2019.

Trotsky, Leon. *The History of the Russian Revolution*. London: Pluto Press, 1997.

Trouillot, Michel-Rolph. *Silencing the Past: Power and the Production of History*. Boston: Beacon Press, 2015.

Tuğal, Cihan. *Passive Revolution: Absorbing the Islamic Challenge to Capitalism*. Stanford, CA: Stanford University Press, 2009.

Turner, Alicia, Laurence Cox, and Brian Bocking. *The Irish Buddhist: The Forgotten Monk Who Faced Down the British Empire*. Oxford: Oxford University Press, 2020.

Vacca, Giuseppe. *Alternative Modernities: Antonio Gramsci's Twentieth Century*. Translated by Derek Boothman and Chris Dennis. Cham: Palgrave Macmillan, 2021.

van Kranenburg, Rob. 'Whose Gramsci? Right-Wing Gramscism'. *International Gramsci Society Newsletter* 9 (1999): 14–18.

van der Linden, Marcel. *Workers of the World: Essays toward a Global Labor History*. Leiden: Brill, 2008.

Van Stekelenburg, Jacquelien, and Bert Klandermans. 'The Social Psychology of Protest'. *Current Sociology* 61, no. 5-6 (2013): 886-905.

Volpi, Frederick, and James Jasper, eds. *Microfoundations of the Arab Uprisings: Mapping Interactions between Regimes and Protesters*. Amsterdam: Amsterdam University Press, 2018.

Wallace, Michelle. *Black Macho and the Myth of the Superwoman*. London: Verso, 1990.

Walton, John K., and David Seddon. *Free Markets and Food Riots: The Politics of Global Adjustment*. Hoboken, NJ: Wiley & Sons, 2008.

Walsh, Catherine E. 'Thinking Andean Abya Yala with and against Gramsci: Notes on State, Nature, and *Buen Vivir*'. In Dainotto and Jameson, *Gramsci in the World*, 190-203.

Wang, Pu. 'Gramsci and the Chinese Left: Reappraising a Missed Encounter'. In Dainotto and Jameson, *Gramsci in the World*, 204-223.

Wedeen, Lisa. 'Acting "As If": Symbolic Politics and Social Control in Syria'. *Comparative Studies in Society and History* 40, no. 3 (1998): 503-523.

West, Cornel, and Christa Buschendorf, *Black Prophetic Fire*. Boston: Beacon Press, 2015.

Wilder, Gary. *Freedom Time: Negritude, Decolonisation, and the Future of the World*. Durham, NC: Duke University Press, 2015.

Williams, Raymond. *The Long Revolution*. London: Chatto & Windus, 1961.

———. *Resources of Hope: Culture, Democracy, Socialism*. Edited by Robin Gable. Introduction by Robin Blackburn. London: Verso, 1989.

Willis, Paul. *Learning to Labour: How Working Class Kids Get Working Class Jobs*. London: Routledge, 2017.

Wynter, Sylvia. 'Beyond the Word of Man: Glissant and the New Discourse of the Antilles'. *World Literature Today* 63, no. 4 (1989): 637–648.

Young, Robert J. *Postcolonialism: An Historical Introduction*. Hoboken, NJ: John Wiley & Sons, 2016.

Zene, Cosimo. 'Self-Consciousness of the Dalits as "Subalterns": Reflections on Gramsci in South Asia'. *Rethinking Marxism* 23, no. 1 (2011): 83–99.

———. 'Justice for the Excluded and Education for Democracy in B. R. Ambedkar and A. Gramsci'. *Rethinking Marxism* 30, no. 4 (2018): 494–524.

Zinn, Howard. *Howard Zinn on History*. New York: Seven Stories Press, 2011.

Note: 'n' after a page number indicates the number of a note on that page

and the war of position, 191, 195–205, 238, 261, 271–73, 306, 314

class, 7, 21, 27–28, 32–33; consciousness, 12, 71, 85–86, 140–43, 164–65, 240–41, 302–3; and culture, 28; and the spirit of cleavage, 142–43; structure, 77, 275, 276; struggle, 25, 30–31, 77, 134, 161, 204, 207, 263. *See also* bourgeois/bourgeoisie; working class

coercion, 18, 57, 84, 257–58, 260–63

collective will, 23, 40, 66, 67, 76, 202, 205, 294; and consent, 190–91, 222, 252; formation of, 50, 56, 61–62, 69, 72, 98, 147–48, 156, 190–91, 223–24, 246; loss of, 63; and the organic party, 214, 306–7; philosophy of praxis and, 290; and popular education, 232; revolution and, 272, 294; synthetic explosion and, 172, 179; theory and, 40, 41, 42

colonialism, 25–26, 34, 93, 165, 183, 203, 231, 247–48, 279, 284

common good, 49–50, 56, 309

common sense, 67, 86–91; and civil society, 87–88; and conservatism, 16; and domination, 86–91; and good sense, 143–46, 229, 232, 300–302; hegemonic, 26, 73, 84; and masculinism, 141; and sexuality, 26

communism, 21, 36, 133, 149–50, 207–8, 215–16, 312

Communist Party, 38, 132, 207–9, 213, 215, 262; Brazil, 3, 135; France, 3, 135, 185; Italy, 2, 135, 189, 206, 207–8, 211–12, 216, 235–37, 241, 256, 278; Soviet Union, 217, 286, 293

conception (of the world), 80, 87–91, 98, 121, 165, 213, 226, 229

conscious leadership (*direzione consapevole*), 92, 173, 185, 190, 192, 193, 229

consciousness: Black, 53, 132, 139–40, 217, 279; class, 12, 71, 85–86, 140–43, 164–65, 240–41, 302–3; contradictory, 11, 12, 73, 120–23, 223, 227, 233–34, 300; critical, 54, 94, 224, 232; group, 85, 96, 102–4, 115, 137–43,

164, 241, 302–3, 310; political, 65–66, 118, 233; social, 50, 80, 83–85, 124, 137–38, 168, 235, 242–43; socialist, 146; working class, 164–65

consent, 66–69, 303–6, 317–18; and adherence, 106, 114; and civil society, 18, 23, 54, 56, 191; and coercion, 79, 257, 263; and collective will, 190–91, 222, 252; and hegemony, 31–32, 122, 169, 185, 190, 200, 205, 220, 233, 257; lack of, 178–79; organization of, 195, 235, 305; and the party, 180, 206, 211, 220–21; and social bloc formation, 241, 243, 304; and the state, 57–58; and subaltern social groups, 66–69, 73, 170, 178–79, 193–94; and vanguardism, 244–47; and the war of position, 195, 198, 200, 203, 205

conservatism, 15–17

conspiracy theory, 101–2, 127, 300

contradictory consciousness, 11, 12, 73, 120–23, 223, 227, 233–34, 300

Cospito, Giuseppe, 57, 58

counterculture, 129, 131, 161–62

counter-hegemony, 137, 190, 199, 217, 239, 242, 243, 260

Coutinho, Nelson, 3, 211, 263, 281, 283, 288

Cox, Laurence, 46, 64, 114

Crehan, Kate, 87–88

crisis of authority, 111, 129–30, 167–72, 205, 302

critical consciousness, 54, 94, 224, 232

Croce, Benedetto, 32, 36, 57, 92, 222, 226, 266

Cronin, Stephanie, 117

cultural hegemony, 35, 77, 261, 269

cultural revolution, 27, 289–290

cultural studies, 28, 30

culture, 27, 56–57, 95–97, 225–26, 231, 289–90, 293, 300, 312. *See also* counterculture

Cuoco, Vincenzo, 265

Dalits, 80–81, 83, 99–100, 122, 141

Davis, Angela, 330n66

Dean, Jodi, 136

de Beauvoir, Simone, 27–28, 79–80, 84–85

decolonial/decolonialism, 3, 21, 24, 27, 29, 141, 314–15

decomposition, 13, 63–64, 67, 125, 256, 299, 309

Del Roio, Marcus, 142

democracy: and bloc formation, 242–43, 269; and domination, 229; popular, 18, 58, 156–58, 238, 287–88, 295; progressive, 283; promotion, 18; radical, 29, 33; social, 3, 135, 208, 256, 269

democratic centralism, 208, 212–14, 217–18, 238, 286

democratic party, 211–14, 216, 278, 317

democratic socialism, 2–3, 146, 153, 155, 210, 242, 269, 288, 306, 309, 311, 319

Desai, Manali, 122, 123

determinism, 21, 41, 50, 98, 148, 191–92

dialectics, 12, 23, 26, 33, 40, 50, 153

domination (*dominazione*), 66–69, 74–79, 81–85, 240, 299–301; and the common good, 49–50; and common sense/good sense, 86–91, 143–45; and contradictory consciousness, 123; and democracy, 229; and intersectionality, 27–28; myth and Utopia, 97–100, 146, 149; and organic intellectuals, 54–55, 92–95, 301; passive/active adherence to, 72, 105–11, 114, 122, 127, 167–70, 179, 301–2, 313; and popular culture, 95–97; and sexuality, 158–61; and subversivism, 100–104

Dostoyevsky, Fyodor Mikhailovich, 228

drama, 56, 68, 72, 80–81

Draper, Hal, 134

Drinot, Paulo, 108

Duggan, Lisa, 161

Dunayevskaya, Raya, 216

ecology, 27, 152

economic-corporate phase, 65, 153–55, 163, 169, 233

economism, 3, 21, 22, 32, 33, 37, 239, 242, 268, 270

economy, 57, 150, 153, 234–35, 304, 307, 310, 319

eco-socialism, 10, 152, 232, 234, 274, 276, 307, 310–11, 319

education, 58, 77, 181, 230–34

Egan, Daniel, 219–20, 260

Egypt: Caesarism, 264; class structure, 275, 276; labour protest, 109–11; moral economy, 106–7; Muslim Brotherhood, 107, 199, 200, 261; popular uprisings, 6, 76, 130, 165, 174, 199–200, 251, 276, 279; subaltern formations, 114, 117, 118, 119, 180, 251–52

El-Fattah, Alaa Abd, 6, 8

Engels, Friedrich, 28, 216, 238, 284

England. *See* Britain

Epstein, Barbara, 136

Eribon, Didier, 23, 26, 80, 83, 114, 116, 159–61

ethico-political, 37, 65, 146, 153–54, 224, 266, 277

Eurocentrism, 10–11, 19, 24–25, 33, 34, 75, 200–201, 278

Eurocommunism, 211, 260, 263, 269, 270

Evans, Daniel John, 267

expressivism, 131, 136–37

EZLN. *See* Zapatistas

factory councils, 29, 131, 133, 149–53, 155, 157, 162–63, 167, 262, 288

faith, 111, 197

Fanon, Frantz, 26, 93, 141, 181–82

Fantasia, Rick, 119

fascism, 2, 8, 36, 98, 101, 174, 189, 204, 211, 236–37, 266

Fatton, Robert, 267

Featherstone, David, 119

feeling, 26, 33, 56, 67, 72, 74, 157, 230, 312

Femia, Joseph, 121–22, 123, 211, 260, 262–63

feminism, 26, 27, 53, 81, 93, 120, 139, 165, 243, 278

Feuerbach, Ludwig, 45, 55, 58

Filippini, Michele, 273

Fonseca, Marco, 17, 18

Fontana, Benedetto, 49

forces, 294; balance and relation of, 11–12, 28, 41, 58, 65, 69, 176, 268

Foucault, Michel, 22–24, 30, 31, 93, 158–60

France, 195, 229, 265, 349n74; bourgeoisie, 176, 254, 269, 275–76; colonialism, 26, 93; Jacobins, 176, 213, 249, 265, 269; Marx on, 284; May 1968, 130, 131–32, 135; Paris Commune, 130, 158, 238, 288; political parties, 3, 135, 168, 185

Freire, Paulo, 231, 232

French revolution, 61, 110, 176, 266, 268, 269, 273, 275–76

Friedan, Betty, 93

Furse, Thomas, 265

gay people, 79, 80, 85, 93, 159–60

Geier, Joel, 208

gender, 27, 157, 158

genus, 16, 84, 126

genus-thinking, 20, 89, 188, 302

Germany, 180–81, 266, 284

Gill, Stephen, 4

Glassman, Jonathon, 109, 111, 123, 146

global civil society, 17–18

globalization, 4, 7, 18, 131, 136, 209

Goffman, Erving, 19

golpismo, 259, 263, 268

good sense, 12, 67, 102, 143–46, 224, 229, 232, 301–3

Gorz, André, 151

Graeber, David, 136, 137, 161–62, 183–84

Gramsci, Antonio: early life and family, 26, 101, 119–20; imprisonment, 8, 26, 43–44, 92, 104–5, 124, 261; *L'Ordine Nuovo* period, 130, 132, 133, 151, 162–63, 206, 215, 292–93; political activism, 38, 142, 207, 241, 256, 277, 280; Sardinian nationalism, 142–43, 241–42, 277–78, 280. See also *Prison Notebooks*

Gray, Kevin, 118

Grayson, John, 233

Green, Marcus E., 49, 52

group: consciousness, 85, 96, 102–4, 115, 137–43, 164, 241, 302–3, 310; formation, 87, 92, 137–40; identifica-

tion, 115. *See also* subaltern social groups

Guha, Ranajit, 4, 75, 170, 284

Gurr, Ted, 74

Hall, Stuart: on civil society, 282–83; on 'authoritarian-populism', 17; on the British Labour Party, 244, 282; on common sense, 91; on the crisis of authority, 171–72; on cultural studies, 3, 312; on democracy, 29; on gender, 27; on good sense, 145; on neo-Kantianism, 33; on popular culture, 95, 161; on socialist construction, 290; on statism, 282; on subaltern formations, 114

Hanchard, Michael G., 123

Hardt, Michael, 179, 276

Harvey, David, 125, 167

Hegel, Georg Wilhelm Friedrich, 63, 187–88, 266, 277

Hegelianism, 35–36, 281

hegemony: and adherence, 105–6, 108, 111; alternative, 67, 233, 276; capitalist, 31, 36, 154, 219, 220; and civil society, 35, 37, 65, 77, 235, 239, 263, 281–83, 311; concentration of, 257; and consent, 31–32, 122, 169, 185, 190, 200, 205, 220, 233, 257; cultural, 35, 77, 261, 269; 'from below', 108; Gramscian concept of, 3, 26, 31–32, 37–38, 119, 152, 270, 294; Said on, 26; socialist, 33, 149–50, 152–53, 311; and vanguardism, 209–10. *See also* counter-hegemony

Hesketh, Chris, 361n239

historical bloc, 85, 241, 261, 268–77, 290, 294–95, 307, 311, 316–17

historical materialism, 21, 37

historicism, 5, 32, 36–37, 39–42, 50, 57, 151, 201

history, 39–43, 89

Hoare, Quintin, 113, 129

Hobsbawm, Eric, 75

Holub, Renate, 26

homosexuality, 26, 93, 160. *See also* gay people; queer

Nowell Smith, Geoffrey, 113, 129
Nunes, Rodrigo, 193, 221

object, 5, 22–24, 26, 43, 49, 83
objectification, 57, 72, 80–82, 93, 96, 122, 127, 167, 171, 274, 307, 310
objective formation, 65, 79, 82–83, 88, 91, 93–94, 113
Occupy Wall Street, 349n72
L'Ordine Nuovo, 130, 132, 133, 151, 162–63, 206, 215, 248, 292–93
organic: crisis, 7, 130, 168, 180, 267, 283; party, 13, 62, 214–22, 238, 240, 271, 294–96, 305–7, 311–12, 318–19; theory, 39–42, 193–95; unification, 11, 37, 40, 49, 63, 280, 298, 299
organic intellectuals, 25–26, 181–84, 188, 197, 213, 219, 298; and civil society, 54; development of theory, 42, 62; and the drive for autonomy, 302–3; efforts to overcome social domination, 54–55, 92–95, 301
organism, 49, 68, 150, 205, 222, 225, 246, 259
organization, 9, 28, 62, 68, 114, 132, 175, 190, 280; autonomous, 29, 131, 153–54, 158, 162–66, 218; collective, 117, 205, 281; of consent, 195, 235, 305; and organic intellectuals, 55; party, 21, 205–22, 238, 291–95, 305, 307; revolutionary, 4, 6, 164, 214, 221; social, 19, 114, 228. *See also* self-organization
Orientalism, 11, 24–25, 26, 94–95, 200–204, 210

Pakistan, 7, 151–52, 267
Palestine, 8, 94, 177, 261, 278
Panizza, Francisco, 135
party: and civil society, 220–22, 292–93, 305, 307, 311; and consent, 180, 206, 211, 220–21; crisis of authority, 167–69, 171; democratic, 211–14, 216, 278, 317; dominant groups, 68–69, 179, 192; and ideology, 215; organic, 13, 62, 214–22, 238, 240, 271, 294–96, 305–7, 311–12, 318–19; organization,

21, 205–22, 238, 291–95, 305, 307; reorganization, 179–81, 222; revolutionary, 136, 206, 211, 214, 239, 291, 294–95; socialist, 130, 153, 161–63, 184, 189, 194, 205–6, 215–16, 218–19, 236, 291–92; vanguardist, 62, 207–11, 218, 240, 305–6. *See also specific parties*
passive revolution, 67, 175, 265–68, 271
passivity, 73, 90, 102, 111–12, 148, 174, 192, 311
patriarchy, 26, 31, 107–8, 157
peasant movements, 4, 74–77, 170, 237, 291
Peru, 108–9
phase, 11–12, 64–69, 134
Philippines, 130, 160, 165, 251
philology, 41–42
philosophy, 289–90
philosophy of praxis, 12, 26–27, 32, 35–37, 192, 213, 220, 315; and collective will, 290; and common sense/good sense, 91, 144, 188, 232; humanism of, 79; and ideology, 222; and self-management, 151
piqueteros, 165–66
Podemos party (Spain), 9, 206, 217
political consciousness, 65–66, 118, 233
political economy, 21, 57, 107, 110, 181
political society, 57, 140, 193, 235, 272, 281–82, 292, 295
politics, 3–6, 16, 31–32, 35, 46, 74, 148–49, 170–71, 179, 195–98
popular: culture, 95–97, 231, 300; definition of, 48–49; democracy, 18, 58, 156–58, 238, 287–88, 295; education, 230–34
popular self-activity, 219; and autonomy, 29, 129–35, 146–47, 151–52; democratic, 155–58; and group consciousness, 139; and the intellectual, 181–84; and myth, 146–49; and sexuality, 158–61; and social consciousness, 137–43; socialist self-management, 149–53; and space/place, 166–67
popular uprising, 10, 12, 51, 172–79, 192, 302, 308, 313. *See also specific countries*

populism, 16-17, 33, 91, 178, 180-81, 256
positivism, 19, 20, 21, 39, 41, 46
postmodern Prince, 4, 62, 221, 291, 305, 318
practice, 5, 16, 21, 22-23, 33, 41-42, 98, 186-87, 213, 309, 315-19
praxis, 40, 55, 56, 232, 316. *See also* philosophy of praxis; revolutionizing praxis
Prison Notebooks (Gramsci), 5, 21, 32, 38, 43-44, 125, 189; common sense in, 86-87; criticism of the PSI, 291-92; economic theories, 57; materialism in, 37; organic 'unification' in, 49; phases in, 65; 'religious-popular' movement of Lazzaretti in, 228; space and time in, 59; subaltern formations in, 52, 79, 113; vision of the party, 207-8, 211-12; war of manoeuvre/war of position, 257, 262
production, 21, 57, 149-52, 232-35, 311
protest: anti-austerity, 176; anti-globalization, 4; bread riots, 106-7; labour, 109, 114, 118, 165-66, 250; nonviolent, 18, 136; and political/theoretical division, 135; structural models of, 19
Proudfoot, Philip, 102

quality and quantity, 51, 60, 63, 142, 248
queer: activism, 18, 24, 158, 161; critique, 8, 198; identity, 23, 79, 80, 83, 116, 137-38, 243, 280; liberation, 160; politics, 159-60, 248; theory, 20, 24, 253

race, 19, 25-26, 52-53, 81-82, 123, 139-40
racism, 94-95, 100, 210
radicalization, 200, 249-52, 308-9, 313, 318
rationalism, 20, 76, 77, 97, 98, 265, 304
Rehmann, Jan, 143, 145-46, 218, 228-29
religion, 58-59, 88, 97, 169, 223, 225, 228
renewal, 2-6, 13, 62-64, 67-68, 187, 256
representation, 33, 83, 140, 157-58
revolutionary party, 136, 206, 211, 214, 239, 291, 294-95

revolutionizing, 13, 144, 230, 271, 273, 306, 308-9, 317, 319
revolutionizing praxis, 55, 56, 272, 298
revolution, 12-13, 254-56; aftermath, 6; and autonomy, 136; and Caesarism, 263-65; and civil society, 281-83, 293, 295; and collective will, 272, 294; consensual, 260; cultural, 27, 289-90; and historical blocs, 268-77, 307; ideological development, 222-23; and maximalism, 245; and organization, 4, 6, 164, 214, 221; passive, 67, 175, 265-68, 271; and the state, 283-88; and synthetic explosion, 173. *See also* war of manoeuvre; war of position
Roberts, Philip, 242, 263
Rojava Revolution, 131, 261, 278, 286-87
Rosengarten, Frank, 207-8
Roy, Srila, 83, 116, 118
ruling groups, 53, 59, 60-61, 63, 67-69, 83-84; crisis of authority, 168-71, 176; and hegemony, 56, 122, 257; knowledge production, 18; populism and, 16-17; reorganization, 179-81, 303; and transformism, 247, 252, 268, 318
Russia, 36, 164, 201, 202-3, 245, 275
Russian revolution, 130, 184, 202, 208, 223, 266, 269, 275-76, 284, 292

Said, Edward, 26, 92-94, 280
Sajjad Akhtar, Aasim, 7-8, 151
Salamini, Leonardo, 87, 112, 126, 269, 281
Salvadori, Massimo, 29
Sanbonmatsu, John, 23, 131-32, 136-37, 193
Sardinia, 25, 87, 142-43, 241-42, 277-78, 280
Sartre, Jean-Paul, 26, 93
scale, 59, 64, 68-69, 73, 100, 119, 151, 220-21, 265
Schucht, Giulia, 50
Schucht, Tatiana, 92, 119-20
Scott, James C., 76, 77, 313
self-activity. *See* popular self-activity
self-changing, 55, 58

Founded in 1893,
UNIVERSITY OF CALIFORNIA PRESS
publishes bold, progressive books and journals
on topics in the arts, humanities, social sciences,
and natural sciences—with a focus on social
justice issues—that inspire thought and action
among readers worldwide.

The UC PRESS FOUNDATION
raises funds to uphold the press's vital role
as an independent, nonprofit publisher, and
receives philanthropic support from a wide
range of individuals and institutions—and from
committed readers like you. To learn more, visit
ucpress.edu/supportus.